NORTH OF AMERICA

C.D. HOWE SERIES IN CANADIAN POLITICAL HISTORY
Series editors: Robert Bothwell and John English

This series offers fresh perspectives on Canadian political history and public policy from over the past century. Its purpose is to encourage scholars to write and publish on all aspects of the nation's political history, including the origins, administration, and significance of economic policies; the social foundations of politics and political parties; transnational influences on Canadian public life; and the biographies of key public figures. In doing so, the series fills large gaps in our knowledge about recent Canadian history and makes accessible to a broader audience the background necessary to understand contemporary public-political issues. Other volumes in the series are

Grit: The Life and Politics of Paul Martin Sr., by Greg Donaghy
The Call of the World: A Political Memoir, by Bill Graham
Prime Ministerial Power in Canada: Its Origins under Macdonald, Laurier, and Borden, by Patrice Dutil
The Good Fight: Marcel Cadieux and Canadian Diplomacy, by Brendan Kelly
Challenge the Strong Wind: Canada and East Timor, 1975–99, by David Webster
The Nuclear North: Histories of Canada in the Atomic Age, edited by Susan Colbourn and Timothy Andrews Sayle
The Unexpected Louis St-Laurent: Politics and Policies for a Modern Canada, edited by Patrice Dutil
Canadian Foreign Policy: Reflections on a Field in Transition, edited by Brian Bow and Andrea Lane
The Rowell-Sirois Commission and the Remaking of Canadian Federalism, by Robert Wardhaugh and Barry Ferguson
A Long Way to Paradise: A New History of British Columbia Politics, by Robert A.J. McDonald
A Cooperative Disagreement: Canada-United States Relations and Revolutionary Cuba, 1959–93, by John M. Dirks
People, Politics, and Purpose: Biography and Canadian Political History, edited by Greg Donaghy and P. Whitney Lackenbauer

The series originated with a grant from the C.D. Howe Memorial Foundation and is further supported by the Bill Graham Centre for Contemporary International History.

NORTH OF AMERICA

Canadians and the American Century, 1945–60

EDITED BY

ASA McKERCHER

AND

MICHAEL D. STEVENSON

UBCPress · Vancouver · Toronto

© UBC Press 2023

All rights reserved. No part of this publication may be reproduced, stored in a retrieval system, or transmitted, in any form or by any means, without prior written permission of the publisher, or, in Canada, in the case of photocopying or other reprographic copying, a licence from Access Copyright, www.accesscopyright.ca.

32 31 30 29 28 27 26 25 24 23   5 4 3 2 1

Printed and bound by CPI Group (UK) Ltd, Croydon, CR0 4YY

Library and Archives Canada Cataloguing in Publication

Title: North of America : Canadians and the American century, 1945–60 / edited by Asa McKercher and Michael D. Stevenson.

Names: McKercher, Asa, editor. | Stevenson, Michael D., editor.

Series: C.D. Howe series in Canadian political history.

Description: Series statement: C.D. Howe series in Canadian political history | Includes bibliographical references and index.

Identifiers: Canadiana (print) 20230224490 | Canadiana (ebook) 20230224547 | ISBN 9780774868839 (hardcover) | ISBN 9780774868846 (softcover) | ISBN 9780774868853 (PDF) | ISBN 9780774868860 (EPUB)

Subjects: LCSH: Canada – Civilization – 1945– | LCSH: Canada – Civilization – American influences. | LCSH: Canada – Foreign relations – United States. | LCSH: United States – Foreign relations – Canada. | LCSH: Canada – Politics and government – 1945– | LCSH: National security – Canada – History – 20th century.

Classification: LCC FC95.4 N67 2023 | DDC 971.064 – dc23

UBC Press gratefully acknowledges the financial support for our publishing program of the Government of Canada, the Canada Council for the Arts, and the British Columbia Arts Council.

This book has been published with the help of a grant from the Canadian Federation for the Humanities and Social Sciences, through the Awards to Scholarly Publications Program, using funds provided by the Social Sciences and Humanities Research Council of Canada.

UBC Press
The University of British Columbia
2029 West Mall
Vancouver, BC V6T 1Z2
www.ubcpress.ca

For Greg Donaghy
1961–2020

Contents

Foreword / ix
Robert Bothwell and John English

Acknowledgments / xi

Introduction: Canada and Canadians in the Shadow of the
American Century / 3
Asa McKercher and Michael D. Stevenson

PART 1: NORTH AMERICA IN A COLD WAR WORLD

1 "A Natural Development": Canada and Non-Alignment in
the Age of Eisenhower / 17
David Webster

2 Cheers to the Canadian Wheat Surplus! Lester Pearson's Visit
to the Soviet Union and the West's Détente Dilemma / 43
Susan Colbourn

3 Living Dangerously: Canadian National Security Policy and
the Nuclear Revolution / 66
Timothy Andrews Sayle

4 From Normandy to NORAD: Canada and the North Atlantic
Triangle in the Age of Eisenhower / 90
Asa McKercher and Michael D. Stevenson

CONTENTS

PART 2: POLITICS AND IDENTITY IN POSTWAR NORTH AMERICA

5 An Emerging Constitutional Culture in Canada's Postwar
Moment / 121
P.E. Bryden

6 Rethinking Postwar Domesticity: The Canadian Household
in the 1950s / 141
Bettina Liverant

7 Racial Discrimination in "Uncle Tom's Town": Media and the
Americanization of Racism in Dresden, 1948–56 / 176
Jennifer Tunnicliffe

8 Between Distrust and Acceptance: The Influence of the United
States on Postwar Quebec / 202
François-Olivier Dorais and Daniel Poitras

PART 3: CULTURAL CONUNDRUMS IN AN AGE OF PROSPERITY

9 Living the Good Life? Canadians and the Paradox of American
Prosperity / 235
Stephen Azzi

10 Make Room for (Canadian) TV: Print Media Cover the
Arrival of Television in the Shadow of American Cultural
Imperialism, 1930–52 / 259
Emily LeDuc

11 Getting Off the Highway: Frederick Gardiner and Toronto's
Transit Policy in the Age of the Interstate Highway, 1954–63 / 288
Jonathan English

12 Talking Jazz at the Stratford Shakespearean Festival, 1956–58 / 315
Eric Fillion

Afterword / 341
Norman Hillmer

List of Contributors / 344

Index / 347

Foreword

American publisher Henry Luce's 1941 declaration that the "American century" had begun proved prophetic. The remainder of the twentieth century saw the United States play the principal role in the creation of a new international order based on an array of new institutions and, after four decades, the collapse of the Soviet Union, the other military superpower that eventually proved to be no match for the liberal democratic capitalist system. This book's title correctly points out that Canadians lived and prospered in the shadow of American dominance, but the chapters illustrate that beneath the shadows Canadians often did things differently and, in some areas, considerably better.

The elegant summary of the volume's contents by Norman Hillmer (see the Afterword) makes a longer foreword unnecessary. This book and the conference on which it is based were conceived in discussions between Greg Donaghy and others. Greg was a brilliant scholar who contributed greatly to our understanding of Canada in the "shadow of the American century." *Grit,* his biography of Paul Martin Sr. was the first book in this series, setting a high standard for its successors. While Greg's voice is now silent, his outstanding scholarship endures.

ROBERT BOTHWELL AND JOHN ENGLISH

The C.D. Howe Series on Canadian Political History is supported by a grant from the C.D. Howe Memorial Foundation. The grant was given to promote greater research and publications on Canada's political history. The Bill Graham Centre for Contemporary International History also supports this series, which has already published important biographies and analytical studies that have attracted academic and popular interest.

Acknowledgments

This project began as separate conversations that each of us had with Greg Donaghy about the need for more attention to the history of Canada-US relations in the 1950s. Greg hit on the idea of a joint effort among the three of us: a monograph examining the Eisenhower administration's dealings with Canada and a symposium leading to an edited collection in which contributors would take a broader view of Canadian interactions with the United States in this period. We secured a SSHRC grant and began both our research and the planning for a symposium to be held at the University of Toronto in May 2020. Needless to say, the COVID-19 pandemic intervened. Then, suddenly, Greg died. This tragic loss did not deter us from seeing our joint project through. The symposium was held, a year late and over Zoom. And this collection rests in your hands. It is dedicated to Greg. A scholar, friend, and mensch, he had a knack for bringing people together – as he did with this project and countless others. Our gratitude to him.

Obviously, this collection is the result of more than just our efforts. First and foremost, thanks go to our contributors, each of whom took the time to prepare an incisive chapter, to respond to suggestions made by the reviewers and by us, and to do both tasks on schedule and amid a pandemic. Our appreciation goes to the reviewers and their efforts to improve our volume. Robert Bothwell and John English honoured us by including this volume in the C.D. Howe Series in Canadian Political History, where it sits among august company. Norman Hillmer graciously provided the Afterword. We would be remiss if we did not thank Randy Schmidt, our editor at UBC Press. His enthusiasm for the project, and his help in seeing it through to fruition so quickly, are much appreciated. Thanks, too, to the members of the editorial and production team at UBC Press, including Carmen Tiampo and Megan Brand, along with freelance copy editor Dallas Harrison, and indexer Noeline Bridge. This book is supported in part by funding from the Social Sciences and Humanities Research Council and the Awards to Scholarly Publications Program, and Jack Cunningham and the Bill Graham Centre for Contemporary International History played host to our virtual symposium. Our thanks to them as well.

Finally, our appreciation goes to our respective families. Michael thanks Roberta for her continued support. Asa thanks Kendall, Calvin, and Harriet, the best people with whom to shelter in place during a pandemic.

NORTH OF AMERICA

Introduction

Canada and Canadians in the Shadow of the American Century

ASA McKERCHER AND MICHAEL D. STEVENSON

In February 1941, American magazine magnate Henry Luce took to the pages of his *Life* magazine to make the case to readers that the United States should reject a posture of so-called isolationism and instead undertake an active role in international affairs. With much of the world embroiled in another conflict, Luce saw that his country was primed to find itself in a position of unprecedented global authority in the years ahead, and he appealed to Americans "to accept wholeheartedly our duty and our opportunity as the most powerful and vital nation in the world" to use that power "to exert ... the full impact of our influence, for such purposes as we see fit."[1] In Luce's view, the basis of that influence was US economic and potential military might and American cultural products – jazz, Hollywood films, "machines and patented products" – that were "the only things that every community in the world, from Zanzibar to Hamburg, recognizes in common."[2] Published nine months before the United States entered the Second World War, Luce's article became famous as a declaration of intent by internationalist-minded Americans aiming to create what Luce called the "first great American Century." This phrase became shorthand for describing the era of US preponderance that began amid the war. The American Century's nature and extent are a subject of debate, but what is clear is that, during the war and in the decades that followed it, the impact of the United States was felt the world over.[3] And it was in Canada that the American presence loomed especially large.

Perhaps it is no surprise that in 1948 Luce himself called not only for closer Canadian-American cooperation to maintain "world order" but also for a "complete and permanent economic union" between the two neighbours.[4]

The Second World War accelerated a process of North American integration that had begun decades earlier, binding Canada and the United States through a series of economic and defence agreements that outlived the conflict – and indeed expanded as the Cold War unfolded. These measures complemented a massive flow of trade and investment across the border, with Canadian natural resources helping to maintain, first, the American arsenal of democracy and, then, the prosperity of the postwar era. In addition, there was an increasing range of cultural and intellectual contacts as well as the cross-border flow of tourists, students, and other travellers, producing what, in 1946, American historian A.L. Burt called an "international intimacy."[5] That same year, Ray Atherton, the US ambassador in Ottawa, told NBC listeners that the bedrock of the close relationship between Canada and the United States was "the free circulation of knowledge and ideas between the two peoples of North America ... a mass phenomenon involving millions and millions of people" that had created an "intellectual and social harmony" between the neighbouring peoples.[6] And, in the view of Canadian political scientist Alexander Brady, seldom was "there a major movement in the neighbouring Republic without its repercussion in Canada."[7] These observations testified to the interchange among Canadians and Americans, but as Brady noted, this process often seemed to be one sided.

At the same time, as many Canadians embraced growing ties with the United States, this intimate relationship also caused disquiet among Canadian nationalists. In 1951, the Royal Commission on National Development in the Arts, Letters and Sciences, or Massey Commission, decried that "our use of American institutions, or our lazy, even abject, imitation of them has caused an uncritical acceptance of ideas and assumptions which are alien to our tradition."[8] "We can only survive," wrote political economist Harold Innis the following year, "by taking persistent action at strategic points against American imperialism in all its attractive guises."[9] Canadians were slow – or reluctant – to heed these warnings, and in 1960 novelist Hugh MacLennan warned of the "Americanization of Canada." Although this was a century-long concern, as he contended, recent increased exposure to "that cluster of ideas, values, habits and thought-patterns called by Mr. Harry Luce The American Way of Life" was actively transforming Canada into "a mental and spiritual colony of the United States."[10] Over the course of the 1960s, many Canadians came to share MacLennan's jaundiced view of the American Century, though their anxiety reflected the immense popularity of the American Way of Life in Canada. The chapters in this volume explore some of these tensions and attractions while providing new light on the history of Canada in the early postwar period, roughly 1945–60, the high-water mark of the American Century – also dubbed the Age of Eisenhower by historian William Hitchcock after one of the period's leading personalities.[11]

Although there is no shortage of works on Canada-US relations, the early postwar era has received relatively scant attention from historians. One reason for this oversight is that many histories of this relationship are surveys in which the postwar years are allotted a chapter, sometimes two, and focus mainly on a handful of high-level bilateral issues such as continental defence, tariffs and trade, and responses to Cold War flashpoints.[12] By necessity, then, these treatments are limited. Moreover, the late 1940s and 1950s are often characterized as a time of consensus between Canada and the United States, and historians are drawn mainly to periods of crisis and confrontation.[13] This volume redresses the lack of attention to an important time period while also underscoring the need for a broader understanding of Canadian-American relations that accounts for the observation made by Michael Behiels and Reginald Stuart that "although the border has separated the countries and their policies, it has had far less impact on cultural values, ideas, ways of life, [and] human relationships."[14] Just as the recent scholarly focus on the British World has allowed historians to trace the impacts of transnational, global, and imperial trends on Canada, so too can growing attention to the influence of the United States and comparisons with the American experience enrich understandings of Canadian history.[15] What is true of the postwar years is the case with other periods as well.

Our collection starts from the premise that the history of the northern part of North America is best explored by looking not only at state-to-state interactions between Canada and the United States but also at the wider gamut of interactions among Americans and Canadians. Whether utilizing international, transnational, or more local historical lenses, our contributors stress the ways in which, from the Canadian perspective, these interactions were often reactive, with actors in Canada – consumers, diplomats, jazz musicians, urban planners – responding to developments in the United States. Of course, not all Canadian actions were reactions to things American. Still, whether considering constitutional reform, engagement with countries in the so-called Third World, or challenges to white supremacy, Canadians were mindful of the United States, often drawing comparisons with American experiences and utilizing these examples for their own purposes. That the United States loomed so large is not a surprise given American preponderance; what is surprising is the extent to which so little has been written about this aspect of postwar Canadian history (or, for that matter, other periods).[16] In contrast, historians of Europe have devoted considerable attention to tracing the US impacts on culture, politics, and society, showing the complicated nature of American-European relations, not just at the elite level but also more widely. As these studies stress, European identities were often crafted in contradistinction to the United States.[17] Although the importance of anti-Americanism in building Canadian identity has long been recognized, there is a need for wider examinations of the US impact in Canada.[18] One reason, for instance, is that, in contrast to the common emphasis on anti-Americanism as a theme in Canada's history, many Canadians have been attracted to American ideals, culture, and commerce. This very fact explains Canadian nationalists' concern with US influences.

With the goal of exploring American influences on Canadian life, this collection provides a new look at Canada's postwar history partially through the lens of Canadian-American relations and partially by tracing the extent to which developments in Canada were part of wider trends in North America. In doing so, the collection offers a mix of topics that gives welcome attention to both elite-level issues and the concerns and perspectives of everyday people. Although transnational and international historians of Canada are now placing a welcome focus on exploring Canadian interactions with the world beyond North America and the North Atlantic,[19] relations with Americans remain of central importance, not only because of matters of propinquity, but also because of the economic, military, diplomatic, and cultural power of the United States, particularly in the American Century.[20]

Importantly, just as the postwar period saw a new sense of power among Americans, so too Canadians seemed to have earned a new prominence in global affairs and developed a nascent perception of their country as a middle power. The notion had begun during the war, when the *Economist* opined that Canada had earned a new international status, making "a category for herself all of her own. Relative to her resources her effort is second to none. In absolute terms the distance which separates Canada from the Great Powers is less than that between her own achievements and that of any other of the smaller powers."[21] Home to huge natural resource deposits, with a booming economy untouched by modern warfare's devastating effects, and a large complement of military forces, wartime Canada seemed to have grown in importance. This appreciation outlived the fighting. "The evidence of Canada's new position in the world is unmistakable," wrote academic Lionel Gelber in 1946. "Henceforth in world politics she must figure as a Middle Power." Historian Arthur Lower agreed that Canada "has risen considerably above the status of a small power and materially (but, in the writer's opinion, not psychologically) possesses far more weight than the size of its population alone would seem to indicate." Journalist Grant Dexter put the matter more simply: "The Canada of 1939 no longer exists."[22] Yet, like Henry Luce, who had invoked the idea of the American Century to urge his compatriots to pursue global primacy, many Canadians who saw their country as a middle power pushed for the adoption of a new, internationally engaged foreign policy. In the closing months of the war, Brooke Claxton – who would serve as defence minister from 1946 to 1954 – gushed that "Canada's part in this war has given her the opportunities and responsibilities of world-wide interests," especially "furthering international co-operation." Similarly, diplomat Hugh Keenleyside explained that along with new power came "new responsibilities." As he emphasized, "*whether Canadians like it or not, their country has to play a new and gravely broadened role in international affairs.*"[23] Historians have cast much doubt recently on whether Canada played this middle power role in the postwar years.[24] Even so, the country had gained more prominence and prosperity, and with Europe and Asia devastated by the war Canada became – albeit briefly and in relative terms – more important.

The idea of Canada as an internationally engaged middle power signified Canadians' hopes for a world without war and economic depression. In September 1945, *Maclean's* magazine expressed this buoyancy: "This is the postwar world, the world for which the toil and sweat, the tears and blood of history's most terrible war were expended. This is the time of freedom, of security, of new life and great hope for which millions fought and died. This is the peace of which scores of millions dreamed."[25] There were reasons for hope. Because of their many wartime sacrifices, Canadians demanded government action to provide social welfare measures and to avoid a return to the privation of the 1930s. The federal and provincial governments responded, with a rapidly growing economy financing an expanded welfare state. As in the past, natural resources were a key element fuelling the postwar boom, whether the oil of Alberta or the mineral wealth of Canada's northern regions. Indeed, the Canadian north seemed to promise unlimited opportunities, signified by the creation in 1953 of the federal Department of Northern Affairs and Natural Resources and Prime Minister John Diefenbaker's articulation in 1958 of a Northern Vision for prosperity.[26] The previous year journalist Bruce Hutchison had predicted that Canada would be "Tomorrow's Giant."[27] Other markers of affluence included increased homeownership in seemingly ever-expanding suburbs and ballooning population growth, the product of high levels of immigration from war-shattered Europe and the baby boom. Historian Doug Owram was right to title his history of Canada's baby boomers *Born at the Right Time.*[28]

Yet the postwar era also produced stresses and strains, including anxieties stemming from the Cold War – both anti-communist paranoia and fear of nuclear holocaust – and dissatisfaction with modern life, whether the "creeping conformity" of suburbia or the shallowness and stultifying nature of mass culture, consumerism, and domesticity.[29] Although Canadian citizenship was legally established in 1946, there remained the questions asked by the *Canadian Forum* that year: "Is Canada a nation, and if not, should she be?"[30] Defining Canadian identity has been a perennial issue, not helped by proximity to a cultural behemoth. In 1951, the Royal Commission on National Development in the Arts, Letters and Sciences voiced concerns about the eclipse of Canadian culture by "a vast and disproportionate amount of material coming from a single alien source."[31] Six years later another royal commission examined Canada's economy and highlighted the related issue of the vast extent of American ownership of Canadian resources and industries, whether through subsidiary operations of US multinationals or via direct investment. Although this situation spurred employment in Canada, the commission warned that "continuing integration might lead to economic domination by the United States and eventually to the loss of our political independence."[32] And, in terms of defence and foreign policy issues, Canadian officials were constantly attuned to the need to protect Canada's sovereignty from their southern neighbour while also supporting a key ally and protector. "To almost every Canadian," Luce's *Time* magazine observed in 1957, "the US is an enveloping fact of life."[33]

Throughout this collection, the contributors examine these issues and more, offering comparisons with the US experience, tracing the impacts of American influences, and charting interactions between Canada and the United States. The book is divided into three thematic sections. The chapters in the first section examine issues of postwar Canadian foreign policy. Here the authors consider how Canadian policy makers had to balance alliance solidarity with the United States against the pursuit of policies meant to advance Canada's own perceived interests. First, David Webster analyzes how Canadians viewed and engaged the so-called Third World during a period in which formal European empires collapsed and the Cold War struggle shifted to the Global South. Next, Susan Colbourn provides an important look at how Canada dealt with Soviet bloc countries – a topic that has received almost no attention from historians – while still toeing a pro-Western line. Then, in his chapter, Timothy Andrews Sayle analyzes how Canadian officials dealt with the stark realities of the nuclear age and the dilemmas of Canada's reliance on the United States for its defence. Finally, in the section's last chapter, Asa McKercher and Michael Stevenson place various developments in the relationship among Canada, Britain, and the United States against the backdrop of the evolving American Century.

In the second section, the chapters explore Canadian political developments and connections to issues of Canadians' evolving identity. From the low-level politics surrounding the nuclear family to high political questions involving the role of Canada's Supreme Court, the United States served Canadians as a point of comparison. First, Penny Bryden traces Canada's evolving constitutional order and emphasizes how judicial activism in the United States served as a point of inspiration – and revulsion – for Canadians. Then, Bettina Liverant examines the nuclear family and its role in setting consumer patterns. Many Canadians were also disgusted by racism in both Canada and the United States, and, as Jennifer Tunnicliffe shows, they utilized the example of Jim Crow segregation in America to challenge Canadian white supremacy. Finally, François-Olivier Dorais and Daniel Poitras offer an important look at changing Québécois attitudes toward the United States and how those views evolved in the postwar period amid changes in Quebec society.

The chapters in the third and final section probe various cultural issues in postwar Canada and the impacts of the United States on Canadians both directly and indirectly. In his wide-ranging chapter, Stephen Azzi reviews how American economic and cultural influences – from television to investment capital – shaped Canada in the years of postwar prosperity. Television is at the heart of the next chapter, by Emily LeDuc, who scrutinizes this new medium's reception by older Canadian media. Jonathan English then uses the urban developer Frederick Gardiner to look at one signature aspect of North American culture from this era: the automobile. Finally, Eric Fillion highlights the role of jazz at the Stratford Shakespearean Festival and how Canadians reacted to this American art form at a venue meant to promote Canada.

Overall, these contributions shed new light on a period of transition in Canada, presaging the later tumult of the Sixties. Moreover, they testify to the need for historians of the United States in the world to pay more attention to Canada, an observation as clichéd as it is true.

INTRODUCTION

NOTES

1 Henry R. Luce, "The American Century," *Life,* 17 February 1941, 63.

2 Ibid., 65.

3 See Michael J. Hogan, ed., *The Ambiguous Legacy: U.S. Foreign Relations in the "American Century"* (Cambridge, UK: Cambridge University Press, 1999); *The Short American Century: A Postmortem,* ed. Andrew J. Bacevich (Cambridge, MA: Harvard University Press, 2012); and William O. Walker, *The Rise and Decline of the American Century* (Ithaca, NY: Cornell University Press, 2018).

4 Henry Luce, "Customs Union with Canada," *Life,* 15 March 1948, 40.

5 A.L. Burt, *Canada: Our Oldest Good Neighbor* (Washington, DC: American Historical Association, 1946), 5.

6 "Our Foreign Policy," transcript, presented by NBC University of the Air, 14 December 1946, Library and Archives Canada (hereafter LAC), External Affairs Records, vol. 6184, file 1415–40-pt. 2.1.

7 Alexander Brady, "Canadian-American Relations," *International Affairs* 29, 2 (1952): 193–94.

8 Royal Commission on National Development in the Arts, Letters and Sciences, *Report* (Ottawa: King's Printer, 1951), 15.

9 Harold Innis, "The Strategy of Culture," in *Changing Concepts of Time* (1952; reprinted, Lanham, MD: Rowman and Littlefield, 2004), 14.

10 Hugh MacLennan, "It's the U.S. or Us," *Maclean's,* 5 November 1960, 59.

11 William I. Hitchcock, *The Age of Eisenhower: America and the World in the 1950s* (New York: Simon and Schuster, 2018).

12 Robert Bothwell, *Your Country, My Country: A Unified History of the United States and Canada* (New York: Oxford University Press, 2015); Stephen Azzi, *Reconcilable Differences: A History of Canada-US Relations* (Don Mills, ON: Oxford University Press, 2014); John Herd Thompson and Stephen J. Randall, *Canada and the United States: Ambivalent Allies,* 4th ed. (Montreal and Kingston: McGill-Queen's University Press, 2008); Reginald C. Stuart, *Dispersed Relations: Americans and Canada in Upper North America* (Baltimore: Johns Hopkins University Press, 2007); J.L. Granatstein and Norman Hillmer, *For Better or for Worse: Canada and the United States into the Twenty-First Century,* 2nd ed.(Toronto: Nelson, 2007).

13 The editors of this book themselves are guilty on this score: Asa McKercher, *Camelot and Canada: Canadian-American Relations in the Kennedy Era* (New York: Oxford University Press, 2016); Michael D. Stevenson, "'Tossing a Match into Dry Hay': Nuclear Weapons and the Crisis in U.S.-Canadian Relations, 1962–1963," *Journal of Cold War Studies* 16, 4 (2014): 5–34.

14 Michael D. Behiels and Reginald C. Stuart, "Introduction: Forging a New American Continent; Transnational Theories and Studies," in *Transnationalism: Canada–United States History into the 21st Century,* ed. Michael D. Behiels and Reginald C. Stuart (Montreal and Kingston: McGill-Queen's University Press, 2010), 5.

15 On the British World, see Phillip Buckner, ed., *Canada and the End of Empire* (Vancouver: UBC Press, 2005); and Phillip Buckner and R. Douglas Francis, eds.,

Canada and the British World: Culture, Migration, and Identity (Vancouver: UBC Press, 2006). For an introduction to the United States in the world, see Frank Costigliola and Michael J. Hogan, eds., *America in the World: The Historiography of American Foreign Relations since 1941* (Cambridge, UK: Cambridge University Press, 2013); and Andrew Preston and Doug Rossinow, *Outside In: The Transnational Circuitry of US History* (New York: Oxford University Press, 2017).

16 Exceptions can be found in several of the essays in Magda Fahrni and Robert Rutherdale, eds., *Creating Postwar Canada: Community, Diversity, and Dissent, 1945–75* (Vancouver: UBC Press, 2007).

17 Reinhold Wagnleitner, *Coca-Colonization and the Cold War: The Cultural Mission of the United States in Austria after the Second World War* (Chapel Hill: University of North Carolina Press, 1994); Rob Kroes, *If You've Seen One, You've Seen the Mall: Europeans and American Mass Culture* (Urbana: University of Illinois Press, 1996); Richard Pells, *Not Like Us: How Europeans Have Loved, Hated, and Transformed American Culture since World War II* (New York: Basic Books, 1997); Victoria De Grazia, *Irresistible Empire: America's Advance through Twentieth-Century Europe* (Cambridge, MA: Harvard University Press, 2005); David Ellwood, *The Shock of America: Europe and the Challenge of the Century* (Oxford: Oxford University Press, 2012).

18 The most useful study of Canadian anti-Americanism remains J.L. Granatstein, *Yankee Go Home? Canadians and Anti-Americanism* (Toronto: HarperCollins, 1996).

19 Asa McKercher and Philip van Huizen, eds., *Undiplomatic History: Rethinking Canada in the World* (Montreal and Kingston: McGill-Queen's University Press, 2019); Karen Dubinsky, Sean Mills, and Scott Rutherford, eds., *Canada and the Third World: Overlapping Histories* (Toronto: University of Toronto Press, 2016); Karen Dubinsky, Adele Perry, and Henry Yu, eds., *Within and without the Nation: Canadian History as Transnational History* (Toronto: University of Toronto Press, 2015).

20 On postwar American power, see Stephen Wertheim, *Tomorrow, the World: The Birth of US Global Supremacy* (Cambridge, MA: Harvard University Press, 2020); and Melvyn P. Leffler, *A Preponderance of Power: National Security, the Truman Administration, and the Cold War* (Palo Alto, CA: Stanford University Press, 1992).

21 "A Foreign Idea?," *Economist*, 29 May 1943.

22 Lionel Gelber, "Canada's New Stature," *Foreign Affairs* 24 (1946): 277; A.R.M. Lower, "Canada, the Second Great War, and the Future," *International Journal* 1, 2 (1946): 99; Grant Dexter, *Canada and the Building of Peace* (Toronto: Canadian Institute of International Affairs, 1944), 18.

23 Brooke Claxton, "The Place of Canada in Post-War Organization," *Canadian Journal of Economics and Political Science* 10, 4 (1944): 421; Hugh L. Keenleyside, "Canada's Department of External Affairs," *International Journal* 1, 3 (1946): 190.

24 Adam Chapnick, "The Canadian Middle Power Myth," *International Journal* 55, 2 (2000): 188–206; Hector Mackenzie, "Golden Decade(s)? Reappraising Canada's International Relations in the 1940s and 1950s," *British Journal of Canadian Studies* 23, 2 (2010): 179–206; Greg Donaghy, "Coming Off the Gold Standard: Re-Assessing the 'Golden Age' of Canadian Diplomacy," paper presented to the symposium A Very

Modern Ministry: Foreign Affairs and International Trade Canada, University of Saskatchewan, Saskatoon, 28 September 2009.

25 "For Good or for Evil," *Maclean's*, 15 September 1945, 1.

26 See the chapters by P. Whitney Lackenbauer and Michel S. Beaulieu in *The Unexpected Louis St-Laurent: Politics and Policies for a Modern Canada,* ed. Patrice Dutil (Vancouver: UBC Press, 2020).

27 Bruce Hutchison, *Canada: Tomorrow's Giant* (Toronto: Longman, 1957).

28 Doug Owram, *Born at the Right Time: A History of the Baby Boom Generation* (Toronto: University of Toronto Press, 1996).

29 Reg Whitaker and Gary Marcuse, *Cold War Canada: The Making of a National Security State, 1945-1957* (Toronto: University of Toronto Press, 1996); Tarah Brookfield, *Cold War Comforts: Canadian Women, Child Safety, and Global Insecurity* (Waterloo: Wilfrid Laurier University Press, 2012); Andrew Burtch, *Give Me Shelter: The Failure of Canada's Nuclear Civil Defence Program, 1945-1963* (Vancouver: UBC Press, 2012); Richard Harris, *Creeping Conformity: How Canada Became Suburban, 1900-1960* (Toronto: University of Toronto Press, 2004); L.B. Kuffert, *A Great Duty: Canadian Responses to Modern Life and Mass Culture, 1939-1967* (Montreal and Kingston: McGill-Queen's University Press, 2003); Valerie Korinek, *Roughing It in the Suburbs: Reading* Chatelaine *Magazine in the Fifties and Sixties* (Toronto: University of Toronto Press, 2000).

30 "Is Canada a Nation?," *Canadian Forum,* June 1946.

31 Royal Commission on National Development in the Arts, Letters and Sciences, *Report,* 18.

32 Royal Commission on Canada's Economic Prospects, *Final Report* (Ottawa: Queen's Printer, 1957), 390.

33 "Canada," *Time,* 5 August 1957.

Part 1

NORTH AMERICA IN A COLD WAR WORLD

1

"A Natural Development"

Canada and Non-Alignment in the Age of Eisenhower

DAVID WEBSTER

It is possible that Secretary of State John Foster Dulles has been given a raw deal regarding his reaction to Cold War neutralism. His views on non-alignment might have been more subtle than is often portrayed. It hardly matters, though. What many in the Global South heard was Dulles calling their abstention from the Cold War an "immoral and short-sighted conception."[1] Showing important continuities between the administrations of Harry Truman and Dwight Eisenhower, Dulles echoed here his Democratic predecessor Dean Acheson, who dubbed neutralism "a shortcut to suicide."[2]

Where did Canada stand on non-alignment in this age of "two camps," of the "us or them" Cold War, of McCarthyism and fallout shelter drills, of "rollback" and "massive retaliation"? Even while Canada's own military expenditure soared and Canada acted as a loyal and active member of the Western alliance headquartered in Washington, policy makers in Ottawa worried about the growth of the US national security state, a major aspect of the "American century" of the 1950s.[3]

Canadian views stood at several removes, reflecting the Canadian diplomatic self-image of Canada as a less aggressive country, aligned with the United States but willing to "constrain" aggressive American impulses when necessary. The trouble with this "diplomacy of constraint" was that it forced Canadian governments to walk a tightrope between criticism of Cold War excesses and the vital need to get along with Washington.[4]

This chapter highlights one area where Canada's government walked that tightrope. As with policy toward the Soviet Union, there was what Susan Colbourn in her chapter calls "a delicate balancing act" that Ottawa managed reasonably well. Canadian policy makers, unlike their US counterparts, welcomed the Asian-African conference in Bandung in 1955, which signalled the arrival of "Third World" assertion in international politics. The word *non-alignment* did not come to the centre until the formation of the Non-Aligned Movement in 1961, but Bandung is generally seen as an expression of non-alignment "avant la lettre."[5]

As Asa McKercher writes, "decolonisation posed a challenge to the stable, familiar global order that Canada had helped to establish following the Second World War."[6] For Canada's Department of External Affairs, gradual decolonization seemed to be a sensible course of action, and it was both unsurprising and unobjectionable that Asian governments that had just won their independence would want to avoid entanglement in the Cold War and the militarism that it entailed. Neither "immoral" nor "short-sighted," Bandung represented "a natural development arising out of the concern of the countries of the area to meet and discuss common problems, and significant [evidence] of the increasing importance of the Asian countries."[7] This was simply another conference and nothing to be feared. It could even help to cool tensions in Asia and improve understanding between the People's Republic of China and its neighbours.

This was a far cry from the attitude both in Washington and in Commonwealth capitals, where polarization between China and neighbouring countries was preferred to the amity of Bandung. The armistice in Korea, where US and Chinese soldiers had confronted each other directly, was less than two years old. Conflict in the Taiwan Strait had soared even more recently. It was just months since the signature of the Treaty of Manila forming the Southeast Asia Treaty Organization (SEATO). Along with the United States, Britain and the "Old Dominions" of Australia and New Zealand joined the new alliance. The Asian Cold War was very much alive.[8]

Bandung was one event in a chain. In this chapter, I treat it as an episode in Canada's approach to Asian non-alignment, taking the same approach as Tim Sayle does in his chapter, which addresses "ducks in a row" rather than individual crisis moments. Canada approached Southeast Asia with a self-conscious non-American tread. It aspired to be a "bridge" to the continent's new states. Policy makers in Ottawa saw no problem if those states wanted to avoid alliances. Canada itself had opted not to join its major US and Commonwealth allies in SEATO, after all. Rather, it backed "constructive" non-communist developments in non-aligned Asia. This meant efforts to build a "special relationship" with India, which "held pride of place in Canadian eyes" among Asian states.[9] So Canada (after initial hesitations) embraced the Colombo Plan, which saw development aid flow not only to India but also to assertive nationalist states such as Indonesia and Burma.

Canadian policy makers found ways to pursue an independent policy toward non-aligned Asian countries while working to win the Cold War. Canada's approach to non-alignment diverged from American policy, yet it also served Cold War goals, as Ottawa interpreted them.

THE COLOMBO PLAN AND THE KOREAN WAR

After independence, Asian and African countries aimed at improved standards of living and economic development, often simply reaffirming late-colonial development strategies. Thus, "the development project was constructed on the shaken foundations – rather than the ruins – of colonialism," as development scholar Molly Kane writes.[10] In responding to the call for aid, donor self-interest clearly operated. Historian Corinna Unger concludes that "there were very few, if any, instances in which aid was not connected to larger political, economic, ideological or strategic positions."[11]

The Commonwealth's Colombo Plan for economic development assistance to South and Southeast Asia was no exception. It aimed, openly, at Cold War motives. Aid to India, Pakistan, and other Asian countries, its boosters hoped, would help to keep Asian governments friendly to the West. This seemed to be all the more important since China was "lost" to communism.[12] Canadian planners hoped to preserve Asia within the non-communist world, and aid seemed to be a way to safeguard "the weakest link in the capitalist chain," as diplomat Escott Reid, citing Soviet leader Josef Stalin, called it. Asia represented, he wrote, a "main base of western Europe," Canada's central strategic preoccupation.[13] Asia mattered. As a result, Reid wrote later, "we in Canada also became conscious of the great value of the new Commonwealth as a bridge between the older democracies of the West and the newer democracies of Asia."[14]

The influence of Reid, a self-described "radical mandarin" on the left wing of the Department of External Affairs, should not be overestimated. His hopes for a "special relationship" between Canada and India generally took a back seat to concerns more central in Ottawa.[15] Still, this mental map of Canada serving as a "bridge" to neutral Asia became a significant if subordinate stream in Canadian diplomatic thinking. "This new commonwealth is providing not only a link between the Asian and the other members that comprise it, but also a very valuable link between the east and the west," Pearson argued.[16] The Colombo Plan, he told Prime Minister Louis St. Laurent, was "one situation where the countries of the Commonwealth can play an important part in bridging the gap between the poverty and therefore the neutrality and indifference of free Asia and the wealth and therefore, at times, the 'interventionist' and impatient tactics of the United States."[17] His Progressive Conservative successor, Sidney Smith, felt just the same. Smith called the plan "one of the particularly productive bridges between Canada and our friends in south and southeast Asia."[18]

India was especially crucial. It was the Commonwealth's largest member, the keystone to the multiracial "new Commonwealth" in the making, and as the great capitalist democracy of Asia it could pave the path for other colonies as they regained their independence. Instructions to Canada's high commissioner in New Delhi expressed hopes that India could become "a durable bridge between the West and Asia" and that India would "look to the Western world for support and understanding."[19] Prime Minister of India Jawaharlal Nehru reciprocated, praising Canada's "very important service in being in some ways a link between the growing countries of Asia and Europe and the Americas."[20]

Canadian policy makers made decisions on a realist calculus of the national interest, one that ironically enough would help to forge the Canadian diplomatic self-image as mediator.[21] That self-image painted Canada as kinder and subtler than the United States. Underpinning the self-image was a different form of public engagement. In Canada, for instance, rightwing "Asia hawks" were rarer than in the United States, where the so-called China Lobby was politically influential, whereas Canadian officials regularly leaned on the work of groups such as the United Nations Association.[22] Certainly, US policy makers, both Democrats and Republicans, were much more skeptical about India than their Canadian counterparts.[23]

Thus, Canadian diplomats tried to work with India in particular during the conflict in Korea and saw the chance to collaborate with their counterparts in India as one argument for joining the truce supervision commissions in Vietnam, Cambodia, and Laos. The existence of non-communist neutral states, Canada and India agreed, was acceptable, despite US objections.[24] In Korea, the "diplomacy of constraint" included efforts to act as a channel between New Delhi and Washington, and there were occasional efforts to mediate in Vietnam between Asian opinion and Washington. This experience shaped Canada's stance toward early Asian constructions of what would become non-alignment.[25]

THE ORIGINS OF ASIAN NON-ALIGNMENT

With African independence lying mostly in the future, the idea of an organized group of countries that chose to abstain from the Cold War formed mainly in Asia, with three countries – India, Burma, and Indonesia – forming the "hard core" of this "Asian neutralism."[26] Yet in 1949 all three appeared to be poised to follow policies broadly sympathetic to the Western powers in the Cold War. The course of events in 1949–53 set each of them on the path to what would become non-alignment. Ironically, US government choices were a big part of why they opted for "neutralism."

In 1945, Asian delegates to the founding conference of the United Nations planned an Asian Relations Conference, meant to be the expression of the continent's resurgence. Nehru, soon to be India's prime minister, hosted the event in 1947, stressing that there was no hostile intent toward Europe.[27] When delegate John Thivy of Malaya "suggested the formation of a neutrality bloc," delegates – including Nehru's sister Vijaya Lakshmi Pandit – shot down the idea.[28] When Nehru and prime minister of Indonesia Mohammad Hatta rejected alignment, it was in response to domestic calls to ally with the Soviet Union. Hatta preferred to "row between two reefs" rather than take up with Moscow. In practice, that meant closer ties to the United States.[29] This stance lined up well with that of Secretary of

State Dean Acheson, who agreed with Nehru's statement that "time was not ripe for a pact corresponding to the North Atlantic Treaty, owing to [internal Asian] conflicts."[30] Whereas Canada and Australia opposed American positions on the UN Temporary Commission for Korea in the late 1940s, India sided with Washington and promised more of the same in exchange for economic aid.[31] A US report on Nehru's tour of Southeast Asia in 1950 noted that "the theme of his speeches was a strong attack against Communism instead of the continued existence of European colonialism in Asia which it might so well have been ... In speaking so frankly Nehru served our purposes admirably."[32]

Early moves toward non-alignment can be traced to the Conference on Indonesia in 1949, the first regional meeting of Asian governments. Proposed by prime minister of Burma U Nu and hosted by Nehru in New Delhi, the conference aimed to mobilize anti-colonial sentiment in support of Indonesia's struggle for independence against Dutch rule. It picked up on moves by Burma, India, Pakistan, and (in its first foreign policy step as an independent government) Ceylon, all of which banned Dutch overflights.[33]

Most of the speeches in New Delhi breathed outrage at Dutch actions. "Those of us," said Ceylon's delegate, Solomon Bandaranaike, "who believe in the democratic way of life and who wish therefore to establish close and friendly relations with other democratic countries, particularly of the West, – I should like to say and quite frankly, – ... have suffered a grievous disappointment."[34] But again this meeting framed itself not as anti-Western but as assisting the United Nations. If alignment was rejected, then it was alignment with the Soviet Union. General Carlos Romulo of the Philippines saw a chance "to strengthen the forces of democracy, to prevent other ideologies from capturing the faith of Asia by default," and to produce "an Asian front against Communism."[35] The same belief seems to have been held in Moscow. According to *Pravda* on 9 February 1949, the goal of the conference was "to create an anti-Communist bloc, which will serve as an instrument of an imperialist war against the USSR, against the new democracy of China and the freedom of Asiatic peoples."[36]

No Asian bloc resulted, but the supports were in place for common action during the Korean War. Asian states, by and large, saw that conflict as a clear case of aggression that had to be halted by UN action. Burma's U Nu told his parliament that "the United Nations was pledged to suppress aggression wherever it occurred and if Burma did not support it now, other member nations might take little interest in Burma, if she was ever faced with a similar situation."[37] Along with Indonesia and India, it pledged non-troop contributions to the UN effort.[38] Yet US government actions and language would start to push them away. A false report that Indonesia would close its ports prompted an angry message from Acheson that accepted Indonesia "maintaining neutrality within limits for a reasonable length of time" but threatened to suspend US aid since "in [the] struggle between USSR and free world Indonesian choice is not only unavoidable but has been made."[39] Indonesia soon reaffirmed its loyalty, and India's parliament voted unanimously to support the "United Nations Command" in Korea.[40]

Then, in Indian diplomat K.N. Pannikar's recollection, the Truman administration "willy-nilly as a result of the Korean incident stepped directly into the Chinese civil war" by guaranteeing support for Chiang Kai-shek's "Republic of China" based in Taiwan.[41] Few in non-communist Asia welcomed the triumph of China's communists and their declaration of a new People's Republic of China (PRC) in late 1949, but it would be necessary for the peace of Asia to recognize the PRC, as most Asian countries soon did. Nehru appealed to Acheson to allow the PRC to assume China's UN seat.[42] Indian observers hoped that the move might avoid too close an alignment between China and the USSR and saw India-China friendship as a way to prevent Soviet advances and keep regional peace.[43] In Korea, India famously warned the United States that its forces should not enter North Korean territory as they advanced for fear of provoking China.[44] India pressed for a UN committee to examine all ideas on Korea, a concept originally proposed by Pearson but that, in the end, he felt he could not support openly in UN voting.[45]

Conversations about a possible league of neutral nations took place between India and Egypt in 1952, but Nehru was not prepared to agree until preparations began for the founding conference of the Non-Aligned Movement in 1961.[46] Instead, he sought an "area of peace" anchored in five principles (Panch Sheel) agreed between India and China in 1954. It was in many ways a self-interested response to China's annexation of Tibet and threats to Nepal, which pointed to the need for a deal between the Asian giants. "By this agreement," Nehru told Premier of China Zhou Enlai, "we ensure peace to a very large extent in a certain area of Asia. I would earnestly wish that this area of peace could be spread over Asia and indeed over the rest of the world."[47] The peace area, Nehru told his parliament, might provide safety from "those great countries that are so explosively bitter against each other."[48] The peace area, "materially speaking, [was] a weak man's policy," in the words of Indian diplomat V.K. Krishna Menon.[49] It was also a step toward non-alignment.

This type of non-alignment could be welcomed in Ottawa, where Pearson saw India as a partner in the quest for peace, even while he knew that Canada itself would side with the United States if the cards were down. Ottawa's smiling policy seemed to be justified when neutral Asian governments appealed to China, as they had earlier to the United States, not to cross the former North-South boundary in Korea. The appeal, in the words of another top Indian diplomat, Benegal Rau, "gave the first indication to a distracted world that the countries of Asia had taken the initiative – as they would be immediately concerned – to prevent the outbreak of hostilities in the East, which might ultimately envelop the entire world."[50] Pearson teamed up with Rau and Iran's Nasrollah Entezam in a General Assembly–mandated peace bid, which he described at length in his memoirs and which carved his path to a Nobel Peace Prize for his later Suez Crisis work.[51] Contrary to the trio's wishes, the United States insisted that China be branded as an aggressor and again drove Asian states away. Once pro-American, Indonesia, for instance, warned the US government against the "second failure" that its policies in Korea seemed to be indicating.[52]

Nehru believed that he had an implicit deal with the Canadians to restrain the United States while India restrained China.[53] Yet the pressure from Washington was too strong for Canada not to support the "aggressor" resolution. Thus, India and Burma joined the Soviet bloc in opposing the US resolution, whereas other Asian countries abstained from voting. Rau noted that "when the world was marching, in our view, toward disaster we – most of the Asian powers – did all we could to halt that march." He did not blame Canada, though. "United States pressure was too great for them, and they were unable to act independently and according to their own better judgment."[54] Canada, in other words, seemed to be more sympathetic than the United States but powerless to act on its convictions.

Peace in Korea was not the top Canadian priority. As a draft memorandum for cabinet noted, "the present negotiations looking toward a cease-fire in Korea, important though they are, must not be allowed to obscure the extreme danger in which the free world now stands and in which it will continue to stand until it has greatly increased its forces in being."[55] Following this first unified Asian action at the United Nations, India would rely less on the Commonwealth bond and more on its neutral neighbours.[56]

When most Asian governments were left out of the Geneva Conference on Korea and Vietnam in 1954, five of them formed a new association of their own to try to promote peace in the region. The Colombo Plan conference of Ceylon, India, Pakistan, Burma, and Indonesia "was going to demonstrate to the world that the people of Asia know what was good for them," said John Kotelawala, Ceylon's staunch anti-communist prime minister.[57]

A peculiar association of Asian nations had formed out of the Korean War. Part of the reason was the effort to restrain the United States and seek good relations with China, the new unavoidable presence in the region. From that came disappointment with American actions. There was disappointment with Canada, too, but it was accompanied by a greater understanding, a sense that Canada had not done the right thing but at least had *wanted* to do so. Krishna Menon told High Commissioner Escott Reid that the Americans were as bad as the Russians, with Canada a little better.[58] Faint praise but an opening nevertheless.

CONSTRAINING DULLES?
THE COLOMBO PLAN CONFERENCE, OTTAWA, 1954

The Colombo Plan, and "the transnational aid impulse"[59] more generally, offered Canadian policy makers a way to expand that opening, widening the "bridge" to Asia and reducing the temptations of communism. Aid, in other words, was harnessed to the national interest.[60] This was no accident:

documents produced at the time make it clear. The "daily practices of people and government" have maintained a system of domination ever since.[61]

Canada's aid policy served the wider Western interest but with more smiles. While Eisenhower and Dulles waved sticks, Ottawa offered some carrots. But did Asian leaders want those carrots? The Colombo Plan was one way to find out. When Canada's turn to host the plan's annual conference arrived, policy makers aimed to advance a very different approach than that of the United States.

Although the Colombo Plan was a proud Commonwealth initiative, much of Canada's attitude toward it revolved around Canada-US relations and the American government's Asia policy. Initially, Prime Minister Louis St. Laurent resisted any Canadian pledge unless the United States also joined it. Yet Congress wanted any aid to Asia framed "in terms of the defence of the free world."[62] It was especially suspicious of India. "To Canada," a dispatch from Ottawa to New Delhi noted, "this means that the economic foundations of the Colombo Plan become more shaky just at a time when the political desirability of Canada showing its support for India becomes more urgent."[63]

In the end, US aid did flow, though most of it went outside Colombo Plan channels. National Security Council document NSC-124 concluded that aid could help to "prevent the countries of southeast Asia from passing into the communist orbit, and to assist them in developing the will and ability to resist communism from within and without and to contribute to the strengthening of the free world."[64]

The Colombo Plan also satisfied the goals of non-Commonwealth Asian states. Burma, Indonesia, and others signed on by 1953, seeing the prospect of modernization with fewer strings attached than other aid sources. Echoing Frantz Fanon, President of Indonesia Sukarno spoke of combining modernization with preservation of Indigenous traditions: "We don't aim to tear off the skin of our cultural and social face, and put on a European or American mask," he told a US audience in 1956. "What we of Indonesia are aiming at, is to rejuvenate our own precious cultural and social heritage by opening our doors for influx from the West."[65]

US allies Japan, the Philippines, and Thailand were ready to join at the plan's conference in 1954, held in Ottawa. Here lay a chance, in the words of a Department of External Affairs memorandum, to "increase support for expenditure to help the under-developed countries" and to "stimulate public awareness of North American interest in the Area from a political point of view."[66] A sense pervades the documents that Canadian officials were trying to convince their American counterparts to take a friendlier stance toward neutral Asia. The plan could still serve Cold War goals. From Moscow, the Canadian embassy reported that "the Soviet Government are genuinely concerned at the possibility of an Asiatic Marshall plan."[67]

The tone of helping the Cold War cause through sunnier ways is clearest in a memorandum from Pearson to St. Laurent seeking increased contributions to the Colombo Plan and UN technical assistance schemes:

> I am sure that you will agree with me that nothing is more important in the fight against Communist penetration of Asia than assistance of the kind we have been giving under the Colombo Plan and the United Nations scheme. I think that Canada can play a more important role in the fight against Asian Communism by assistance of this kind than by joining organizations such as SEATO ... Something really big and imaginative has to be done in Asia in the social, economic and technical assistance fields if the ground that is being lost because the Communists have been able to identify themselves with nationalism and change ... is to be regained.[68]

With the apparent success of the Colombo Plan, US diplomats began to wonder whether it could be the basis for a non-communist regional association, a valuable economic counterpart to SEATO. "We could gain a great deal of advantage in using the Colombo Plan as a springboard for an Asian development program," one State Department official argued.[69] The prospect worried some Asian neutrals. Indonesia's foreign minister, for instance, shared his "fear that the United States would tend to dominate what has been, up to now, a very agreeable and acceptable form of aid."[70]

Thus, Ottawa followed a dual policy. On the one hand, US consideration of increased economic aid was welcome. "The growing appreciation of the importance of economic assistance as a major means of promoting stability in the area is very much to the good," External Affairs telegrammed the embassy in Washington. On the other hand, any linkage to SEATO and US strategy had to be avoided. As External Affairs put it, there was a "real need ... for the type of association in which the Asian 'neutrals' can rest easily. The Commonwealth is one such association and the Colombo Plan is another. We therefore think it highly important to preserve the present character of the Colombo Plan."[71] The plan represented an "important factor in the effort to create basically stable conditions in the area, and it is performing a useful service as a common meeting ground for the free nations of Asia and the West."[72]

The primary goal, then, was to educate the Americans, especially if the secretary of state himself attended. The Colombo Plan gathering could "be a good experience for Mr. Dulles and might give us an opportunity to impress upon him one aspect of the general approach to the countries of South and [S]outheast Asia which we think constructive," one External Affairs memorandum argued.[73] Furthermore, it "might help him to appreciate the importance of the United States seeking in this field [economic development] the free co-operation of all the Asian countries and not limiting participation to those which might be prepared to join SEATO."[74] There were shades here of the Washington elite's perception of Dulles as "an awkward dinner guest, often inelegantly dressed in off-green suits," somehow needing to be educated in proper ways.[75]

Dulles did not attend, and the conference did not see closer Colombo Plan alignment with SEATO. Asian neutrals and Commonwealth member states retained their leading role. Still, US development aid to Asia soared in the years that followed. The Mutual Security Act of 1956 authorized this aid given "international communism and the nations it controls by threat of military action, use of economic pressure, internal subversion and other means to attempt to bring under their domination peoples now free and independent."[76]

Canada's approach to aid also had Cold War goals, though it stressed non-military aid and a charm offensive directed at the neutral Asian governments. That approach continued as Asian and African independent states gathered as a group in 1955.

BANDUNG: "A NATURAL DEVELOPMENT"

When Indonesia hosted the twenty-nine-member Asian-African conference at Bandung in 1955, only one Western alliance member sent greetings. Perhaps as a result, Prime Minister Louis St. Laurent's relatively anodyne wish that "the Conference will contribute to the welfare of the people of Asia and Africa and promote the settlement by peaceful means of all disputes" featured prominently on the opening page of one issue of the Bandung Conference daily bulletin.[77]

St. Laurent did not speak in a daring fashion. Still, his words were a far cry from views in Washington, where the news that an Asian-African conference would take place drew fears that China would hoodwink the "relatively inexperienced Asian diplomats" into opposing SEATO and US policy and ultimately aid "the communist engulfment of these nations."[78] Britain and France opposed the conference and initially urged invitees not to attend it, then joined the United States in accepting that it would take place but pressing for it to avoid strong positions.[79] Australian foreign minister R.G. Casey wrote to Lester B. Pearson to "greatly regret the holding of this conference, which is the first attempted large-scale line-up of non-Europeans against Europeans."[80] Against this background, polite good wishes from Canada must have looked like a whole-throated endorsement, breaking with the United States, France, and the Commonwealth.

"Bandung introduced a fundamentally anticolonial discourse," writes Sara Lorenzini.[81] This anti-colonialism crossed and linked nations, advancing what Vijay Prashad calls the "Third World project" of national and global liberation.[82] Both historians cite Sukarno's declaration that Bandung marked Asians and Africans becoming "masters in our house." The conference aimed not to create a new regional organization but to change the norms of international relations.[83] But in regard to economic aspects, there was no fundamental challenge. Rather, as development scholar Gilbert Rist argues, Bandung accelerated rather than opposed the promotion of Western development models.[84]

The conference in the end did not launch any head-on challenges to existing global norms or signal any advances for the Soviet Union. True, China improved relations with its Asian neighbours, but this was possible only by replicating the existing China-India accord on a larger scale. China acquiesced to neutral governments in Asia cracking down on their local communist parties, even seeking friendship with the Philippines as it backed US Cold War aims and suppressed leftist movements.[85] Bandung accepted the United Nations as the major channel for economic change, welcomed aid and foreign investment, and shied away from calls to establish a permanent Asian-African organization.

In a circular to Canada's overseas posts, diplomat Arthur Menzies praised the "responsible attitudes in the discussions" and "spirit of moderation." Calling the Bandung final declaration on world peace and cooperation "a thoughtful and construct[ive] document" that lacked "any aura of Communist peace propaganda," Menzies speculated that the conference "may have the final result of bringing closer the time when Asia will be able to co-operate with the West without any of the afterthoughts of colonialism which have impeded good relations until now. If this is so, the beneficial results of the Asian-African Conference from the Western point of view will outweigh Communist China's undoubted success there."[86]

There was no doubt that Canada's stance was still dictated by Cold War goals – to hide that would have been "absurd," one External Affairs official wrote.[87] Hopes in India that Canada itself would move toward non-alignment were "mistaken," in the words of Chester Ronning from his perch as high commissioner in New Delhi.[88] Ottawa diverged but did not break ranks. Its positive attitude toward the conference seemed to be justified when both the United States and Britain expressed relief at the moderation of the event.[89]

The diverging Canadian attitude lingered, for instance, during the Suez Crisis in 1956, when

> the Colombo Plan has taken on even greater significance as a means of preserving the ties of friendship and mutual interest among the Asian and Western members of the Plan (Commonwealth and non-Commonwealth alike), and in presenting to the world at large an example of successful co-operation in the field of economic development among countries whose political relationships have been subjected to recent strains.[90]

CANADA AND THE INDONESIAN CIVIL WAR, 1956–57

It is possible that the Canadian divergence led to three of its main allies leaving Canada out of a covert effort to overthrow the Indonesian government in 1956–57. The Eisenhower administration was much concerned that "Asian dominoes" might fall in the face of advancing communist tides and entirely happy to engage in "secret wars" to topple non-communist nationalist governments in the Global South.[91] Generally, these covert actions, which most famously saw US-backed coups in Iran (1953) and Guatemala (1954), are associated with Secretary of State John Foster Dulles and his brother, Allen Dulles, director of the Central Intelligence Agency (CIA). But Eisenhower, in this as in other aspects of his administration, was also an active participant. To cite Allen Dulles, the White House had "an intense interest in every aspect of covert action."[92]

American embassy, State Department, military, and CIA officials all maintained contacts with opponents of President Sukarno in Indonesia. In 1956, they encouraged plans by these dissidents, linked to Indonesia's more conservative political parties, to declare a dissident "emergency government." The "Revolutionary Government of the Republic of Indonesia" also drew covert support from Britain and Australia, and US flights in support of the rebels came from bases in Taiwan and the Philippines. In tandem with covert intervention in this Indonesian civil war, American, Australian, and British officials became much more hostile to Sukarno's government.

For Canada, nothing changed.[93] None of the three governments trying to topple Sukarno informed their Canadian counterparts of their intentions. Thus, Ottawa continued to seek cordial, if not close, relations with Sukarno's government and to negotiate possible aid projects through the Colombo Plan. When External Affairs signalled that it planned to approve the sale of trucks made by Ford Canada to the Indonesian army, the news drew a rebuke from Australia. The tone of injured surprise in an External Affairs report indicates the gulf between views in Canberra and Ottawa:

> To the extent that we had considered that these trucks might have some influence on developments within Indonesia we had for our part regarded it as important to ensure that the trucks would in fact

remain under the control of the central government; otherwise our release of this might encourage dissident groups to undertake (or assist them in undertaking) armed revolt ... To act otherwise could be interpreted as giving tacit support to the opponents of the central government, and surely would tend sooner or later to drive the government further towards the Communists and hence render substantially less likely a stabilization of the situation on terms reconcilable with western interests.[94]

The question of how best to promote Western interests explained the divergence. Canadian officials believed that aid to Sukarno's government would "strengthen the position of the political moderates in Djakarta," whereas their Australian counterparts feared that aid would encourage Indonesians already "turning to communism."[95]

Officials in Ottawa quickly realized what their allies were up to, and it was undeniable after Indonesian forces captured a CIA operative bombing their country. Diplomat John Holmes urged a quiet Canadian effort at constraint, wondering "if we could not prod our NATO colleagues into revising an attitude towards Indonesia that is quite clearly accelerating the drift to catastrophe."[96] Ottawa duly instructed Canadian missions in London and Washington to stress the "danger that resentment against alleged 'foreign interference' may inflame anti-Western feeling in Indonesia and may force the moderates in the Djakarta Government to adopt a more extreme position."[97]

It was military victory by the Indonesian army, rather than Canadian urging, that ended covert operations against Sukarno. He emerged stronger from the episode and far more skeptical of the West. Canada's stance, though not decisive, marked another example of a different approach to neutral Asia, one that sought to advance Western interests in ways that welcomed rather than condemned Asian assertiveness.

THE ROAD TO BELGRADE

This discussion has concentrated on uncommitted Asian states. Africa appeared on Ottawa's agenda later. When Ghana became the first Black

African member of the Commonwealth in 1957, some hoped that it might look to Canada for guidance, but relations remained low key. Canada's high commissioner in Ghana was unimpressed with the All-African People's Conference in 1958, and Canada showed limited interest in francophone Africa, even going so far as to side with France over the non-aligned states in the Algeria conflict.[98] It was not until 1960 that the Commonwealth established an African counterpart to the Colombo Plan.

Non-alignment did not become official until the Belgrade conference of 1961 founded the Non-Aligned Movement. Along with the UN Declaration on the Granting of Independence to Colonial Peoples and Countries passed in December 1960, it might be called the end of the "age of Eisenhower" for the Global South and the non-aligned world. (Unlike the United States, Britain, France, and most other colonial powers, Canada voted for the declaration.[99]) For some, the high hopes of non-alignment were dashed by 1960, even before Belgrade sought to revive them. Gamal Abdel Nasser, for instance, "spoke of non-alignment in the past tense" and "had lost faith in the UN," according to the report of Canadian ambassador Arnold Smith as 1960 drew to a close.[100]

Changes under the presidency of John F. Kennedy can be read as a belated American embrace of Canada's softer stances toward non-alignment and the Global South. Kennedy pledged to be more sympathetic to anti-colonial struggles than Eisenhower, and it would be for his administration to determine the US stance toward non-alignment as the Eisenhower presidency ended. Kennedy modified rather than abandoned the Eisenhower stress on a Cold War national security state and US global leadership. On non-alignment, the Kennedy administration was closer than its predecessor to the Canadian stance that had emerged in the 1950s toward Asian desires to abstain from the Cold War and plot an independent course in global affairs – an "independent and active" policy, as Indonesia's government called it, or "positive neutralism" in Egypt's formulation. Eventually, it was willing to embrace the Belgrade conference's call for "peaceful co-existence."[101]

Non-alignment was born in the 1950s before the word was applied. So too was Canada's attitude toward it. The difference simply might have been more tactical than substantive, part of what Escott Reid described as a preference to follow "the main lines of the larger world strategy" over "consideration of short-run gains or losses to our Western cause."[102] Still, it was a genuine divergence. On this, the St. Laurent and Diefenbaker governments made similar choices. Diefenbaker preferred pro-Western Pakistan to non-aligned India but still tried to work with the whole Asian Commonwealth. The prime minister cherished the Commonwealth "mission and mandate of freedom" and its capacity to act as a "dynamic incubator of new nations."[103] Thus, he fought to keep it united – prioritizing African non-aligned states' wishes over that of South Africa, for instance.[104]

All this made a good fit with the Canadian diplomatic self-image, which sought differentiation from the United States. As Janice Cavell concludes, "anti-American nationalism" served Diefenbaker electorally.[105] It simply developed Pearson's statement in 1951 that the "relatively easy and automatic relations" with Canada's mighty ally had ended.[106] Diefenbaker's stance on Eisenhower-era crises such as the deployment in 1958 of US troops to Lebanon was little different from Canadian foreign policy under St. Laurent or Pearson.[107]

Canadian generosity as an aid donor should not be overestimated. Canada was a laggard in the 1950s, as it is today, scoring below average among donors in terms of aid as a percentage of gross national income. In 1957, Canada stood with the United States and Britain in voting against a Special United Nations Fund for Economic Development (SUNFED), which "died on the vine" despite the hopes of poorer countries.[108] Canada in the 1960s would attempt to side with demands for decolonization in order to moderate African governments but abandoned the effort and came to side with the West.[109]

Nor should any of this be taken to suggest Canadian altruism. Canada's dilemma lay in a fervent wish to avoid any "white versus Asiatic" split, coupled with a determination to remain "loyal" to one team in the Cold War.[110] This was true at both national and global levels. Canada's relations with Egypt, for instance, were "more as a member of 'the West' than bilateral," as Arnold Smith noted.[111] Similarly, Pearson stressed that "membership in the Atlantic group, of which the US was the leader ... did not prevent us from speaking with our own voice or making our own decisions."[112] Canada's friendlier attitude toward non-alignment is best seen as a different tactic aimed at winning the same Cold War battles.

Canadian policy makers, more than their American and other Western counterparts, saw the prevalence of assertive, "independent," and "active" positions in Asia and later Africa as a "natural development" that was no threat to the Western alliances that formed the core of Canadian foreign policy. Canada was able thereby to abstain from some aspects of the hardline Cold War of the Eisenhower years. Seen from Ottawa, non-alignment was not "immoral" but natural. It deserved quiet Canadian sympathy, even while Canada remained firmly anchored in its own alliances.

NOTES

Acknowledgments: This chapter was originally to be co-authored with the late Greg Donaghy, whose thoughts inspire much of its approach. Errors of content and interpretation are entirely mine.

1 P.K. Menon, "The Non-Aligned Countries in the Global Arena," *Indian Journal of Political Science* 27, 3–4 (1966): 37–47, Dulles cited on 37.

2 Vijay Prashad, *The Darker Nations: A People's History of the Third World* (New York: New Press, 2007), 48. On US policy toward the Third World, see H.W. Brands, *The Specter of Neutralism: The United States and the Emergence of the Third World, 1947–1960* (New York: Columbia University Press, 1989); and Kathryn C. Statler and Andrew L. Johns, eds., *The Eisenhower Administration, the Third World, and the Globalization of the Cold War* (Lanham, MD: Rowman and Littlefield, 2006).

3 William I. Hitchcock, *The Age of Eisenhower: America and the World in the 1950s* (New York: Simon and Schuster, 2018). Ironically, Canada was constructing its own national security state at the same time; see Reg Whitaker and Gary Marcuse, *Cold War Canada: The Making of a National Insecurity State, 1945–1957* (Toronto: University of Toronto Press, 1994).

4 Denis Stairs, *The Diplomacy of Constraint: Canada, the Korean War, and the United States* (Toronto: University of Toronto Press, 1974); Robert S. Prince, "The Limits of Constraint: Canadian-American Relations and the Korean War, 1950–51," *Journal of Canadian Studies* 27, 4 (1992–93): 129–52.

5 For US and British reactions to Bandung, see Jason Parker, "Cold War II: The Eisenhower Administration, the Bandung Conference, and the Reperiodization of the Postwar Era," *Diplomatic History* 30, 5 (2006): 867–92; Jason Parker, "Small Victory, Missed Chance: The Eisenhower Administration, the Bandung Conference and the Turning of the Cold War," in *The Eisenhower Administration, the Third World, and the Globalization of the Cold War,* ed. Kathryn C. Statler and Andrew L. Johns (Lanham, MD: Rowman and Littlefield, 2006), 153–74; Cary Fraser, "An American Dilemma: Race and Realpolitik in the American Response to the Bandung Conference, 1955," in *Window on Freedom: Race, Civil Rights, and Foreign Policy, 1945–1988,* ed. Brenda Gayle Plummer (Chapel Hill: University of North Carolina Press, 2003), 115–40;

Matthew Jones, "A 'Segregated' Asia? Race, the Bandung Conference, and Pan-Asianist Fears in American Thought and Policy, 1954–1955," *Diplomatic History* 29, 5 (2005): 841–68; and Nicholas Tarling, "'Ah-Ah': Britain and the Bandung Conference of 1955," *Journal of Southeast Asian Studies* 23, 1 (1992): 74–111.

6 Asa McKercher, "The Centre Cannot Hold: Canada, Colonialism, and the 'Afro-Asian Bloc' at the United Nations, 1960–1962," *Journal of Imperial and Commonwealth History* 42, 2 (2014): 329–49.

7 Secretary of State for External Affairs to High Commissioner in India, 12 April 1955, in *Documents on Canadian External Relations* (hereafter *DCER*), vol. 21, 1955, ed. Greg Donaghy (Ottawa: Department of Foreign Affairs and International Trade, 1999), 1615.

8 Stephen Hugh Lee, *Outposts of Empire: Korea, Vietnam, and the Origins of the Cold War in Asia, 1949–1954* (Montreal and Kingston: McGill-Queen's University Press, 1996); Bruce Cumings, *The Korean War: A History* (London: Penguin, 2011); Greg Donaghy, "Canadian Diplomacy and the Offshore Islands Crisis, 1954–1955: A Limited National Interest," *International Journal* 68, 2 (2013): 242–54.

9 Robert Bothwell, "Pearson and Pearsonianism," in *Mike's World: Lester B. Pearson and Canadian External Affairs,* ed. Asa McKercher and Galen Roger Perras (Vancouver: UBC Press, 2017), 25. On the special relationship, see Ryan Touhey, *Conflicting Visions: Canada and India in the Cold War World, 1946–76* (Vancouver: UBC Press, 2015).

10 Molly Kane, "Canada and the Third World: Development Aid," in *Canada and the Third World: Overlapping Histories,* ed. Karen Dubinsky, Sean Mills, and Scott Rutherford (Toronto: University of Toronto Press, 2016), 94. On the late colonial development model, see Frederick Cooper, *Africa since 1940: The Past of the Present* (Cambridge, UK: Cambridge University Press, 2002), 84.

11 Corinna Unger, *International Development: A Postwar History* (London: Bloomsbury, 2018), 97–98.

12 Ademola Adeleke, "Ties without Strings? The Colombo Plan and the Geopolitics of International Aid" (PhD diss., University of Toronto, 1996); Douglas V. LePan, *Bright Glass of Memory* (Toronto: McGraw-Hill Ryerson, 1979); Jill Campbell-Miller, "The Mind of Modernity: Canadian Bilateral Foreign Assistance to India, 1950–60" (PhD diss., University of Waterloo, 2014). German-speaking readers might also consult Ursula Lehmkuhl, *Kanadas Öffnung nach Asien der Colombo-Plan; Das "New Commonwealth" und die Rekonstruktion des Sterlinggebietes 1949–52* (Bochum: Brockmeyer, 1990).

13 "General Principles of India's Foreign Policy," memorandum from Escott Reid to Jules Léger on the occasion of Jawaharlal Nehru's visit, 20 October 1949, Library and Archives Canada (hereafter LAC), Lester B. Pearson Papers, MG 26 N1, Pre-1958 Correspondence Series, file "India-Canada Relations 1947–1957."

14 "Canadian Foreign Policy, 1947–1951," draft speech by Escott Reid, Canadian High Commissioner in India, 15 February 1957, LAC, Pearson Papers, vol. 12, file "Reid, Escott – Canada – External Affairs 1951–57."

15 Greg Donaghy and Stéphane Roussel, eds., *Escott Reid: Diplomat and Scholar* (Montreal and Kingston: McGill-Queen's University Press, 2004); Escott Reid, *Radical Mandarin*

(Toronto: University of Toronto Press, 1989); Escott Reid, *Envoy to Nehru* (Delhi: Oxford University Press, 1981).

16 Lester B. Pearson, speech, 22 February 1950, in *House of Commons Debates (HCD)*, 21st Parliament, 2nd session, vol. 1, 129–37.

17 Lester B. Pearson to Louis St. Laurent, 27 December 1950, in *DCER*, vol. 16, 1950, ed. Greg Donaghy (Ottawa: Department of Foreign Affairs and International Trade, 1996), 1276–77.

18 Sidney Smith, speech, 26 February 1959, in *HCD*, 1959, vol. 2, 1397–1408.

19 Extract from letter of instruction to the Canadian High Commissioner Designate to India, 31 August 1949, LAC, Pearson Papers, vol. 22, file 1950 pt. 1; Touhey, *Conflicting Visions*, 39.

20 Quoted in "M. Nehru Visits Ottawa," *External Affairs* 9, 1 (1957): 19.

21 Adam Chapnick, *Canada on the United Nations Security Council: A Small Power on a Large Stage* (Vancouver: UBC Press, 2019), 43.

22 Tarah Brookfield, "Save the Children/Save the World: Canadian Women Embrace the United Nations," in *Canada and the United Nations: Legacies, Limits, Prospects,* ed. Colin McCullough and Robert Teigrob (Montreal and Kingston: McGill-Queen's University Press, 2016), 104–36; Chapnick, *Canada on the United Nations Security Council*; Ted Cogan, "Building a Base: The Growth of Public Engagement with Canadian Foreign Aid Policy, 1950–1980," in *A Samaritan State Revisited: Historical Perspectives on Canadian Foreign Aid,* ed. Greg Donaghy and David Webster (Calgary: University of Calgary Press, 2019), 191–221.

23 Andrew Rotter, *Comrades at Odds: The United States and India, 1947–1964* (Ithaca, NY: Cornell University Press, 2000).

24 Bothwell, "Pearsonianism," 39.

25 Robert Bothwell, *Alliance and Illusion: Canada and the World, 1945–1984* (Vancouver: UBC Press, 2007); Douglas A. Ross, *In the Interests of Peace: Canada and Vietnam 1954–73* (Toronto: University of Toronto Press, 1984); Stairs, *The Diplomacy of Constraint*; Prince, "The Limits of Constraint"; Greg Donaghy, "Diplomacy of Constraint Revisited: Canada and the UN Korean Reconstruction Agency, 1950–55," *Journal of the Canadian Historical Association* 25, 2 (2014): 159–85; John Price, "The 'Cat's Paw': Canada and the United Nations Temporary Commission on Korea," *Canadian Historical Review* 85, 2 (2004): 297–324.

26 Ton That Thien, *India and South East Asia 1947–1960* (Geneva: Librairie Droz, 1963), 88; David Wu-wei Chang, "A Comparative Study of the Neutralism of India, Burma and Indonesia" (PhD diss., University of Illinois, 1960), 57.

27 Jawaharlal Nehru, inaugural address at the Asian Relations Conference, 23 March 1947, in *India's Foreign Policy: Selected Speeches, September 1946–April 1961,* by Nehru (New Delhi: Ministry of Information and Broadcasting, 1961), 248–53.

28 ARC proceedings, cited in G.H. Jansen, *Afro-Asia and Non-Alignment* (London: Faber and Faber, 1966), 57–61.

29 Jawaharlal Nehru, speech, 7 September 1946, in Nehru, *Speeches,* 2; Mohammad Hatta, speech, 2 September 1948, in *Portrait of a Patriot,* by Hatta (The Hague: Mouton, 1972),

446; Paige Johnson Tan, "Navigating a Turbulent Ocean: Indonesia's Worldview and Foreign Policy," *Asian Survey* 3, 3 (2007): 147–81.

30 Dean Acheson, comments at news conference, 18 May 1949, in *Foreign Relations of the United States* (hereafter *FRUS*), 1949, vol. 7, part 2, ed. John G. Reid and John P. Glennon (Washington, DC: United States Government Printing Office, 1976), 1143.

31 Surendra K. Gupta, *Stalin's Policy towards India 1946–1953* (New Delhi: South Asian, 1988), 90–91; memorandums of conversations with G.S. Bajpai, Secretary General of the Indian Foreign Ministry, 2 April 1948, in *FRUS*, 1948, vol. 5, part 1, ed. Herbert A. Fine and David H. Stauffer (Washington, DC: United States Government Printing Office, 1975), 502–8.

32 Assistant Secretary of State Raymond Hare, memorandum, 3 July 1950, in *FRUS*, 1950, vol. 5, ed. Herbert A. Fine et al. (Washington, DC: United States Government Printing Office, 1978), 1466–68.

33 H.S.S. Nissanka, *Sri Lanka's Foreign Policy: A Study in Non-Alignment* (New Delhi: Vikas, 1984), 117.

34 Text of speeches in S.L. Poplai, ed., *India 1947–50, Volume Two: External Affairs* (London: Oxford University Press, 1959), 660–81.

35 Jansen, *Afro-Asia and Non-Alignment*, 95. See also Carlos P. Romulo with Beth Day Romulo, *Forty Years: A Third World Soldier at the UN* (New York: Greenwood, 1986).

36 Cited in Gupta, *Stalin's Policy*, 119.

37 Cited in Uma Shankar Singh, *Burma and India 1948–1962* (New Delhi: Oxford, 1979), 165.

38 *Yearbook of the United Nations* (hereafter *YUN*), 1950, 227; *YUN*, 1953, 216–17.

39 Secretary of State to US Embassy in Jakarta, 26 July 1950, in *FRUS*, 1950, vol. 6, ed. Neal H. Petersen et al. (Washington, DC: United States Government Printing Office, 1976), 1039–40.

40 William Stueck, *The Korean War: An International History* (Princeton, NJ: Princeton University Press, 1995), 80.

41 K.M. Panikkar, *In Two Chinas: Memoir of a Diplomat* (London: George Allen and Unwin, 1955), 103.

42 K.P. Karunakaran, *India in World Affairs 1950–3* (New Delhi: Oxford University Press, 1952), 102–3; Panikkar, *In Two Chinas*, 104; Gupta, *Stalin's Policy*, 107; Loy Henderson to Department of State, 13 July 1950, in *FRUS*, 1950, vol. 7, ed. John P. Glennon (Washington, DC: United States Government Printing Office, 1976), 371–72; Parvathi Vasudevan, *Non-Alignment as a Factor in Indo-American Relations: The Nehru Era* (Delhi: Kalinga, 1996), 27–28.

43 Nirmal Bhattacharya, "Foreign Policy of the People's Republic of China," in *Indian Yearbook of International Affairs 1952* (Madras: Indian Study Group of International Affairs, 1952), 233.

44 Loy Henderson to Department of State, 23 September 1950 and 27 September 1950, *FRUS*, 1950, vol. 7, 763, 791; Panikkar, *In Two Chinas*, 108–10; "Factors Affecting the Desirability of a UN Military Conquest of All of Korea," CIA memo, 18 August 1950, *FRUS*, 1950, vol. 7, 600.

45 Lester B. Pearson, speech, Victoria, 21 August 1950, External Affairs Statements and Speeches 50/31; UN Delegation to External Affairs, 31 August 1950, in *DCER*, 1950, 158–60; Canadian UN Delegation to External Affairs, 5 October 1950, in *DCER*, 1950, 177–79; Stueck, *Korean War*, 63–64.

46 Magali Grolleau, "Les relations indo-égyptiennes sous Nehru (1947–1964)," in *Le Tiers-Monde postcolonial: Espoirs et désenchantements*, ed. Maurice Demers and Patrick Dramé (Montreal: Les Presses de l'Université de Montréal, 2014), 66, 73.

47 Jawaharlal Nehru, speech, 15 May 1954, in Nehru, *Speeches*, 304.

48 Jawaharlal Nehru, speech to Lok Sabha, 12 June 1952, in Nehru, *Speeches*, 58.

49 Michael Brecher, *India and World Politics: Krishna Menon's View of the World* (London: Oxford University Press, 1968), 8.

50 Cited in Jansen, *Afro-Asia and Non-Alignment*, 106.

51 Lester B. Pearson, *Mike: The Memoirs of the Right Honourable Lester B. Pearson, Volume 2: 1948–1957*, ed. John A. Munro and Alex I. Inglis (Toronto: University of Toronto Press, 1973).

52 External Affairs to UN Delegation, 19 January 1951, in *DCER*, vol. 17, 1951, ed. Greg Donaghy (Ottawa: Department of Foreign Affairs and International Trade, 1996), 60; Loy Henderson to Department of State, 27 January 1951, in *FRUS*, 1951, vol. 7 (Washington: US Government Printing Office, 1977), 140–42; L.N. Palar, Indonesian Ambassador to the United Nations, remarks, cited in Department of State to Embassy in Indonesia, 9 January 1951, in *FRUS*, 1951, vol. 7, 43–44.

53 Nehru reminded St. Laurent of this understanding, and that the aggressor resolution violated the agreed Commonwealth policy, in a letter of 19 January 1951, in *DCER*, 1951, 60–61.

54 Quoted in Jansen, *Afro-Asia and Non-Alignment*, 107.

55 Draft memorandum for cabinet, 19 December 1950, sent from External Affairs to UN Delegation, in *DCER*, 1950, 1149–52.

56 Nehru proclaimed in a speech on 30 September 1954 that "the two countries closest to India in policy were Burma and Indonesia. They are far closer than our Commonwealth link." Cited in Singh, *Burma and India*, 180.

57 John Kotelawala, *An Asian Prime Minister's Story* (London: George G. Harrop, 1956), 119.

58 Reid, *Envoy to Nehru*, 52.

59 Will Langford, *The Global Politics of Poverty in Canada* (Montreal and Kingston: McGill-Queen's University Press, 2020), 213.

60 See, for instance, Jill Campbell-Miller, "Encounter and Apprenticeship: The Colombo Plan and Canadian Aid in India, 1950–1960," in *A Samaritan State Revisited: Historical Perspectives on Canadian Foreign Aid*, ed. Greg Donaghy and David Webster (Calgary: University of Calgary Press, 2019), 27–52; and Ryan Touhey, "'A One-Way Street': The Limits of Canada's Aid Relations with Pakistan, 1958–1972," in *A Samaritan State Revisited: Historical Perspectives on Canadian Foreign Aid*, ed. Greg Donaghy and David Webster (Calgary: University of Calgary Press, 2019), 105–22. On Canadian aid history, see also François Audet, Marie-Eve Desrosiers, and Stéphane Roussel, eds.,

L'aide canadienne au développement (Montreal: Les Presses de l'Université de Montréal, 2008); Pierre Beaudet, *Qui aide qui? Une brève histoire de la solidarité internationale au Québec* (Montreal: Boréal, 2009); David R. Morrison, *Aid and Ebb Tide: A History of CIDA and Canadian Development Assistance* (Waterloo, ON: Wilfrid Laurier University Press, 1998); and Stephen Brown, Molly den Heyer, and David R. Black, eds., *Rethinking Canadian Aid* (Ottawa: University of Ottawa Press, 2016).

61 Maika Sondarjee, *Perdre le sud: Décoloniser la solidarité internationale* (Montreal: Ecosocieté, 2020), 65.

62 Memorandum from Under-Secretary of State for External Affairs (USSEA) to Secretary of State for External Affairs (SSEA), 22 January 1951, in *DCER*, 1951, 1046–48.

63 SSEA letter E-264 to New Delhi, 30 January 1951, LAC, External Affairs records, vol. 6575, file 11038–40 [5.2].

64 NSC-124/2, 25 June 1952, in *FRUS*, 1952–54, vol. 12, part 1, ed. David W. Mabon (Washington, DC: United States Government Printing Office, 1984), 125–34.

65 Sukarno, "Herodians and Zealots in Indonesia," speech at the ceremony for receiving doctorate honoris causa, Columbia University, New York, 24 May 1956, LAC, External Affairs records, vol. 7751, file 12371–40 [1.3].

66 Memorandum to the Minister, 1 September 1953, LAC, External Affairs records, vol. 6576, file 11038–40 [13.1].

67 Canadian Embassy in Moscow to SSEA, 5 November 1954, LAC, External Affairs records, vol. 6590, file 11038–5-40 [1].

68 Memorandum from SSEA to Prime Minister, 9 September 1954, in *DCER*, vol. 20, 1954, ed. Greg Donaghy (Ottawa: Department of Foreign Affairs and International Trade, 1997), 814–15.

69 "The Colombo Plan as a Vehicle for an Asian Economic Aid Program," memorandum by Director of the Office of Financial and Development Policy to Assistant Secretary of State for Economic Affairs, 24 August 1954, in *FRUS*, 1952–54, vol. 12, part 1, 781–82.

70 Sunario, remarks cited in Canadian Embassy in Jakarta to External Affairs, 6 April 1955, LAC, External Affairs records, vol. 6590, file 11038–4-40 [1].

71 SSEA to Canadian Embassy in Washington, 21 August 1954, LAC, Department of Finance records, vol. 4272, file 8055–04–1 [2].

72 SSEA to Canadian High Commission in London, 21 August 1954, LAC, Department of Finance records, vol. 4272, file 8055–04–1 [2].

73 Memorandum for the Minister, 3 June 1954, LAC, External Affairs records, vol. 4409, file 12025–40.

74 SSEA to Canadian Embassy in Washington, 14 July 1954, LAC, Department of Finance records, vol. 4272, file 8055–04–1 [2].

75 Stephen Kinzer, *The Brothers: John Foster Dulles, Allen Dulles, and Their Secret World War* (New York: Times Books, 2013), 126.

76 PL 726, 84th Congress, 2nd Session, 18 July 1956.

77 "Good Wishes from Canada," *Asian-African Conference Bulletin*, 23 April 1955, 2. All conference bulletins are digitized at http://historybeyondborders.ca/?p=142.

78 Minutes of meeting with the Secretary of State, 7 January 1955, cited in Ang Chen Guan, "The Bandung Conference and the Cold War International History," in *Bandung*

Revisited: The Legacy of the 1955 Asian-African Conference for International Order, ed. See Seng Tan and Amitav Acharya (Singapore: NUS Press, 2008), 29.

79 Darwis Khudori, *La France et Bandung: Batailles diplomatiques entre la France, l'Afrique du Nord et l'Indochine en Indonésie (1950–1955)* (Paris: Les Indes Savantes, 2020), 279.

80 R.G. Casey, personal and confidential letter to Lester B. Pearson, 28 January 1955, LAC, Pearson papers, vol. 2, file "Casey, R.G.; Australia – External Affairs – 1951–57."

81 Sara Lorenzini, *Global Development: A Cold War History* (Princeton, NJ: Princeton University Press, 2019), 41.

82 Prashad, *The Darker Nations*, xvi.

83 Amitav Acharya and See Seng Tan recall the words of Bandung Conference secretary-general Ruslan Abdulgani on this score in "Introduction: The Normative Relevance of the Bandung Conference for Contemporary Asian and International Order," in *Bandung Revisited: The Legacy of the 1955 Asian-African Conference for International Order*, ed. See Seng Tan and Amitav Acharya (Singapore: NUS Press, 2008), 3–4. See also Kane, "Development Aid," 91.

84 Gilbert Rist, *The History of Development: From Western Origins to Global Faith*, 4th ed. (London: Zed Books, 2014), 84–88. On the significance of the Bandung Conference, see Christopher J. Lee, ed., *Making a World after Empire: The Bandung Moment and Its Political Afterlives* (Athens: Ohio University Press, 2010).

85 Bandung Conference bulletins; Romulo, *Forty Years*.

86 SSEA circular, 27 July 1955, in *DCER*, 1955, 1616–25.

87 S. Morley Scott to Jules Léger, 27 August 1954, LAC, External Affairs records, vol. 6590, file 11038-5-40 [1].

88 High Commissioner in India to SSEA, 19 May 1060, in *DCER*, vol. 27, 1960, ed. Janice Cavell (Ottawa: Foreign Affairs and International Trade Canada, 2007), 825.

89 Guan, "Bandung Conference," 36.

90 "Amount of Canada's Contribution to the Colombo Plan in Financial Year 1957–58," memorandum from Lester B. Pearson to Cabinet, 28 November 1956, in *DCER*, vol. 22, part 1, 1956–57, ed. Greg Donaghy (Ottawa: Department of Foreign Affairs and International Trade, 2001), 1214–16.

91 The quotations are chapter titles from Hitchcock, *Age of Eisenhower*.

92 Kinzer, *The Brothers*, 117; see also Audrey R. Kahin and George McT. Kahin, *Subversion as Foreign Policy: The Secret Eisenhower and Dulles Debacle in Indonesia* (New York: New Press, 1995).

93 This section draws from my book *Fire and the Full Moon: Canada and Indonesia in a Decolonizing World* (Vancouver: UBC Press, 2009).

94 Memorandum for the Minister, 13 February 1958, LAC, External Affairs records, vol. 6985, file 5495-G-40 [3.1].

95 Documents cited in Webster, *Fire and the Full Moon*, 71.

96 John Holmes to P. Campbell, Far Eastern Division, 6 May 1958, LAC, External Affairs records, vol. 6985, file 5495-G-40 [3.1].

97 Memorandum for the Minister, 16 May 1958, LAC, External Affairs records, vol. 6985, file 5495-G-40 [3.2]; memorandum of conversation, Walter Robertson with Canadian

Ambassador Norman Robertson, 16 May 1958, in *FRUS*, 1958–60, vol. 17, microfiche supplement.

98 Kevin A. Spooner, "The Diefenbaker Government and Foreign Policy in Africa," in *Reassessing the Rogue Tory: Canadian Foreign Relations in the Diefenbaker Era*, ed. Janice Cavell and Ryan Touhey (Vancouver: UBC Press, 2018), 186–208. On francophone Africa, see Robin S. Gendron, *Towards a Francophone Community: Canada's Relations with France and French Africa, 1945–1968* (Montreal and Kingston: McGill-Queen's University Press, 2006).

99 McKercher, "The Centre Cannot Hold."

100 Ambassador in the United Arab Republic to SSEA, 28 December 1960, in *DCER*, 1960, 1045–51.

101 Prashad, *The Darker Nations*, 95–96.

102 Memorandum from Escott Reid to John Diefenbaker, 10 September 1957, cited in Chapnick, *Canada on the United Nations Security Council*, 51; Robert Rakove, *Kennedy, Johnson, and the Nonaligned World* (Cambridge, UK: Cambridge University Press, 2012).

103 Francine McKenzie, "A New Vision for the Commonwealth: Diefenbaker's Commonwealth Tour of 1958," in *Reassessing the Rogue Tory: Canadian Foreign Relations in the Diefenbaker Era*, ed. Janice Cavell and Ryan Touhey (Vancouver: UBC Press, 2018), 31, 32.

104 Daniel Manulak, "'An African Representative': Canada, the Third World, and South African Apartheid, 1984–1990," *Journal of Imperial and Commonwealth History* 49, 2 (2021): 368–99.

105 Janice Cavell, "The Spirit of '56: The Suez Crisis, Anti-Americanism and Diefenbaker's 1957 and 1958 Election Victories," in *Reassessing the Rogue Tory: Canadian Foreign Relations in the Diefenbaker Era*, ed. Janice Cavell and Ryan Touhey (Vancouver: UBC Press, 2018), 67–84.

106 Department of External Affairs, *Statements and Speeches* 51/14, 10 April 1951.

107 Greg Donaghy, "When the Chips Are Down: Eisenhower, Diefenbaker, and the Lebanon Crisis, 1958," in *Reassessing the Rogue Tory: Canadian Foreign Relations in the Diefenbaker Era*, ed. Janice Cavell and Ryan Touhey (Vancouver: UBC Press, 2018), 85–102.

108 Keith Spicer, *A Samaritan State?* (Toronto: University of Toronto Press, 1966), 16.

109 McKercher, "The Centre Cannot Hold."

110 John Price, *Orienting Canada: Race, Empire, and the Transpacific* (Vancouver: UBC Press, 2011), 207.

111 Memorandum from Arnold Smith to Prime Minister John Diefenbaker, 8 September 1960, in *DCER*, 1960, 1044.

112 Pearson, *Mike*, 132.

2

Cheers to the Canadian Wheat Surplus!

*Lester Pearson's Visit to the Soviet Union
and the West's Détente Dilemma*

SUSAN COLBOURN

Lester and Maryon Pearson touched down in Moscow on a beautiful autumn day. The Soviet capital glistened in the October sun, "the golden domes and spires ... glittering under a vast blue sky like that of the Canadian West."[1] Over the next week, between 5 and 13 October 1955, Pearson criss-crossed the Soviet Union, accompanied by Mitchell Sharp, the associate deputy minister of trade and commerce; a small delegation from the Department of External Affairs (DEA), made up of John Holmes, George Ignatieff, and Ray Crépault; and a handful of Canadian journalists, including the CBC's René Lévesque and Richard Needham from the *Globe and Mail*.

Pearson's October 1955 visit to the Soviet Union was a historic occasion, the first such trip by a foreign minister from a member of the North Atlantic Treaty Organization (NATO).[2] The visit's tangible outcomes were modest, such as paving the way for a trade agreement signed the next February. But Pearson's stop in Moscow was, above all, "a voyage of reconnaissance," coming at a critical juncture as the Cold War struggle between East and West settled into a protracted standoff.[3]

That Pearson travelled to the Soviet Union at all was testament to the transformations under way in international politics during the 1950s. A hallmark of that decade was the acceptance that the Cold War would endure and that, to wage it, the West would need to be prepared to do so over the long haul. With that transformation came new challenges. Pearson's visit – and the careful cautions that the secretary issued both before and after – spoke to a fundamental paradox inherent in any diplomatic engagement with the Soviet Union, one that shaped NATO's policies from the 1950s to the final days of the Cold War nearly four decades later. How could the Western allies continue to wage the Cold War, garnering the necessary public support for their policies (and their defence spending) even as the threat from Moscow seemed to recede?

Soviet leaders hammered the theme of peaceful coexistence, the popular refrain adopted after Josef Stalin's death in 1953. With these calls, those in the Kremlin sought to modulate and transform the Cold War confrontation, not diminish it. For all the change in Soviet rhetoric, the substance of Moscow's policies seemed to be yet more of the same. Despite "some interesting and important variations in tactics," Pearson counselled that the Soviet Union's basic aims and overall strategy appeared to be unchanged. Those in charge in Moscow had not yet "abandoned the dangerous paths" first charted under Stalin.[4] Despite these reservations, Pearson was willing to talk. With the advent of the atomic age, the risks inherent in international politics demanded nothing less.

Moscow's latest moves had taken the Cold War "out of the trenches," as Pearson put it, and into the open. The Soviets' shifting tactics created new opportunities to negotiate, and alongside those opportunities came new risks for the Western allies, not least the danger of unreasonable and lofty expectations. Pearson worried that Canadian voters – and those across the Atlantic Alliance – might come to believe that the various outstanding issues dividing East and West could be resolved quickly, despite their obvious complexities.[5]

Herein lay the rub, the crux of the West's détente dilemma. The Western allies might be tempted to make the most of the current opportunities to negotiate with the Soviet Union, "to relax tensions and reduce the threat of a nuclear war." If they entered into negotiations, the Soviets were almost certain to name their price. What would happen if that price was simply too high for Western governments to pay?[6]

Figuring out how and on what terms to engage the communist world was fraught, hardly surprising given the stakes. Here I consider how Canadian policy makers interpreted Moscow's calls for peaceful coexistence, grappling with both the promise and the peril for the Western allies. Pearson and his visit to the Soviet Union in October 1955, I argue, illustrated starkly the delicate balancing act required of the Western allies as they prepared to wage the Cold War over the long haul. It was critical, at once, to demonstrate a willingness to engage the Soviet Union but to do so with eyes wide open about the prospects for meaningful change.

Pearson appreciated the dangers of peaceful coexistence but also the potential to encourage change. The Cold War bolstered the Kremlin's power both at home and abroad. And so, by whittling down the various tensions between East and West, he saw the strategic advantages of a policy of détente. Canada and its allies across "the free world" could undercut the elements that made the Soviet Union seem so dangerous in the first place.[7]

STIRRINGS IN MOSCOW

Change, it seemed, might come rapidly to Soviet foreign policy in the spring of 1953. After Stalin's death in early March, Moscow's tone altered almost overnight. The new collective leadership wasted little time, even making overtures in their remarks at Stalin's funeral. Devoid of the "old abuse of the West," Soviet leaders instead trotted out "almost fervent declarations of peaceful intentions."[8] A few days later, before the Supreme Soviet, Georgy Malenkov insisted that there were no outstanding issues in relations between East and West that could not be resolved through negotiations.[9]

Canadian officials embraced the need for open lines of communication with the Soviet Union. At the University of British Columbia, Undersecretary of State for External Affairs Dana Wilgress insisted that "the free nations must seriously welcome and realistically follow up every opening for a settlement of outstanding differences."[10] But Wilgress also took pains to highlight the dangers inherent in Moscow's concept of peaceful coexistence and prevent the erosion of public support for defence spending and collective security arrangements including the Atlantic Alliance.[11]

These cautionary words echoed the conclusions circulating within the DEA. Before March was through, just weeks after Stalin's death, the chargé d'affaires at the Canadian embassy in Moscow, Robert Ford, cabled back to Ottawa with a comprehensive overview of the recent Soviet moves and overtures, along with his attempts "to estimate what the intentions of the regime are."[12]

Before diving into the policies of the new Soviet leadership, Ford set the stage, dismissing arguments that Stalin had been some sort of "great moderator, the man who really could keep the Soviet Union from plunging the world into war." If anything, the opposite was true. The fundamental sources of the current confrontation between East and West, in Ford's estimation, stemmed from Stalin's actions and policy choices. "The world could hardly have reached its present sorry state without Stalin," he concluded, "and peace could have been had at any time in the last three years by a word from him." There was little question, at least in Ford's mind, about where to lay blame.[13] Did Stalin's exit from the scene mean an opportunity to wind down the Cold War?

The new collective leadership's tone had softened, accompanied by a steady string of seemingly small gestures. Press attacks on the United States declined. In Moscow, Western diplomats were treated with greater courtesy. The Chinese and the North Koreans offered to exchange sick and wounded prisoners of war. In isolation, each of these shifts might be easily dismissed. Taken together, however, Ford concluded, "they make a fairly impressive list of Soviet acts which, compared with the negative attitude of the last few years, certainly points towards a more co-operative attitude."[14]

"We should accept these at their face value," Ford recommended, "and exploit present Soviet policy for the purposes of peace, without necessarily accepting the view that the Russians have modified their ultimate aims."[15] Cautious about Soviet intentions, Ford's assessment mirrored conclusions reached in capitals across the West. Although still "too early to determine the exact meaning of recent gestures of a seemingly conciliatory nature," in the words of one State Department circular, "the Department is inclined to doubt that they indicate any change in basic Soviet long-range objectives."[16] The Kremlin's tactics might have changed, but the Soviet Union's overriding objectives had not. "They still aim at dividing the North Atlantic Powers," one NATO report asserted, "and in the long run at the overthrow of democratic governments."[17]

In Washington, the Eisenhower administration swung into action. On 16 April 1953, in a sweeping speech, Dwight Eisenhower tackled the prospects for peace. "The new Soviet leadership now has a precious opportunity to awaken, with the rest of the world, to the point of peril reached and to help turn the tide of history," the president remarked. "Will it do this? We do not yet know."[18]

Eisenhower's central message was unmistakable and his tone cautious. "He spoke not only for American people," one Swiss newspaper concluded, "but for [the] entire West."[19] The president's speech, Secretary of State John Foster Dulles confidently proclaimed two days later, had turned back the Soviets' "peace offensive," transforming it into a "peace defensive."[20]

Eisenhower's remarks triggered a flurry of speculation about when and from where additional initiatives might appear, designed to break the stalemate in East-West relations.[21] Such reactions hinted at a much larger problem facing the Western allies, one that would appear and reappear in the years to come. If the Soviet threat subsided, what would that mean for the future of the Atlantic Alliance? The State Department's official press guidance, circulated to US official information outlets regarding Eisenhower's speech on 16 April, stressed the need for continued vigilance. "There is still no repeat no occasion to relax," the guidance cautioned. "Friendly nations, particularly in Western Europe, must continue to push forward defense efforts in support of NATO and EDC," the European Defence Community currently being debated, "and for greater unity."[22]

Officials at NATO already worried about a waning interest in the alliance. The softening Soviet attitude could amplify these problems, posing "psychological (public and parliamentary opinion), military, economic, and financial" difficulties for the various NATO allies.[23] NATO's secretary-general, Lord Ismay, minced few words. "There appears to be a decline in the belief that the North Atlantic Alliance is a fundamental and necessary element," he warned in the summer of 1953. That negative trend seemed to be sweeping through the alliance, present in each and every one of its fourteen members. "If we do not forthwith remove that impression, and regain the initiative," Ismay warned, the outcome might be dire. "We may wake up to find that the Soviets have succeeded, by a simple change in tactics which has cost them nothing, in attaining their supreme desire –

the disruption of the North Atlantic Pact and the prevention of European integration."[24]

The prospect of a relaxation in East-West tensions represented a double-edged sword. Should the perceived threat from the Soviet Union recede, could it unravel the Atlantic Alliance entirely? "One of the dangers implicit in the present Soviet peace overtures," as Deputy Undersecretary of State for External Affairs Charles Ritchie concluded in a memorandum in May 1953, "is the disillusionment which may follow." Should the Soviet Union prove to be unwilling to participate in meaningful negotiations or talks drag on, it could easily lead to a situation even more hostile and dangerous than the present state of international affairs. "Such a mood of disillusionment and impatience," Ritchie warned, "particularly if it should develop in the United States, would be most dangerous."[25]

The Western allies could not afford to dismiss Soviet calls for dialogue out of hand. But there was a fundamental difference between professions of peace and meaningful change. Distinguishing between the two remained critical, and the Eisenhower administration hammered this theme in the days and months after Stalin's death. "If the Soviet leaders demonstrate constructive *action* – as differentiated from mere propaganda – on serious matters," the administration vowed, then "they will not find us wanting."[26]

The Western allies fretted about the damage that might be done as a result of undue euphoria among their constituents. It would be critical to develop – and sustain – realistic public expectations of what might be achieved in relations with the Soviet Union. Ideally, "public opinion in Western countries should view the possibility of negotiation with realism." In practice, this meant a healthy appreciation of the nature and conduct of Soviet diplomacy. "Any agreements which the Soviet Union enters into will be honoured only until the next twist of the Party line makes it desirable to dishonour them," Ritchie warned, adding that Moscow "will always implement its international obligations in the fashion most advantageous to the Soviet Union." Public appreciation of these realities, officials insisted, was all the more significant given the complexity of the problems at hand. German unification and that of the two Koreas divided East and West, as did the future of Indochina, Formosa, and the People's Republic of China's recognition and admission into the United Nations.[27]

COEXISTENCE AND NON-EXISTENCE

In July 1954, Pearson asked Ford, now preparing to take over as head of the European Division, to pull together a memorandum on relations with the Soviet Union. Ford's mandate was sweeping, framed by a single question: "How could we find a stable relationship with a hostile regime?"[28]

Pearson's query – and Ford's subsequent report – were landmarks. "This was the first time," Ford later noted, that "an effort had been made to assess the USSR and our interest in it, and I think it served as the basis for our relations for many years."[29] Decades later that 1954 report still resonated with him. An early draft of his memoirs included a full chapter dedicated to its drafting, but it ended up on the cutting room floor, deemed "too cerebral" for a general audience by his publishers.[30]

His assessment was blunt. "We must admit that to all practical purposes we have reached a complete impasse in our relations with the USSR," Ford wrote. Neither side, East nor West, was willing to compromise on its basic positions.[31]

The change in Moscow's recent tone, dating back to Stalin's death, seemed to be "a fairly clear attempt to reduce international tension," to normalize relations without making any real concessions – what Charles "Chip" Bohlen, the US ambassador to the Soviet Union, referred to as a "peace at no price." Certainly, from the Soviet perspective, the current circumstances were preferable to "a contest of arms." But the fact remained that the basic thrust of Soviet foreign policy had not changed. Moscow had simply decided to wage the Cold War struggle on a different plane.[32] However sweeping, this overview held out little hope of immediate change.

At a string of public appearances in the summer and autumn of 1954, Pearson took up the same theme. He spoke of this curious new refrain in Soviet diplomacy, the opportunities, and the potential pitfalls. "A strange new word has lately been insistently and clearly pushed by the communists," he remarked before a gathering of the Canadian Federation of Mayors and Municipalities in August: *coexistence.*[33]

The Soviet Union's affinity for peaceful coexistence scarcely seemed to be a surprise. "Perhaps it is not surprising," Pearson told that same audience in Windsor, "that this appealing but ambiguous slogan, 'co-existence,' should have been launched by men who have inherited and maintain the device known as the 'iron curtain,' that complex of ingenious barriers, physical and psychological."[34]

Whatever the Soviet motives, Moscow's calls for peaceful coexistence could not be easily brushed aside. "We cannot escape the challenge of what is called 'co-existence,'" Pearson told an audience at Detroit's Economic Club in November 1954, "because we live in a divided world, and under the menacing shadow of a thermo-nuclear cloud." But, in recent years, *co-existence* had taken on new meaning. "The word has now acquired a suspect specialized meaning – most words do which are taken over and debased by communism," he noted. Co-existence's typical prefix, *peaceful,* had fared little better thanks to Soviet semantics.[35]

"What we need," Pearson argued, "is not some blind and wishful faith that 'peaceful co-existence' with communism on honourable, or at least tolerable terms, is possible, but a sober realization that it may only be possible if our own politics and actions make it so, by their wisdom, steadiness and firmness."[36] This did not mean that coexistence should be dismissed out of hand. "It would be dangerous for the West not to be prepared for deceit," Pearson cautioned, "but it would be stupid not to take advantage of every reasonable opportunity for sincere negotiation."[37]

Casting coexistence aside, dismissing it as little more than a trick or an illusion, would be to embrace the logic of thermonuclear conflict. "Such a grim and despairing view," as Pearson put it, "would restrict the area of human control, to not much more than deciding where and when the global smash-up is to take place."[38] The realities of the new hydrogen age emerged time and again in Pearson's remarks, a state of affairs that coloured his thinking about how and on what terms to engage the Soviet Union in critical ways.

Convinced that the collective strength of the Western allies had diminished the threat of war with the Soviet Union in recent years, Pearson maintained that the men of the Kremlin were "realists." Soviet leaders fully appreciated the risks of an attack, and as a result their calls for coexistence could be sincere, motivated by a desire to avoid that outcome. Even if that were the case, it did not mean that Soviet motives were purely altruistic. Those calling the shots in Moscow, Pearson insisted, "undoubtedly also hope that we may ourselves weaken the strength, unity and resolve that make co-existence as essential for them – as for us."[39]

Nor was Pearson afraid to identify and champion the Western allies' advantages. "We have the right to believe that the dynamism of a free society, despite all its faults and weaknesses, has a greater vitality and capacity to adapt itself to new conditions and, therefore, to survive than rigid, monolithic Soviet Communism can ever hope to achieve." Those stark differences between East and West, to Pearson's mind, were prime indicators that the Western allies could embrace the Soviet Union's calls for peaceful coexistence. "We can welcome 'peaceful co-existence,'" he argued, "not as a way of avoiding a contest but of winning it without war."[40]

To meet the challenge inherent in the Soviet Union's sustained calls for peaceful coexistence, then, demanded patience and creativity. It would not only require continued strength and confidence ("we cannot afford – indeed it would be most foolish," Pearson told the audience in Detroit, "to reduce our strength or relax our vigilance") but also a willingness to consider, sincerely and without prejudice, how and on what terms coexistence could be converted into more durable and stable forms of cooperation between East and West.[41] That war might easily break out by accident, through miscalculation or error, underscored the need to keep an open mind.[42]

The potential pitfalls for Western governments were not lost on Pearson. Asking whether or not one believed that peaceful coexistence with communism was possible, he quipped in one instance, was a bit like asking whether a man still beat his wife. "You are condemned by your mouth whether you answer 'yes' or 'no.'"[43]

NATO's members, Canada included, faced charges of inconsistency as they championed arms control proposals at the United Nations while also building up their military strength and adding new members to the Atlantic Alliance, including bringing the Federal Republic of Germany into the fold. "There is no inconsistency here," Pearson argued, for these policies were complementary. "We must not reduce our collective strength relative to that of the Soviet Empire," he insisted. "We must not slacken our vigilance as long as the present danger persists. But we must also never adopt a position so rigid or follow a diplomacy so frozen that we refuse any reasonable offer to negotiate in order to reduce that danger and eliminate current tensions."[44] His framing foreshadowed the formulations of the late 1960s, for NATO's members explicitly defined the alliance's functions as twofold: to maintain sufficient strength to deter aggression and, based on that strength, to pursue "a more stable relationship" with the Soviet Union such that the broader political problems might be resolved.[45] As for his own policies, Pearson remained convinced of the fact that dealings with the Soviet Union should be grounded in a position of collective strength and a proper Western deterrent.[46] He saw the potential of détente, yet he recognized the dangers inherent in any change to the international order. It was a blend of realism and idealism, something quintessentially Pearson.

"A VOYAGE OF RECONNAISSANCE"

On the margins of the United Nations' meeting marking the organization's tenth anniversary, Vyacheslav Molotov waylaid Pearson after a session. The Soviet foreign minister was flanked by a number of Soviet officials who "encircled" the Canadian and steered him "into a sort of tunnel."[47] There Molotov extended a roundabout invitation to his Canadian counterpart to visit the Soviet Union.[48] Molotov's offer was part of a spate of similar invitations, including to India's Jawaharlal Nehru and Konrad Adenauer, the chancellor of the Federal Republic of Germany.

A few weeks later, in early July, Pearson responded favourably. Writing to Molotov, the secretary of state for external affairs indicated that he would be able to stop in Moscow en route to Singapore for a ministerial meeting of the Colombo Plan conference that autumn. This plan was deliberate, an attempt to mitigate undue enthusiasm and temper expectations in advance of the visit. By folding his visit to the Soviet Union into part of a larger trip, a six-week world tour with stops in the United Kingdom, France, divided Berlin, Singapore, India, Pakistan, Iraq, Ceylon, Egypt, and Belgium, Pearson hoped to blunt Moscow's efforts to make hay of the visit and exploit it for propaganda purposes.[49] The same caution infused his public remarks in the months leading up to the visit as he tried to dampen any hope of a dramatic – and immediate – breakthrough. "The hopeful developments in the last year of relations with Moscow," Pearson told an audience in Vancouver, "are proof positive of the unreality and unwisdom of basing a policy on irrevocable hostility; of allowing your diplomacy to become frozen in fear and stagnation." But change would not be easy or immediate.[50]

To be sure, there were glimmers of hope, however fleeting. In July, the leaders of the Big Four – the United States, the Soviet Union, the United Kingdom, and France – gathered for a summit in Geneva, the first such meeting in almost a decade.[51] Pearson, attuned to the potential for undue optimism, repeated his earlier refrain, this time in the popular American outlet *Foreign Affairs*. (That he took to the pages of an American publication perhaps indicated his concern that Americans were among the most susceptible to this kind of euphoria.) The Geneva Summit was a beginning, not an end, and "it would be foolish, perhaps dangerous, to draw premature and exuberantly optimistic conclusions." Global realities demanded a search for solutions, not least the "fantastic development of nuclear weapons" and the prospect that these terrible arsenals could spread. The sheer destruction made possible by these weapons had "already created what many consider to be the greatest deterrent to war."[52] Here, again, the dangers of the thermonuclear age underscored Pearson's case that dialogue between East and West should remain open.

His decision to accept the Soviet invitation coincided with an acrimonious showdown in cabinet over a study of national security policy. Concerned about the rising pressure from the United States, including overflights of Canadian airspace and the deployment of nuclear weapons, Pearson pressed for a short, public-facing paper to be prepared on the implications of the atomic age and the advent of delivery technologies such as missiles and long-range bombers. Such a paper, drafted jointly by External Affairs and National Defence, could then be considered by the House of Commons.[53] A sweeping assessment of the current landscape, as Timothy Andrews Sayle illustrates in his chapter in this volume on this jumbled review, it would bear on the policies that Ottawa had pursued for almost a decade and their continued significance in the face of new weapons technologies.

Louis St. Laurent backed Lester Pearson's recommendation. Even with prime ministerial support, the paper went nowhere. General Charles Foulkes, the chair of the Chiefs of Staff, resisted the initiative outright. Drafting a paper of this kind, he argued, would jeopardize his personal ties to key interlocutors in the United States, including the chair of the

Joint Chiefs of Staff, Admiral Arthur Radford, and General Omar Bradley, the head of the US Army. Instead, the Department of National Defence simply ignored St. Laurent's request. Pearson let it drop rather than press the issue. George Ignatieff, then serving as defence liaison at External Affairs and knee-deep in this interdepartmental turf war, later described this choice as "a typical Pearsonian reaction."[54] The status quo remained unchanged, even in the light of a changing Cold War.

Pearson's trip to Moscow, according to Ignatieff, was a direct response to this simmering crisis in cabinet. Pearson intended to size up the Soviet Union himself to get a sense of just how likely a war might be.[55] The temptation to see the Soviet system up close was not new, though. "When will I be able to go to Moscow in disguise?," Pearson had wondered in a dispatch to John Watkins in the autumn of 1954. "I have been talking so much about co-existence these days I think I should examine it on the spot."[56] Molotov's invitation provided the opening to see the Soviet Union first hand.

Conventional wisdom in Ottawa held that a war was unlikely. A September 1955 assessment, prepared by Ford, argued that the Cold War had settled into a stalemate, an acknowledgment of the military balance between the two sides and the sheer destruction that could be unleashed by their respective nuclear arsenals. Given these realities, Ford recommended policies that would enable and encourage the "gradual transformation of the Soviet Union." To do so, he saw a clear logic in embracing "every Soviet move which might prolong and deepen the present détente, while maintaining our strength and our collective policies."[57]

Touching down in Moscow in the afternoon of 5 October 1955, the Pearsons were greeted by Molotov. That evening there was a performance of *Don Quixote* at the famed Bolshoi Theatre, a choice that Molotov embraced wholeheartedly as he peppered the conversation with references to the West's propensity for "tilting at windmills." Pearson took it in stride, noting that all foreign offices likely had their Don Quixotes and their Sancho Panzas.[58]

It was the start of a packed itinerary, with stops in Moscow, Leningrad, Stalingrad, and Crimea. The city of Leningrad pulled out all the stops, lining the streets with Soviet and Canadian flags. In Stalingrad, Lester Pearson and John Watkins, the Canadian ambassador to the Soviet Union, laid a wreath at one of the city's innumerable war memorials. (Shortly before, George Ignatieff insisted on a change of location, after the Soviets tried to get Pearson to lay a wreath at a monument dedicated to "the victims of the white guardist executioners" – in other words, Bolsheviks killed by White Russian forces during the civil war.[59]) But the central aim of the visit was simply an exchange of views. "The Canadians," as one *Globe and Mail* reporter summed up the trip, "are going to have a look at Russia, and Russia is going to have a look at the Canadians."[60]

Even these simple exchanges mattered after years without them. What if these high-level diplomatic visits paved the way for others to do the same? That idea was hardly far-fetched. Already, the month before, in September, Konrad Adenauer had visited Moscow. And as Pearson toured the Soviet Union, journalists peppered Soviet officials with questions, wondering if the US secretary of state, John Foster Dulles, might follow in Pearson's footsteps. Molotov's deputy, Valerian Zorin, made sure to keep the possibility open. "It is completely up to him," Zorin told reporters. "We would welcome him at any time."[61]

The biggest breakthroughs came in the realm of trade, in which Soviet and Canadian officials indicated that a bilateral trade agreement seemed to be possible. "There was a sufficient measure of agreement," as the final communiqué summed up the trade talks during Pearson's visit, "to warrant resumption of negotiations shortly," with an eye toward a deal based on most-favoured nation status.[62] "The superficial impression," one US reporter remarked about the communiqué, "was that new life would be given [to] East-West trade."[63]

"New life" was an exaggeration, to put it mildly. Bilateral trade between the two countries was minuscule prior to 1955, and the prospects for growth remained slim. That American reporter assumed that the most likely area of growth remained grain sales, a market for Canadian products that depended on the continued failures of the Soviet Union's own grain industry.[64]

Exploratory in nature, many of the conversations broke little new ground. As part of the trade talks, the Soviets tried to secure advantageous agreements that would undercut restrictions and export controls backed by the members of NATO. Noting the Soviet desire to place a large order to purchase Canadian wheat, Ivan Kabanov, the Soviet minister of foreign trade, lobbied for a formulation of most-favoured nation status that would weaken these strategic export controls.[65]

Pearson, too, opposed any attempt to undercut Canada's ties to the Atlantic Alliance, even semantic ones. When Molotov praised the secretary's visit as evidence that Canada could serve as a "bridge" or an "interpreter," Pearson chafed.[66] He had no interest in cultivating impressions that the Canadians might serve as a go-between, somehow out of step with the Western camp.[67] His insistence is worth dwelling on, given the subsequent popularity of his image as an "honest broker" and the impartiality, perhaps even neutrality, implicit in that formulation. Pearson was anything but. Time and again, including in the Soviet Union, the secretary of state for external affairs rebuffed even the slightest suggestion of neutrality.

The Canadians were scarcely impressed with Soviet posturing. Molotov's remarks were "discursive, ambiguous and followed the familiar current Soviet line." The Soviet foreign minister touted the "spirit of Geneva," invoking the popular slogan for the possible thaw in East-West relations surrounding the four-power meetings in the Swiss capital, and he insisted on the need to find common ground where possible. But, on the substantive questions that divided East and West, he showed little flexibility. Molotov asserted, for example, that German unification need not take priority and could serve as a stumbling block in European security questions.[68]

Pearson rejected this argument; the two could not be separated. "Europe could not be secure," he told the Soviet foreign minister, "if it included two German states bitterly hostile to one another and each in an opposing camp."[69] John Holmes, who accompanied the secretary, later recalled Pearson's sense of disappointment with the Moscow leg of his trip. "Pearson really wanted a frank talk," Holmes remembered. Instead, he was treated to a spate of pat speeches from Molotov about "how we were neighbours over the pole, and that kind of thing."[70] (Such appeals were a staple of Soviet diplomacy, offering up banal references to a shared geography with an unmistakable subtext: Moscow's nuclear arsenal was just over the pole.) Pearson, for all his efforts to dampen public enthusiasm, still had a few outsized expectations of his own it seems.

His meetings with Nikita Khrushchev were a far cry from the generic expressions of goodwill between neighbours. Instead of sweeping statements and predictable generalizations like those from Molotov, the Soviet general secretary launched into a tirade almost immediately. Khrushchev started in on Pearson, hounding him about Canada's membership in NATO and offering some "friendly advice" that the Canadians leave the alliance.[71] It was "well laced with persiflage," as John Watkins later put it.[72] Khrushchev, in the words of another Canadian diplomat, was "as blunt and volatile as only a Ukrainian peasant, turned one of the most powerful political figures in the world, can be."[73]

The substance of the Soviet general secretary's remarks was nothing new. Khrushchev repeated Molotov's warnings about the German problem and the forthcoming meeting of the Big Four's foreign ministers in Geneva. Warning that the "main stumbling block" would be the future of Germany, he noted that the current proposals, backed by the three major Western powers, remained unacceptable to the Soviet Union. Moscow could not accept unification on terms that would strengthen NATO, an alliance, as Khrushchev hammered home once more, directed against the Soviet Union. It was better, he remarked, to "have 2/3 of Germany against us than the whole of it. We cannot be so stupid as to agree to strengthening the organization which is directed against us."[74]

Pearson dismissed such accusations. NATO, he maintained, was a "purely defensive organization." But Khrushchev quickly interjected, insisting that the West should let the Soviet Union into the Atlantic Alliance. "We have been knocking at the door for two years," he reminded the prime minister, before backing away from the line of conversation that this argument invited. Rather than engage Pearson's calls for the Soviet Union to make the UN system effective, Khrushchev doubled down on his charges against NATO. The Soviet Union, he boasted, "could afford to wait for the break up of NATO" as the result of the alliance's internal tensions. Pearson sounded a note of caution in return. Without the Atlantic Alliance, the Soviets might be in an even worse position. They could be faced with a unilateral United States and a "free-wheeling" Germany, all without "the cautious and restraining influence of countries like the United Kingdom, Belgium, France and Canada."[75]

Even before these meetings, Canadian reporters presumed that this would be Pearson's preferred line of attack, rebutting Soviet concerns about the

Federal Republic of Germany's place in the European system. "The Canadian answer," one reporter told readers, in strikingly similar language to that used by Pearson, "will probably be that the disintegration of NATO would put Europe back to where it was in 1935, with a free-wheeling Germany doing as she pleased, and with the US withdrawing to its own continent, where it has all the resources to destroy Russia."[76]

After their at-times heated exchange, Khrushchev gave the visiting Canadians a tour of his "country home" – in fact a former palace – on the way to a conference room. Along the way, Khrushchev studiously alerted them to the various bathrooms, "whether," as Watkins put it, "in anticipation of the results of his subsequent assault on our digestions or simply as a house-proud ex-plumber eager to exhibit the wonders of his ex-Yussupov mansion."[77] What ensued ranks among the most infamous – and intoxicating – incidents in the history of Canadian foreign relations.

Over dinner that evening, Khrushchev plied the table with alcohol, offering rapid-fire toasts and goading George Ignatieff to "drink up like a Russian."[78] (Decades later, Ignatieff indicated that he'd had little desire to accompany Pearson; "Why should I have been, as Defence Liaison, brought into this journey to the Soviet Union, which I certainly did not want as an ex-Russian?"[79]) Khrushchev poked fun at Ignatieff's title and inquired about the various branches of his family tree. At one point, he referred to Ignatieff as "Tovarish" before quickly joking that he should have referred to him as "Graf" (Count) or "vache siatelstvo" (my lord), then laughing at his own jokes.[80] Plied with vodka, Ignatieff escaped to "one of the washrooms Khrushchev had so thoughtfully pointed out," where he was "violently sick."[81] Pearson later recalled that someone tallied the toasts, which came in at eighteen or so. "I do remember we even drank to the Canadian wheat surplus."[82]

STAYING THE COURSE

Pearson's visit to the Soviet Union confirmed much of his earlier thinking. The basic principles and objectives animating Soviet foreign policy had not changed; Moscow's policies were still designed to break the Atlantic Alliance and evict the United States from the European continent.[83] "The

Soviet leaders," Dana Wilgress, now the Canadian permanent representative to NATO, told his colleagues on the heels of Pearson's visit, "had expressed in the bluntest terms their continuing hostility to NATO, and their desire to see it replaced by a European security system acceptable to them."[84]

In the weeks and months after the trip, Pearson discussed his time in the Soviet Union in interviews and speeches (scarcely a surprise given the conventions of diplomacy, let alone the significance of the visit). The purpose of the trip, he reiterated, had been a simple one, "to exchange views about current international issues, particularly those of direct concern to our two countries, in the hope that such an exchange might assist in some small way in the resolution of differences."[85]

His postmortems were plain. Pearson was not shy about alerting audiences that the Soviet Union still wished to undermine and unravel NATO. "To the Soviet rulers," he told listeners of one CBC speaker series, "peaceful co-existence means competitive co-existence – and that in this competition, which they expect to win, they are bound only by their own rules."[86] Moscow's enthusiasm for peaceful coexistence did not bely a fundamental shift in thinking but a new type of competition.

This general line had been adopted widely in Canadian press coverage, the Canadian delegation to NATO reported. "While the new trend in Soviet policy has been generally welcomed," one assessment noted in November 1955, "hopeful editorials and news articles have usually been tempered by an attitude of 'wait and see,' by reminders that the Communist and Western worlds are still far apart and that problems remain great, and by warnings that Canada and NATO cannot afford to relax vigilance."[87] Canadians, at least those who expressed an opinion, tended to view the Soviet Union's recent overtures with a healthy dose of skepticism; 34% of respondents in one Gallup poll in 1955, for instance, indicated that the recent "Russian geniality" was intended "to give the West a false sense of security." Another 22% thought the overtures genuine and sincere. Perhaps most telling was the fact that a whopping 36% expressed no opinion on the matter.[88] Such was the attention given to the wider world during the so-called golden age of Canadian foreign policy.

In the corridors of power, Canadian thinking continued to be guided by the potential advantages of ties criss-crossing the Iron Curtain. It would require the careful coordination of various national policies, Wilgress told his colleagues at the North Atlantic Council, but provided that those policies were "carefully supervised" the advantages of increased connections easily could outweigh the potential pitfalls and dangers.[89]

CONCLUSION

Canadians needed to be prepared for the Cold War situation in the mid-1950s to last for months and even years. "We must, above all, realize we're going to have to live with this situation for a long time – this isn't a sprint," Pearson remarked in late 1955. "It's at least middle distance."[90]

As the Cold War settled into a protracted stalemate, Pearson and his colleagues at the Department of External Affairs grappled with fundamental tensions and trade-offs that would shape strategic debates in the West for decades to come. How should the Western allies respond to the Soviet Union's professions of peace and overtures to improve relations? Canadian assessments differed, at times, from views south of the border, in Washington, and across the Atlantic. But these differences were a matter of tactics, not of broad aims or objectives in the ongoing Cold War struggle. Yet these divergences tended to loom larger in other theatres, such as the Canadians' desire to bridge the gap between free Asia and the Western bloc – with an "impatient" United States at its helm – discussed in David Webster's chapter in this volume.

There were limitations, of course, to what Canadian officials could achieve on their own. Asked in the summer of 1957 about the value of direct negotiations between the United States and the Soviet Union, Pearson was blunt. "We may tell them that we think it is a good time to have a Geneva conference: you ought to meet the Russians," he told *Maclean's* Blair Fraser and Lionel Shapiro. "We can advise perhaps, and influence them, but not determine."[91]

Yet Pearson remained adamant about the value of dialogue. "I think we ought to be doing more than we do to use the ordinary channels of diplomacy for getting in touch with the Russians more," he remarked. "I think we should never treat our differences with them as though they are untouchable or untalkable."[92]

NOTES

1 Richard J. Needham, "Molotov at Airport as Pearson Arrives," *Globe and Mail,* 6 October 1955.

2 Pearson's visit is well covered in memoirs, many of them cited here. Historians have offered brief treatments of the trip. See, for example, John English, "Lester Pearson Encounters the Enigma," in *Canada and the Soviet Experiment: Essays on Canadian Encounters with Russia and the Soviet Union, 1900–1991,* ed. David Davies (Toronto: Centre for Russian and East European Studies, University of Toronto, 1994), 105–16; Leigh Sarty, "A Middle Power in Moscow? Canada and the Soviet Union from Khrushchev to Gorbachev," *Queen's Quarterly* 98, 3 (1991): 557–61; Jamie Glazov, *Canadian Policy toward Khrushchev's Soviet Union* (Montreal and Kingston: McGill-Queen's University Press, 2002), 40–51; and Timothy Andrews Sayle, "A Cold Warrior? Pearson and the Soviet Bloc," in *Mike's World: Lester B. Pearson and Canadian External Affairs,* ed. Asa McKercher and Galen Roger Perras (Vancouver: UBC Press, 2017), 229–50.

3 George Ignatieff, *The Making of a Peacemonger* (Toronto: University of Toronto Press, 1985), 127.

4 "New Year's Message by the Secretary of State for External Affairs, Mr. L.B. Pearson," December 1954, Department of External Affairs, *Statements and Speeches* No. 54/61.

5 Standing Committee on External Affairs, 24 May 1955, House of Commons Committees, 22nd Parliament, 2nd Session, 550.

6 "Memorandum from Under-Secretary of State for External Affairs to Secretary of State for External Affairs," 28 June 1955, in *Documents on Canadian External Relations* (hereafter *DCER*), vol. 21, 1955, ed. Greg Donaghy (Ottawa: Department of Foreign Affairs and International Trade, 1999), 379–83.

7 Sayle, "Cold Warrior?," 230–31.

8 "Chargé d'Affaires in Soviet Union to Secretary of State for External Affairs," 31 March 1953, in *DCER,* vol. 19, 1953, ed. Greg Donaghy (Ottawa: External Affairs and International Trade Canada, 1991), 1458.

9 "Working Group on Trends in Soviet Policy: Selected List of Soviet Moves since Stalin's Death on 5th March, 1953," annex to Ismay note, "Calendar of Events since Stalin's Death and Points to Be Considered by Ministers," 14 April 1953, NATO, C-M(53)38.

10 "The Unity of the Free World," 19 May 1953, Department of External Affairs, *Statements and Speeches* No. 53/22.

11 Ibid.

12 "Chargé d'Affaires in Soviet Union to Secretary of State for External Affairs," 31 March 1953, in *DCER,* 1953, 1457.

13 Ibid.

14 Ibid., 1459.

15 Ibid.

16 "The Soviet 'Peace Offensive,'" state circular telegram, 22 April 1953, Dwight D. Eisenhower Library (hereafter DDEL), White House Central Files, Subject Files, box 65, folder "Russia – Stalin's Death and Reaction and Results of President's Speech of 4-16-53 (2)."

17 "Report on Trends of Soviet Policy, April to December, 1953," 3 December 1953, NATO, Annex to C-M(53)164.

18 Dwight D. Eisenhower, "Chance for Peace," 16 April 1953, The American Presidency Project, https://www.presidency.ucsb.edu/documents/address-the-chance-for-peace-delivered-before-the-american-society-newspaper-editors.

19 Bern to Secretary of State No. 1198, 19 April 1953, DDEL, White House Central Files, Subject Files, box 65, folder "Russia – Stalin's Death and Reaction and Results of President's Speech of 4-16-53 (3)."

20 "The Soviet 'Peace Offensive,'" state circular telegram, 22 April 1953, DDEL, White House Central Files, Subject Files, box 65, folder "Russia – Stalin's Death and Reaction and Results of President's Speech of 4-16-53 (2)."

21 Moscow to Secretary of State No. 1512, 22 April 1953, DDEL, White House Central Files, Subject Files, box 65, folder "Russia – Stalin's Death and Reaction and Results of President's Speech of 4-16-53 (2)."

22 Department of State circular No. 1036, 16 April 1953, DDEL, White House Central Files, Subject Files, box 65, folder "Russia – Stalin's Death and Reaction and Results of President's Speech of 4-16-53 (1)."

23 "List of Points to Be Considered by Ministers," annex to Ismay note, "Calendar of Events since Stalin's Death and Points to Be Considered by Ministers," 14 April 1953, NATO, C-M(53)38.

24 "NATO: The Present Position," covering note, 25 June 1953, NATO, C-M(53)87.

25 "Memorandum from Deputy Under-Secretary of State for External Affairs to Secretary of State for External Affairs," 2 May 1953, in *DCER*, 1953, 1465.

26 "The Soviet 'Peace Offensive,'" state circular telegram, 22 April 1953, DDEL, White House Central Files, Subject Files, box 65, folder "Russia – Stalin's Death and Reaction and Results of President's Speech of 4-16-53 (2)."

27 "Memorandum from Deputy Under-Secretary of State for External Affairs to Secretary of State for External Affairs," 2 May 1953, in *DCER*, 1953, 1465–66.

28 Sayle, "A Cold Warrior?," 232, 234, notes that this framing bore a striking similarity to a question that Lester Pearson had posed to William Lyon Mackenzie King nearly a decade earlier.

29 Quoted in Charles A. Ruud, "The Reports of Robert A.D. Ford, Canadian Ambassador to the Soviet Union, 1964–1980," in *Diplomatic Documents and Their Users,* ed. John Hilliker (Ottawa: Department of Foreign Affairs and International Trade, 1995), 179. Ruud, ibid., 183, wholeheartedly agreed, referring to it as "my most important single source" in writing a biography of Ford's career.

30 Ibid., 180. Ford's memoirs appeared in 1989 as *Our Man in Moscow: A Diplomat's Reflections on the Soviet Union* (Toronto: University of Toronto Press, 1989).

31 "Memorandum by European Division," 1 November 1954, in *DCER*, vol. 20, 1954, ed. Greg Donaghy (Ottawa: Department of Foreign Affairs and International Trade, 1997), 1570.

32 "Memorandum by European Division," 1 November 1954, in *DCER*, 1954, 1575, 1588.

33 "Co-Existence," 30 August 1954, Department of External Affairs, *Statements and Speeches* No. 54/38.

34 Ibid.

35 "The Challenge of Co-Existence," 8 November 1954, Department of External Affairs, *Statements and Speeches* No. 54/47.

36 Ibid.

37 "New Year's Message by the Secretary of State for External Affairs, Mr. L. B. Pearson," December 1954, Department of External Affairs, *Statements and Speeches* No. 54/61.

38 "The Challenge of Co-Existence," 8 November 1954, Department of External Affairs, *Statements and Speeches* No. 54/47.

39 "Co-Existence," 30 August 1954, Department of External Affairs, *Statements and Speeches* No. 54/38.

40 "The Challenge of Co-Existence," 8 November 1954, Department of External Affairs, *Statements and Speeches* No. 54/47.

41 Ibid.

42 "Co-Existence," 30 August 1954, Department of External Affairs, *Statements and Speeches* No. 54/38.

43 Ibid.

44 "The Challenge of Co-Existence," 8 November 1954, Department of External Affairs, *Statements and Speeches* No. 54/47.

45 "Future Tasks of the Alliance," 28 November 1967, NATO, C-M(67)74. On the Harmel Report, see Timothy Andrews Sayle, *Enduring Alliance: A History of NATO and the Postwar Global Order* (Ithaca, NY: Cornell University Press, 2019), 151–60.

46 Sayle, "Cold Warrior?," 230.

47 Lester B. Pearson, *Mike: The Memoirs of the Right Honourable Lester B. Pearson*, vol. 2, 1948–57, ed. John A. Munro and Alex I. Inglis (Toronto: University of Toronto Press, 1973), 191.

48 "Memorandum from Secretary of State for External Affairs to Prime Minister," 28 June 1955, in *DCER,* 1955, 1159–60.

49 "Secretary of State for External Affairs to Ambassador in Norway," 8 July 1955, in *DCER,* 1955, 1160–61.

50 "Excerpts from an Address by the Secretary of State for External Affairs, Mr. L.B. Pearson, to the Women's Canadian Club, Vancouver, B.C.," 25 August 1955, Department of External Affairs, *Statements and Speeches* No. 55/30.

51 On the Geneva Summit, see William I. Hitchcock, *The Age of Eisenhower: America and the World in the 1950s* (New York: Simon and Schuster, 2018), 270–78.

52 Lester B. Pearson, "After Geneva: A Greater Task for NATO," *Foreign Affairs* 34, 1 (1955): 14–23.

53 George Ignatieff interview, in *In Alliance: An Oral History of Canadian Involvement in NATO,* ed. Roger Hill (Ottawa: Canadian Institute for International Peace and Security, 1991), 55.

54 Ibid., 55–56. In his memoirs, Ignatieff obliquely hints at how strange the request might have seemed, noting that he was "not dealing with Soviet affairs at the time." Ignatieff, *The Making of a Peacemonger,* 127.

55 Ignatieff, interview, *In Alliance,* 55–56.

56 Quoted in English, "Lester Pearson Encounters the Enigma," 108.

57 "Memorandum from Secretary of State for External Affairs to Prime Minister," 29 September 1955, in *DCER*, 1955, 1158–59; John Hilliker and Donald Barry, *Canada's Department of External Affairs*, vol. 2, *Coming of Age, 1946–1968* (Montreal and Kingston: McGill-Queen's University Press, 1995), 112.

58 Ignatieff, *The Making of a Peacemonger*, 128–29.

59 Ibid., 140.

60 Needham, "Molotov at Airport as Pearson Arrives."

61 "Molotov Hopeful on Geneva Parley," *New York Times*, 7 October 1955.

62 Department of External Affairs, press release, 12 October 1955, No. 79.

63 Brendan M. Jones, "Red Trade Boom Seems Unlikely," *New York Times*, 16 October 1955.

64 Ibid.

65 Ignatieff, *The Making of a Peacemonger*, 132.

66 "Memorandum," 17 October 1955, in *DCER*, 1955, 1163.

67 Sarty, "A Middle Power in Moscow?," 560; Glazov, *Canadian Policy towards Khrushchev's Soviet Union*, 42.

68 "Memorandum," 17 October 1955, in *DCER*, 1955, 1161–62.

69 Ibid.

70 John Holmes interview, *In Alliance*, 35. George Ignatieff indicated that this "'neighbours over the pole' theme was ubiquitous" during the visit. See "Summary Record of Address Delivered to the Joint Intelligence Committee by Mr. George Ignatieff," 23 November 1955, Library and Archives Canada (hereafter LAC), External Affairs records, vol. 7903, file 50028-B-40, part 5.

71 "Khrushchev Attacks N.A.T.O.," *Manchester Guardian*, 13 October 1955.

72 John Watkins, letter, 5 November 1955, in *Moscow Despatches: Inside Cold War Russia* (Toronto: Lorimer, 1987), 123.

73 "Ambassador in Federal Republic of Germany to Secretary of State for External Affairs," 15 October 1955, in *DCER*, 1955, 1169.

74 Ibid., 1171.

75 Ibid.

76 Needham, "Molotov at Airport as Pearson Arrives."

77 Watkins, letter, 5 November 1955, *Moscow Despatches*, 123–24. The palace had been owned by the Yousoupov family.

78 Pearson, *Mike*, 209.

79 Ignatieff interview, *In Alliance*, 56.

80 Watkins, letter, 5 November 1955, *Moscow Despatches*, 125–26.

81 Ignatieff, *The Making of a Peacemonger*, 143.

82 Pearson, *Mike*, 209.

83 "Secretary of State for External Affairs to Permanent Representative to North Atlantic Council," 21 October 1955, in *DCER*, 1955, 418–19; "Extract from Cabinet Conclusions," 16 November 1955, in *DCER*, 1955, Doc. 538; Standing Committee on External Affairs, Minutes of Proceedings and Evidence No. 1, House of Commons Committees, 22nd Parliament, 3rd Session (1956), 9–10.

84 "Summary Record of a Meeting of the Council Held at the Palais de Chaillot, Paris, XVIe, on Tuesday, 25th October, 1955, at 3 p.m.," NATO, C-R(55)48.

85 "The Visit to the Soviet Union," 27 November 1955, Department of External Affairs, *Statements and Speeches* No. 55/41.

86 Ibid.

87 "Public Reaction in Canada to Recent Soviet Moves," note by the Canadian Delegation at the Committee on Information and Cultural Relations, 4 November 1955, NATO, AC/52-D/125.

88 Canadian Delegation, Committee on Information and Cultural Relations, "Public Reaction in Canada to Recent Soviet Moves," supplementary note, 14 November 1955, NATO, AC/52-D/128.

89 "Summary Record of a Meeting of the Council Held at the Palais de Chaillot, Paris, XVIe, on Tuesday, 25th October, 1955, at 3 p.m.," NATO, C-R(55)48.

90 "Pearson Questions Red Intentions," *Globe and Mail*, 3 December 1955.

91 Quoted in Blair Fraser and Lionel Shapiro, "Where Canada Stands in the World Crisis," *Maclean's*, 6 July 1957, 55–56.

92 Ibid., 56.

3

Living Dangerously
Canadian National Security Policy
and the Nuclear Revolution

TIMOTHY ANDREWS SAYLE

"The thing has gone off." The note passed from Malcolm MacDonald, the high commissioner of Great Britain in Ottawa, to C.D. Howe, the minister of munitions and supply and of reconstruction, announced the explosion of an atomic weapon over Hiroshima on 6 August 1945. The revolution had begun.[1]

Canadians suspected that a revolution was approaching even before the *Enola Gay* dropped the first atomic bomb. In April 1944, C.J. Mackenzie, the acting president of the National Research Council, encouraged Howe to authorize Canadian participation in "a project which is not only of the greatest immediate military importance; but which may revolutionize the future world in the same degree as did the invention of the steam engine and the discovery of electricity."[2] And participate Canada did, one of the three countries, along with the United States and United Kingdom, that in the wartime race to develop the atomic bomb gained "the secret of its production."[3]

After the bombs were dropped over Japan, Lieutenant General Maurice Pope, then the senior Canadian army member on the Permanent Joint Board of Defence, observed that "participants in a revolution rarely ever perceive the ultimate or even the short-run consequences of their action."[4] But Canadians in 1945 had no doubt, and talk of revolution was everywhere. Lester B. Pearson, the ambassador to the United States, wrote that the bomb was "not merely a new weapon in the long succession of weapons, since man first began to fight with clubs, but something revolutionary and unprecedented; a new departure in destruction and annihilative effect."[5] Hume Wrong, the acting undersecretary of state for external affairs, agreed that the bomb might change how wars were fought. But he thought the implications even more significant, with "revolutionary results ... in the political field." The bomb might shake the very basis of international affairs, he argued, calling into question the principle of sovereignty and raising the need for an "international government" to control atomic energy.[6]

Pearson wrote that "it has been said that the discovery of atomic weapons is the most revolutionary event in human history since Noah launched the Ark." But the relationship between the ark and the bomb was nearly diametrical: the former was designed to save and preserve life, the latter to take it away. As Pearson noted in late 1945, atomic weapons might one day make it "possible for the government of a parliamentary democracy to destroy a menacing power by pressing a button," just as "buttons presumably could be pressed a few seconds later in the other country as well."[7]

The nuclear revolution posed an irresolvable dilemma for Canada. The most striking element of Canadian thinking about the atomic and nuclear revolution was the conviction of Canadian officials, both civilian and military, and expressed both in prose and in policy, that Canada's supreme national interest was best served by enabling, if necessary, the United States to "press a button," to ensure that the bombers of the US Strategic Air Command (SAC) could convincingly threaten to destroy an opposing country.

Yet, though Canadian officials agreed that enabling the nuclear deterrent was the single most important tool for preventing nuclear war, they disagreed about whether Canada's national security was best ensured by a singular focus on defending North America or whether Canada should also maintain its military commitment in Europe, the location of the previous two general wars. The dilemma posed by the nuclear revolution came to a sharp point during the presidency of Dwight D. Eisenhower, years that saw a huge expansion of the US nuclear arsenal.[8] The question of how best to use Canada's sparse resources to ensure that nuclear war did not begin was never fully answered in or after the Eisenhower years.[9] The issue was vital for Canada, the neighbour of two nuclear-armed superpowers, one of which was Canadians' closest ally and trading partner. In short, although Canadian policy makers perceived that they were witnessing a revolution, policy itself failed to account adequately for the changes afoot.

* * *

By the time that Eisenhower became president of the United States in 1953, Canadians had already thought carefully about the role of atomic weapons in shaping world affairs. Canada had participated in diplomatic efforts at the United Nations (UN) to develop international control of atomic energy.[10] These hopes had been dashed by the time that Eisenhower became president (although he would rekindle the idea of an international solution to nuclear energy in his first term). Canada's Joint Intelligence Committee had conducted several years of assessments seeking to determine the likelihood of general war with the Soviet Union and the likely scale of an atomic attack on North America. And Ottawa had established a pattern of agreements with Washington that allowed the United States to request that SAC bombers, laden with their nuclear payloads, fly over Canada.[11] Given Canada's location, standing "athwart the trans-polar air routes,"[12] Canadians lay between the atomic superpowers. In a future war, American bombers would receive permission to attack the Soviet Union by flying over Canada, while Soviet bombers seeking targets in North America would be engaged by air defence fighters over Canadian territory.

During the Truman presidency, the increasingly frightening possibility of a US-Soviet war, with airplanes criss-crossing northern North America, was only one of the diplomatic and defence policy challenges facing Ottawa. The other two lay in Europe and Asia. In 1949, Canada had acceded to the Washington Treaty, positioning it as a member, along with the United States and ten European states, of the North Atlantic Treaty Organization (NATO). In 1950, after the outbreak of the Korean War, Canada sent ships and later combat troops to the Korean Peninsula under UN auspices. Fearing that the invasion of South Korea by the Soviet-backed North Koreans might lead to a Soviet attack in Western Europe, Canada deployed ground and air forces to Europe in support of NATO allies.

By the time that Eisenhower was inaugurated, the poles of Canadian defence policy were clear: a need to participate in continental defence (to defend North America but especially to protect the SAC airfields); a continental commitment of a different kind, in the deployment of forces to Europe; and the chance of being called on to engage in a future war in Asia. But there was an uneasy balance among these three poles. Existing defence commitments were expensive in terms of dollars and human resources, and there were political dimensions to each commitment that were risky. But in the atomic age, Canadians could hardly imagine abandoning continental defence (which would mean ceding the responsibility to the United States), nor could they abandon the notion of securing Europe when most officials lived with the haunting memory of at least one world war, and often two, begun there. Nor could they write off their affiliation with the United Nations and the real possibility – as had been demonstrated in Korea – of the United Nations calling for members to provide military forces.

The nuclear revolution, particularly its stark manifestation as revealed by events and policies in the early Eisenhower administration, underscored the dilemma faced by the government of Canada. Officials concerned with defence policy – those in the Department of National Defence (DND) and especially the Chiefs of Staff Committee – increasingly favoured a reduction in Canada's European commitment and a shift of resources to North American continental defence to protect the SAC airfields and bombers that served as the ultimate deterrent to war with the Soviet Union. This was in contrast to officials in the Department of External Affairs (DEA) who focused on the broader contours of Canada's foreign policy. DEA officials recognized the importance of continental defence – especially the domestic political imperative to ensure that the defence of North America not be achieved by handing over the responsibility for defending Canada to the United States. But they were also convinced that Canadian forces in Europe strengthened NATO and thus deterred war.

In late 1954, DEA officials, recognizing the conundrum, sought to find a way to reconcile the various arms of Canadian policy in an interdepartmental "Study of National Security Policy." The study was not successful in that it did not produce a formal "national security policy" for Canada;

instead, the government of Canada would continue to navigate the Cold War with foreign and defence policies that lay in tension with each other. But the study serves as a time capsule and challenges the notion that policy-making in the Cold War was easy, predetermined, and without choice. The records of the study, finally declassified over six decades later, point to the ultimately unsolvable dilemma between Canadian political and strategic instincts brought about by the nuclear revolution.[13]

* * *

On a Friday afternoon toward the end of October 1954, Jules Léger, the undersecretary of state for external affairs, gathered several senior DEA officials in his East Block office. The purpose of the meeting was to discuss a paper written by W.H. Barton, a DEA officer with responsibilities for defence affairs, arguing that it was necessary "to set in motion a reassessment of Canadian national security policy."[14] The men agreed that such a policy was desirable and concluded that a reassessment would require a working party, including all of the Chiefs of Staff, a representative each from External Affairs and Finance, and two from the armed services. Memorandums were prepared and sent up the chain to the minister – then Secretary of State for External Affairs Lester Pearson – and then from Pearson to the minister of national defence and the prime minister.[15]

Ottawa, or so the DEA officials thought, was about to embark on its first study of national security policy. It was not, and purposefully not, to be simply a study of foreign policy, or defence policy, or economic policy, but something grander: an exploration of Canadian grand strategy for the nuclear age.[16] In the end, the study was only half finished. Officials did one half of the hard job – they generated crucial questions that highlighted the challenges of both defining and resourcing Canadian national security policy in the thermonuclear era. The other half of the task, finding answers to hard questions and making difficult choices about priorities, was never completed. For the rest of the Cold War, the government of Canada would be faced with the same challenges presented by the nuclear revolution. The questions posed by the study, about how and where efforts should be focused to preserve Canadian national security, remained unanswered.

Barton's paper, entitled "Canadian National Security," had a special, possibly unique, classification: "External Affairs Eyes Only."[17] The marking, no doubt, resulted from the fact that the paper was part response, part repudiation, of the recent White Paper prepared by the minister of national defence setting out Canada's three defence policy objectives: to defend Canada and North America; to make good on any undertaking required of Canada by the United Nations, NATO, or other agreements; and to maintain the organization necessary to build up strength in case of total war.[18]

The problem, Barton noted, was that by this point in 1954 Canada had "committed fully the military manpower and financial resources available." It had no "strategic reserve," and it would have been impossible, without an entirely new policy, to assign any more men or money to any one of these objectives without reducing resources assigned to another objective. The suggestion in the White Paper that Canada could "make good" on any new undertaking was hollow.

For the previous five years, since the signing of the Washington Treaty creating NATO, the balance had been acceptable: Canadian policy had assumed that Canada itself was relatively insulated from attack and that the front lines of any future war would be in Europe. Canada spent some resources on air defence in North America, but it also sent troops to Europe as part of NATO's standing forces. But in 1954 it seemed that change was coming fast. Barton warned that the events of the past year in the USSR, Europe, North America, and Asia might have thrown that balance out of whack.

The most important event had been the explosion of a Soviet thermonuclear bomb in 1953. Russia had, Barton argued, "or will have shortly, the power to launch a surprise attack on North America" that would destroy the continent's industrial centres and strategic air bases.[19] The possibility of such an attack meant not only that air defence would become more expensive but also that the cost of civil defence efforts in Canada, designed to allow Canada to survive such an attack, would increase dramatically.[20]

Compounding these issues was Secretary of State John Foster Dulles's declaration in 1954 of an American strategy of "Massive Retaliation," suggesting that the United States was ready and willing to let loose its atomic arsenal in response to Soviet provocations. This seemed to be in stark contrast to American exhortations to NATO allies to train more conventional troops for NATO's defences. Eisenhower himself ended up downplaying

Dulles's speech, assuring the world that the policy was "not new or revolutionary."[21] Even so, it had important ramifications for Canada. The first, as Pearson told Prime Minister Louis St. Laurent, was that the United States had halted its effort to encourage allies to build up their NATO forces in Europe. Instead, the United States would rely on its "massive retaliatory power" to deter the Soviet Union. Pearson understood that, with Washington no longer pressing allies to increase their NATO forces, and with a potential reduction of US forces in Europe, it was "not going to be easy, politically," for Canada to maintain its forces in Europe.[22]

Dulles's remarks were accompanied by signals from Washington to Ottawa that the Americans considered continental defence more important than ever.[23] Dana Wilgress, the Canadian permanent representative to NATO, shrewdly observed the implications for Canada: as the United States concentrated its strategic nuclear forces, "the protection of this retaliatory power will assume progressively greater importance and, in the end, it will become inseparable from the power itself." North America would become "a fortress as well as the power house of [the] Western ability to deter and defeat aggression." Canada, Wilgress wrote, would "inevitably be part of the fortress 'America,'" and it was clear that a "greater part of our military effort than hitherto will have to be devoted to the integrated defence system of the American continent."[24] However, with finite resources, more military effort in North America would have implications for the Canadian commitment in Europe. Pearson, borrowing one of Dulles's more pungent phrases, warned that it "may be that the American administration will not be the only ones who will have to make an 'agonizing reappraisal' of foreign policy."[25]

There had been change in Europe, too, in 1954. The occupation of West Germany came to a formal end, and the Federal Republic of Germany (FRG) joined the Brussels Treaty, a necessary prelude to the FRG joining NATO in 1955. This meant that, before long, German military power would be incorporated into NATO defences, strengthening the alliance's forces in Europe. In Asia, too, with the collapse of the French position in Indochina and the onset of the First Taiwan Strait Crisis, Canadians started to sense the danger of conflict there and the "possibility that Canada might become increasingly involved in commitments in Asia."[26]

All of these factors, Barton wrote, meant that Canada had to "live dangerously," trying to balance possible threats to peace in North America, Europe, and Asia. This swirl of events, he wrote, necessitated a "review of all the factors affecting Canada's security and an analysis of the possible effects of a shift in policy would have to be made."[27]

After the initial meeting, Barton's memorandum was redrafted, no doubt to blur the rather bald suggestion in the initial "External Affairs Eyes Only" draft that the formal policy of the minister of national defence was in need of reconsideration. The new, more polite, version stressed the importance of thermonuclear weapons in the making of future Canadian policy. It raised questions about how such a bomb changed the likelihood of war, which civil defence measures were feasible, whether Canadian and allied political and military strategy needed to change, and how Canadian disarmament policy would be affected.[28] Pearson, upon receiving the new draft, sent a copy to the prime minister and to Ralph Campney, the minister of national defence, suggesting a "comprehensive study ... of the implications for Canadian national security of recent developments in air-nuclear power."[29]

As the DEA waited for Campney's reply (which never did come), George Ignatieff, the head of the Defence Liaison (1) Division, was tasked with drawing up some questions to guide the study.[30] On 1 February 1955, Ignatieff completed a list of "Some Specific Questions on Future National Security Policy." He asked fourteen pointed questions about whether and how to reconsider the most fundamental aspects of Canada's postwar foreign and defence policy. What, for example, would be "the effects over the next ten years of the technological advance in nuclear and thermonuclear weapons upon the offensive capacities and intentions of the US and USSR"? (The ten-year period was chosen to account for the development of intercontinental ballistic missiles or ICBMs.) How much more vulnerable was North America in the thermonuclear era? If war came between the United States and China, would it be feasible for Canada to remain neutral? How should Canada decide how much to contribute to continental defence, and what would happen if the United States took over this role in Canada? Should Canada keep its Air Division in Europe? What about the Brigade Group? Was atomic disarmament still feasible after the Soviet thermonuclear test? Intriguingly, Ignatieff even posed the question:

"Should Canada be armed with nuclear and thermonuclear weapons and intercontinental missiles in the next ten years?"[31]

Ignatieff's questions were sent to General Foulkes, along with the suggestion that any study could build on the work done in the DEA and by the Joint Intelligence Committee and the Joint Planning Committee that reported to the Chiefs of Staff Committee.[32] These efforts to draw Foulkes in came up empty; there was no response from the Chiefs of Staff or from DND. The matter escalated to the ministerial level, with Pearson writing to Campney noting the "urgency and importance" of the study, but still there was no response from National Defence.[33]

* * *

By the spring of 1955, the general questions about future policy raised in 1954 had settled into the minds of DEA officials as two discrete but interconnected concerns: the need to assess the balance of Canadian deployments in support of European versus North American defence and a looming possible war between the United States and China.

The United States continued to signal that continental defence was its most important priority, and Canadian officials, even in the DEA, did not disagree. One DEA paper on the topic stated that the "most important development" was that "now, by general agreement" (i.e., agreement between Americans and Canadians), "swift and effective H bomb retaliation [has] become the chief deterrent against Soviet attack." Such a deterrent was effective only if the bases and facilities from which the retaliation would be launched were protected against surprise attacks. "Continental defence," then, had become "of primary importance, not only for North America but for all the NATO countries and indeed the rest of the free world as well." In terms of the geography of global security, the "sector of greatest importance is not now Western Europe, as it certainly was four years ago, but North America."[34] After reading the paper on continental defence, Pearson requested another paper, ultimately titled "The Strategic Concept of the Nuclear Deterrent." Drafted by Ignatieff but with contributions from several senior officials, it stands as the best and clearest encapsulation of the DEA's vision of Canada's role in the deterrent. Ignatieff defined the main aim of Canadian policy as preserving peace without sacrificing interest, and the "chief means of doing this is by building and maintaining deterrent strength," especially the "capacity to retaliate instantly against aggression with nuclear weapons."[35]

There is a nagging paradox in Ignatieff's paper, one that represents the early roots of the difficult choices that Canadians faced. Ignatieff recognized that Canada's position between the United States and the Soviet Union put Canada "in a position to contribute to the deterrent power of the allies by providing facilities for the Strategic Air Command and through continental defence." And he argued, as did other Canadians at this time, that supporting the nuclear deterrent was the "chief" or "main" means of preserving peace. But Ignatieff pointed out that the existence of a nuclear deterrent gave the Soviet Union every reason to avoid general war. To him, a Soviet surprise attack on North America was unlikely. Instead, "the most dangerous possibility," and the more likely road to war, were "the use of force in a local and limited might conflict" that "might lead to general war by accident or miscalculation." The danger, then, lay not in a surprise attack by the Soviet Union against the United States but in a conflict at the edge of Europe or in Asia that might lead to a general war that no one sought.[36]

Even when the Canadians set aside the question of how war might start, and instead focused on how to defend the deterrent, thorny questions arose. Who was going to defend this now most-important sector? There could be no continental defence without the use of Canadian territory. But it was politically impossible for the government of Canada to allow the necessary installations on Canadian territory to be managed by the United States alone.[37] If the US government planned the defence of North America alone, the Canadians feared, then the US Air Force commanders would, as Ignatieff warned, treat the populated parts of Canada "as the scene of the air battle" rather than an area to be defended.[38] Yet it was economically impossible for Canada to take on the defence of this territory by itself. The only solution was the joint management of continental defence by Canada and the United States.[39]

Joint efforts to defend Canadian territory, while helping to dodge political and economic consequences, had strategic consequences for Canada. The first was the obvious limit on Canada's freedom of action by having its air defences jointly coordinated with another state. The more tangible consequence of joint defence was a worry that such close integration with the United States might lead to Canada being caught up in "emergency situations for which Canada has no direct responsibility."[40] In 1955, there appeared to be the real possibility of a fight between Chinese Communist and Chinese Nationalist forces over Chinese coastal islands, with US forces supporting the Nationalists.[41] The Canadians worried that, if US forces did intervene in the defence of the islands, they might "extend hostilities to the mainland." This was the "'nightmare' situation" for the Canadians. And the nightmare went like this: if fighting broke out between the United States and China, then the United States might request that Ottawa allow the deployment of SAC bombers and the nuclear weapons at Goose Bay. If the war between the United States and China developed into a more serious confrontation, then Washington might ask Ottawa for "full mobilization measures of continental air defence" and the clearance to fly over Canadian territory in preparation for air strikes. Although the DEA thought it "difficult to identify any precise Canadian interests in the denial of the coastal islands to the Chinese Communists," American requests for ferrying nuclear weapons over or from Canada would "pose the most serious problem to the Canadian government." Such precautionary measures requested by the United States might "lead to a chain reaction of events which would tend to precipitate general war." And, though Canada did not share the US commitment in China, if it came to war, then "we are not likely to escape its consequences."[42]

The one method by which Canada could help to ensure that the nature of joint continental defence truly aligned with Canadian interests and policy was to make a larger contribution. But, as Barton had noted, the cupboard was bare. Did the growing importance of continental defence mean that Canada would or should transfer its military commitments to Europe back to North America? The effects on NATO would be significant, and Europe was one of the sites where a local conflict might escalate.

The DEA effort to examine the problem had raised questions that the External Affairs officials believed could be answered only by a larger examination of national security policy with the DND. The scenarios that loomed in 1955 only underscored the need for the study.[43] Yet DND still had not replied to the suggestion.

It took an exogenous force, in this case a rather peculiar request from the United Kingdom, to jump-start interdepartmental conversations in Ottawa. In late 1954 and early 1955, American officials had hinted that the United States was prepared to use smaller nuclear weapons, sometimes referred to as "tactical" nuclear weapons, in a contest with the PRC. This worried the British. They asked Ottawa to join with London in sending a formal submission to Washington raising concerns about American policy. The Canadians were puzzled by the British request but ultimately determined just what it was that bothered the British: London was trying to warn Washington that dividing up nuclear weapons between those that were small and tactical and therefore "morally justifiable," and those that were "large and therefore immoral," would weaken the nuclear deterrent on which NATO's defences rested. Even if such a distinction were possible, it would be undesirable.[44] The British idea of a joint submission (ultimately rejected by Ottawa) gave Pearson an opportunity to raise the study of national security policy once more with Campney, who now agreed that his department would participate.[45]

In April 1955, officials from the DEA, DND, and Privy Council Office met to discuss the questions raised by the British and to talk about the proposed study of national security policy. They discussed the possible use of nuclear weapons in Asia and decided that the best way to reduce the US need to use nuclear weapons would be to support US efforts in Asia with conventional forces. But they acknowledged that Canada and its allies were not in a position to provide troops, so it was nearly impossible to tell their American allies "how to resist Communist attacks in the Far East."[46]

The Canadian officials returned to the larger issue of the "moral" distinction between large and small weapons that had so concerned London. Deputy Minister of National Defence C.M. "Bud" Drury and Charles Foulkes warned that, if the public became convinced that the use of nuclear weapons was immoral, then it might "rule out or place a restraint upon the use of our main arm of defence – the nuclear deterrent – as being immoral."[47] There was no question in the halls of Ottawa, neither in DND nor, as the Ignatieff paper had made clear, in the DEA, that Canada had a supreme interest in defending and enabling the ability of SAC to wage war. What would happen if Canadians rejected this interest?

The officials continued to discuss the details of North American defence, following closely the conclusions already reached by External: neither the Canadian public nor the Canadian economy could support the sole defence of Canadian territory, and Canada did not want to be "incidentally" protected by the United States alone, which might turn Canadian airspace into a "no man's land," so closer cooperation was necessary. "In the past, the risk in a unified command has been too much US presence in Canada." Now, however, "given the vast extent of Canadian territory and the very limited resources available to the Canadian Government to defend it, we must balance against this the risk of too little US presence in Canada."[48]

Robert Bryce, secretary to cabinet, sought to guide the discussion toward the broader study of a national security policy because, as had been clear in the DEA for months, any decision on continental defence would affect Canada's stance in Europe and elsewhere in the world. Léger laid out the case again for an interdepartmental study of national security policy to deal not only with "day to day matters such as that which had been discussed earlier in the meeting but also to have a more intimate and up to date knowledge of the field of defence." The DND officials pushed back against his suggestions, noting that the DEA really wanted two distinct things: a discussion of "long range 'ephemeral' matters" and a discussion of the equipment and human resources that made up the defence program.[49]

Foulkes dismissed the notion that there was any value in trying to look ten years into the future; instead, he said, any study should "start by looking at the aim of Canadian defence policy." This aim, he made clear, was "to defend Canada." Canada had joined NATO and "agreed to play our part in the Cold War." But Canada's postwar defence commitments had been "entered in a piecemeal fashion," and it was "time to review them to see if Canada was making the most effective contribution to the defence of NATO that it could, having regard to finances and manpower limits." It was no secret what Foulkes meant: he singled out the brigade in Europe as the result of decisions "taken some years ago." Another item on his list was the practice by the Royal Canadian Air Force (RCAF) of fielding one type of airplane in Canada and another in Europe. Was that sensible? One gets the strong sense that his skepticism about a broader study, and perhaps the explanation for the DND refusal to respond to the DEA entreaties, rested on his view that the NATO brigade should be withdrawn and that he wanted to avoid a policy study in which the DEA raised the political importance of NATO. This would undercut the case, fairly straightforward in a narrow defence perspective, to bring the brigade home. Foulkes proposed starting with a close examination of Canadian defence programs and then moving to the "long-term study of the overall national security policy."[50]

Building on his suggestion, Bryce pointed out that there was general agreement that a study should examine both "present defence arrangements" and "general long-term questions." Again, the DND officials present balked, arguing that the department was "really not designed to take part in such a study" and that there were "not many officers available qualified to do long-range thinking." "It was a 'terrible commentary' on the Department of National Defence," said Drury, its deputy minister, "but the fact was that the personnel were just not available to do the job of finding the answers to such questions as what should be the proportion of Canada's effort to that of the United States in continental defence?"[51] Still, Bryce, Drury, and MacKay agreed to try to develop more detailed plans for a study of national security policy in the coming weeks.[52]

A month later there still had been no progress toward a joint study. Yet DEA officials wrote that "we are daily learning of new projects which will involve the establishment and operation by the United States of additional defence facilities in Canada." The pressure to increase Canadian continental defence efforts led DEA to look seriously at the idea proposed by Foulkes of "transferring Canadian commitments from Europe to North America."[53]

This transfer, as he presented it, was a matter of defence policy. But for the diplomats in External, it was a larger political question. The Soviet Union had begun a concerted effort to undermine NATO. Moscow was determined "to bring about the withdrawal of North American forces from Western Europe, or from Germany initially, as the price for German reunification." This would throw the alliance into disarray, and DEA feared that it would also lead to political agitation for pro-communist popular front governments in other NATO countries such as France and Italy.[54]

For political reasons, then, the DEA officials thought it "unwise," even dangerous, to make known, even to allies, that Canada was considering reducing its military commitment in Europe. But External saw a strategic or defence policy angle here too: its officials worried that the more forces were withdrawn from Europe "the more Canada would represent the only buffer area between the United States and the Soviet Union." This would lead Americans to "ever-increasing demands upon us for further measures of defence."[55] The officials, it seems, were worried not only about the political implications of ending the European commitment but also about DND getting the strategic equation wrong.

Finally, after so many letters from External, Foulkes forwarded his own paper to the department. It is a key document setting out his views, and its title made clear its purpose: a reassessment of Canadian defence policy over the next five years. He argued, plainly, that Canada's "primary task in NATO," which should "take priority over our other endeavours," was to provide air defence in North America. Such air defence, first, would allow SAC to "get off the ground and avoid destruction" and, second, help to "blunt the initial enemy strikes so that we can survive until the full weight of our retaliation can have its effect." In light of the importance of this task, Canada's other "arrangements for assisting in winning the Cold War" needed to be reconsidered. It was time to examine the "wisdom of continuing to plan our whole defence on the basis of defending the NATO area [Europe]."[56]

DEA officials were concerned that Foulkes was singularly focused on defence questions and not on "the review of the effects upon policy of the revolutionary developments in the methods of warfare." But he had agreed to the study, and with his paper he had come out swinging. DEA officials were now in the position of scrambling to ensure that the study was organized so that service representatives did not outweigh civilian representatives and that Foulkes did not dictate the scope of the project and run "away with the ball."[57] MacKay wrote to Foulkes, emphasizing what the DEA thought so crucial about the study: "We have to find some way of resolving our defence commitments in Europe and our desire to participate in continental defence activities to the extent necessary to safeguard our autonomy."[58]

The first formal meeting of the "review of national security policy in the light of developments in air-nuclear warfare" convened on 20 July 1955. Early in the meeting, Bryce – building on Ignatieff's earlier work – posed a set of broad, crucial questions. Would Canada provide forces for small wars outside NATO? Would Canada ever face the prospect of a large but non-nuclear war? What was the proper role for Americans in Canada? What was the proper role for Canadians in Europe? What were "our attitudes toward large and small atomic weapons? Should Canada use small atomic weapons?"[59]

The discussion returned to the perennial question of North American versus European defence. Foulkes continued to make his case: already the "new defence concept" of both Canada and its allies was "based on the long-term aim of avoiding war by means of the nuclear deterrent." Along with Drury, Foulkes argued that Canada and its allies should focus on maintaining the deterrent "and, if necessary, win, or at least not lose, a war in the first phase" – the first phase, in this case, represented a general nuclear exchange between the United States and the Soviet Union. Foulkes again questioned the role of the Canadian ground forces across the Atlantic: "Originally our maximum effort had been placed in Europe but things had now changed." The brigade "had perhaps a very valuable moral purpose when it was originally sent to Europe, but was it of such great value now?" He pointed out, too, the major problem of Canadian air defence: Canada had committed eighteen squadrons to the defence of North America, half of them regular forces and the other half auxiliaries. The auxiliary pilots, it turned out, could not operate the CF-100s, effectively cutting in half the number of squadrons that Canada could use to defend North America. If the United States asked how Canada would fill in the gap, "and if the Canadians answered it could not be done for the present, the US would then suggest that it meet the deficiency." The easiest solution, from the perspective of Foulkes, was to bring back the Canadian squadrons from Europe. And perhaps bringing back the Brigade Group and restructuring the human resources of the Canadian forces would help to provide what DND predicted were the additional 10,000 men required for the control stations and ground-to-air missiles that defended North America. Foulkes summarized his point plainly: "If we accepted the defence of the nuclear deterrent, it seemed to him that our defences should be weighted in favour of this continent, because of the importance of protecting the deterrent capability of the Strategic Air Command against the increasing capacity of the USSR to attack this continent by air."[60]

Léger offered the DEA's counter-argument: withdrawing Canadian forces from Europe would help the Soviet Union to achieve its political goal of weakening NATO.[61] The Soviets had been sowing discord in the alliance, painting the Federal Republic of Germany as the aggressive heir of the Nazis. Moscow had made concessions on Austria and was now positioning itself as the champion of peace and disarmament in Europe, implying that NATO was worthless, or worse, warmongering. Those in External worried that this would be attractive to "large elements" of the electorate in France, Italy, and even the United Kingdom. The "Europeans," Léger warned, "might be in a mood where they no longer thought our troops were necessary on their continent for defence." The result could be a radical shift in public and then government opinion, in both Europe and the United States, against NATO. The Canadian troops had been deployed to Europe for symbolic reasons; their withdrawal would be equally symbolic. As Bryce put it, speaking about Canadian defence policy in general, "we are a prisoner of the past."[62]

Pearson read the minutes of the first official discussion of the national security policy and deemed it "a very interesting, important and satisfactory meeting."[63] The key questions had been posed, and both DEA and DND had made strong cases for their priorities.

The July meeting led to a flurry of papers exchanged between DND and DEA officials. Foulkes distributed a paper that ostensibly traced the development of Canadian defence policy in the postwar period. The historical overview, however, barely disguised the familiar refrain from Foulkes that the "first objective of Canada's defence policy has been the defence of Canada and North America from direct attack." Despite the Canadian troops and squadrons in Europe, the paper argued, "our primary task in NATO is to implement our part in the provision and protection of the retaliatory forces and the provision of an early warning system." Previously, "the right place to defend Canada and what Canadians believe in is as far away from Canada as possible," that is, with the forward deployment in

Europe. So what had changed? The "change of concept is due to the development of mass destruction weapons and the means of delivering them" creating the need to protect retaliatory forces in North America – the next stage of the nuclear revolution.[64]

External Affairs also revised and distributed its "nuclear deterrent" paper, which continued to align with many DND views: nuclear weapons, jets, and guided missiles had "revolutionized warfare." These "revolutionary developments" required "a re-thinking of our concepts of defence." And the DEA agreed that the "chief means" for preserving peace lay in "the capacity to retaliate instantly with nuclear weapons in the event of aggression."[65]

But the DEA paper went beyond the calculations of defence strategy, pointing out that the "communist threat by no means poses a straight military problem." DEA officials argued that the very power of the West's nuclear deterrent would lead the Soviets to seek their aims through other means and to use "communist methods of diplomatic manoeuvre and political warfare designed to weaken the unity and effectiveness of the Western Coalition." Maintaining the unity of NATO was a principal goal of Canada's foreign policy. It was obvious from Léger's comments and other departmental memorandums, even if it was not directly stated in the "deterrent paper," that Canada's force deployments in Europe helped to reinforce NATO's unity, that a Canadian withdrawal would undercut the coalition, that a weakened NATO might lead to political upheaval and conflict on the continent, and that this would threaten Canadian national security.

The DND and DEA papers were rendered into a short joint draft paper grandly titled "National Security Policy."[66] But the paper dodged the fundamental question of how to allocate Canadian resources and did not reconcile the two departments' views. The policy listed five aims for Canadian national security policy, and the first two were poles apart. The first aim was the "immediate defence of Canada and North America from direct attack, in co-operation with the United States." This recognized the DND preference for continental defence and the DEA acknowledgment of the overriding importance of enabling the deterrent. The second aim, however, was "co-operation within the North Atlantic Treaty Organization for the provision of a collective force capable of deterring aggression and for defence of the NATO area." It is impossible to see how this could be achieved by removing Canadian forces from Europe.

The contradictory elements of the policy grew more stark in two sections called "Military Assumptions" and "Political Assumptions." The first category included the statement, again reflecting DND views, that "general war, if it cannot be averted, will most likely come with little or no warning and will involve the use of nuclear weapons against targets in North America." The DEA view of the political assumptions was that the Soviet Union would have every reason to avoid nuclear war. "The most dangerous" possibility, then, was "that the use of force in a local and limited conflict might lead to general war by accident or miscalculation."

The fundamental tensions between the two views of a national security policy resulted from different military and political assumptions about how war might occur and the best means to prevent the conditions that could lead to nuclear apocalypse. On the one hand, the military perspective began with an analysis of the worst-case scenario, a Soviet surprise nuclear attack against North America. Given these military assumptions, a single-minded focus on North American defence, and the withdrawal of forces from Europe, comprised the logical solution. On the other hand, the political assumption – that Soviet political warfare in Europe might split the alliance and create the conditions for local conflicts and misunderstandings of intentions – made it imperative for Canada to strengthen NATO or at least not to weaken it by removing Canadian forces. But this did not help to resolve the question of North American defence.

* * *

In the American Century, Canadian national security policy was made in the shadow of American atomic power. The conundrums that Canada faced as the result of the nuclear revolution would rear up throughout the Eisenhower years and spill over across multiple Canadian governments and multiple American presidencies. The questions posed by Ignatieff and other DEA officials during the formulation of the study would be answered partially and only after excruciating difficulty. The first, chronologically, was the question of organizing North American air defence. The decision came to a head with the creation of the North American Aerospace

Defence Command (or NORAD) in the Diefenbaker years, the result of a messy policy process that truly did see Foulkes "run away with the ball."[67] The second was the question, raised several times during preparation of the study, but never fully addressed, of whether and how to equip Canadian forces in both North America and Europe with nuclear weapons. The "decision making" on this issue, if it truly can be called that, cost Prime Minister John Diefenbaker his office and led to years of wrangling and comic posturing. The third matter, so crucial to the discussions of 1955, was whether or not to maintain Canadian troops in Europe and at what level. When the government of Prime Minister Pierre Trudeau finally addressed this issue directly by reducing forces, his decision was held up as evidence that he just did not understand strategy, military affairs, and hard power. But his decision to question the utility of the Canadian deployment to Europe echoed the hard-headed thinking of the chairman of the Chiefs of Staff over a decade earlier.

Too often such particular moments of crisis in Canadian policy-making have been treated as singular events, the results of the peculiarities of the prime minister of the day. They are all, ultimately, ducks in a row – the forced and belated answers to the questions lined up by Ignatieff and the others who understood the tough choices that Canada would have to face, one day, as a result of the nuclear revolution.

NOTES

1 High Commissioner of Great Britain to Minister of Munitions and Supply and of Reconstruction, August 6, 1945, in *Documents on Canadian External Relations* (hereafter *DCER*), vol. 11, part 2, 1944–45, ed. John F. Hilliker (Ottawa: External Affairs and International Trade Canada, 1990), 973.
2 Memorandum No. 1, "General Status of Radiological Project," from C.J. Mackenzie to C.D. Howe, 10 April 1944, ibid., 961.
3 Canada's junior role in the development of the bomb had been something of a sticking point in trilateral relations. See the document from which this quotation is drawn, "Deputy High Commissioner, High Commission of Great Britain, to Minister of Munitions and Supply and Reconstruction," ibid., 975. See also Elisabetta Kerr et al., "Draft History of US-UK-Canadian Atomic Energy Cooperation, 1953–1954," Canada Declassified, https://declassified.library.utoronto.ca/exhibits/show/draft-history-of-us -uk-canadia/summary. The authoritative treatment remains Robert Bothwell, *Eldorado: Canada's National Uranium Company* (Toronto: University of Toronto Press, 1984).

4 Memorandum from Senior Canadian Army Member, Permanent Joint Board on Defence, to Associate Undersecretary of State for External Affairs, 21 September 1945, in *DCER*, 1944–45, 992.

5 Memorandum by Ambassador in United States, "Canadian Memorandum on Atomic Warfare," 8 November 1945, ibid., 1026.

6 Memorandum from Acting Undersecretary of State for External Affairs to Undersecretary of State for External Affairs, 29 October 1945, ibid., 1005.

7 Memorandum by Ambassador in United States, "Canadian Memorandum on Atomic Warfare," 8 November 1945, ibid., 1027–29. See also the observations on nuclear war made by Diamond Jenness in "Memorandum from Chief, Interservice Topographical Section, to Canadian Joint Intelligence Committee," 20 August 1945, ibid., 979–82.

8 The most thorough account of US nuclear policy in the Eisenhower era remains Richard G. Hewlett and Jack M. Holl, *Atoms for Peace and War, 1953–1961: Eisenhower and the Atomic Energy Commission* (Los Angeles: University of California Press, 1991).

9 For a sustained discussion of Canada's post-1945 approach to nuclear strategy, see Andrew Richter, *Avoiding Armageddon: Canadian Military Strategy and Nuclear Weapons, 1950–1963* (Vancouver: UBC Press, 2011).

10 Katie Davis, "Very Close Together: Balancing Canadian Interests on Atomic Energy Control, 1945–46," in *The Nuclear North: Histories of Canada in the Atomic Age*, ed. Susan Colbourn and Timothy Andrews Sayle (Vancouver: UBC Press, 2020), 17–39.

11 On the origins of the overflight agreement, see Timothy Andrews Sayle, "A Pattern of Constraint: Canadian-American Relations in the Early Cold War," *International Journal* 62, 3 (2007): 689–705. For the implications of SAC exercises over Canadian air space, see Asa McKercher and Timothy Andrews Sayle, "Skyhawk, Skyshield, and the Soviets: Revisiting Canada's Cold War," *Historical Journal* 61, 2 (2018): 453–75.

12 "The Policy Implications of the Nuclear Deterrent," 15 July 1955, Library and Archives Canada (hereafter LAC), External Affairs records, file 50333-40, CDNW00142. All records cited in this chapter with a "CD" number are available online at *Canada Declassified*. To view a document, proceed to https://declassified.library.utoronto.ca, click the magnifying glass symbol, and search for the Canada Declassified identifier, i.e., "CDNW00142."

13 The study itself is the subject of a small editorial note in *DCER*, vol. 21, 1955, ed. Greg Donaghy (Ottawa: Department of Foreign Affairs and International Trade, 1999), 1640–41. Despite the publication of a handful of records in *DCER*, the full archival record of the study was released only after I made an Access to Information Act request.

14 Barton was assigned to Defence Liaison (1) Division and was the Canadian secretary of the Permanent Joint Board of Defence. "Proposed Study on Canadian National Security," 28 October 1954, LAC, External Affairs records, file 50333-40, CDNW00004.

15 "Canadian National Security," 1 November 1954, LAC, RG 25, file 50333-40, CDNW00005.

16 I do not intend to discuss whether Canada had a grand strategy during the Cold War. But what I describe below – that an effort to draft a grand strategy resulted in failure – is instructive.

17 "Canadian National Security," n.d. [completed on 1 November 1954], LAC, External Affairs records, file 50333-40, CDNW00006.

18 "White Paper on Defence," presented by the Honourable Paul Hellyer and the Honourable Lucien Cardin, 1964, http://publications.gc.ca/collections/collection_2012/dn-nd/D3-6-1964-eng.pdf.

19 In 1954, the Soviet Union did not have the bombers required for such an attack, but Barton was working with Canadian intelligence assessments that put that possibility soon – in 1956.

20 "Canadian National Security," n.d. [completed on 1 November 1954], LAC, External Affairs records, file 50333-40, CDNW00006.

21 Dispatch No. 610 from Washington to SSEA, 1 April 1954, LAC, External Affairs records, file 50115-P-40, part 3, CDTT00030.

22 The quotations are from the first draft of "Memorandum" from Lester Pearson, 16 January 1954, LAC, External Affairs records, file 50115-P-40, part 2, CDTT00015. The version sent to the prime minister made the same points but in less strident language. See "United States Defence Policy," Memorandum for the Prime Minister, 2 February 1954, ibid, CDTT00018.

23 "Canadian National Security," n.d. [completed on 1 November 1954], LAC, External Affairs records, file 50333-40, CDNW00006.

24 Letter No. 586 from the Canadian Delegation to the North Atlantic Council to the USSEA, 25 February 1954, LAC, External Affairs records, file 50115-P-40, part 2, CDTT00020.

25 "Memorandum" from Lester Pearson, 16 January 1954, LAC, External Affairs records, file 50115-P-40, part 2, CDTT00015.

26 "Canadian National Security," n.d. [completed on 1 November 1954], LAC, External Affairs records, file 50333-40, CDNW00006.

27 Ibid.

28 "National Security Policy," 17 November 1954, LAC, External Affairs records, file 50333-40, CDNW00009; "National Security Policy," 18 November 1954, LAC, External Affairs records, file 50333-40, CDNW00010.

29 "National Security Policy," 25 November 1954, LAC, External Affairs records, file 50333-40, CDNW00011; Lester Pearson to Ralph Campney, 25 November 1954, LAC, External Affairs records, file 50333-40, CDNW00014.

30 "Study of National Security Policy," 4 February 1955, LAC, External Affairs records, file 50333-40, CDNW00020.

31 "Some Specific Questions on Future National Security Policy," 1 February 1955, LAC, External Affairs records, file 50333-40, CDNW00015.

32 "Study of National Security Policy," R.A. MacKay to Charles Foulkes, 4 February 1955, LAC, External Affairs records, file 50333-40, CDNW00020.

33 "National Security Policy," 11 February 1955, LAC, External Affairs records, file 50333-40, CDNW00021; Lester Pearson to Ralph Campney, 11 February 1955, LAC, External Affairs records, file 50333-40, CDNW00023; "National Security Policy," 28 February 1955, LAC, External Affairs records, file 50333-40, CDNW00024; Lester Pearson to Ralph Campney [draft], 3 March 1955, LAC, External Affairs records, file 50333-40,

CDNW00028; "National Security Policy," 16 March 1955, LAC, External Affairs records, file 50333-40, CDNW00031. The DEA drafted one more letter to Campney, but it was not sent. Lester Pearson to Ralph Campney [not sent], 16 March 1955, LAC, External Affairs records, file 50333-40, CDNW00032.

34 "Continental Defence," 17 March 1955, LAC, External Affairs records, file 50333-40, CDNW00034.

35 "The Strategic Concept of the Nuclear Deterrent," 26 March 1955, LAC, External Affairs records, file 50333-40, CDNW00041.

36 Ibid.

37 "Continental Defence," 17 March 1955, LAC, External Affairs records, file 50333-40, CDNW00034.

38 "The Strategic Concept of the Nuclear Deterrent," 26 March 1955, LAC, External Affairs records, file 50333-40, CDNW00041.

39 "Continental Defence," 17 March 1955, LAC, External Affairs records, file 50333-40, CDNW00034.

40 Ibid.

41 "Problems which Might Be Posed for Canada, if the United States Were to Become Involved in Hostilities over the Chinese Offshore Islands," 17 February 1955, LAC, External Affairs records, file 50333-40, CDNW00022.

42 Ibid.

43 "Comments on the Draft Memorandum on Continental Defence of March 7, 1955," 18 March 1955, LAC, External Affairs records, file 50333-40, CDNW00037. See also "The Strategic Concept of the Nuclear Deterrent, Its Implications and Limitations," n.d., LAC, External Affairs records, file 50333-40, CDNW00036.

44 High Commissioner for Canada, London, No. 537, to SSEA, 18 April 1955, LAC, External Affairs records, file 50333-40, CDNW00063.

45 "Policy for the Employment of Nuclear Weapons," Lester Pearson to Ralph Campney, 19 April 1955, LAC, External Affairs records, file 50333-40, CDNW00069.

46 "Notes on a Discussion [21 April] between Representatives of the Departments of External Affairs and National Defence on Views Received from London about Distinction between Large and Tactical Nuclear Weapons and a Study of National Security Policy," 25 April 1955, LAC, External Affairs records, file 50333-40, CDNW00079.

47 Ibid.

48 Ibid.

49 Ibid.

50 "Minutes of Meeting to Discuss Distinction between Large and Tactical Nuclear Weapons and a Study of National Security Policy, 21 April 1955," LAC, External Affairs records, file 50333-40, CDNW00077.

51 "Notes on a Discussion [21 April] ... " 25 April 1955, LAC, External Affairs records, file 50333-40, CDNW00079.

52 "Minutes of Meeting ... " 21 April 1955, LAC, External Affairs records, file 50333-40, CDNW00077.

53 "Canadian Defence Commitments in North America and in Europe," 10 June 1955, LAC, External Affairs records, file 50333-40, CDNW00109. See also "Canadian Defence

Commitments in North America and in Europe," 10 June 1955, LAC, External Affairs records, file 50333-40, CDNW00108.

54 "Canadian Defence Commitments in North America and in Europe," memorandum for the Minister, 10 June 1955, LAC, External Affairs records, file 50333-40, CDNW00108.

55 Ibid.

56 "Reassessment of Canada's Defence Policy, Aims and Programmes for the Next Five Years – 1955–1960," 16 June 1955, LAC, External Affairs records, file 50333-40, CDNW00122.

57 "Letter to General Foulkes on National Security Study Policy Study [sic]," George Ignatieff to R.A. MacKay, 6 July 1955, LAC, External Affairs records, file 50333-40, CDNW00126.

58 R.A. MacKay to Charles Foulkes, 8 July 1955, LAC, External Affairs records, file 50333-40, CDNW00133.

59 "National Security Policy Study," memorandum for the Minister, 21 July 1955, LAC, External Affairs records, file 50333-40, CDNW00147. The prospect of war with China was another major element of this meeting.

60 "Minutes of Meeting to Discuss Study of National Security Policy," 20 July 1955, LAC, External Affairs records, file 50333-40, CDNW00153.

61 "Their major aim is undoubtedly to secure the withdrawal of United States forces from Europe ... and the detachment of ... Germany from NATO." R.A.D. Ford, "Soviet Policy in Europe," 30 May 1955, in *DCER*, vol. 21, 1955, 1147–48.

62 "Minutes of Meeting to Discuss Study of National Security Policy," 20 July 1955, LAC, External Affairs records, file 50333-40, CDNW00153.

63 "Study of National Security Policy," memorandum for the Minister, 26 July 1955, LAC, External Affairs records, file 50333-40, CDNW00151.

64 "The Development of Canadian Defence Policy," 3 August 1955, LAC, External Affairs records, file 50333-40, CDNW00166.

65 "The International Setting of Canadian and Allied Defence Policy Aims in the Light of the Nuclear Deterrent," 2 August 1955, LAC, External Affairs records, file 50333-40, CDNW00162.

66 "National Security Policy (Joint External Affairs–National Defence Draft Paper)," 9 August 1955, LAC, External Affairs records, file 50333-40, CDNW00169.

67 Foulkes would claim later that he "stampeded" Diefenbaker into the NORAD agreement. House of Commons Committees, 26th Parliament, 1st Session, Special Committee on Defence, vol. 1, 510.

4

From Normandy to NORAD

*Canada and the North Atlantic Triangle
in the Age of Eisenhower*

ASA McKERCHER AND MICHAEL D. STEVENSON

In this chapter, we examine Canada's place within a changing "North Atlantic Triangle." The term was popularized in 1945 by Columbia University historian John Bartlet Brebner. Penning the ultimate volume of a twenty-five-book series on Canadian-American relations for the Carnegie Endowment of International Peace, Brebner had set out to chart the "interplay" between Canada and the United States, "the Siamese Twins of North America." Yet, as he had concluded, both countries "could not eliminate Great Britain from their courses of action, whether in the realm of ideas, like democracy, or of institutions, or of economic and political processes." Brebner had not been able to exclude Britain either. So, rather than a bilateral study, his book had become the *North Atlantic Triangle: The Interplay of Canada, the United States and Great Britain,* a historical examination of this trilateral relationship. Writing as he had been in the midst of the Second World War, Brebner had also looked ahead to the future, affirming that no countries were "more experienced or more capable of contributing to collective security" in the postwar period than the triangle's members.[1]

The idea of a triangular relationship reaches back to the end of the nineteenth century and sprang from conceptions of racial, cultural, and historical solidarity within a so-called Anglosphere. Indeed, in the foreword to Brebner's book, series editor James Shotwell enthused about an international order modelled after the peace achieved within the "Anglo-Saxon polity."[2] In common usage, the North Atlantic Triangle often equated to a special tripartite relationship, within which Canada was touted – by Canadians at least – as playing an important role between the other two members. William Lyon Mackenzie King himself outlined this notion, to Adolf Hitler of all people, stating "that we, in Canada, had frequently to be explaining the English attitude on some matters to the Americans, and the American attitude on some matters, to the English."[3] Expectations and rhetoric aside, there seem to be few instances in which Canadians played the role of Anglo-American interpreter or mediator.

Although Canada's mediatory record was limited, the idea of the North Atlantic Triangle is helpful for understanding and delineating Canada's most important international relationships – economically, militarily, politically – particularly at the dawn of the American Century. The 1940s and 1950s saw the collapse of British power and the emergence of the United States as *the* global power, developments of vital importance to Canada. As we showcase, triangular thinking was central for Canadian officials as they charted Canada through the difficult waters of the Second World War and the early Cold War era.

That the North Atlantic Triangle was important to Canada in this period is not a new viewpoint. One long-standing notion posits that either purposefully or through lack of forethought King's Liberal government took Canada out of its British orbit and transformed it into a satellite of the United States. As a result, Canada, in historian W.L. Morton's colourful phrasing, was left "so irradiated by the American presence that it sickens and threatens to dissolve in cancerous slime."[4] Another view stresses that the Anglo-American transition of power was a prime reason for the increasing imbalance within the North Atlantic Triangle or, as Jack Granatstein ably put it, *How Britain's Weakness Forced Canada into the Arms of the United States*.[5] Although there is no doubt that Canada-US relations grew closer during the Second World War and the early Cold War period, Canadian policy makers were wary of being drawn too closely to their southern neighbours, and Britain still provided something of a counterweight to American influences. Overall, the dawn of the American Century witnessed key transitions in global power that reverberated through the triangular relationship that Canada maintained with Britain and the United States.

* * *

A good starting point is 1940. In that year, historian Frank Underhill later reflected, Canada had "passed from the British century of our history to the American century."[6] The signal event was the Ogdensburg Agreement on 18 August between Prime Minister King and President Franklin Delano Roosevelt establishing a Permanent Joint Board on Defence (PJBD) to coordinate continental defence efforts. The move came amid a period of crisis: France had fallen to Nazi Germany in June, and Britain, with its empire and commonwealth, stood alone against Hitler. Roosevelt's offer to protect Canada despite his own country's neutrality in the war was taken as a sign of magnanimity, and King seized the opportunity. Canada's prime minister was less enthused about the president's request that King ask Winston Churchill, his British counterpart, whether, in the event that Britain collapsed, London would transfer its fleet to the United States, thereby keeping it out of German hands. Writing to King regarding Ogdensburg and this naval request – as the Luftwaffe assaulted the British Isles – Churchill snapped that, if the Nazis failed to defeat Britain, then "all these transactions will be judged in a mood different to that while the issue still stands in the balance."[7] Here was a fleeting moment in which Canada played the role of Anglo-American mediator and was chastised for it. In discussing Ogdensburg in Parliament, King was careful to portray it as contributing not just to "the effective defence of Canada" but also to "the defence of the British commonwealth of nations as a whole."[8]

Ogdensburg was followed by the Hyde Park Declaration in 1941, an economic arrangement that harmonized the production of war material, allowed Canadian-made munitions to be purchased by Britain via the Lend-Lease Program, and offset a trade imbalance via increased US purchases in Canada. As with Ogdensburg, King publicly defended the Hyde Park arrangement on triangular grounds, stating that it was not only "a common plan for the economic defence of the western hemisphere" but also "a joint agreement between Canada and the United States for aid to Britain."[9] Together these two informal arrangements – neither was a formal treaty – signified a closer Canada-US relationship in which the easy rapport between King and Roosevelt played an important role. A report in 1942 by Canada's Department of External Affairs (DEA) characterized the "personal friendship" between prime minister and president as "one of the really significant factors in Canadian-American affairs." Although Ogdensburg, Hyde Park, and other smaller agreements represented what was "probably an historically inevitable development," DEA officials contended that the personal tie meant that "they were all effected more quickly, with less of a bargaining or of a bullying spirit involved in the negotiations, and with greater and more mutual satisfaction in the results."[10] Roosevelt himself recognized this factor. In a letter to King, he raised the "thoroughly sanctimonious and pharisaical thought that it is a grand and glorious thing for Canada and United States to have the team of Mackenzie and Roosevelt at the helm for times like these," adding that though "probably both nations could get along without us ... our association has brought some proven benefits to both nations."[11]

The friendly relations between Roosevelt and King belied wartime tensions in the Canada-US relationship. Canadians welcomed American entry into the conflict in December 1941, but concerns quickly emerged about the preponderant power of the United States. Only weeks after the US declaration of war, Norman Robertson, the undersecretary of state for external affairs, saw that Americans were discovering their strength and "showing a new sense of their 'manifest destiny' and a corresponding disposition to take decisions and accept responsibilities." This was an encouraging development as far as the war effort was concerned, but Robertson nonetheless predicted significant changes in "the special relationship" between the two countries.[12]

In the name of wartime cooperation, the range of contacts between both governments expanded over a wide array of economic, military, and intelligence issues. Often Canadian officials felt that their American counterparts had little regard for Canadian sensitivities or interests. In early 1943, Lester B. Pearson, the deputy at Canada's Washington embassy, wrote that US officials "consider us not as a foreign nation at all, but one of themselves," a flattering but dangerous outlook.[13] Similarly, Escott Reid, a rising star in the DEA, complained that Canada had "not won from London complete freedom to make our own decisions on every issue – including that of peace and war – in order to become a colony of Washington."[14] This triangular formulation, of Canada moving from colony to nation to colony, would be common by the 1960s as various Canadian nationalists worried about their country's place alongside the United States.

As for the war, a specific complaint emerged about American-built infrastructure projects in Canada's north: an oil pipeline, weather stations, airfields, and the massive Alaska Highway. Ottawa had obliged the United States in granting permission to build these projects, but concerns about sovereignty were soon apparent. "They have apparently walked in and taken possession in many cases as if Canada were unclaimed territory inhabited by a docile race of aborigines," groused Vincent Massey, the high commissioner in London.[15] The Alaska Highway, King grumbled, "was less intended for protection against the Japanese than as one of the fingers on the hand which America is placing more or less over the whole of the Western hemisphere."[16] Such complaints belied the chumminess of Roosevelt and King, exposing tensions in the supposedly special bilateral relationship.

Wartime Anglo-Canadian relations were also marked by ups and downs. Canada had entered the conflict in support of Britain – albeit waiting a week to declare war so as to assert its independence – and particularly from the crisis of 1940 onward had assumed huge financial and military burdens. Over 1.1 million Canadians served in uniform – British uniforms with a "Canada" patch sewn on them – mainly under overall British command: in No. 6 Group Royal Canadian Air Force as part of RAF Bomber Command and in the army's I Canadian Corps as part of the British Eight Army in the Mediterranean or in the First Canadian Army as part of the British 21st Army Group in Northwest Europe. Hundreds of Canadian officers served in British units via the CANLOAN program, and Canada played a major part in the British Commonwealth Air Training Program, which trained tens of thousands of Allied aircrew. Further, Ottawa providing billions of dollars to London in the form of industrial production and gifts and loans.[17] Beyond the battlefield, more than half a million Canadian personnel spent part of the war in Britain, sometimes for several years, forging personal bonds, even if a reputation for rowdiness offended some locals.[18]

Among Canadians, there was some irritation over treatment at the hands of the British. One story that Dwight Eisenhower liked to tell was of General A.G.L. McNaughton, commander of the First Canadian Army, who resented his British colleagues. "Remember, General," Eisenhower would laugh as he delivered his punchline, "we are fighting the Germans, not the British!"[19] King, meanwhile, was ever on the lookout for instances of British reassertion of imperial control. In early 1944, Lord Halifax, the British ambassador in Washington, publicly called for more frequent and formal consultation and cooperation among Commonwealth members. To Canada's prime minister, Halifax's speech was evidence that London sought a unified imperial foreign policy. "If Hitler himself wanted to divide the Empire – get one part against the other," King ranted, "he could not have chosen a more effective way, or a better instrument."[20] Such complaints aside, other Canadian officials forged cooperative relations with their British allies. Among Canadian army officers, for instance, positive experiences of common Anglo-Canadian wartime service left a lasting legacy.[21] At the same time, Canadians also developed fond feelings for Americans. Thousands of well-wishers greeted Eisenhower when he visited Ottawa and Toronto in January 1946, with King capping off the trip by renaming Castle Mountain, near Banff, Mount Eisenhower, a testament to the general's "steadfastness and the security of his leadership."[22]

Many Canadian concerns about treatment by the Americans or British were the result of Canada's subordinate status within the overall war effort, which King, for all his complaints, accepted. In December 1941, he remarked to his cabinet colleagues that it was a *fait accompli* that "the US and Britain would settle everything between themselves." Later King admitted to Churchill that "strategy had to be left in the hands of the British and Americans."[23] Ever cautious, Canada's prime minister did little to alter this status quo. He hosted the senior-most British and American officials at two summits (1943 and 1944) at Quebec City, but Canadians played little part in these meetings. King stayed for the photo ops and banquets, but later he equated his role "to that of the General Manager of the Chateau Frontenac."[24] The busts of Churchill and Roosevelt that now stand on Rue Saint-Louis inside the gates to Quebec's old town testify to the figures who mattered most. Lamenting King's supine attitude, Escott Reid put the matter bluntly: Canadians were "being treated as children because we have refused to behave as adults."[25] In the opinion of C.D. Howe, who as minister of munitions and supply directed Canada's wartime economy, the "Anglo-American monopoly" was a concern because the "British unwillingness to give Canada a place where the measure of our contribution would justify it" was pushing the country "into very close relations with the United States."[26]

As part of his ministerial remit, Howe oversaw Canadian participation in the development of the atomic bomb. Canada's part in the Manhattan Project was small – some research and uranium – but it came about at British insistence. The use of the resulting bombs against Japan in August 1945 was heralded in some quarters in Canada as an "Anglo-American-Canadian victory" and the "culmination of a process in which the American-British-Canadian forces have earned for themselves an unchallenged and unchallengeable reputation. We are the great destroyers."[27] These grim sentiments testified to the harsh attitudes prevailing during the war and to the exultation of victory.

For Canada and the United States, there were some grounds to consider the Second World War a "good war." Certainly, in economic terms, the mass industrial and military mobilizations and huge infusions of government money had put an end to the Great Depression, and neither North American country had suffered the destruction of its cities or industries. Yet Canada's economic situation was precarious, with much of the country's wartime production involving exports to Britain financed through Canadian government loans or the Lend-Lease Program. As victory approached, the question remained whether a bankrupt Britain could continue to import Canadian goods. To keep exports flowing, in March 1946 Ottawa extended a $1.25 billion loan to London, followed by long-term contracts to supply the British with agricultural goods and other foodstuffs. As one Canadian trade official later admitted, the Canadians "put a great many eggs" in the British basket.[28] Doing so was vital because Canada faced a trade and resulting dollar imbalance with the United States. Canadian policy makers feared that the situation would only grow more dire as wartime American purchases from Canada ended and as Washington announced the European Recovery Program, or Marshall Plan, aimed at rebuilding war-shattered Europe but requiring that much of the aid money be spent in the United States.

Thankfully for Canada's short-term economic health, US authorities were willing to be helpful just as Roosevelt had been at Hyde Park in 1941.

State Department officials urged their colleagues in the armed services to continue purchasing raw materials from Canada, asserting that "the Canadian economy should be treated as nearly as possible like our own in peacetime as well as in war, based always on mutual reciprocity."[29] As for the Marshall Plan, Washington included an offshore purchases clause – akin to the Hyde Park Agreement – letting Europeans buy Canadian goods. One American official explained that "it was in the United States self-interest that there should be a strong Canada."[30] A further solution to Canada's economic situation was the possible expansion of an existing trade agreement into a full-blown customs union with the United States. Talks between officials began in 1947, and the following year a draft agreement was concluded. American diplomats observed a willingness among the Canadian public to accept such an arrangement. "Economic union between the two countries," the US ambassador in Ottawa stated, "is taken as a natural parallel development with intimate military ties existing since early in the late war and close political collaboration as now manifest at the UN."[31] Judging public opinion differently, King nixed the proposal, for "while it might be sound economically ... it would be fatal politically."[32]

Apart from the customs union's collapse, the postwar era saw the continuation of close Canada-US economic ties, a development parallelled by continuing military links. The immediate impetus was the emerging Cold War. In September 1945, shortly after Japan's surrender, Igor Gouzenko, a cipher clerk at the Soviet embassy in Ottawa, defected, bringing with him evidence of a spy network reaching throughout the Canadian government and into the British foreign service. King was hesitant about acting on the information, but arrests soon followed, and American, British, and Canadian officials began to look increasingly askance at the Soviet Union. Privately, King mused about the need for "some larger design to help keep the English-speaking peoples together and of furthering international goodwill."[33] A government panel analyzing future trends in the postwar period had reported in early 1945 that, with the USSR a potential military threat, Canada's defence "should be closely coordinated with the United States after the war."[34] The PJBD provided the basis for this coordination, though, as King remarked, this wartime arrangement was "not in fact a military alliance."[35] The Ogdensburg Agreement was simply a press release, and as the Cold War began Canadian and American officials sought to create a more formal tie. In January 1947, Minister of Defence Brooke Claxton explained to King that international tensions and technological developments required continental defences, urging that in this task "self interest and our good relations with the United States should lead Canada to play an adequate part."[36] The next month the Canadian and American governments issued a joint statement – again not a formal treaty – affirming the continued functioning of the PJBD and listing a host of areas for military cooperation.

A year earlier, in his famous speech at Fulton, Missouri, Winston Churchill cited the PJBD favourably. It was, the now former British prime minister affirmed, "more effective than many of those which have often been made under formal alliances." His speech, made with President Harry Truman in the audience, was famous not only for its invocation of the "Iron Curtain" dividing Europe but also for the "special relationship between the British Commonwealth and Empire and the United States" and for his call for a "fraternal association of the English-speaking peoples."[37] After listening to this statement on the radio – and judging it "the most courageous made by any man at any time" – King called Churchill and was pleased to find him with Truman. "I felt," he explained to them, that "we must all work together ... to see that our position was made secure."[38] It was within this context that Ottawa renewed the PJBD. At the same time, Ottawa took the lead in seeking an agreement with London and Washington to standardize the production of some munitions, an important consideration for Canada, whose industry was tooled largely along American lines but whose military equipment was mainly British. "As in so many other fields," noted one senior Canadian, "our objective, it is felt, should be to bring the British and Americans together."[39] An agreement was hammered out in 1947. "The standardization of screw threads may sound trivial," reflected A.G.L. McNaughton, "but it was one of the greatest things we ever did."[40] Meanwhile, these three allies undertook to continue one of the most important aspects of their wartime collaboration, intelligence sharing.[41]

There was also triangular action in the wider field of military cooperation. The dire situation in Europe led Belgium, France, Luxembourg, Netherlands, and Britain to pursue a defensive alliance, the Brussels Pact of March 1948. Several days before the agreement was reached, King reviewed the situation with Claxton, Pearson, and Secretary of State for External Affairs Louis St. Laurent. "We were all agreed that collective security was essential," King recorded in his diary, adding that "if we did not join in at once with the United Kingdom and the United States in seeking to arrange a solution that might help to preserve peace, we would certainly be destroyed in no time."[42] Talks toward an Anglo-American-Canadian defensive pact soon began, occurring at the moment when King withdrew Canada from the proposed customs union with the United States. As he remarked soon after, the "long objective of the Americans was to control the continent [and] to get Canada under their aegis."[43] Clearly, King – tarred by nationalists for selling Canada out to the United States – had mixed views on the propriety of closer relations with his country's southern neighbour. In any event, negotiations over a defence agreement among the triangular powers expanded to become the North Atlantic Treaty Organization (NATO).

For Canada, NATO solved several problems. First, it ensured an American commitment to European security. Second, as a multilateral organization, it presented a means of counterbalancing the United States. Third, it offered the allies a measure of control over US actions, something that appealed to Pearson, who admitted that he had "more confidence" in European diplomacy getting the West out of a crisis than he did in American problem-solving abilities.[44] Nor was Pearson alone in this assessment. At a meeting of senior national security officials in 1951, General Guy Simonds, the chief of the general staff, asserted that it was "essential to foster and maintain within the Western democratic alliance a 'balance of power' which could effectively restrain to some degree arbitrary unilateral action. The practical application of this concept in NATO at the present time would be to counter-balance the disproportionate and preponderant power of the US."[45] It was because of his influence that Canada's NATO contingent was attached to the British Army of the Rhine, a sign of lingering British ties. Still, there remained what diplomat Dana Wilgress had earlier identified as the problem of "our proximity to the United States," which would make it increasingly difficult for Canada to diverge from US policy. This lack of autonomy, he predicted, would "bring us into still greater dependence upon the United States and to this extent away from the United Kingdom."[46]

Canada's shifting position within the North Atlantic Triangle was evident, but this development's impact was a source of speculation. In 1948, the US ambassador in Ottawa had traced a variety of ways in which "Canada's orientation" was changing, with British decline forcing the Canadians to turn to the United States for "economic welfare and military security." Indeed, because of the spread of American culture in Canada, this reorientation was actually "discernible."[47] The Royal Commission on National Development in the Arts, Letters and Sciences, or the Massey Commission, convened in 1949 in part to study the "American invasion by film, radio and periodical" and the resulting growth of "ideas and assumptions which are alien to our tradition." Among many recommendations to safeguard Canadian culture, the commission's report accounted for the wider context of Canadian-American relations. "Our military defences must be made secure," it affirmed, "but our cultural defences equally demand national attention."[48]

As a result of the Massey Commission, Ottawa launched varied initiatives meant to nurture Canadian identity. Concurrently, over half a million British migrants came to Canada in the decade after the war, a wave of immigration that reinforced Britain's role as a counterweight to the United States.[49] British diplomats recognized the "peaceful penetration" of US influence in Canada. After just eight months in Ottawa, in 1953 High Commissioner Archibald Nye was convinced that "the overwhelming impact" of the United States was changing Canada in fundamental ways, and he urged means of strengthening "those influences working towards a distinctive Canadian culture with a strong sense of Commonwealth attachment." Failure to help the Canadians, he feared, would mean that Canada would become "inexorably a virtual satellite" of the United States.[50] Two years later Nye still observed "a considerable Americanization of the Canadian way of life," but he had a greater appreciation of Canadian resilience and what he saw as "a growing determination to be neither British nor French nor American, but just Canadian." In terms of foreign affairs, Nye applauded the extent to which Ottawa refused "to be dominated by US foreign policies," instead asserting its own views and positions.[51]

The beginning of the Korean War in June 1950 had raised questions in Ottawa about the room for manoeuvre. Initially, Pearson was of two minds about the conflict. On the one hand, he remarked that, if US military intervention to defend South Korea "was effective, the result would be helpful generally in the Cold War" by affirming American willingness to oppose communist aggression. On the other hand, he worried about US bellicosity. The Canadians made it clear to Washington that Ottawa would only give "help to the United Nations, fulfilling our obligations under the Charter, and not help to the United States."[52] Ottawa committed naval, air, and ground assets to the UN mission. In a sign of continued Anglo-Canadian ties, Canada's ground forces were assigned to a Commonwealth Division, alongside troops from Britain, Australia, New Zealand, and India. In pushing for Canadian participation, St. Laurent emphasized that, to avoid upsetting the newly independent nations of Asia, which might resent a seeming assertion of British imperialism, it was important that this force was seen to be organized around "considerations of efficiency and practicability rather than on Commonwealth ties."[53] However, Canadians found themselves chafing over some British officers' tendency, complained General John Rockingham, the commander of the Canadian brigade, "to treat my staff as mere colonials."[54]

It was American direction of the Korean War that proved to be worrying for officials not just in Ottawa but also in London. The autumn 1950 expansion of the conflict into North Korea and the entry of Red Chinese forces in response to approaching US troops on their border alarmed both the British and the Canadians, who feared the escalating situation and worried that Korea was a sideshow to the Cold War standoff in Europe. Statements by General Douglas MacArthur about expanding the war into China and an incautious comment from President Truman about the battlefield utility of nuclear weapons led Prime Minister Attlee to head for Washington to urge prudence.[55] Concurrently but independently, Pearson polled friendly countries on the viability of pressing for a ceasefire and reaching a settlement with Beijing. He also had a memorandum sent to the State Department outlining that the atomic bomb was "the ultimate weapon" and that, given the consequences surrounding its use, "there should be consultation among the governments principally concerned."[56] Whether Attlee's and

Pearson's initiatives influenced the Truman administration's avoidance of using nuclear weapons is doubtful. But it was clear that Korea had exposed differences within the North Atlantic Triangle.

In April 1951, two months after Canadian ground forces were engaging for the first time in combat in Korea, Pearson asserted publicly that Ottawa was no longer concerned "whether the United States will discharge her responsibilities, but how she will do it and how the rest of us will be involved." He followed up by contending that "relatively easy and automatic relations with our neighbour are, I think, over."[57] The statement soon made headlines in the United States when, days later, Truman fired MacArthur, leading some commentators to blame Canada for his termination.[58] Although Pearson regretted some of his language, he defended his statement, which stemmed from a "feeling of dependence on the United States and the frustration over the fact that we can't escape this no matter how hard we try."[59] With the Korean War dragging on, Canada backed several efforts to achieve an armistice, including a successful Indian initiative. There was discontent over the Canadian course of action, leading Secretary of State Dean Acheson to dub Pearson "an empty glass of water" and to confide to British officials a desire to bring Canada "to heel."[60] Overall, the Korean experience was an unhappy one, not least for the Koreans themselves. Whatever hopes Pearson and other Canadian policy makers had for the Korean intervention to reaffirm the founding principles of the United Nations were dashed by the bloody stalemate.

Concern about American actions in Asia continued to unite Canadian and British officialdom. In 1954, diplomats from Britain, France, the United States, the USSR, and communist China gathered in Geneva to find a Korean peace agreement and a settlement for the French colony of Indochina, where an anti-colonial insurgency was raging. As a belligerent in Korea, Canada attended the portion of the conference dealing with that conflict – the talks failed to produce a peace treaty – and en route to the summit Pearson met with British Foreign Secretary Anthony Eden. Pearson found his British counterpart anxious about potential American intervention in Indochina to aid beleaguered French forces. The men agreed that this action would be unwise, a point seconded by Prime Minister Louis St. Laurent, who reminded Pearson that Canada was "not now committed to anything in respect of Indo-China" and would steer clear of the conflict.[61] Pearson followed this line, but he fretted about the "real danger" of Anglo-American disagreement. Indicating one of the few instances when Canada acted as a triangular mediator, in a debriefing to the prime minister he divulged that he had "once or twice suggested to both sides its danger, and ways of avoiding it in respect of specific suggestions made by one side (say the United States) which would be obviously unwelcome to the other."[62] The Eisenhower administration held back from intervening in Indochina, and eventually the Geneva Conference produced an agreement partitioning the colony into Laos, Cambodia, and North and South Vietnam and creating several international commissions to oversee this process as well as an eventual Vietnamese unity election. As a result of its international reputation, Canada was asked to sit on the commissions as the Western representative, a role that Pearson agreed to with some hesitancy.

Canada's reputation was burnished during the Suez Crisis in November 1956, a nadir for relations among the members of the North Atlantic Triangle. Not only did Washington refuse to back London, despite stoking Anglo-Egyptian tension, but also following the invasion the Eisenhower administration applied economic thumbscrews to force a British withdrawal. Meanwhile, for St. Laurent and Pearson, the British, French, and Israeli attack on Egypt came as a shock. The potential sundering of Anglo-American relations, of NATO, of the United Nations, and of the Commonwealth was disastrous; the result was not just Ottawa's refusal to back London but also a successful Canadian *démarche* introducing a UN peacekeeping force allowing the British and French to withdraw with a modicum of face. Yet Canada's opposition to the armed intervention rankled imperialists on both sides of the Atlantic. One Canadian diplomat in London reported "that the bitterness about the Canadian attitude on Suez was as great as that against the Americans."[63] Tory opposition spokesperson Howard Green accused the Liberals of acting as "the United States chore boy" and of "knif[ing] Canada's best friends in the back." Pearson retorted that "it is bad to be a chore boy of the United States. It is equally bad to be a colonial chore boy running around shouting 'Ready, aye, ready.'"[64] For Canadians, Suez was very much a Rorschach test of Canada's place within the North Atlantic Triangle.

For the British, Suez proved to be disastrous: Prime Minister Anthony Eden resigned, and his successor, Harold Macmillan, was left to repair Britain's shattered reputation and the Anglo-American and Anglo-Canadian relationships. He found willing partners in both North American capitals. A meeting to patch things up between London and Washington was held in Bermuda in March 1957: Eisenhower and Macmillan, old colleagues since the Second World War, met for jovial talks in the Caribbean sun. With the British prime minister unable to arrange a concurrent trip to Canada, St. Laurent and Pearson travelled to Bermuda. In advance of the meeting, British officials advised Macmillan that "the essential question for Canada at this stage is the restoration of UK-US relations," advice that fit the new prime minister's own goal for the Bermuda summit.[65] Fresh from his happy meetings with Eisenhower, Macmillan was upbeat about the Anglo-American relationship and even "expressed in warm terms thanks to Mr. Pearson for all the understanding and assistance" that he had given during Suez.[66]

Despite Macmillan's optimism, the Suez Crisis, an increasing sense of economic and cultural nationalism in Canada, and a diplomatic crisis in the spring of 1957 over the US release of classified security information that led to the suicide of Canada's ambassador to Egypt, E.H. Norman, played a major role in the realignment of Canadian politics. The St. Laurent government had dissolved Parliament and called an election for 10 June 1957 convinced that its record of managing a buoyant postwar economy would extend the Liberals' twenty-two-year hold on power. The Progressive Conservative Party, however, conducted an effective election campaign featuring the dynamism and populist oratory of its new leader, John Diefenbaker, who promised a new national development strategy and a renewed relationship with the United Kingdom and the Commonwealth. Although many pundits predicted a Liberal win despite the lethargic campaign, the Conservatives secured a minority government by winning 112 of 265 seats in the House of Commons; a majority followed in March 1958.

In the aftermath of the Conservative victory, senior American and British diplomats in Ottawa reflected on the direction that the Diefenbaker government would take. The US ambassador, Livingston Merchant, counselled the State Department that the Conservatives would be "both professionally more sensitive to what [they] may consider indignities inflicted on Canada's sovereignty and philosophically more instinctively reverential to British policy."[67] In practical terms, Merchant emphasized, there was "every likelihood" that Diefenbaker would try to develop stronger links with the United Kingdom.[68] From Earnscliffe, Sir Saville Garner focused his post-election analysis on Diefenbaker himself. Fired with "the zeal of an Old Testament Prophet," Diefenbaker initially impressed Garner as "a man of great integrity, considerable force, but little real depth or breadth of mind, little charm of personal manner, and no sense of humour." Nonetheless, the high commissioner gave Diefenbaker "full credit" for engineering the election victory and demonstrating great vitality on the campaign trail that would translate well to Canada's highest elected political office. If Diefenbaker surrounded himself with capable advisers, Garner predicted, then he would be successful. But he also noted that the emotion-driven Diefenbaker "may attempt to be too quick ... His judgment is faulty at times and there have been occasions when he has shown himself politically inept."[69]

Garner's evaluation proved to be prescient. The prime minister's first engagement on the international stage occurred in London at a meeting of Commonwealth prime ministers. Diefenbaker lobbied his colleagues to support the convening of a Commonwealth economic and trade conference and warned of the baleful influence of American investment in Canada. His call for an economic summit was rejected by Commonwealth leaders, although they agreed that the matter would be considered by Commonwealth finance ministers during an upcoming meeting at Mont Tremblant, Quebec, in September 1957. Undaunted by this rebuff, Diefenbaker returned to Ottawa and announced to the press an off-the-cuff promise to divert 15% of Canada's trade with the United States to Britain. Basil Robinson, who would become Diefenbaker's personal assistant liaising with the Department of External Affairs, described this proposal as "a political impulse" to show that the prime minister "was still planning to deliver closer and more profitable relations with Britain and to achieve greater economic independence from the United States."[70] A subsequent Department of Finance analysis revealed the scope of Diefenbaker's incaution; a 15% diversion in the value of imports from the United States would have required a corresponding 130% increase in Canadian purchases from Britain over import levels in 1956.[71]

The Canadian government continued publicly to support closer ties to the United Kingdom during 1957 even as Diefenbaker backed away from promoting his diversion proposal, an example of "offhand thinking" that Secretary of State John Foster Dulles – paying an informal visit to Ottawa in July 1957 – reminded the prime minister required deeper study.[72] The meeting of Commonwealth finance ministers ultimately endorsed Diefenbaker's cherished goal of a trade and economic conference to be held in Montreal in 1958. But the British government short-circuited any awkward Canadian attempts to reorder Canada-UK economic relations by proposing a free-trade agreement between the two countries, an offer that British officials knew Diefenbaker would reject. The year closed with the dispatch of a Canadian trade delegation to the United Kingdom, and though the trip was a public relations success the tangible financial benefits of the mission were limited. Nevertheless, British officials continued to appreciate the spirit of these often clumsy initiatives. Although the Diefenbaker government had shown itself "somewhat inept and feeble," Garner informed Macmillan, "this should not blind us to the fundamental fact of their goodwill towards Britain and to their anxiety to work for close Commonwealth co-operation."[73]

If these early attempts by the Diefenbaker government to strengthen ties with Britain did not directly involve the United States, the first United Nations Conference on the Law of the Sea (UNCLOS I) that commenced in Geneva in February 1958 tested the traditional strength of the triangular relationship. The central issue of the conference involved the delineation of the territorial sea adjacent to national coastlines. Traditional maritime powers such as the United States and the United Kingdom favoured a narrow three-mile territorial sea. Canada, though, found itself at odds with its two primary allies after adopting a pre-conference position of supporting the narrow territorial sea with an additional nine-mile contiguous zone in which countries would control fishery resources. British officials were "very much distressed" with Ottawa's stance, and the UK delegation received instructions to "strain every nerve" to hold the line at a three-mile sea with no contiguous fishing zone, which would be ruinous to British fishing interests.[74]

Conference negotiations on the breadth of the territorial sea proved to be bruising. Britain's steadfast refusal to consider Canada's three-plus-nine proposal exasperated George Drew, Canada's high commissioner to London helming the Canadian delegation. Drew introduced a revised Canadian resolution in the committee stage of the conference calling for a six-mile territorial sea with an additional contiguous fishing zone extending twelve miles from the coast. The United States, meanwhile, introduced a similar six-plus-six proposal with the exception that a state that traditionally had fished in the outer six-mile contiguous zone could continue to do so during a five-year phase-out period. When delegations voted on proposals in the committee stage, only the operative paragraph of the Canadian resolution calling for a state to control fisheries in a zone twelve miles from the coast received narrow majority support – Britain and the United States opposed the Canadian resolution.

Subsequently, the Canadian and American delegations lobbied furiously in the plenary session of the conference to swing the required two-thirds support behind their respective positions after the United States successfully reintroduced its resolution through a procedural manoeuvre. Ultimately, neither measure received the required two-thirds support to become binding in international law, and not a single NATO member except for Iceland and Greece supported Ottawa's proposal. Drew subsequently reported that his efforts to syphon support from the US resolution represented a major victory for Canadian maritime interests in the face of Washington's "dollar imperialism."[75] Arthur Dean, the US delegation's leader, placed responsibility for the failure of the American initiative squarely on Drew's shoulders and took "a certain satisfaction" in the failure of the Canadian proposal.[76]

As the first anniversary of the Conservative election victory in 1957 passed, Prime Minister Diefenbaker hosted visits from Macmillan and Eisenhower. Macmillan came to Ottawa in June 1958 after meeting with Eisenhower in Washington, and he devoted considerable attention to the upcoming Commonwealth trade and economic conference. Although he believed that the meeting in Montreal would be a "notable success," Macmillan reminded his Canadian host that the goal of the conference should be to avoid placing artificial restrictions on trade with non-Commonwealth countries and that conference initiatives should "facilitate, and not hinder, economic cooperation with the United States."[77] President Eisenhower magnified Macmillan's mild rebuke of Diefenbaker's ill-fated trade diversion proposal during his visit to Ottawa in July, particularly in his speech to Parliament emphasizing the free-market determination of trade flows. "The United States government does not place goods in Canada as part of a state-directed program," Eisenhower stressed. Without directly identifying the Tories' proposal to substitute imports from the United States for Commonwealth sources, he reminded his audience that the "artificial redirection" of commerce was inconsistent with the principles of the General Agreement on Tariffs and Trade.[78]

Ultimately, the much-hyped Commonwealth trade and economic conference held in Montreal in September was unable to achieve substantive outcomes. Senior trade, finance, and external affairs officials had concluded before the conference that the Commonwealth "involved a clash between form and substance" and provided "little of real substance" in terms of economic benefits to Canada.[79] The conference's singular achievement was the establishment of Commonwealth education scholarships.

In addition to the trade and economic conference in Montreal, DEA officials planned a world tour on Diefenbaker's behalf to emphasize further the prime minister's belief in a strengthened Commonwealth. Leaving Ottawa on 28 October 1958 and stopping briefly in New York, Diefenbaker proceeded to London for a week-long stay. In his primary conversation with Macmillan, he trumpeted the Montreal conference's success and played up the mild increase in Canadian imports from the United Kingdom and a decline in Canadian imports from the United States. "This trend," Diefenbaker informed his host, "improved Canada's relationship with both the USA and the UK."[80] After stops in Paris, Bonn, and Rome, Diefenbaker and his party arrived in Pakistan in mid-November, with subsequent visits to India, Ceylon, Malaya, Singapore, Australia, and New Zealand before returning to Canada in mid-December. Although "hints of anti-Americanism, an overly personalized approach to foreign policy, lack of nuance, mistrust of officials, and the politicization of foreign policy" certainly marked the tour,[81] Diefenbaker nonetheless succeeded in convincing many Canadians of the increasing importance of Britain and the wider Commonwealth in Ottawa's conduct of foreign affairs.

But apart from positive public attitudes in Canada toward these initiatives, American and British officials did not believe, by the spring and early summer of 1959, that Diefenbaker's attempt to alter the balance of the trilateral relationship had succeeded. Washington had laboured assiduously to solve thorny issues in its relationship with Ottawa and paid little attention to the Conservative government's efforts to gravitate toward traditional British Empire and Commonwealth loyalties. "The number of abrasive issues with the Canadians is remarkably few," Woodbury Willoughby, the head of the State Department's Office of British Commonwealth and Northern European Affairs, reported to his superiors. "To be sure," he maintained, "some new ones have developed but on the whole the Canadians are pleased with our recent attitudes on bilateral relations."[82]

No such positive appraisal of the Diefenbaker government could be found within British circles. In a biting review in April 1959, Saville Garner noted that "it would not be wise to pin any hopes on the present Diefenbaker administration playing a broad and constructive role in our affairs." Ottawa had "virtually done nothing" to increase imports significantly from Britain, and the bilateral trade deficit had only increased in Canada's favour in 1958 compared with 1957. Garner conceded that the Diefenbaker government was "entirely genuine" in its support for the United Kingdom and the Commonwealth, but domestic political considerations prevented bold measures from being adopted that might be unpopular with the Canadian electorate. There was "no dramatic prescription" to secure more cooperation from the Conservative government, but by handling relations carefully and cautiously Canada would continue generally to be supportive of British initiatives in the international arena. "I recognise that this is perhaps not an heroic course," Garner concluded, "but we are not dealing with an heroic government."[83]

A new appointment in Diefenbaker's cabinet in June 1959 injected an important level of vitality into Canada's conduct of foreign relations for the final eighteen months of Eisenhower's presidency. Howard Green, the vocal critic of Pearson's conduct during the Suez Crisis, assumed the position of secretary of state for external affairs following his predecessor's death. British officials described Green as "a passionate admirer of the United Kingdom and all its works" who "can be counted upon to back the British line uncritically."[84] In their initial evaluation of his appointment, though, US officials in Ottawa supported the view of a Canadian contact who, while noting his "high principle, complete integrity, and real stature," believed that Green "did have some old fashioned, practically antediluvian ideas on foreign affairs which could be expected to cause problems."[85]

Green immediately turned his attention to the United Nations following his appointment as foreign minister and became the leading proponent of international disarmament within the Western alliance. During the fourteenth session of the United Nations, in the fall of 1959, the Canadian delegation endorsed a resolution constructively addressing disarmament in the shortest possible time by working with the Disarmament Commission and the new ten-power Disarmament Committee. Green also directed efforts crafting a resolution on atomic radiation that would allow nations with advanced laboratory facilities to help compile information on the deleterious impacts of nuclear tests. Although US and UK officials grudgingly supported this resolution, they frequently expressed their concern about Green's increasing willingness to work with communist bloc states. "We had a last-minute alarm from the British," Green recalled after the passage of the resolution, "who were not very keen about it but they did not try moving an amendment. I thought they were stupid in their moves but I was not surprised, as we have a low opinion of their representative at the UN."[86]

Green carried this disarmament advocacy into the North Atlantic Council ministerial meeting in December 1959. He arrived in Paris determined to ensure that "the voices of the smaller nations are heard."[87] In his primary speech, he cautioned that the Canadian government had no illusions about the "very real difficulties" that confronted Western nations in their dealings with the USSR, but he advocated that "while remaining watchful and realistic, and avoiding unilateral concessions, we should resist the tendency we sometimes have of placing the worst construction of Soviet actions and pronouncements."[88] Press reports across Canada noted Green's role in pursuing a more independent foreign policy. Under his leadership, the *Globe and Mail* asserted, Canada had "earned many new friends in the

United Nations by gaining a reputation for independent thought and judgment."[89]

The contentious issue of an international territorial sea regime returned to the forefront of trilateral relations ahead of the opening of the second UN Conference on the Law of the Sea (UNCLOS II) in Geneva in March 1960. In a marked change from the antagonism exhibited by the United States and United Kingdom toward Canada at the conference in 1958, Ottawa and Washington worked to craft two complementary preliminary proposals, with the Macmillan government choosing to withdraw from actively championing its own proposal hopefully to accept a compromise final resolution agreed to by the three nations. The Canadian delegation received authorization initially to submit a plain proposal of a six-mile territorial sea and a contiguous six-mile fishing zone. Washington tasked its delegation with holding the limit of the territorial sea at six miles at any cost, with a six-mile contiguous fishing zone beyond the territorial sea in which states could continue to harvest catches that did not exceed a pre-conference level. These initial proposals immediately encountered opposition, and Canada and the United States co-sponsored a new six-plus-six resolution with a ten-year phase-out period for traditional fishing rights in the six-mile contiguous zone. This proposal received strong support at the committee stage.

Ahead of the voting on committee proposals in the plenary session, the United States, United Kingdom, and Canada lobbied conference delegations to accept the revised Canadian-American proposal. Eisenhower personally contacted the heads of state of five allies who had abstained or voted against the committee resolution, and British and Canadian delegates worked to change the negative votes of Commonwealth members, India in particular. These efforts came to naught. In plenary voting, the Canada-US proposal failed to reach the required two-thirds threshold by a single vote. India remained recalcitrant to the end, casting a critical negative vote, and two South American states expected to favour the resolution opposed it. Despite the best cooperative efforts of the Canadian, British, and American delegations at UNCLOS II, no international agreement could be reached demarcating the limits of the territorial sea and contiguous fisheries zones.

Green also could not carry the momentum from his UN efforts in 1959 forward into the fifteenth session of the General Assembly. In the First Committee, Green crafted a resolution to establish an ad hoc committee of UN members not possessing nuclear weapons to report on ways to advance the goals of complete and general disarmament. The US delegation initially refused to support this initiative. Green's special disarmament adviser, General E.L.M. Burns, noted that American hostility "might be an attack on Green because they think him pro-disarmament and anti-US ... Looks like more trouble, either for Green, or US-Canadian relations, or both."[90] As the resolution began hemorrhaging support, Green forced a vote on the measure that resulted in its defeat. Privately, Canada's foreign minister lamented the inability to count on established allies, but he judged that "at least everyone knew we meant business."[91]

The resilience of the North Atlantic Triangle was beginning to be tested when Eisenhower left office in January 1961. In terms of Canada-US relations, Canadian officials lamented Diefenbaker's lack of a personal relationship with the incoming president, John F. Kennedy, of whom the prime minister seemed to have formed "some rather unfavourable early impressions."[92] From Washington, the new administration immediately adopted a more direct approach toward the Conservative government. The fundamental problem facing the United States in its bilateral relations, Kennedy was briefed, lay in "an evolving Canadian attitude of introspection and nationalism" and the development of a Canadian "inferiority complex" because of the wealth and power of the United States.[93] Although the Kennedy administration attempted to work through some problematic issues in the field of continental defence, the vacillation of Diefenbaker over the nuclear arms issue led to the collapse of the Progressive Conservative government, although the cooperative tenor of diplomatic relations that generally had marked Washington's connection to Ottawa before 1957 eventually would be restored.

The Macmillan government adopted a similar attitude toward its Canadian counterpart at this time. Diefenbaker's attempts to move closer to the United Kingdom and away from the American orbit had been largely unsuccessful, and cracks in the bilateral relationship emerged by the end of 1960 over the Commonwealth reaction to apartheid South Africa and the United Kingdom's attempt to join the European Economic Community, which Ottawa viewed as a threat to Canadian access to British markets. Assessing the merits of the Canadian government in January 1961, Garner maintained that Diefenbaker "does not appear to have developed at all" and that Green found it advantageous "to appear to stand up to pressure from Washington and London and to assert that the Great Powers are not going to twist his elbow." Nonetheless, Garner noted that Diefenbaker's government was one with which the Macmillan government should "be able to enjoy frank, fruitful, and close relations and our cooperation, based on enlightened self-interest, can be practical, sensible, and helpful – if still not dynamic."[94]

As the Eisenhower era closed, the lustre that once marked the North Atlantic Triangle relationships had faded. In early 1962, reflecting in his diary on the squabbles between Canada and its two closest allies, Charles Ritchie, Canada's ambassador in Washington, observed that "at one time we had pretensions to consider ourselves a 'bridge' between the United Kingdom and the United States. What a bad joke that looks now!"[95] Yet squabbling and tension had been constant in the triangular relationship, the result of natural differences among states with their own interests. Canada, the United States, and the United Kingdom would continue to engage each other productively in keeping with their respective foreign policy goals and opportunities. However, notions of a special tripartite relationship, forged during the crucible of war, continued to fade.

NOTES

1 J.B. Brebner, *North Atlantic Triangle: The Interplay of Canada, the United States and Great Britain* (New Haven, CT: Yale University Press, 1945), xi, 336.

2 Ibid., vii; see also Duncan Bell, *Dreamworlds of Race: Empire and the Utopian Destiny of Anglo-America* (Princeton, NJ: Princeton University Press, 2020).

3 William Lyon Mackenzie King, memorandum on a talk with German leaders, 29 June 1937, The National Archives (hereafter TNA), PREM 1/344.

4 W.L. Morton, "Review of *William Lyon Mackenzie King. II. The Lonely Heights, 1924–1932*," *Canadian Historical Review* 45, 4 (1964): 320–21; Donald Creighton, *The Forked Road: Canada 1939–1957* (Toronto: McClelland and Stewart, 1976).

5 J.L. Granatstein, *How Britain's Weakness Forced Canada into the Arms of the United States* (Toronto: University of Toronto Press, 1989).

6 F.H. Underhill, "Canada and the North Atlantic Triangle," in *In Search of Canadian Liberalism* (Toronto: Macmillan, 1961), 256.

7 John English, "Not an Equilateral Triangle: Canada's Strategic Relationships with the United States and Britain, 1939–1945," in *The North Atlantic Triangle in a Changing World*, ed. B.J.C. McKercher and Larry Aronsen (Toronto: University of Toronto Press, 1996), 147–83.

8 William Lyon Mackenzie King, speech, 12 November 1940, *House of Commons Debates*, 19th Parliament, 2nd session, 59.

9 William Lyon Mackenzie King, speech, 28 April 1941, *House of Commons Debates*, 19th Parliament, 2nd session, vol. 3, 2289.

10 American and Far Eastern Division to USSEA, Report on Canadian Representation with the United States of America, 31 March 1942, Library and Archives Canada (hereafter LAC), External Affairs records, vol. 6786, file 1415–40.

11 Franklin Delano Roosevelt to William Lyon Mackenzie King, 5 November 1941, Franklin Delano Roosevelt Library, Roosevelt PSF, file "PSF 1 Diplo correspondence – Canada."

12 Norman Robertson to William Lyon Mackenzie King, 22 December 1941, in *Documents on Canadian External Relations* (hereafter *DCER*), vol. 9, 1942–43, ed. John Hilliker (Ottawa: Department of External Affairs, 1980), 1125–31.

13 Lester Pearson to Leighton McCarthy, "Certain Developments in Canada–United States Relations," 18 March 1943, in ibid., 1138–42.

14 Escott Reid, "Some Problems in the Relations between Canada and the United States," 16 April 1943, LAC, Escott Reid papers, vol. 6, file 10.

15 Shelagh Grant, *Sovereignty or Security: Government Policy in the Canadian North, 1936–1950* (Vancouver: UBC Press, 1988), 71.

16 William Lyon Mackenzie King, Diary (hereafter King Diary), 21 March 1942, LAC.

17 Iain Johnston-White, *The British Commonwealth and Victory in the Second World War* (London: Palgrave Macmillan, 2016).

18 Jonathan Vance, *Maple Leaf Empire: Canada, Britain, and Two World Wars* (Don Mills, ON: Oxford University Press, 2012), 147–219.

19 Quoted in A.D.P. Heeney, *The Things that Are Caesar's: The Memoirs of a Canadian Public Servant* (Toronto: University of Toronto Press, 1972), 117.

20 Quoted in Adam Chapnick, "Testing the Bonds of Commonwealth with Viscount Halifax: Canada in the Post-War International System, 1942–1944," *International History Review* 31, 1 (2009): 24.

21 John A. English, *Monty and the Canadian Army: A Military Triumph* (Toronto: University of Toronto Press, 2021).

22 Asa McKercher and Michael D. Stevenson, "'Under Your Inspired Leadership': Dwight Eisenhower, Canadians, and the Canada–United States Consensus, 1945–1961," *International Journal* 75, 4 (2020): 472.

23 Cabinet War Committee Minutes, 29 December 1941, LAC, Privy Council Office records, series A-5-B, Reel C-04654, file M; King Diary, 20 May 1943.

24 Lord Moran, *Churchill: Taken from the Diaries of Lord Moran* (Boston: Houghton Mifflin, 1966), 117n3.

25 Escott Reid, "The United States and Canada," 12 January 1942, LAC, MG 31 E46, vol. 13, file "US and Canada."

26 Quoted in Vincent Massey, *What's Past Is Prologue* (Toronto: Macmillan, 1963), 352.

27 "Atomic Bomb Rocks Japan," *Globe and Mail*, 7 August 1945; "Pre-Eminence of the Anglo-Saxon," *Canadian Forum*, September 1945.

28 A.F.W. Plumptre, *Three Decades of Decision: Canada and the World Monetary System, 1944–75* (Toronto: McClelland and Stewart, 1977), 98.

29 Butt to Browning, 27 April 1945, National Archives and Records Administration (hereafter NARA), Department of State records, file 842.20 Defense/4–2745.

30 Foster to Wailes, 31 December 1947, NARA, Department of State records, file 842.00/12–3147.

31 Ray Atherton to George Marshall, 29 October 1947, NARA, RG 59, file 611.4231/10–2947.

32 King Diary, 25 March 1948.

33 King Diary, 8 November 1945; Hector Mackenzie, "Canada's International Relations in the Early Cold War: The Impact and Implications of the Gouzenko Affair," in *The Gouzenko Affair: Canada and the Beginnings of Cold War Counter-Espionage*, ed. J.L. Black and Martin Rudner (Manotick, ON: Penumbra Press, 2006), 15–37.

34 Post-Hostilities Problems Committee, "Post-War Canadian Defence Relations with the United States: General Considerations," 2 March 1945, LAC, External Affairs records, vol. 5749, file 52-C(s).

35 William Lyon Mackenie King to Lester Pearson, 13 March 1946, LAC, Lester B. Pearson papers, vol. 7, file "King W.L. Mackenzie 1942–1950."

36 Brooke Claxton to William Lyon Mackenzie King, "Re. Defence Policy," 7 January 1947, in *DCER*, vol. 13, 1947, ed. Norman Hillmer and Donald Page (Ottawa: External Affairs and International Trade Canada, 1993), 1482.

37 Winston Churchill, "The Sinews of Peace," in *Winston Churchill: His Complete Speeches, 1897–1963*, vol. 7, ed. R.R. James (London: Chelsea House, 1974), 7289.

38 King Diary, 5 March 1946.

39 A.D.P. Heeney to William Lyon Mackenzie King, "Re: Standardization of Military Equipment between the United Kingdom, the United States and Canada," 6 September 1946, in *DCER*, vol. 12, 1946, ed. Donald M. Page (Ottawa: Department of External Affairs, 1977), 1750.

40 Quoted in John Swettenham, *McNaughton*, vol. 3, 1944–66 (Toronto: Ryerson Press, 1969), 188.

41 Wesley Wark, "The Road to CANUSA: How Canadian Signals Intelligence Won Its Independence and Helped Create the Five Eyes," *Intelligence and National Security* 35, 1 (2020): 20–34.

42 King Diary, 11 March 1948.

43 King Diary, 30 March 1948.

44 Lester Pearson to Hume Wrong, 21 May 1948, in *DCER*, vol. 14, 1948, ed. Hector Mackenzie (Ottawa: Department of Foreign Affairs and International Trade, 1994), 1794–95.

45 Minutes of the 503rd Meeting of the Chiefs of Staff Committee, 14 August 1951, Department of History and Heritage, Kardex 112.3M2 (D296).

46 Minister Designate in Switzerland to SSEA, 25 April 1947, in *DCER*, 1947, 365.

47 Laurence Steinhardt to George Marshall, 24 November 1948, NARA, RG 59, State Department Decimal File 1945–49, box 5884.

48 Canada, Royal Commission on National Development in the Arts, Letters and Sciences, *Report* (Ottawa: King's Printer, 1951), 275, 15, 18, 15.

49 Marilyn Barber and Murray Watson, *Invisible Immigrants: The English in Canada since 1945* (Winnipeg: University of Manitoba Press, 2015).

50 Archibald Nye to Viscount Swain, Dispatch No. 65, 9 April 1953, TNA, DO 35/10797.

51 Archibald Nye to Crookshank, Dispatch No. 115, 20 October 1955, TNA, DO 35/10797.

52 Cabinet conclusions, 27 June 1950, LAC, Privy Council Office records, vol. 2645; extract from memorandum from SSEA to Prime Minister, 27 June 1950, in *DCER*, vol. 16, 1950, ed. Greg Donaghy (Ottawa: Department of Foreign Affairs and International Trade, 1996), 49–50.

53 Cabinet conclusions, 31 August 1950, LAC, Privy Council Office records, vol. 2645.

54 William Johnston, *A War of Patrols: Canadian Army Operations in Korea* (Vancouver: UBC Press, 2004), 140–41.

55 Peter Lowe, "Waging Limited Conflict: The Impact of the Korean War on Anglo-American Relations, 1950–1953," in *War and Cold War in American Foreign Policy, 1942–62*, ed. Dale Carter and Robin Clifton (Basingstoke, UK: Palgrave Macmillan, 2001), 133–55.

56 DEA telegram, 2 December 1950, in *DCER*, 1950, 252; Lester Pearson, "Korea and the Atomic Bomb," 3 December 1950, in ibid., 254–55; Greg Donaghy, "Pacific Diplomacy: Canadian Statecraft and the Korean War, 1950–53," in *Canada and Korea: Perspectives 2000*, ed. Rick Guisso and Yong-Sik Yoo (Toronto: University of Toronto Press, 2002), 81–100.

57 Department of External Affairs, *Statements and Speeches* 51/14, 10 April 1951.

58 George Sokolsky, "These Days," *Washington Times-Herald*, 23 April 1951; "Canadian Plaint," *Washington Post*, 29 April 1951.

59 Lester Pearson to Hume Wrong, 16 April 1951, LAC, Lester B. Pearson papers, vol. 35, file "Korea: Canadian Policy 1950–1951."

60 Evelyn Shuckburgh, *Descent to Suez: Foreign Office Diaries, 1951–1956* (New York: Norton, 1987), 54.

61 Paris to DEA, tel. 181, 24 April 1954, and DEA to Geneva, tel. 3, 25 April 1954, LAC, RG 25, vol. 4627, file 50052–40.

62 Lester Pearson to Louis St. Laurent, 6 May 1954, LAC, Lester B. Pearson papers, vol. 34.

63 Norman Robertson to Lester Pearson, 1 November 1956, LAC, Lester B. Pearson papers, vol. 39.

64 Lester Pearson, speech, 27 November 1956, *House of Commons Debates*, 22nd Parliament, 4th session, vol. 1, 51.

65 Saville Garner to Lord Home, 26 February 1957, TNA, DO 35/7136.

66 Notes by Secretary to Cabinet on Bermuda Discussions, 26 March 1957, in *DCER*, vol. 23, part 2, 1956–57, ed. Greg Donaghy (Ottawa: Department of Foreign Affairs and International Trade, 2002), 1374–75.

67 Livingston Merchant to John Foster Dulles, 14 June 1957, NARA, RG 59, Central Files, 1950–63, box 3210, file 742.00/1–757.

68 Ottawa Telegram 640, 11 June 1957, NARA, RG 59, Central Files, 1950–63, box 3210, file 742.00/1–757.

69 Saville Garner to Gilbert Laithwaite, 12 June 1957, TNA, PREM 11, 1957–62 – Canada.

70 H. Basil Robinson, *Diefenbaker's World: A Populist in Foreign Affairs* (Toronto: University of Toronto Press, 1989), 14.

71 "Diversion of Canadian Imports from the United States to the United Kingdom," 9 August 1957, in *DCER*, vol. 24, part 1, 1957–58, ed. Michael D. Stevenson (Ottawa: Department of Foreign Affairs and International Trade, 2003), 750–63.

72 John Foster Dulles to Dwight Eisenhower in London to State Department, DULTE 2, 29 July 1957, Dwight D. Eisenhower Library (hereafter DDEL), Dulles-Herter Series, box 9, Whitman file.

73 Saville Garner to Harold Macmillan, 17 October 1957, TNA, DO 35/5403.

74 Memorandum by Assistant Deputy Minister of Fisheries, 24 January 1958, in *DCER*, vol. 24, 1957–58, 112.

75 Geneva Telegram 397, 26 April 1958, in *DCER*, vol. 24, 1957–58, 190.

76 Geneva Telegram 1277, 26 April 1958, in *Foreign Relations of the United States*, vol. 2, 1958-1960, ed. Suzanne E. Coffman and Charles S. Sampson (Washington, DC: United States Government Printing Office, 1991), Document 371.

77 Cabinet Document 181–58, 23 June 1958, in *DCER*, vol. 24, 1957–58, Document 1026.

78 Dwight Eisenhower, speech, 9 July 1958, *House of Commons Debates*, 24th Parliament, 1st session, vol. 2, 2084–85.

79 Summary note attached to Louis Couillard to A.F.W. Plumptre, 2 April 1958, in *DCER*, vol. 24, 1957–58, 805.

80 London Telegram 4171, 4 November 1958, in *DCER*, vol. 24, 1957–58, 889.

81 Francine McKenzie, "A New Vision for the Commonwealth: Diefenbaker's Commonwealth Tour of 1958," in *Reassessing the Rogue Tory: Canadian Foreign Relations in the Diefenbaker Era*, ed. Janice Cavell and Ryan Touhey (Vancouver: UBC Press, 1989), 39.

82 Woodbury Willoughby to Livingston Merchant, 24 June 1959, NARA, RG 59, Bureau of European Affairs Files, Alphanumeric Files Relating to Canadian Affairs, 1957–63, vol. 5, file 16.22.

83 Saville Garner to Lord Home, 3 April 1959, TNA, PREM 11, file 1957–1962 – Canada.

84 Ottawa Telegram 1151, 23 October 1959, TNA, PREM 11, file "Prime Minister to See Mr. Howard Green, Canadian Minister for External Affairs, during His Visit to the UK in November 1959."

85 Ottawa Telegram 961, 4 June 1959, NARA, RG 59, Central Files, 1950–63, box 3216, file 742.13/3–1358.

86 Howard Green to Mother, 22 November 1959, City of Vancouver Archives, Howard Charles Green papers, Series 593-E-5, file 6.

87 "Green Scores Disarmament," *Vancouver Province,* 14 December 1959.

88 NATO Telegram MM-11, 16 December 1959, LAC, External Affairs records, vol. 4800, file 50102-X-40.

89 "The Voice of Commonsense," *Globe and Mail,* 28 November 1959.

90 E.L.M. Burns, Diary, 31 December 1960, LAC, E.L.M. Burns Papers, vol. 8, file "Diaries 1960."

91 Howard Green to Mother, 23 December 1960, City of Vancouver Archives, Green papers, Series 593-E-5, file 7.

92 Basil Robinson to A.D.P. Heeney, 18 January 1961, LAC, Heeney papers, vol. 1, file "United States – Ambassador to Washington, Correspondence and Memoranda, 1961–1962."

93 Dean Rusk to John Kennedy, 17 February 1961, John F. Kennedy Library, President's Office Files, box 113, file "Canada Security, 1961."

94 Saville Garner to Duncan Sandys, 27 January 1961, TNA, DO 182/84, "The Canadian General Political Scene – 1960."

95 Charles Ritchie, *Diplomatic Passport* (Toronto: Macmillan, 1981), 186.

Part 2

POLITICS AND IDENTITY IN POSTWAR NORTH AMERICA

5

An Emerging Constitutional Culture in Canada's Postwar Moment

P.E. BRYDEN

In 1976, Canada's "greatest living historian," a "master of his material," published a very bad book. Donald Creighton's *The Forked Road: Canada 1939–1957,* the second-last volume in McClelland and Stewart's Centenary Series, was panned for its thin research, unsubstantiated claims, and overblown caricature.[1] But where it failed to capture the history of the period, it profoundly captured the way that that history was experienced, at least by Creighton and presumably others of his particular middle-class, Anglo-Saxon, central Canadian Tory identity. And Creighton viewed the Canada of the mid-twentieth century with deep and abject hopelessness. Although the evidence that he presented might not have convinced all of his readers, it was clear what was in his mind: Canada had not selected the "high road leading to commonwealth cooperation, east-west economic integration and a lusty national sovereignty" but had been taken along the low road of "sinister continentalism" by a villainous band of Liberal politicians and bureaucrats.[2] At the fork in the road, Canada had turned in the wrong direction, bringing to its natural conclusion the Laurentian thesis that "had been both a story of Canada's origins and a prophecy of its defeat." Canada had deeply disillusioned its most prominent chronicler, leaving Creighton in the "depths of despair."[3]

That despair led to bad history – angry and one-sided. *The Forked Road* would be dismissed as little more than the last gasp of a once-great historian. But it also illustrates the profound emotions attached, of all things, to *constitutional* decisions and directions. Creighton's angst was inchoate, directed haphazardly at the American economic and cultural domination that the historian saw developing under the King Liberals and picking up speed after 1945 – an anxiety shared with other Canadians, as Stephen Azzi shows in his contribution to this collection. In railing against the direction that Canada was taking, however, Creighton was really rattling the constitutional scaffolding built by decisions about the balance of power between Ottawa and the provinces, about the role of the Judicial Committee of the Privy Council, and about the capacity to share a continent with a superpower. He was far from alone, but in showing his anguish so conspicuously he reminds us of the existence of a deeply felt constitutional culture in Canada, one increasingly affected by propinquity to the United States.

The 1950s saw that culture emerge and evolve. Where a constitutional culture existed in much of the first century after 1867, it was steeped in British traditions and a sense of belonging. It was given space to develop in the language of the British North America Act, which "eschew[ed] precise prescriptions [and] allowed a diversity of views and political orientations";[4] the vagueness of the Constitution itself allowed the emergence of a homegrown constitutional framework. Two endings, however, those of the Second World War and appeals to the Judicial Committee of the Privy Council (JCPC), opened up the possibility of new directions and demanded more concrete action than was necessary in the first eight or nine decades of the existence of Canada. With general economic security, government stability, and increasing autonomy from Britain, it was possible to consider broad questions of rights and responsibilities. It was possible to consider real constitutional change rather than simply constitutional meaning. Yet this was occurring at the dawn of the so-called American Century, which had an effect on the extent of the direction of those constitutional possibilities.

Far from being the exclusive concern of courts and chambers, moreover, the possibility of changes to Canada's constitutional direction fuelled a much broader public conversation. Much attention has been directed at the ways in which lawyers and politicians, judges and monarchs, viewed, debated, and shaped the Constitution both as it was being written and when it was being interpreted.[5] We have spent less time considering the ways in which people understood that Constitution and lived it. We know relatively little about what farmers and shopkeepers, labourers and doctors, thought about Confederation and the document that marked it, let alone what they thought about the progression of the BNA Act in the years that followed.[6] That lack of attention, however, does not imply an absence of sentiment: the Canadian Constitution, in fact, was "planted deep in the affections of the people," as John Sanborn argued in 1865, so we just need to look for it.[7]

Constitutional conversations had a particular resonance in the 1950s. If a constitution, as one American scholar has suggested, is "*always in a state of becoming,*" then it was doing so in Canada faster in the 1950s than it had before.[8] Inspired by the autonomy of the end of appeals, the civil rights agenda apparent under the Warren Court in the United States, and the security provided by economic growth, Canadians embraced constitutional possibilities. Some, like Creighton, did so with one eye on what used to be and one eye on American influences, but others considered how the constitutional future could be shaped through education, representation, and case law. In doing so, average Canadians demonstrated with surprising emotional intensity that even the most "mundane set of provisions" offering "a reasonably workable and effective system of government" could provide the foundation for a robust constitutional culture.[9]

An examination here of the public response to the end of appeals and to appointments to the Supreme Court of Canada, a consideration of how key cases were understood by Canadians, and finally an analysis of how the BNA Act was incorporated into the postwar education system will illuminate the tug-of-war for constitutional affection. In the shadow of two mature constitutional systems, one monarchical and one republican, Canadians of all walks picked through the meanings of their own constitutional culture, weaving a new level of affection into the dry language of the law. They also opened a new area of Canadian-American relations as the similarities between the two constitutional democracies became apparent and the search for differences became more passionate. As in so many other areas, constitutional culture in the years immediately following the Second World War offered another lesson in the narcissism of small differences.

* * *

The end of appeals to the Judicial Committee of the Privy Council was achieved in the fall of 1949 after more than a decade of on-again, off-again consideration and some last-minute objections from various quarters. It marked a major transition in constitutional development: no longer would Canadian cases be considered outside the country by a court populated by people with little or no intimacy with the Canadian context. The end of appeals, not surprisingly, received considerable attention from both the legal profession and academia both at the time and since then. The public reception was more muted, however, but not entirely absent.

Minister of Justice Stuart Garson introduced the legislation in the House of Commons in the fall of 1949 that would make the Supreme Court the last court of appeal. In doing so, he placed particular emphasis on the significance of acquiring the "full powers of self-government." Ending appeals would cut the judicial umbilical cord, allowing Canadian law makers the right to interpret Canadian laws. In all other areas, Garson argued, Canada had already "attained a complete and honourable nationhood"; the time had come "that we should act ourselves as the citizens of a great country to make our Canada achieve the destiny to which she is capable." To do otherwise would only demonstrate "smallness of mind."[10]

The United States surely cast a long shadow over the debate – a neighbouring nation, hardly suffering from "smallness of mind," offered a proximate example of self-governing federalism. Its Supreme Court was supreme. Garson was wise enough not to invoke the American example, however, leaving his audience in the House of Commons and beyond it to draw the parallels themselves. The United States remained an awkward partner, necessary yet still a threat to Canadian autonomy and identity; the former prime minister, William Lyon Mackenzie King, had only recently refused to go down the road of free trade for fear of a repeat of Wilfrid Laurier's electoral loss on the issue in 1911. To model an independent Supreme Court on the American example was dangerous, and Garson knew enough to keep quiet. Those opposed to the end of appeals used the spectre of Americanization to advantage: Howard Green, the Conservative MP from Vancouver-Quadra, insisted that "all the talk of winning autonomy for Canada is faking the issue. If there is an autonomy problem," he argued, it had to do with the United States, not Britain.[11]

There was no doubt that the legislation would pass; the Liberals had a clear majority and were united in their desire to see the amendment to the Supreme Court Act. Many Conservatives were also happy enough with the change. But after the argument that this was a necessary step on the road to nationhood, it remained to be seen how the people of that nation would greet the newly acquired independence of the Supreme Court. Indeed, if the enthusiasm for abolishing appeals was largely about appearances – ending Canada's appearance of being less than fully autonomous – then surely the start of a new era must also offer an appeal to the imagination. The idea of a supreme Supreme Court would need to take root in the public mind. Garson tried to stir up interest among Canadians through their wallets, suggesting that a national court would be more financially accessible than the imperial court: "The extra appeal to the privy council," he argued, "gives a great advantage to the more wealthy, reckless litigant" who can afford the costs associated with trying a case before the law lords in London.[12]

To some extent, the ploy worked. Identifying the savings of an independent court was one way to interest Canadians in judicial changes. But there were costs involved as well, and the few newspapers that went beyond the mere acknowledgment of the end of appeals, for example, often raised this issue. "Now Supreme in Law," the *Globe and Mail* noted in the headline to its photo essay on the new Canadian court, "Seven Jurists Get Higher Pay." Chief Justice Thibaudeau Rinfret would now earn $25,000 per year rather than the $20,000 that he had been making when appeals to London were still possible; the associate justices saw their salaries increase from $16,000 to $20,000.[13] There were other costs too: two new judges were added to the court, bringing the total to nine (with an additional $40,000 in personnel costs), and there were more clerks and additional office requirements. The particularly cynical could even point to the new $3 million Supreme Court building, completed in 1940 but not occupied by the justices until 1945, as another cost of independence. These changes, though costly, also ensured that Americans took notice of events north of the border.[14]

There were reasons for these changes. With no more appeals, the Supreme Court was expected to hear more cases; two more judges would make that feasible. Nine judges brought more heft to the court. It also, not incidentally, replicated the court in the United States, telegraphing gravitas and weighty judgments with the increase in size. Cabinet was careful not to signal profligacy, though, refusing to allocate funds for celebrations for the opening of the new Supreme Court building, or a dinner for the new independent court, or a reception. Any more attention to the court might "give rise to many difficulties, and possibly some unpleasantness."[15]

For a court establishing its reputation, though, there was another side to the image being created. The Supreme Court was a Canadian court, proximate, familiar, and, to a "surprising" degree, "informal."[16] The judges were real people – in 1949, all of them were "married, some grandfathers."[17] There was an intimacy to the descriptions of the old court with new responsibilities that implied the intention to establish it more firmly in the Canadian imagination. "Lawyers address the bench in conversational tone, never bursting into the oratory employed to sway juries," reported one newspaper. With justices from across the country, it could be embraced as an accessible, homegrown institution.[18]

Nurturing a constitutional culture is slow and inadvertent work, destined to take root in erratic ways and random places. Beyond newspaper notice of the end of appeals, and commentary in small-circulation journals such as *Queen's Quarterly*, there was little attention given to the change in Canada's judicial status by anyone other than lawyers.[19] As a ceremonial or symbolic occasion that could be expected to stir public sentiment, the end of appeals fell flat; in this, the Canadian experience was too far removed from that of the United States, where ideological conflict was more likely to elicit public interest.[20] Still, the stage had been set as the 1950s dawned: an independent court could make its mark not just on jurisprudence, in which early debate focused on the degree to which the precedents set by the Judicial Committee would be observed in Canada, but also on a nation's fancy. The set was appropriately majestic, and the characters were familiar, but a constitutional culture required an audience that felt invested in the action that unfolded. It demanded that the court's decisions affect the everyday, not just in the ways that laws were followed but also in the ways that people thought about the nation.

* * *

The American Supreme Court, by the 1950s, had a long history of attracting periodic attention and then slipping from public view for long stretches. Franklin Delano Roosevelt's court-packing scheme in the 1930s, which saw the addition of up to six judges to the court in order to water down opposition to his New Deal, led voters to write to their congressional representatives and the neophyte Gallup organization to query Americans on their views about both the Constitution and the proposal.[21] But by the end of the Second World War, less than ten years later, both the Constitution and the Court had once again receded from view, although there were indications that public opinion could soon be stirred again. Segregation, not only in schools but also elsewhere, was being questioned in court, bringing civil liberties to the forefront of the American constitutional debates.

Canadians watched, and commentators viewed the events favourably.[22] In 1950, Chief Justice Frederick Moore Vinson "made a hash of the subterfuge" of race-based education considered "separate but equal" in a series of rulings against racial segregation that was "cause for rejoicing." A *Globe and Mail* editorial noted that "we do not recall a single American agitation carried on by liberal Americans for such a long period as that which now seems crowned with success."[23] But the Canadian rejoicing itself was separate, if not equal, offered from a distance that obscured the possibility that a newly independent Canadian court might also have the opportunity to weigh in on matters affecting civil rights. The decisions of the Vinson Court were only the opening act, however; by the time that Dwight Eisenhower moved into the presidency, the role of the courts in protecting civil liberties, and the concomitant growth in attachment to the Constitution, not only had become more apparent in Canada but also had implications for Canada's burgeoning constitutional culture.

The American case that would have the greatest impact on the reputation of the court, and on the evolving constitutional culture in the United States, if not necessarily on the process of desegregation, was *Brown v Board of Education.* As Eisenhower prepared to take office in January 1953, the case – or really the series of five intertwined cases – was before the Supreme Court. The court would not release a final verdict until May 1954, by which time a great deal had changed. Most importantly among those changes, Chief Justice Vinson, who had issued an order setting the *Brown* case reargument in the fall of 1953 and had requested that the administration answer five specific questions dealing with enforcement, died suddenly, necessitating a mid-case readjustment of the court.[24]

Eisenhower, and perhaps the United States more generally, was at a crossroads in the summer of 1953. On the one hand, it was clear that the eyes of the world were on the United States. Responding to the request of the court to answer a series of questions pertaining to *Brown,* the attorney general filed an *amicus* brief, or a "friendly report," offering relevant information. In it, he stressed the international significance of the ruling, citing a letter from Secretary of State Dean Acheson: "The continuance of racial discrimination in the United States remains a source of constant embarrassment to this Government in the day-to-day conduct of its foreign relations; and it jeopardizes the effective maintenance of our moral leadership of the free and democratic nations of the world."[25] International opinion about the United States was already on shaky ground: the McCarthy hearings had undermined American authority in the fight against communism, and now the desegregation case threatened to bring further attention to American inequities.

Eisenhower used the vacancy on the Supreme Court to try to counterbalance the mounting attention to judicial matters in the United States. Earl Warren, a three-term Republican governor of California who had decided recently not to run for a fourth term, was a bit of a surprise choice as chief justice. He had little judicial experience, but he did have "recognized integrity ... experience in government [, and a] national stature in reputation so as to be useful [to Eisenhower's] effort to restore the Court to the high position of prestige it once enjoyed."[26] At least these were the qualities that Eisenhower privately remarked he wanted in his new chief justice. He was also clear that he wanted someone with "middle-of-the-road" views, another quality that he believed Warren exhibited. The new chief justice, according to Eisenhower, was expected to guide the court quietly through the stormy waters ahead.

Warren was not the chief justice that Eisenhower expected. The unanimous decision on *Brown* was just the first example, but it set the stage. Steering what had been a deeply divided court toward a unanimous decision was an extraordinary feat: "This is a day that will live in glory," wrote

Justice Felix Frankfurter to Warren on the day of the decision. "It's also a great day in the history of the court, and not in the least for the course of deliberations which brought about the result. I congratulate you."[27] The public took notice, accusing or praising the court for judicial activism, for relying on social science more than law, or for issuing a second emancipation proclamation. Whether embraced or rejected, the decision was unquestionably momentous and regarded as such from the outset.[28] That it was so quickly digested beyond the courtroom owed much to Warren's insistence that the decision be "short, readable by the lay public, non-rhetorical, unemotional and, above all, non-accusatory."[29] But in the Oval Office, the reaction was considerably more muted: "The Supreme Court has spoken ... And I will obey."[30]

What Eisenhower might have preferred will remain unknown. He had guessed that the decision would be "very moderate" and leave "a maximum of initiative to local courts." In both regards, he would have been sorely disappointed. We also know that the president was widely reported to have described his appointment of Warren to the chiefship as "the biggest damn fool thing I ever did."[31] We know that the developing storm in the southern states over the process of desegregation would occupy his attention for the remainder of his administration. And we have some evidence that he cautioned states to move even more slowly toward racial equality than the glacial pace that many had adopted initially.[32] Of his own opinion on the civil rights turn that the court had taken with the *Brown* decision, the record remains relatively silent.

The same is true of opinion in Canada. Although newspapers reported the verdict and noted its significance, there is little evidence of any broader response by the public. As the civil rights movement gathered momentum through the 1950s and 1960s, Canadians viewed events to the south with some detachment, a separate and superior perspective frequently adopted but rarely valid.[33] Although commentators could regard race relations as "*that* country's most explosive internal issue,"[34] the broader significance of the *Brown* decision began to seep into a Canadian understanding of the role of courts and constitutions in everyday life. Rights rhetoric increasingly found a place not just in the American conversation but also in the Canadian understanding of the law.

Whereas American jurisprudence foregrounded race in its consideration of civil rights, and did so by building on a long-standing body of law that reached back to decisions such as *Plessy v Ferguson* and *Dred Scott*,[35] in Canada the twinning of law and rights was really beginning in earnest only in the years following the Second World War. That was a function in part of dependence on the Judicial Committee and in part of the absence of a Bill of Rights. But the confluence of circumstances in the 1950s that included not only the end of appeals and the example of the United States but also the debate over stare decisis, or the role of precedent in the work of the newly independent Supreme Court of Canada, all pointed to the possibility that the Canadian court would set out in new directions.

Agreeing on how closely to follow the precedents set at the Judicial Committee was the first "substantial and contentious jurisprudential issue" to confront the newly free Supreme Court. The issue was never addressed head on, and the Supreme Court remained "content to chip away at the doctrinal legacy of the Judicial Committee without openly asserting its emancipation."[36] One of the justices most responsible for making those initial chips in the edifice was Ivan Rand, who noted that the JCPC had "modified the language" of the BNA Act, and so could the Supreme Court, "with the same authority," modify the "formulations that have come down to us." If Rand was instrumental in pulling the court away from JCPC precedent, he was also the chief articulator of an "implied bill of rights" in his decisions in the 1950s and 1960s. Nowhere was this more apparent than in his iconic judgment in *Roncarelli v Duplessis* in 1959, which "captivated the entire country."[37]

Rand undoubtably was influenced by his years at Harvard University, where ideas of citizenship loomed large and had a profound influence on his concept of the "rights of a Canadian citizen." Fundamental principles of equality and non-discrimination came to Canada, at least in part, through the rhetoric of judges trained on the promise of the Fourteenth Amendment in American law schools.[38] But ideas of fundamental rights were wafting out of less rarified spaces than Harvard. When Quebec Jehovah's Witness Frank Roncarelli had his liquor licence removed for posting bail for fellow witnesses arrested by the conservative government of Maurice Duplessis, 12,000 McGill University students signed a petition in his support. The Civil Liberties Association joined the fray along with the Presbyterian Church in Montreal and numerous other groups that had not, until recently, considered the issue of "rights" one that might have a place in the Canadian Constitution.[39]

Legal scholar F.R. Scott saw more potential in Canada's Constitution than most and was probably a key factor in the strong views that McGill students seemed to have on the *Roncarelli* case. Writing about the case in 1947 in the pages of *Canadian Forum,* the McGill law professor sought an audience beyond the classroom for his argument for "the need for judicial review of administrative acts," in this case the "dictatorial powers" under the Alcoholic Liquor Act.[40] On the basis of that opening salvo, Scott was invited to join Roncarelli's legal team, and his arguments about human rights were honed in front of new audiences. By the time that the case was heard before the Supreme Court, Roncarelli's "rights" had become a central feature of a trial that initially revolved around damages under the Civil Code of Lower Canada.[41]

The Constitution was also central to the case, with Scott arguing in closing that Duplessis had subverted "the roots of our constitution and basic human rights." Indeed, Scott's position, taken in the years prior to a Canadian Bill of Rights, let alone an entrenched Charter of Rights, hinged on the idea of a national citizenship, with inherent rights, that fell under exclusive federal jurisdiction.[42] Canadian constitutionalism still revolved largely, if not entirely, around the relative reach of sections 91 and 92, and Scott knew that rights would need to be pinned on federalism, at least for the short term, in order to find a sympathetic hearing in court. But combining rights rhetoric with federalism also served to imbue the BNA Act with more meaning for the average Canadian and was a key stage in the evolution of a domestic constitutional culture. As Scott later stated, "the law surrounds and clothes the body politic and economic, and as that body stirs restlessly so does the surface of the law disclose where the tensions and the pressures are being most felt"; although cases regarding federalism are "always with us," in recent years "we cannot but be struck by the emergence in our law of a remarkable combination of cases and legislative purposes which we can properly classify under the heading of human rights."[43] Scott's argument, then, bridged the American origins of entrenched rights, then being discussed publicly in the cases on segregation that the Warren court was so accessibly deciding, and the Canadian familiarity with cases of federalism. Using jurisdictional arguments to make the argument for the constitutional protection of human rights was a gateway to both the Charter of Rights (through the "implied bill of rights" argument) and a more public embrace of a domestic constitutional culture. As Scott said, "a good constitution is like a good poem. Both are concerned with the spirit of man."[44]

His arguments had little impact on most of the Supreme Court justices who heard the *Roncarelli* case, save for Justice Rand, whose decision remains studied in law schools today. Rand shifted the focus from Duplessis's fault in removing the liquor licence, where other justices had staked their decision, to Roncarelli's rights to associate and to post bail for whomever Roncarelli wanted, which emerged "as a fundamental postulate of our constitutional structure." Here was a line of argument, a basis for decision, that Canadians could understand. By using the language of individual rights, Rand's decision cut through the complexities, ambiguities, and contradictions of the divided decision that the Supreme Court presented and offered an understanding of the relationship between individuals and the Constitution that struck a chord. In much the same way that the brief, unanimous decision of the Warren court in *Brown v Board of Education* said something about rights that the public could understand, Scott's arguments and Rand's decision brought the same sort of clarity to Canada. In the English Canadian media in particular, the decision was presented as rooted in fundamental freedoms – the freedom to worship, the freedom to sue authority, the freedom to associate.[45]

Roncarelli and the other Jehovah's Witnesses cases heard at the Supreme Court in the 1950s – *Bourcher v R* and *Saumur v Quebec (City of)*[46]– were key components of the "civil liberties decade" in Canada, much as *Brown v Board of Education* heralded the beginning of the postwar civil rights moment in the United States. Canadians owed much to American civil rights advocates, whose strategies informed their own;[47] the arguments that lawyers such as Frank Scott presented, and the reasoning that justices such as Ivan Rand employed, were both influenced by legal thought in the United States; and the suggestion that the Constitution could have implications for how people interacted – in restaurants and churches and their daily lives – arose within an environment heavily influenced by the civil rights movement south of the border.

Precisely what this shift toward a more American understanding of rights meant, however, was open to interpretation. Obviously, the Donald Creightons of Canada viewed the turn with suspicion. The division wasn't really between right and left, though it often looked that way, with traditionalists leery of moving too far from British jurisprudence and those on the left, like Scott, keen to see Canada move in a new direction. That vast majority in the middle, represented by Liberal governments through the 1940s and much of the 1950s, walked a careful line. Violent clashes in the United States following the *Brown* ruling led to some debate over how successful an entrenched Bill of Rights could be, lending some weight to the argument that parliamentary supremacy provided a better guarantee of Canadians' rights and freedoms than any Bill of Rights ever could.[48] Successive Liberal governments avoided confronting the issue head on, content with having ended appeals to the Judicial Committee of the Privy Council.

The election of crusading civil rights advocate John Diefenbaker as prime minister, however, brought a change in strategy. Hardly known for his rejection of British traditions, Diefenbaker nevertheless was keen to protect rights in a way that was more American than British. Indeed, in introducing his bill, one day before prorogation in September 1958, he made particular note of the American example: "There are many who contend that we do not need a bill of rights," he said, "because parliament ... can be trusted ... to safeguard our rights and freedoms." Not Diefenbaker, though. "The United States found it necessary to provide for a bill of rights [rather than] to trust to the discretion and whims of the majority." He then proceeded to recount the occasions in Canada when those whims were responsible for the trampling, rather than the protection, of rights and freedoms.[49] Moreover, he explicitly tied the Bill of Rights to the public, saying that it would "act as a landmark by means of which Canadians, through parliament, would have redeclared those things which have made Canada great ... It would give Canadians the realization that wherever a Canadian may live, whatever his race, his religion or his colour, the parliament of Canada would be jealous of his rights and would not infringe upon those rights which are dear to us all."[50]

Diefenbaker's bill did not entrench rights, so it did not elevate them beyond the control of Parliament, but it did move Canada one step closer to the constitutional protections that existed in the United States. It also encouraged people to think about the role that the Constitution might play in the protection of human rights in Canada; many had pressed for a constitutional amendment in the years between the introduction of the bill in 1958 and its passage into law in 1960. There was little enthusiasm for embarking on the sort of political negotiation that constitutionalizing rights would mean, however, and the draft bill remained virtually unchanged from the beginning of the process to the end.[51]

Although Diefenbaker's Bill of Rights had little impact, reportedly being invoked in only a dozen cases in its first year of existence, it pulled members of the Canadian public ever closer to a consideration of the constitutional meaning within their daily lives. They indicated that interest by ordering copies of the Bill of Rights for use in classrooms and buying their own copies for a dollar each.[52] It was not an American Bill of Rights, nor a judicial advance toward equality, but a tentative step in the direction of the constitutional protection of rights in Canada and a more certain step in the direction away from the British system. That it was Diefenbaker who brought about this change, despite his suspicious views of the United States, underlined the degree to which the American Century affected even the most resistant of Canadians.

* * *

The influence of American thinking on the decisions of Justice Ivan Rand, on the arguments of Frank Scott, and on the public response to civil liberties infractions inherent in cases such as *Roncarelli* in Quebec suggests the seepage of American ideas into Canadian minds. Rand studied in the United States, Scott read about the United States, and the public witnessed events in the United States, but the influence was more than merely passive. Legal scholars there, for example, showed a long-standing interest in legal developments in Canada. Felix Frankfurter, a professor of law at Harvard University during the interwar years and an associate justice of the Supreme Court from 1938 through the Eisenhower years, had a particular interest in Canada. Through friends such as Loring Christie, he kept abreast of the growing disillusionment with the Judicial Committee and the "cockeyed mess [that its decisions] have made of [Canada's] constitution."[53] He exerted influence on the direction of Canadian policy, drafting the Ogdensburg Agreement that Prime Minister King and President Roosevelt signed in 1940, signalling a commitment to joint defence. He noted, in the aftermath of war, his support for the investigation into the Gouzenko Affair.[54] In all sorts of ways, then, Frankfurter and others expressed an interest in what was happening in Canadian legal developments.

Canadian legal thought exerted influence too. Although law schools in Canada were hardly on par with that of Harvard University, ideas emanating from established institutions such as the University of Toronto and Osgoode Hall,[55] and new law schools such as those at the University of British Columbia and the University of Alberta, were woven into the public record in ways that reached far beyond the legal community. The growth of legal education in Canada parallelled the establishment of an independent Supreme Court, an emerging rights conversation, and took off in the shadow of an increasingly muscular American conversation about constitutional rights. Deeply influenced by the legal philosophy of Oliver Wendell Holmes, the dominant orientation of the Harvard Law School at which so many Canadian legal scholars had been trained, Canadians exhibited a "sociological jurisprudence" that emphasized "the felt necessities of the time." Holmesian ideas emphasized the law in practice, a forward-looking legal pragmatism well suited to the developing constitutionalism in Canada.[56] As legal historian Eric M. Adams notes, the discipline's "modest beginnings [were] followed by the dramatic influence of the Second World War, and finally the emergence of a new professional identity and confidence in the postwar decades."[57]

However, in addition to the proliferation of opportunities to study the law and join the profession as practitioners, Canadians in all walks of life had increasing contact with the Constitution through the nonprofessional education system. The Departments of History and Political Economy at the University of Toronto had tousled over which would get to teach constitutional history (the former won, at least initially), with the founding dean of the law school, W.P.M. Kennedy, publishing much of the key literature in Canadian constitutional history in the interwar years. He was planning, apparently, on revising his work in the postwar period, but the promised volume never emerged. The field would have to wait for Peter Hogg's *Constitutional Law in Canada* for its complete assessment, but the broader – and more accessible – study of government and the Constitution was much in evidence in the 1950s.

The Canadian government series, under the editorship of Toronto political scientist R. MacGregor Dawson, had produced two volumes by 1950. The first positioned Canada's constitutional system within "its appropriate international and philosophical setting," which meant somewhere between Great Britain and the United States.[58] With its emphasis on democracy and its manifestation in a number of "authorities, functions and agencies," J.A. Corry's *Democratic Government and Politics* was "planned and written as a textbook" but should have "a far wider group of readers among the general public."[59] Indeed, as one reviewer suggested, people who live in democratic nations "must know not only the types of government under which they live but also their significance in society and in the everyday life of those who take a greater or lesser part in ruling themselves."[60] Just like Corry's volume, the second in the series was also designed to reach outside the academy. MacGregor Dawson's own contribution to the series, *The Government of Canada,* examines the apparatus of government, the structure of the BNA Act, and the relationship between the two with "robust wit [and] penetrating judgement."[61]

The book is a celebration, on the one hand, of British institutions. On the other, though, it positions Canada on the edge of a bold move into new constitutional territory. Dawson's analysis of the BNA Act identifies its "most serious defect" in the "absence of any provision giving special protection to the civil liberties of the citizen" and implores "public vigilance" in addition to the inclusion of a constitutional Bill of Rights.[62] Thus both a primer and a prescription, the volume went on to be revised and reissued multiple times, shaping the way that generations of Canadians understood both the Constitution and their relationship to it. That first edition, however, was unique. It offered the first guide to Canadian structures and customs, the first homegrown analysis of what worked and what did not, and the first suggestion that the Constitution belonged to everyone, not just lawyers and judges and politicians. Adopted widely across Canada, it gave people the tools to develop a constitutional culture.

In the decade and a half between the end of the Second World War and the dawn of the 1960s, Canadian constitutional culture underwent a dramatic transformation, emerging from under the cloak of British authority and flirting with the possibilities promised by American-style entrenched rights. Canadian constitutional culture set off in a distinct direction. It was cautiously rights based and carefully independent, as seen in the response to the end of Judicial Committee appeals and the interest in Quebec civil rights cases, and piqued Canadians' interest in understanding the constitutional tools available, as the growth of both legal education and domestic constitutional analyses demonstrates. The emergence in Canada of a more overt constitutional culture was possible only at the particular moment when judicial independence and international civil rights rhetoric converged to offer Canadians an opportunity to understand, to shape, and to embrace a document – the British North America Act – that until recently seemed to be dry and elitist and foreign. Flexing constitutional muscles – what was possible? what should be possible? – was one important feature of Canada's postwar arrival on the world stage. That the shift seemed to be more American than British was a concern for people such as Donald Creighton; in his anguish, though, he demonstrated just how deeply the Constitution had seeped into the public consciousness. Events of the 1950s in London, Ottawa, and Little Rock, Arkansas, had made that possible.

NOTES

1 Donald Creighton, *The Forked Road: Canada 1939–1957,* Centenary Series (Toronto: McClelland and Stewart, 1976); Reg Whitaker, review of *The Forked Road: Canada 1939–1957,* by Donald Creighton, *Canadian Historical Review* 59, 1 (1978): 105–7; Paul Fox, "The Forked Road," *Globe and Mail,* 6 November 1976, 43.
2 Marg Conrad, "Studies in Canada's Recent History," *Acadiensis* 6, 2 (1977): 121.
3 Donald Wright, *Donald Creighton: A Life in History* (Toronto: University of Toronto Press, 2015), 296, 321.
4 Eric M. Adams, "Canadian Constitutional Identities," *Dalhousie Law Journal* 28, 2 (2015): 318.
5 John T. Saywell, *The Lawmakers: Judicial Power and the Shaping of Canadian Federalism* (Toronto: University of Toronto Press, 2002).

6 P.E. Bryden, "'Putting Flesh on the Bones': The Meaning of the *BNA Act* in Confederation-Era Canada," paper presented at The Other 60s Workshop, University of Toronto, April 2017. Peter Price has considered recently the broader meaning given to the Constitution in the nineteenth century in his examination of the magazine literature of post-1867 Canada. See Peter Price, *Questions of Order: Confederation and the Making of Modern Canada* (Toronto: University of Toronto Press, 2020), 58–81.

7 Quoted in Adams, "Canadian Constitutional Identities," 313.

8 Arthur S. Miller, "Toward a Definition of 'The' Constitution," *University of Dayton Law Review* 8 (1982–83): 637.

9 Benjamin L. Berger, "Children of Two Logics: A Way into Canadian Constitutional Culture," *International Journal of Constitutional Law* 11, 2 (2013): 320.

10 Stuart Garson, House of Commons, *Debates*, 20 September 1949, 21st Parliament, 1st session, vol. 1, 74–75.

11 Howard Green, House of Commons, *Debates*, 27 September 1949, 21st Parliament, 1st session, vol. 1, 287.

12 Stuart Garson, House of Commons, *Debates*, 20 September 1949, 21st Parliament, 1st session, vol. 1, 73.

13 "Seven Jurists Get Higher Pay," *Globe and Mail*, 20 December 1949, 13.

14 E.K. Williams, "The Supreme Court of Canada Moves into Its 'New' Building," *American Bar Review Journal* 32, 2 (1946): 68–70.

15 Justice Kerwin, quoted in James G. Snell and Frederick Vaughan, *The Supreme Court of Canada: History of the Institution* (Toronto: The Osgoode Society, 1985), 196.

16 "Supreme Court to Become 'Supreme,'" Victoria *Daily Colonist*, 17 August 1952, 29.

17 "Time Grows Near When Supreme Court Will Become Highest Court of Appeal," Victoria *Daily Colonist*, 21 December 1949, 2.

18 "Supreme Court to Become 'Supreme,'" Victoria *Daily Colonist*, 17 August 1952, 29.

19 Wilfrid Eggleston, "Public Affairs: Amending the Canadian Constitution," *Queen's Quarterly* 56, 1 (1949): 576–85.

20 Michael Kammen, *A Machine that Would Go of Itself: The Constitution in American Culture* (New York: Alfred A. Knopf, 1986), 357, 385.

21 William D. Blake, "'Justice Under the Constitution, Not Over It': Public Perceptions of FDR's Court Packing Plan," *Presidential Studies Quarterly* 49, 1 (2019): 205–18.

22 "Supreme Court Rulings Hit Race Segregation; South Shouts Defiance," *Globe and Mail*, 6 June 1950, 1.

23 "Another Emancipation," *Globe and Mail*, 27 June 1950, 6.

24 Herbert Brownell, "*Brown v. Board of Education* Revisited," in *Black, White and* Brown: *The Landmark School Desegregation Case in Retrospect*, ed. Clare Cushman and Melvin I. Urofsky (Washington, DC: Supreme Court Historical Society, 2004), 193–95.

25 Quoted in Ruth Bader Ginsberg, "'A Decent Respect to the Opinions of [Human]kind': The Value of Comparative Perspective in Constitutional Adjudication," *Cambridge Law Journal* 64 (2005): 587. On *Brown*'s international dimensions, see Mary L. Dudziak, "*Brown* as a Cold War Case," *Journal of American History* 91, 1 (2004): 32–42.

26 James F. Simon, *Eisenhower vs. Warren: The Battle for Civil Rights and Liberties* (New York: Liveright, 2018), 136–37.

AN EMERGING CONSTITUTIONAL CULTURE

27 Quoted in Melvin I. Urofsky, "'Among the Most Humane Moments in All Our History': *Brown v. Board of Education* in Historical Perspective," in *Black, White and* Brown: *The Landmark School Desegregation Case in Retrospect,* ed. Clare Cushman and Melvin I. Urofsky (Washington, DC: Supreme Court Historical Society, 2004), 24.

28 Ibid., 24–27.

29 Ibid., 28.

30 Quoted in Simon, *Eisenhower vs. Warren,* 195.

31 Quoted in ibid., 197, 198.

32 "'Go Slower': Racial Plea by President," *Globe and Mail,* 28 August 1958, 1.

33 For an awkward defence of segregation, see Aileen Taylor Smith, as told to June Callwood, "A Southerner in Canada Makes a Frightening Journey Home," (*Maclean's,* 11 June 1961, 5; and, for a news primer, Christina Newman, "The American Negro: His Fight for Equality," *Chatelaine,* October 1961, 31. For a look at varied Canadian reactions to the wider civil rights movement, see Asa McKercher, "Too Close for Comfort: Canada, the US Civil Rights Movement, and the North American Colo(u)r Line," *Journal of American History* 106, 1 (2019): 72–96.

34 Newman, "The American Negro," 31.

35 *Plessy v. Ferguson,* 163 US 537 [1896] and *Dred Scott v. Sandford,* 60 US (19 How.) 393 [1857].

36 Saywell, *The Lawmakers,* 238, 241.

37 Christopher MacLennan, *Toward the Charter: Canadians and the Demand for a National Bill of Rights, 1929–1960* (Montreal and Kingston: McGill-Queen's University Press, 2003), 114.

38 Matthew Lewans, "*Roncarelli's* Green Card: The Role of Citizenship in Randian Constitutionalism," *McGill Law Journal* 55, 3 (2010): 537–62.

39 William Kaplan, *State and Salvation: The Jehovah's Witnesses and Their Fight for Civil Rights* (Toronto: University of Toronto Press, 1989), 245–46.

40 F.R. Scott, "Duplessis *versus* Jehovah," *Canadian Forum* 26 (1947), reprinted in Frank R. Scott, *Essays on the Constitution: Aspects of Canadian Law and Politics* (Toronto: University of Toronto Press, 1977), 195–96.

41 Eric M. Adams, "Building a Law of Human Rights: *Roncarelli v. Duplessis* in Canadian Constitutional Culture," *McGill Law Journal* 55 (2010): 442–43.

42 Ibid., 444; see also Gerald LeDain, "F.R. Scott and Legal Education," in *On F. R. Scott: Essays on His Contributions to Law, Literature and Politics,* ed. Sandra Djwa and R. St. J. Macdonald (Montreal and Kingston: McGill-Queen's University Press, 1983), 103–5.

43 F.R. Scott, "Expanding Concepts of Human Rights," *Canadian Bar Journal* 3 (1960), reprinted in Scott, *Essays on the Constitution,* 353.

44 Ken Lefolii, "The Poet Who Outfought Duplessis," *Maclean's,* 11 April 1959, 76.

45 Adams, "Building a Law of Human Rights," 451–52.

46 *Roncarelli v. Duplessis,* [1959] S.C.R. 121, *Bourcher v. The Queen,* [1955] S.C.R. 16, and *Saumur v. City of Quebec,* [1953] 2 S.C.R. 299.

47 MacLennan, *Toward the Charter,* 110–11.

48 Ibid., 155.

49 John Diefenbaker, House of Commons *Debates*, 5 September 1958, 24th Parliament, 1st session, vol. 4, 4640-41.

50 Ibid., 4644.

51 MacLennan, *Toward the Charter*, 136–41.

52 Langevin Cote, "A Ripple not a Splash: Canada's Bill of Rights One Year Later," *Globe and Mail*, 11 August 1961, 7.

53 Loring Christie to Felix Frankfurter, 30 January 1937, Library of Congress, Felix Frankfurter Papers, vol. 43, file 769.

54 Joshua Kastenberg, "National Security and Judicial Ethics: The Exception to the Rule of Keeping Judicial Conduct Judicial and the Politicization of the Judiciary," *Elon Law Journal* 12, 2 (2020): 290–91, 316.

55 Of course, the relationship between Osgoode Hall and the University of Toronto was fractious in the middle of the twentieth century as the two institutions vied for control of legal education in Canada. See C. Ian Kyer and Jerome E. Bickenbach, *The Fiercest Debate: Cecil A Wright, the Benchers, and Legal Education in Ontario, 1923–1957* (Toronto: Osgoode Society for Legal History, 1987).

56 Martin L. Friedland, *Searching for W.P.M. Kennedy: The Biography of an Enigma* (Toronto: University of Toronto Press, 2020), 165–70.

57 Eric M. Adams, "The Dean Who Went to Law School: Crossing Borders and Searching for Purpose in North American Legal Education, 1930–1950," *Alberta Law Review* 54, 1 (2016): 4.

58 Frederick W. Gibson, "How Canada Is Governed," *Queen's Quarterly* 57, 1 (1950): 479–80.

59 George W. McCracken, "Defining Democracy," *Queen's Quarterly* 54, 1 (1947): 233, 235.

60 George de T. Glazebrook, review of *Democratic Government and Politics*, by J.A. Corry, *Canadian Historical Review* 33, 2 (1952): 176–77.

61 Gibson, "How Canada Is Governed," 498.

62 Ibid.

6

Rethinking
Postwar Domesticity
The Canadian Household in the 1950s

BETTINA LIVERANT

Despite three decades of historical revision, the 1950s in Canada and the United States continue to be seen as a period of broad prosperity characterized by the baby boom and suburban mass conformity driven by pent-up demand, rising wages, and the yearning for traditional family life. The idealization of domestic life remains largely unshaken and continues to influence scholarly research and policy-making. The popular image of the American Century continues to be viewed with nostalgia in the United States and Canada alike.

In recent decades, Canadian historians have sought to unsettle conventional narratives of postwar domesticity with new research strategies, inverting conventional paradigms through detailed studies of consumer citizens, wage-earning wives, politicized domesticity, masculine domesticity, and a proposed shift in periodization with the introduction of a fifteen-year postwar interregnum. American historians, looking at the same era, similarly have questioned popular and academic stereotypes, adding the experiences of minority groups and challenging romanticized visions as "the way we never were." In both nations, focused studies, often using oral history, have made clear that lived experiences do not conform to pre-existing categories, including those of producer/consumer, private/public, and male breadwinner/female housewife. Lives are multi-dimensional, boundaries are porous, and contexts of home life are always evolving. But historiographic challenges clearly remain.[1]

The postwar era has long been considered one of the peak periods of America's global influence, and the American way of life, anchored by the suburban family home, has been regarded as one of America's principal exports. The reassessment of postwar domesticity coincides with new approaches to the study of Americanization and the exercise of American economic power.[2] The "one-lane highway" model of cultural imperialism evolved as historians, economists, and cultural theorists developed new paradigms, noting patterns of selective appropriation and varieties and trajectories of consumer capitalism. American business practices and consumption-oriented domesticity were not adopted intact but filtered through local traditions. Anti-Americanism emerged as a useful foil, deployed by critics on both the left and the right of the political spectrum in Europe, Britain, and Canada to bolster diverse nation-building projects. The postwar American ideal, in short, represented only one of many possible forms of modern domesticity.

The conventional Canadian narrative of broad-based, middle-class affluence, happy families, consensus, and conformity has been unsettled. New scholarship increased awareness of the strains that accompanied new patterns of domesticity and how tensions were carried forward within households without being resolved. The ambivalence of Canadians as they navigated changes in domestic life extended to their views of America. Canadians often positioned their experiences and choices as a middle way between the extremes that they associated with the American model. Conservatism, in general, was less reactionary in Canada than in America, and the pressures on individuals to conform were less intense, but there were those who regarded new goods and increased comforts as examples of rampant American materialism. Others had more positive views, welcoming direct investment in the Canadian economy and business practices that promised increased profits. America was a source of popular entertainments and consumer goods not readily available in Canada. Improving domestic comfort could be good for the economy and good for the family.

Despite their proximity, Canadians and Americans held different visions of what was possible and what was desirable. In most of Canada, modernization was more gradual, constrained by smaller, decentralized populations, government policies, local traditions, and the particular challenges of geography and climate. Canadian households generally were less prosperous, with lower average incomes than American households. With expectations tempered by lower incomes and the limited availability of goods, Canadians often seemed to make a virtue out of necessity, pursuing domestic comforts rather than advertised novelties, guided by an ethic of responsible spending and cautious consumerism.

As American historian Kathryn Kish Sklar recently proposed, using domesticity as a category of historical analysis can help historians to contextualize daily life in new ways, see everyday patterns more deeply, and view change over time more clearly.[3] This chapter builds on her suggestion with a data-driven approach that situates the intimate spaces of the household as they emerge not in distinction to but within long-term social, economic, and political frameworks. Attention to the long term does not diminish agency; as numerous fine-grained studies have shown, women and men directly participate in the creation of new patterns of daily life. At the same time, understanding consumption choices and the decisions of daily life solely as choices made freely and constrained primarily by income obscures the degree to which longer-term histories of capitalism, policy, tradition, and statistically common ways of being shape the available alternatives.

THE DEMOGRAPHICS
OF CANADIAN DOMESTICITY

Despite the boom in marriages and babies, most postwar demographics actually conform to long-term trends.[4] The nuclear family living in a single-family dwelling consistently has been the most common household type in Canada among non-Indigenous families from the time of settlement onward in all settings, including backwoods, farms, villages, and urban locations. Average household size declined steadily, fluctuating with the family life cycle, economic conditions, and the availability of affordable housing (see Table 6.1). The two-child, two-parent family was already the norm by the end of the interwar period. There was a temporary increase in the average number of children per family at the peak of the baby boom, but

TABLE 6.1

Populations and households in Canada, 1881–1971

Year	Total population	Number of households	Average persons per household	Census family per household	Average persons per census family	Average number of children in families
1881	4,324,810	800,410	5.3	–	–	–
1931	10,362,833	2,252,729	4.4	0.95	4.2	–
1941	11,489,263	2,575,744	4.3	0.98	3.9	1.9
1951*	14,009,429	3,409,284	4.0	0.96	3.7	1.7
1956	16,080,791	3,923,646	3.9	0.95	3.8	1.8
1961	18,238,247	4,554,736	3.9	0.91	3.9	1.9
1966	20,014,880	5,180,473	3.7	0.87	3.7	1.9
1971	21,568,310	6,041,305	3.5	0.85	3.7	1.7

Notes: On changes in the census definition of the family and household over time, see Wargon and Statistics Canada, *Canadian Households and Families,* 15–19.

* Includes Newfoundland after 1951.

Sources: Wargon, "Household and Family in Canada," 55–56, and *Historical Statistics of Canada,* Household and Family Statistics, Table A248-253.

the number of very large families declined, and the number of small families rose in every decade since the turn of the century.

More significant than the rate of marriage was the change in the timing of marriage (see Table 6.2). Before the war, marriage was regarded generally as the final step into adulthood, but in the late 1940s and 1950s young adults began marrying earlier, often before securing financial independence or building up savings. Marriage became part of growing up rather than the end point of the process.[5] Young married couples also started families earlier, waited less time between children, and finished having children earlier. As the absolute number and relative prevalence of children aged four and younger rose, the differential in age between parents and children narrowed, resulting in a cohort of youthful families.

Young families, however, were only part of the overall picture, and the focus on babies has been disproportionate in some ways. Babies, after all, are very photogenic, and they were especially noticeable following the

TABLE 6.2

Age at first marriage, 1941–61

	Males		Females	
Year	Median	Average	Median	Average
1941	26.3	28.9	23.0	25.1
1951	24.3	28.3	22.0	25.3
1961	24.0	27.7	21.1	24.7

Source: Median ages from Ellen Margaret Gee, "Fertility and Marriage Patterns in Canada, 1851–1971" (PhD diss., University of British Columbia, 1978), 168.

decline in the number of young children during the decade 1931–41. The most dramatic change in household formation through the 1950s was not the short-term increase in the number of young families with children but the equally dramatic and sustained increase in non-family households as young adults, never-married singles, and elderly individuals "uncoupled" from families and established independent households. During the 1950s, the population of Canadians sixty-five years of age and older increased by 38.4 percent, approximately twice the rate of increase of the population as a whole. By the mid-1950s, public health officials were discussing the impending problems of an aging population.[6] Longer life spans, however, did not result in multi-generational households. Canadians were living increasingly in age-segregated households. More people than ever before were living alone.[7] The rate of household formation exceeded the rate of total population growth. Between 1951 and 1961, over 1 million new private households were formed with significant implications for overall patterns of consumption and for the structure of domestic life going forward.

CHANGING HOUSEHOLD ECONOMIES

Histories of Canadian household economies reference a persistent series of mythological households: self-sufficient pioneer farm families, breadwinners and housewives, and suburban mass consumers. These conceptions continue to be used even though they are recognized as ideological constructions unrepresentative of lived experiences. From the period of settlement onward, households were involved in local, regional, and global markets. Settler colonists brought, bartered, and self-provisioned, and they also bought. Families produced goods for market exchange as well as for household use, making calculated trade-offs about what to make and what to buy.[8]

The ideals of breadwinner-housewife domesticity that emerged through the nineteenth century and early twentieth century were no more accurate. Domesticity ("the self-conscious construction of domestic life"[9]) emerged as the counterpart to the industrial workplace in the nineteenth century. Housework by definition was non-market work, carried out in the privacy of the home, gendered feminine, and coded as caring and "a labour of love."[10] Economically important work was subject to the time disciplines of industry, done for wages, and associated with masculinity. The patriarch of the agrarian household became the breadwinner of the working-class family.[11]

Although the ability of a male head of the household to support his wife and family through paid employment was regarded as the cornerstone of masculine identity, it was seldom attainable.[12] Studies made midway through the interwar period revealed that almost half of Canada's wage-earning families required the earnings of other family members, as well as the most stringent budgeting, to achieve a minimally adequate standard of living. Most homes by necessity were places of income earning for working-class families.[13] Wives and mothers added to household income informally by taking in sewing, laundry, ironing, and lodgers, offering child care and house cleaning for others, and taking in piecework, primarily from the clothing trades. This income was typically part time, low status, low paid, and under-reported. Regarded as domestic by its nature, work in the home was less visible and objectively less remunerative, but the additional income made a crucial difference to families on the margins of subsistence.[14] In a study of working-class families in Montreal during the Great Depression, wives in eighteen of the thirty families worked for pay, both within and outside their homes. Fifteen wives were already working to bring money into the home before the Depression. Thirteen of the husbands in the study earned income from various sidelines in addition to their regular jobs in the struggle to make ends meet.[15]

While working-class families fell short on the breadwinner side of the ideal, middle-class families (perhaps one-quarter of all Canadian non-farm households) were already grappling with changes in domestic standards and practices. Housework was becoming industrialized with new sources of energy (electricity, oil, and gas), new equipment (central heating, flush toilets, hot and cold piped running water), mass-produced appliances, prepared prepackaged foods, and commercial cleaning products, all of which promised to save labour and improve efficiency, hygiene, nutrition, and food safety. New technologies did not reduce housework overall – changing practices and rising standards used up the time saved – but did reduce the physical drudgery of housekeeping for those who could afford them. The pattern of change was typically Canadian: varying by region and adopted by urban households before rural households and by upper income earners before all others.

The economic value of unpaid domestic labour was captured for the formal economy, commodified, commercialized, and sold back with improved benefits. Advice on changing standards and how to achieve them was also commercialized, dispensed by product manufacturers and household experts in articles and advertisements in mass-market women's magazines and the daily press, by trusted department stores, by interior designers, and by professional home economists. Well before the 1950s, domestic competence required ownership of modern appliances, and the absence of modern goods and services was associated with lower standards of living. The home was no longer seen as a refuge from modernity; instead, it had become a place of modernity.

THE NORMALIZATION
OF THE DUAL-EARNER FAMILY

Despite the fears of many, there was no postwar recession. By the end of 1948, 5 million Canadians were working, 700,000 more than the number of civilians employed at the peak of the war effort in 1943 and 1.3 million more than in 1939 at the end of the Depression.[16] Although remembered as a period of steady growth and prosperity, there were recessions during 1947–48, 1951, 1953–54, 1957–58, and 1960–61 of sufficient severity to affect both GDP and employment.[17] Unemployment rose steadily after 1952; average male unemployment reached 7 percent by the end of the decade. The overall strength of the labour markets reflected not simply the expansion of the economy but also significant shortages in the working-age population exacerbated by the low birth rates during the Depression, deaths during both world wars and the influenza pandemic, young people spending more time in schools and entering the workforce at later ages, and men retiring at younger ages.[18] Demand was high for workers to fill good-paying, male-oriented jobs in manufacturing, construction, resource extraction, and middle and upper management. These were often the best jobs, the jobs that provided incomes sufficient to support a family on a single wage.

But it was the rise in labour participation rates for women, especially married women, that was particularly dramatic, as Table 6.3 indicates.[19] By 1961, married women accounted for nearly half of the entire female labour force, and that number does not include those women who worked for wages at some point during the year but not at the time of the census. Almost all of the half-million women who entered the labour force in the 1950s were employed in the rapidly expanding but relatively low-waged clerical, retail, and service sectors.[20]

The postwar employment of many married women followed a two-phase pattern. Young women entered the labour force after high school and continued to work during the early years of marriage before having children, helping to build savings. Women returned to the workforce after their children entered school to improve family purchasing power. With

TABLE 6.3

Female labour force participation, 1941–61

Year	Married	Single	Other	Total	Married women as a percentage of total women in labour force
1941	4.5	47.2	17.3	20.3	12.7
1951	11.2	58.3	19.3	24.1	30.0
1961	22.0	54.1	22.9	29.5	49.8

Source: Lappin, "'Irreconcilable Differences?,'" Appendix 4, 133.

changes in the age at marriage and age at child-bearing, the labour force participation of married women increased steadily even during the "baby boom" years.[21]

Although it was taken for granted that working-class women were likely to work outside the home, the entry of married women – especially of middle-class mothers – into the workforce generated headlines and feature stories in the mainstream media. Negative reactions were especially strong from conservative social critics. Wives and husbands in working-class and middle-class households themselves were ambivalent.[22] Regardless, pragmatics overcame mixed feelings. Jobs in the formal economy, even if relatively underpaid, paid more than work in the home. In any case, opportunities to earn income in the house were disappearing as labour-saving appliances became more affordable, lodgers moved into apartments, and piecework was consolidated in factories. There were new opportunities in direct sales (Tupperware and Avon are best known), in typing (especially of academic papers), and providing child care to other families, but new municipal zoning bylaws restricted many home-based businesses.[23] These various pull and push factors increased pressures to override institutional and cultural barriers limiting the employment of married women. A mother's time in and out of formal paid work became part of a family life cycle. Women did not need to stay at home to support the domestic ideal; indeed, aspirations for the material goods associated with the domestic ideal were drawing women into the labour force.

In the decade 1951–61, the average annual income of non-farm households rose from $3,185 to $4,815, a gain of more than 50%. This increase was offset partially by rising prices, so in real terms it was about 30%. The proportion of households described by the government as low income fell from 42% to 27% through the 1950s, but expectations for domestic comforts and consumer goods were rising.[24] By 1959, a middle-class standard of living required an estimated income of $8,000. Somewhere between 25% and 33% of Canadian families earned enough to be considered middle class; two of three of these families were dual-income families (see Table 6.4). The families supported by a single male wage earner were found increasingly at the extremes of income: that is, in the poorest and the richest of Canadian households.[25]

TABLE 6.4

Percentage of families with and without working wives by income group, year ending 31 May 1961

Income group	With working wives (dual incomes)	Without working wives
$10,000 and over	9.5	9.4
$7,000 to $9,999	24.0	13.0
$5,000 to $6,999	31.3	22.5
$3,000 to $4,999	24.9	33.1
Under $3,000	10.4	22.0

Source: Lappin, "'Irreconcilable Differences?,'" Appendix 6, 135.

THE POLITICIZATION OF DOMESTICITY

Support for preferred forms of domesticity was integral to the politics of settler colonialism and nation making but did not generally include direct financial support. When programs of income supplementation did appear, they were tied to male wages and support for breadwinner roles rather than the needs of household budgets. Unemployment insurance, workman's compensation, and old-age pension required contributions from employers. Mothers' allowance payments were calibrated to male wages – always at the lower end – and conditional on the oversight of government welfare agents who would ensure that mothers were "fit and proper" and their allowances spent in a manner consistent with the conventions of Anglo-Celtic respectability. As the Ontario Mothers' Allowances Commission explained, "the mother is regarded as an applicant for employment as a guardian of future citizens of the State."[26] Through the twentieth century, cycles of inflation and recession spurred protest, prompting successive inquiries by federal, provincial, and municipal governments into costs of living and household spending patterns.[27] Politicians began actively to encourage voters, particularly new women voters, to make household spending the basis of their political identification, linking purchasing power to tariff policies, wartime conservation, and employment. The crisis of the Great Depression invested domestic consumption with unprecedented political and economic urgency. By the time of the 1935 election cycle,

FIGURE 6.1 Government advertising promoting the sale of Victory Bonds conflated support for the war effort with saving for future spending. The prospect of peace was widely associated with images of happy families in modest new homes, well equipped with modern appliances, backyard gardens, and a car in the driveway. | "Keep on Saving till the Job Is Done ... " advertisement, circa 1939–45, Library and Archives Canada, Acc. No. 1983-30-581.

political legitimacy had become linked to promises of economic well-being in the home across the political spectrum.

The imperatives of total war dramatically increased the involvement of the state in Canadian households. Wage and price controls, rationing, production restrictions, and propaganda were deployed specifically to reduce household consumption in order to limit inflation and preserve materials for the war effort. Private acts of household spending were redefined as duties to the nation. The constant monitoring of prices and mobilization of Canada's homemakers as "house soldiers" on the home front encouraged a hyper-awareness of domestic spending.

FIGURE 6.2 Canada's Official Food Rules were introduced in 1942 to promote nutrition during wartime and improve the general health of Canadians. Periodically updated in accordance with scientific evidence, household practices, the influence of agricultural lobby groups, and graphic standards, they are one of the most requested government publications and a constant presence on the bulletin boards of the public school system. | "Eat Right-Feel Right," approved by the Canadian Council on Nutrition, c. 1942, *Eat Right – Feel Right* (Swift Canadian Co. Limited, 1942), 15.

Images of idealized postwar domesticity were used widely by governments in the Allied and Axis nations to rally support for their respective war efforts.[28] Commercial advertising similarly promised that the technologies used to win the war would soon be available to improve daily life.

In planning for the postwar period, Canada's senior bureaucrats regarded consumer spending as both a potential problem and a possible solution to the challenges of transition. Whereas American policy makers embraced mass consumption as a driver of economic growth, Canadian policy makers

RETHINKING POSTWAR DOMESTICITY

FIGURE 6.3 The Veterans Charter promised to "give a new meaning to land settlement" by assisting ex-service men and women to purchase and equip homes in cities, towns, and surrounding acreages. | "Home Ownership – In Town or Suburb," advertisement, *Globe and Mail*, 31 October 1944, 4.

saw inflationary risks and counselled moderation. Wartime restrictions on household spending were prolonged to curb inflationary pressures even as the physical apparatus of war was demobilized. Controls were maintained or added to limit the production and purchase of a wide range of household goods, including appliances and building materials, to ensure adequate

FIGURE 6.4 Canada's Family Allowance program (nicknamed the Baby Bonus) supported families by increasing the purchasing power of private households rather than by expanding social services. | "Need for Family Allowances," poster, circa 1944, Canadian War Museum, Artifact Number 20070104-009.

supplies for industrial conversion. Yet, at the same time, Canadian policy makers believed that modest amounts of household spending could be useful, filling the gap left by the withdrawal of government spending until foreign markets recovered. New programs were created to direct domestic spending to sectors of the economy where policy makers believed that it would be most effective in stabilizing and supporting the economy during the critical period of transition.

A universal family allowance was introduced in 1944 with monthly payments to be made directly to every family, regardless of income, to be spent at its discretion. The program was devised not by welfare agencies but by senior bureaucrats in the Departments of External Affairs and Finance in collaboration with the governor of the Bank of Canada, directly linking domesticity and fiscal policy.[29]

The emotional and political significance of the home had been amplified by the experiences of the Depression and wartime, but Canada's housing shortages were well known, well documented, and long standing. Despite prewar initiatives, in the mid- to late 1940s, the majority of new homes were still being built by owners and small contractors and financed by private savings and personal loans. To avoid going into debt and keep costs down, many Canadians chose to build in stages as their finances permitted, often on property outside city limits, where taxes were lower, land minimally serviced, and development largely unplanned and unregulated. Families who qualified for mortgage financing from a life insurance or trust company were expected to put down between 50 and 60 percent of the equity to obtain a term loan with interest payable monthly and repayment expected in full at the end of the term, typically five years or less. These were not processes that would solve Canada's housing problem.

Provisions were made in the Veterans Charter to encourage home ownership, but the turning point in the federal government's efforts to stimulate house building was the creation of the Central Mortgage and Housing Corporation (CMHC) in 1946 and the passage of Canada's fourth National Housing Act (NHA) in 1954. The surge in house construction through the 1950s was not simply the result of an unprecedented "yearning for home"; rather, it was the result of new legislation that lowered entry costs, dramatically expanded mortgage financing, and helped to increase the speed and amount of new house construction.

CMHC, in conjunction with revisions to the National Housing Act, modernized mortgage lending and made home ownership more broadly affordable by reducing down payment requirements, regulating interest rates, extending amortization periods, and blending equity with mortgage loan repayments. The government promoted a market approach to home ownership, with houses seen as "mortgageable units" and "packages for sale."[30] The NHA removed barriers limiting the participation of Canada's charter banks in mortgage lending. Mortgage insurance underwritten

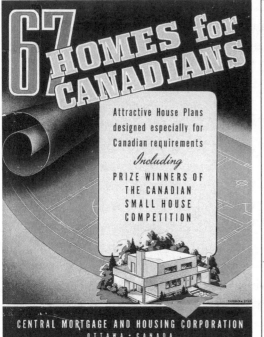
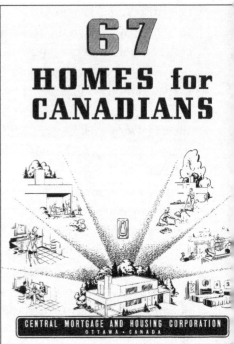

by the CMHC and new nation-wide building codes minimized risks for financial institutions and corporate builder-developers. By 1950, close to 50 percent of all new housing starts were financed with NHA assistance.[31]

Programs that brought home ownership within reach of blue- and white-collar middle-class households were matched by changes in the construction process that increased the speed and volume of house construction. The nation's largest land development and house-building companies adopted vertical integration, rationalized workflows, and assembly line construction techniques already in use in America. Drywall, windows, doors, and trusses were constructed offsite in factory settings. Central heating, up-to-date electrical wiring, hot and cold running water, and flush toilets were standard – they had to be in order for homes to meet new building codes and qualify for NHA mortgages.[32] The CMHC encouraged designs that were simplified and standardized to facilitate mass production and the integration of modern appliances.[33] After they were built,

RETHINKING POSTWAR DOMESTICITY

FIGURE 6.5 The federal government promoted modern home designs through the CMHC and the Canada Housing Design Council with exhibitions and contests and by distributing advice and small house plans to potential homeowners, builders, and the media. | "67 Homes for Canadians," poster, Central Mortgage and Housing Corporation, Ottawa, 1947; "Build a Home," *Ottawa Citizen*, 22 August 1955, 8.

homes were advertised, branded, and sold as any other consumer good. The industrialization of residential construction did not lower costs substantially, but it did make more homes faster. Large developers in particular benefited from the focus on scale and speed, with tax benefits and zoning changes that made it cost effective to assemble and subdivide large blocks of raw land and construct homes rapidly. With the addition of retail stores concentrated in shopping plazas, suburban development was geared to mass selling and profit making.

THE FINANCIALIZATION OF DOMESTICITY

Although earned income remained the key determinant of economic and social well-being, institutional fixed rate debt became a permanent part of household budgets. The postwar expansion of consumer lending was driven by changes in Canada's financial services sector. Legislation allowing for the entry of chartered banks into consumer finance was critical both in expanding the amount of capital available to be loaned and in reducing the stigma of debt. Debt structured with small fixed payments, scheduled regularly over time, encouraged consumers to plan their spending and to purchase more expensive items. The nation's total consumer debt as a percentage of total disposable income rose steadily from 8.3% in 1949, to 12.6% in 1954, to 15.4% in 1959, to 17.8% in 1963.[34] By 1962, nine of ten Canadian households were carrying consumer debt.[35] Contrary to popular thinking, the biggest credit users were not working-class families but middle-income families associated with the Canadian ideal (white, educated, married, with salaried, white-collar jobs). It was not unusual to find 40 percent of their household income tied up in mortgage and instalment payments.[36]

Purchasing a new home often lowered a family's immediate overall standard of living. Taking on the burden of a mortgage committed families to an ongoing stream of expenditures and instalment payments. Suburban migration, one expert noted, was creating a debtor society.[37] Yet experts argued that credit could be a tool to achieve higher standards of living. Mass-market periodicals aimed at middle-class readers regularly featured advice on borrowing, explaining interest rates, financing charges, credit ratings, and the increasing number of ways to borrow, in effect giving Canadians permission to improve their domestic well-being through the responsible use of debt.[38] Planned payments required a steady income and aligned with the pattern of regular payroll deductions that many earners were experiencing. Structured debt blurred the difference between saving and spending and made it possible for families to spread costs over time and continue to save even as they spent. Traditional budgeting virtues of self-discipline and thrift were consistent with instalment purchases and mortgage payments. When spending was associated with higher standards of living, Canadians could practise self-discipline comfortably without self-denial.

CHANGING DOMESTICITIES AT MID-CENTURY

Surveys of household equipment regularly conducted by the Dominion Bureau of Statistics show that, by the early 1960s, more than 90% of

TABLE 6.5

Percentage of Canadian households with certain types of household equipment, 1941–63

	1941	1948	1951	1953	1958	1963
Hot and cold running water	–	–	–	63	74	85
Gas or electric stove	–	48	–	63	77	87
Mechanical refrigerator	21	29	48	66	86	94
Electric washing machine	–	59	74	76	84	87
Electric or gas clothes dryer	–	–	–	–	–	22
Vacuum cleaner	24	32	42	48	60	72
Electric sewing machine	–	–	–	23	36	49
Telephone	40	–	60	–	–	87
Radio	78	–	93	96	–	96
Television set	–	–	–	39	–	90
Automobile (one or more)	37	–	43	–	–	73

Note: These figures do not include households in the Yukon, in the Northwest Territories, or on Indigenous reservations.
Sources: Margrit Eichler, *Families in Canada Today: Recent Changes and Their Policy Consequences* (Toronto: Gage, 1983), 149; Slater, *Consumption Expenditures,* Table 49; Porter, *Vertical Mosaic,* 130.

Canadian households had electric refrigerators and radios; more than 80% had automatic washing machines, telephones, and television sets; and more than 70% had vacuum cleaners and cars. These items made up the "standard package" of domestic commodities, affordable by a large number of households, albeit at different levels of quality (see Table 6.5).

The commoditization of domesticity in this way required changes on the supply side (innovations in mass production, distribution, and supply chain management that lowered costs and generated a stream of new and improved consumer goods), changes in purchasing power (regular and slowly rising wages, dual incomes, low inflation, government programs of financial support and social security, and a dramatic expansion in the availability of new forms of credit), as well as structural changes in the volume and character of demand. Economic theory assumed that families would reduce spending on basic necessities as incomes rose, but Dominion Bureau of

Statistics surveys showed that Canadians were spending much the same proportion of their income on food, shelter, clothing, and fuel as they had a quarter of a century earlier, but they were now buying higher-quality goods and more conveniences.[39] The self-service grocery supermarket emerged as the dominant mode of food retailing and a symbol of progress, modernity, and abundance. Canadian supermarket chains made record sales and earned record profits every year for the two decades following the end of the war.[40] Dominion Stores opened a new store every twenty-one days in the early 1950s. New supermarkets opened with fanfare, and existing stores were enlarged and modernized. The average store size doubled, and food production changed to meet the needs of food retailers, transforming what people ate as well as how they shopped. When food expenditures plateaued, stores added non-food lines that sold at higher profit margins – including automotive accessories, outdoor cooking supplies, and garden tools – to appeal to growing numbers of male shoppers. Cold War rhetoric was less pronounced in Canada than in America, but Canadian newspapers and magazines also celebrated the abundance of fresh, frozen, instant, and prepared foods, doors that opened automatically, abundant free parking, and longer store opening hours as expanded freedom of choice.

Rapid changes in domestic practices through the 1950s are frequently associated with non-specific terms such as "wartime savings," "pent-up demand," "persuasive advertising," and "Americanization" (the last term explored more fully in Stephen Azzi's chapter). These were no doubt factors, but the sustained and ongoing acquisition of domestic goods and services was more complex. By the late 1950s, the North American mass market was becoming a series of mass markets, segmented by region, income, gender, and age. A closer look at the components of consumer demand is especially revealing. During the 1950s, Canada's population grew by 23%, the overall number of households grew by more than 1 million, and construction was completed on 794,712 single-family homes and 357,535 units in multiple-unit dwellings, including duplexes, rowhouses, and apartments.[41] Rising home ownership (from 57% to 66%) generated an ongoing stream of practical and aspirational purchases, particularly for young suburban families. Net immigration provided 8% of the population growth in the 1940s and 25% in the 1950s. Immigration policies were deliberately altered to admit families to support the development of home markets for Canadian goods and services.[42]

The gap between patterns of rural and urban domesticity lessened in the postwar era. Changes in the economics of farming drove out marginal operations, leaving rural areas with fewer, larger, more specialized, and commercially oriented farms. Longer life expectancies delayed intergenerational land transfers. Young adults continued to migrate to larger centres for education and employment. Responding to declines in the number of rural farm families and the development of low-density, quasi-urban districts on the peripheries of growing towns and cities, the Dominion Bureau of Statistics developed new definitions of rurality and began to record rural household income as either farm or non-farm starting with the 1941 count. By 1956, the number of non-farm households surpassed the number of farm households within rural Canada.[43] By 1965, two-thirds of the rural population were no longer living on farms, and an estimated 80% to 90% of rural households had little to do with agriculture.[44]

Of course, Canadian farms were never entirely self-sufficient. Rural households had long obtained farm equipment and consumer goods in stores, from peddlers, and by mail order. Rural women earned income by selling butter, eggs, dairy, and handwork. In many households, women had control over the money that they earned, using it to purchase goods that raised household standards of comfort and convenience. After the war, improvements in road networks, falling transportation costs, and expanding suburbs made it easier for rural residents to work and spend off the farm. It was increasingly common for one or both spouses, often beginning with the wife, to commute to jobs in larger centres. Multiple streams of income soon became the norm.

Rural wives described their motivations for off-farm work in much the same terms used by urban wives. They worked to earn income that would reduce their families' financial risk, raise their standard of living, and pay for the postsecondary education of their children. With access to mail order catalogues, radio programs, meetings of local women's organizations, and trips to larger communities, rural women were well aware of trends in modern homemaking; however, the supply of electrical and fossil fuel energy needed to operate modern equipment was limited and unreliable.[45] New labour-saving appliances were often unsuited to rural conditions. Many households continued to rely on dependable hand-operated equipment, including water pumps and older-model wringer washers. Rural families, in effect, were consumers in waiting. Programs of rural electrification undertaken by provincial governments opened the way to new purchases. In 1941, when virtually all urban homes had electrical service, only 20% of rural homes had electric lighting; by the 1951 census, two-thirds of rural homes were electrified, and by 1961 the question had been dropped from the census.[46] In 1941, 12% of rural farm dwellings, 30% of rural non-farm dwellings, and 91% of urban dwellings had inside running water. By 1961, these numbers had grown to 61%, 68%, and 98% respectively. In 1941, 3.6% of rural farm dwellings, 15.6% of rural non-farm dwellings, and 31% of urban dwellings had mechanical refrigeration. By 1961, these numbers had grown to 80%, 78%, and 95% respectively.[47] As more goods and services became available, the benefits of a stable middle-class income from off-farm employment were increasingly attractive, and the average number of days of off-farm work rose steadily. In rural districts, as elsewhere in Canada, many of the tasks that previously were the responsibility of the family unit were taken over either in whole or in part by government agencies and commercial providers. Many of these benefits, including ease of access to modern amenities and steady incomes, were still unavailable to isolated households in remote rural regions. They remained beyond the reach of energy grids, clean water, and modern sanitation systems, and they continued to carry the burden of high transportation costs.

By the early 1960s, many Canadians regarded living in the country as a lifestyle preference that combined the advantages of rural and city life. The encroachment of development on the agricultural lands surrounding Canada's larger towns and cities, including small and mid-sized hubs, and the emergence of new regional service centres were ongoing. Districts designated rural were home to growing numbers of middle-class and professional income earners. Many regarded the decision to live rural and work urban as a choice about the quality of domestic experience. In these locations, rural households had much the same consumption patterns, economic needs, and aspirations as suburban households.[48]

The immediate postwar decades were times of significant retrofitting and upgrading in both rural and urban homes. Urban working-class households, like those in Denyse Baillargeon's study of families in Montreal, had lost the use of appliances during the Depression when they were unable to afford payments, repairs, or electrical bills. They began to purchase new, more efficient stoves and subscribe to telephone systems as soon as incomes improved in the 1940s and then more costly items such as new refrigerators in the 1950s.[49] There were also a significant number of renovations, including those by renters who purchased the houses in which they were already living. According to estimates in 1956, two-thirds of the appliances that Canadians bought were replacements for older units.[50]

Income and taste also guided choices inside the home. Working-class women tended to buy furniture incrementally and associated traditional styles, regarded as timeless, with respectability, greater comfort, and domestic stability. Working-class households also preferred large-capacity, sturdy appliances over those with new automatic features.[51] Upper-middle-class urban families, in comparison, favoured current decorating trends and efficient appliances with the most up-to-date features, but they made strategic decisions about which household goods to retain, in order to maintain a link with important traditions, and which to replace, in order to denote upward mobility.[52] As it became easier to own material goods, they became less relevant as markers of social status. Upper-middle-class consumer goods were those associated more directly with leisure time (high-fidelity stereo systems, cottages, outboard motorboats, and new domestic-sized power tools) and cultural values (privacy, education, access to better health services and extracurricular activities, travel abroad, season tickets to concert series).[53]

New suburban households were not just city dwellers transplanted to new settings. They tended to be younger and better educated, and though temporarily house poor the majority had solid incomes and prospects for higher earnings over time. Houses were constructed at different price points and grouped together in similarly priced neighbourhoods; families typically bought up to or slightly beyond what they could afford. House purchases, determined almost entirely by affordability, created relatively homogeneous neighbourhoods.[54] Overall, though, suburban householders were well informed of and interested in new products, including new foods, and new lines of merchandise, especially goods related to home improvement.

There were specific regional differences even within urban Canada. Montrealers spent more on clothes, dining out, and taxis. Vancouverites owned the most cars. Edmontonians were the thriftiest in personal indulgences and gave the least to charity but spent the most on home furnishings.[55] Spending by teens became a significant factor, reaching $100 million a year by 1957. With higher wages and dual incomes, the after-school earnings of young adults were less critical to family incomes.[56] The growing number of one-person households in Canadian cities increased demand for fast-preparation and ready-mix foods, health and beauty aids, and dietary and drug items. New kinds of products were being specially marketed to senior citizens, including digestive aids, analgesics, dietary supplements, and products for denture wearers.[57]

More dollars were being spent on recreational activities, hobbies, and sports equipment for use both in and out of the home. Fewer Canadians worked in agriculture, and the average hours of work per week in key male employment sectors, including manufacturing and construction, declined through the century, from fifty hours per week in 1926 to forty hours per week by 1960. Many companies provided two weeks of paid vacation for employees with three or more years on the job. Some men used their extra non-work hours for part-time work, often off the books, but increases in leisure activities also provided a bridge for men to create new forms of domestic masculinity.

Both genders tended to prefer activities of making and fixing that added to the home, activities with an aura of productive leisure and at least theoretical market value. Men were encouraged to become more involved in family and domestic life as outdoor cooks "manning" the barbecue and handymen engaged in do-it-yourself home improvements. There were also new roles in family-oriented leisure: coaching little-league sports and driving the car (when the whole family was present) for family shopping nights and family vacations. Modern masculinity was strongly associated with rising home ownership and consumer goods, including new domestic-sized power tools, barbecues and accessories, and family recreational activities, including spending on cottages and travel.[58] Modern appliances and compulsory schooling for younger children opened the way to new leisure experiences for many women. Women's leisure tended to be less capital intensive than men's leisure. Activities resonant of traditional feminine skills were redefined as creative play when undertaken voluntarily by women who took up knitting, gourmet cooking, rejuvenating second-hand furniture, painting furniture, and home decorating as hobbies.[59]

NEW TRADITIONS OF DOMESTICITY[60]

By the late 1950s, a Canadian home was a container for consumer goods and a venue for consumption, notably of energy, food, appliances, furniture, clothing, and mass media (which also promoted consumption). Decades of incremental change fundamentally altered how households sourced and used goods, which kinds of goods were available, which technologies were available, which things were regarded as basic necessities of modern living, and what was appropriate to buy or what should be made in the home. The lists of commodities and conveniences being systematically recorded by the Dominion Bureau of Statistics denoted new patterns of domesticity and changes in what constituted homemaking and housework.

Activities had been transferred from the home to other sectors of the economy. The industrialization of housework had substituted capital for unpaid labour in the home. Cheap sources of energy and new household equipment brought dramatic changes in domestic comfort and reductions in the physical labour of housework. Time savings came with second-generation appliances such as automatic washing machines, self-defrosting combination refrigerator-freezers, and Mixmasters and new, easier-to-clean materials such as linoleum and Canadian-made Arborite. By 1950, it was estimated that a typical American housewife had the productivity that required a staff of three to four in 1850; Canadian housewives were not far behind.[61] Much of the work of food production and preparation was transferred to the commercial sector, available for purchase as frozen foods, prepared breakfast foods, fresh and cleaned vegetables, prepared

FIGURE 6.6 Frank and Irene Camisso purchased the millionth home built in Canada after the end of the Second World War. Their monthly mortgage payments were similar to what they paid in rent, and, as a contractor working in the construction industry, Frank calculated that the $16,500 price of the Wishing Well Acres home was less than the cost of building the same house by themselves. The family received the keys on 14 September 1956 in a well-publicized ceremony attended by local leaders and representatives from provincial and federal housing authorities. "Everything was just about the way we wanted it," Frank told reporters. "Conventional layout, six rooms and a wonderful heating system, hot water on oil with cast iron baseboard radiators." "And," he noted, "the roof was green." | Jack Dobson, "And the Roof Was Green: 1,000,000th House Built in Canada since War Is Sold to Young Family of Four," *Globe and Mail,* 15 September 1956, 22.

salad dressings, cake mixes, roasted chickens, and more. Other domestic responsibilities were outsourced to governments. Payroll deductions and higher taxes provided greater security for old age, medical care, and basic education and with it, daytime care for children ages four to sixteen, and they helped to subsidize family investments in higher education. Provisions for social security freed consumers to spend after-tax disposable income more readily.

The rhythms of domestic life changed; most obvious were the changes in paid work outside the home, but there were many other changes. Shopping for food became a weekly rather than a daily chore. Despite increases in real per capita income and average household income, the proportion of income devoted to food, clothing, shelter, and household maintenance had not changed substantially over the past quarter century. The difference was that household needs included many more consumer items, such as durables and a steady input of consumables. Managing the household budget involved keeping abreast of product developments and planning future purchases to determine best value for money. Ownership of durable goods (even on instalment) and houses (even with twenty-five and thirty-year mortgages) extended time horizons, promising a new kind of stability.

At mid-century, it was no longer possible to see the Canadian household as a refuge from capitalism. Changes in financing increased the purchasing power of Canadian households and transformed buying practices. Standards of living, as measured by the ability to accumulate and consume the products of modern industry, reached new high levels. Everyday life had become more central to politics; residential construction and consumer goods became important sectors of the Canadian economy. Domesticity was the site of increased capital investment by households, financial services industries, manufacturers, retailers, mass media, and advertising industries. Mass-produced goods were remaking household routines, and the rising tertiary sector was drawing women into the workforce. As paid work for women became more available outside the home, unpaid work inside the home came to be perceived as having lower social status.

Changes in postwar domesticity involved new ways of organizing households. Home life became more commercially defined and housekeeping more organized around commodities; some were regarded as durable, whereas others were purchased, consumed, and purchased again according to weekly shopping schedules. Managing a relative abundance of goods was central to a new cautious consumerism, underwritten by dual incomes, expanding consumer debt, and policies targeted to grow the economy, in part by increasing household spending. Spending patterns that previous generations would have regarded as self-indulgent and irresponsible were becoming more broadly accepted. New habits were established, setting in motion many years of future buying.

These changes were general, if far from universal. Not all Canadians participated, and new structural inequalities and vulnerabilities were created. Rising home ownership represented more than security of tenure; it was an opportunity to build equity, but this opportunity was not available to all. There were meaningful differences in the quality of goods bought at different income levels. Access to credit and the costs of borrowing were unequal. Daily practices continued to be shaped by the resources available to each household (resources of financial, physical, social, and cultural capital) and by networks of constraints and supports. Household economies continued to operate in a dynamic relationship with changes in the economy, particularly the demand for labour. Cheaper supplies of power and the decreasing costs of mass production had broadened the market for household appliances but left households more vulnerable to escalations in energy prices and long-term ecological impacts. Single persons, one-parent families, and households fully dependent on the incomes of two wage earners had little flexibility to respond to rapid rises in inflation and interest rates, rising unemployment, and changes in government policies and commitments that were to come.

Domesticity, it has been said, is never finished, and homemaking is a work in progress. Even those tasks that remain the same can always be done in new ways. "Domesticity" is not an easy term to define. It is used in reference to lived practice, ideology, and tradition. In each context, domesticity is subject to change over time, and the rate of change is different in each case. Traditions constrain practices, and practices remake traditions. Conceptual distinctions between male wage earners and female housewives, between public life and private life, and between producers and consumers exist in tension and often in largely unacknowledged contradiction. The decisions that shape households are made in the present, with awareness of what could be and should be and what was. But domesticity as it is lived is not the result of averages, trends, and ideals. On balance, despite fluctuations in business cycles, the 1950s were a decade of increased domestic comfort for most Canadians and increased financial security for many Canadians, even if not for the reasons generally assumed.

NOTES

1 For recent overviews, see Nancy Christie and Michael Gauvreau, *Cultures of Citizenship in Postwar Canada, 1940–1955* (Montreal and Kingston: McGill-Queen's University Press, 2003), especially 3–26; Magda Fahrni and Robert Rutherdale, eds., *Creating Postwar Canada: Community, Diversity, and Dissent, 1945–1975* (Vancouver: UBC Press, 2008); Wendy Gamber, "Women and Domesticity in the 1950s," *Oxford Research Encyclopedias, American History,* https://doi.org/10.1093/acrefore/9780199329175. 013.423; Joanne Meyerowitz, "Rewriting Postwar Women's History, 1945–1960," in *A Companion to American Women's History,* ed. Nancy Hewitt (Oxford: Wiley Blackwell, 2002), 382–96; and Stephanie Coontz, *The Way We Never Were: American Families and the Nostalgia Trap* (New York: Basic Books, 2016).

2 The reappraisal of Americanization is ongoing, most recently with attention to the transnational circulation of business practices and popular culture, with transmission now seen as akin more to a turntable than a highway. See Volker R. Berghahn, "The Debate on 'Americanization' among Economic and Cultural Historians," *Cold War History* 10, 1 (2010): 107–30; Peter Clark and Emanuela Todeva, "Review Article: Unmasking Americanization: De Grazia's Irresistible Market Empire Advancing through Twentieth Century Europe," *Prometheus* 24, 1 (2006): 101–15; Richard Kuisel, "Commentary: Americanization for Historians," *Diplomatic History* 24, 3 (2000): 509–15; and Richard Kuisel, "The End of Americanization? Or Reinventing a Research Field for Historians of Europe," *Journal of Modern History* 92, 3 (2020): 602–29.

3 Kathryn Kish Sklar, "Reconsidering Domesticity through the Lens of Empire and Settler Society in North America," *American Historical Review* 124, 4 (2019): 1258.

4 The demographic discussion here draws from A. Gordon Darroch and Michael Ornstein, "Family and Household in Nineteenth-Century Canada: Regional Patterns and Regional Economies," *Journal of Family History* 31, 2 (1984): 158–77; O.A. Lemieux, "Changes in the Population Pattern as Revealed by the 1951 Census," *Canadian Journal of Public Health* 45, 12 (1954): 524–32; Emily M. Nett, "Canadian Families in Social-Historical Perspective," *Canadian Journal of Sociology* 6, 3 (1981): 239–60; Sylvia Wargon, "Household and Family in Canada: A General Review of Recent Demographic Trends," *International Journal of Sociology of the Family* 8, 1 (1978): 53–68; Sylvia Wargon and Statistics Canada, *Canadian Households and Families: Recent Demographic Trends* (Ottawa: Minister of Supply and Services, 1979); and Cynthia Comacchio, "'The History of Us': Social Science, History, and the Relations of Family in Canada," *Labour/Le travail* 46 (2000): 167–220.

5 For attitudinal explanations, see Jessica Weiss, *To Have and to Hold: Marriage, the Baby Boom and Social Change* (Chicago: University of Chicago Press, 2000), 4, 17, 21–27. For economic explanations, see Wargon and Statistics Canada, *Canadian Households,* 86; and Steven Ruggles, "Patriarchy, Power, and Pay: The Transformation of American Families, 1800–2015," *Demography* 52, 6 (2015): 1797–1823.

6 Lemieux, "Changes in the Population Pattern," 528–29, 531.

7 Urbanization, smaller household units, and greater availability of appliances, services, and food products made it easier to live independently. A strong economy meant

that young adults did not need to contribute to the family income, and pensions supplemented the savings of elderly Canadians. Wargon and Statistics Canada, *Canadian Households,* 21–22, 41–42.

8 For a recent discussion of the myth of the self-sufficient pioneer household, see Douglas McCalla, *Consumers in the Bush: Shopping in Rural Upper Canada* (Montreal and Kingston: McGill-Queen's University Press, 2015), 3–22.

9 Sklar, "Reconsidering Domesticity," 1249.

10 Jeanne Boydston, cited in Joan C. Williams, "From Difference to Dominance to Domesticity: Care as Work, Gender as Tradition," *Chicago Kent Law Review* 76 (2001): 1446.

11 For a recent overview of key historiography, see Sklar, "Reconsidering Domesticity." On the emergence of domesticity as the redemptive counterpart to industrial capitalism, see Nancy Cott, *The Bonds of Womanhood: "Woman's Sphere" in New England, 1780–1835,* 2nd ed. (New Haven, CT: Yale University Press, 1997), 64, 70–71, 97–98. On the transition from the family economy to the waged economy, see Sara Horrell and Jane Humphries, "The Origins and Expansion of the Male Breadwinner Family: The Case of Nineteenth-Century Britain," *International Review of Social History* 42 (1997): 25–64. On the legacies of the ideal of domesticity, see Kathryn Abrams, "Destabilizing Domesticity," *Connecticut Law Review* 32 (1999): 281–89; and Joan C. Williams, "From Difference to Dominance to Domesticity: Care as Work, Gender as Tradition," *Chicago Kent Law Review* 76 (2001): 1444–93. For the breadwinner ideal as a convention structuring domestic life in Canada and in Canadian historiography, see Cynthia R. Comacchio, "Beneath the 'Sentimental Veil': Families and Family History in Canada," *Labour/Le travail* 33 (1994): 279–302; Comacchio, "'The History of Us'"; and Joy Parr, *The Gender of Breadwinners: Women, Men, and Change in Two Industrial Towns, 1880–1950* (Toronto: University of Toronto Press, 1990), especially 241–46.

12 An urban family required an annual income of $1,040 for mere subsistence and $1,500 to be self-supporting with better housing and clothing, though still without room for contingencies. Two-thirds of all married wage earners earned less than $1,200 a year; 40% earned less than $500 a year. Leonard Marsh, *Canadians in and out of Work: A Survey of Economic Classes and Their Relation to the Labour Market* (Montreal: McGill Social Research Series, 1940), 166–67, 170–73, 193, 195–96.

13 The wages contributed by sons and daughters, who were generally unskilled or semiskilled and reached the age of marriage before reaching their maximum earnings, were less critical than the earnings of wives and mothers. Because more income earners also meant more consumers, the earnings of children helped to stabilize but did not tend to increase their family's overall standard of living. Ibid., 170–73.

14 By 1921, one-quarter of the formal labour force was female; however, the majority of female wage earners were single. Married women's contributions to family businesses and family farms would not have been recorded in the census. Significant participation of married women was a postwar phenomenon.

15 Denyse Baillargeon, "'If You Had No Money, You Had No Trouble, Did You?': Montréal Working-Class Housewives during the Great Depression," *Women's History Review* 1, 2 (1992): 217–37. The Depression tested but did not fundamentally alter the commitment

of Canadian families and governments to maintaining the framework, however illusory, of the breadwinner wage. On the pressures to meet breadwinner-housewife ideals, see Denyse Baillargeon, *Making Do: Women, Family and Home in Montreal during the Great Depression*, trans. Yvonne Klein (Waterloo: Wilfrid Laurier University Press, 1999); Lara Campbell, *Respectable Citizens: Gender, Family and Unemployment in Ontario's Great Depression* (Toronto: University of Toronto Press, 2009); Suzanne Morton, *Ideal Surroundings: Domestic Life in a Working-Class Suburb in the 1920s* (Toronto: University of Toronto Press, 1995); and Parr, *The Gender of Breadwinners*.

16 Robert Bothwell, Ian Drummond, and John English, *Canada since 1945: Power, Politics, and Provincialism*, rev. ed. (Toronto: University of Toronto Press, 1989), 68–69.

17 See Philip Cross and Phillippe Bergevin, *Turning Points: Business Cycles in Canada since 1926*, Commentary No. 366 (Ottawa: C.D. Howe Institute, 2012), 9–10, https://www.cdhowe.org/sites/default/files/attachments/research_papers/mixed/Commentary_366_0.pdf.

18 "Labor Force and Employment Trends in Canada, 1950–60," *Monthly Labor Review* 85, 6 (1962): 668–72; Steven Ruggles, "Patriarchy, Power, and Pay: The Transformation of American Families," *Demography* 52, 6 (2015): 1797–1813.

19 Opportunity as well as patriotism and necessity encouraged women to enter the workforce during the war. By 1943, women made up 30.3% of the civilian labour force. As the war drew to a close, changes in policies and social expectations encouraged and often forced women, particularly married women, to exit the workforce. For a positive interpretation of the legacy of women's wartime work, see Jeff Keshen, "Revisiting Canada's Civilian Women during World War II," *Histoire sociale/Social History* 30, 60 (1997): 239–66. On the institutional barriers limiting the participation of married women in the labour force, see Chelsea Michelle Lappin, "'Irreconcilable Differences?' The Experiences of Middle-Class Women Combining Marriage and Work in Post-War English Speaking Canada (1945–1960)" (MA thesis, University of Ottawa, 2018), 23–27, 35–37, 44–46; and Jennifer Stephen, *Pick One Intelligent Girl: Employability, Domesticity, and the Gendering of Canada's Welfare State, 1939–1947* (Toronto: University of Toronto Press, 2007).

20 "Labor Force and Employment Trends in Canada, 1950–60," *Monthly Labor Review* 85, 6 (1962): 668–72. Rising demand for women in the labour force reflected the long-term movement from farm to non-farm employment, the relative rise of the tertiary sector, and the corresponding decline of jobs in manufacturing, construction, and resource extraction. Tertiary-sector employment rose from 53.4% of total non-farm employment in 1950 to 60.3% in 1960. Women working full time typically earned 59% of male earnings for the same labour categories.

21 Wargon, "Household and Family in Canada," 66.

22 Iacovetta, *Such Hardworking People*, 73–74; Lappin, "'Irreconcilable Differences'?," 23; Joan Sangster, "Doing Two Jobs: The Wage Earning Mother, 1945–1970," in *A Diversity of Women, 1945–1980*, ed. Joy Parr (Toronto: University of Toronto Press, 1995), 231–36, 242–46; Veronica Strong-Boag, "'Their Side of the Story': Women's Voices from Ontario Suburbs, 1945–1960," in *A Diversity of Women, 1945–1980*, ed. Joy Parr (Toronto: University of Toronto Press, 1995), 46–74.

23 For an especially noteworthy example, see Donica Belisle and Kiera Mitchell, "Mary Quayle Innis: Faculty Wives' Contributions and the Making of Academic Celebrity," *Canadian Historical Review* 99, 3 (2018): 456–86.

24 Twenty-seven percent of Canada's non-farm families spent 60 percent or more of their income on basic food, clothing, and shelter. Alvin Finkel, *Our Lives, Canada after 1945*, 2nd ed. (Toronto: Lorimer, 1997), 6–10.

25 Veronica Strong-Boag, "Canada's Wage-Earning Wives and the Construction of the Middle Class, 1945–1960," *Journal of Canadian Studies* 29, 3 (1994): 8. On the prominence of immigrant women in paid labour in the postwar period, see Iacovetta, *Such Hardworking People*, 92.

26 Quoted in Veronica Strong-Boag, "'Wages for Housework': Mothers' Allowances and the Beginnings of Social Security in Canada," *Journal of Canadian Studies/Revue d'études canadiennes* 14, 1 (1979): 27. Also see Comacchio, "History of Us," 206, 210.

27 Bettina Liverant, *Buying Happiness: The Emergence of Consumer Consciousness in English Canada* (Vancouver: UBC Press, 2018), 44–61, 89–109; Ruth Frager, *Sweatshop Strife: Class, Ethnicity, and Gender in the Jewish Labour Movement of Toronto, 1900–1939* (Toronto: University of Toronto Press, 1992); Julie Guard, "A Mighty Power against the Cost of Living: Canadian Housewives Organize in the 1930s," *International Labor and Working-Class History* 77, 1 (2010): 27–47.

28 Despite divergent experiences, idealized images of home were central to wartime propaganda in all of the combatant nations. Domestic concerns were especially central in the "radical reconstruction" of postwar Europe. Paul Betts and David Crowley, "Dreamworlds: Notions of Home in Post-1945 Europe," *Journal of Contemporary History* 40, 2 (2005): 219, 220–21.

29 For a full discussion of the multiple factors leading to the Family Allowance Act, see Robert Douglas Weaver, "Understanding the Present by Exploring the Past: An Analysis of Family Allowance and Child Care in Canada" (MA thesis, University of Regina, 2000), 19–29.

30 Humphry Carver, cited in Steven Logan, "Modernist Urbanism in the Age of Automobility: Producing Space in the Suburbs of Toronto and Prague" (PhD diss., York University, Toronto, 2015), 181. These policies were specific to single-family homes. Laws creating condominiums, making it possible to own and obtain mortgages for units in multi-unit buildings, date in Canada from 1966.

31 J.V. Poapst, "The National Housing Act, 1954," *Canadian Journal of Economics and Political Science* 22, 2 (1956): 234–43; John Belec, "Underwriting Suburbanization: The National Housing Act and the Canadian City," *Canadian Geographer* 59, 3 (2015): 341–53; Miron, *Postwar Housing in Canada*, 266–67.

32 On the importance of the CMHC and NHA in standard setting, see Miron, *Postwar Housing*, 266.

33 George Thomas Kapelos, "The Small House in Print: Promoting the Modern Home to Postwar Canadians through Pattern Books, Journals and Magazines," *The Journal of the Society for the Study of Architecture in Canada/Le Journal de la Société pour l'étude de l'architecture au Canada* 34, 1 (2009): 33–60. Also see Joy Parr, *Domestic Goods: The Material, the Moral, and the Economic in the Postwar Years* (Toronto:

University of Toronto Press, 1999), 40–63. On a similar program in Europe, see Betts and Crowley, "Dreamworlds," 222.

34 James Hadden, "A Study of the Consumption Function in Canada" (PhD diss., University of Windsor, 1965), 73, https://scholar.uwindsor.ca/etd/6384.

35 General-purpose credit cards did not exist before 1950 and were not common in Canada until the later 1960s and early 1970s. Eric Hutton, "Money, Suddenly Everybody's Owing It," *Maclean's,* 10 August 1963, 11.

36 Sidney Margolius, "How Much Money Should Your Family Owe?," *Chatelaine,* January 1956, 22.

37 S.D. Clark, *The Suburban Society* (Toronto: University of Toronto Press, 1966), 120.

38 For example, Sydney Margolius, "How to Borrow Money," *Maclean's,* 15 March 1950, 21, 42–43, 45; Mary Jukes, "How to Borrow Wisely," *Chatelaine,* February 1951, 53–54, 64; Sydney Margolius, "How Good Is Your Credit?," *Maclean's,* 1 April 1951, 12–13, 45–46; Sydney Margolius, "How Much Money Should Your Family Owe?," *Chatelaine,* January 1956, 22, 27–31; and Hutton, "Money," 11–12, 39–42.

39 Slater, *Consumption Expenditures,* 2–3.

40 Barry Boothman, "Mammoth Market: The Transformation of Food Retailing in Canada, 1946–1965," *Journal of Historical Research in Marketing* 3, 3 (2011): 279–301.

41 Miron, *Housing in Postwar Canada,* 153.

42 On the considerations of consumer demand as a factor in postwar immigration policy, see James Walsh, "Mass Migration and the Mass Society: Fordism, Immigration Policy and the Post-War Long Boom in Canada and Australia, 1947–1970," *Journal of Historical Sociology* 25, 3 (2012): 363–64; and Peter C. Newman, "How Long Can the Boom Last?," *Maclean's,* 31 March 1956, 12, 64.

43 From 1871 to 1941, census distinctions between rural and urban were based upon governance. Residents of incorporated villages, towns, and cities, regardless of the size of the community, were classified as urban; rural was the residual category. The term "rural" was redefined in the census years 1941, 1951, and 1961 and measured by population density. In 1931 and 1941, a census farm was a holding of one acre or more that produced, in the year prior to the census, agricultural products valued at fifty dollars or more, was under a crop of any kind, or was used for pasturing in the census year. For the 1951 and 1956 counts, a census farm was defined as a holding on which agricultural operations were carried out and that was three acres or more in size, or from one to three acres in size, with agricultural production in the year prior to the census valued at $250 or more. For the 1961, 1966, and 1971 counts, a census farm became a farm, ranch, or other agricultural holding of one acre or more with sales of agricultural products of fifty dollars or more during the twelve-month period prior to the census.

44 Gerald Fortin, "The Challenge of a New Rural World," in *Rural Canada in Transition,* ed. M.A. Tremblay and W.J. Anderson (Ottawa: Agricultural Economics Research Council of Canada, 1966), 375.

45 On discussions of consumer spending in rural Women's Institutes in the 1920s, see Donica Belisle, *Purchasing Power: Women and the Rise of a Canadian Consumer Culture* (Toronto: University of Toronto Press, 2020), 98–123. For the postwar period,

see E.A. (Nora) Cebotarev, "From Domesticity to the Public Sphere: Farm Women, 1945-86," in *A Diversity of Women, 1945-1980*, ed. Joy Parr (Toronto: University of Toronto Press, 1995), 200-31; Parr, *Domestic Goods*, 218-42; and Ruth Sandwell, "Pedagogies of the Unimpressed: Re-Educating Ontario Women for the Modern Energy Regime, 1900-1940," *Ontario History* 107, 1 (2015): 36-59.

46 Miron, *Housing in Postwar Canada*, 185; David Schulze, "The Politics of Power: Rural Electrification in Alberta" (MA thesis, McGill University, 1989), 53-57; Ruth Sandwell, "How Households Shape Energy Transitions: Canada's Great Transformation," *RCC Perspectives* 2 (2019): 23-30, https://www.jstor.org/stable/pdf/26631558.pdf.

47 Donald White, "Rural Canada in Transition," in *Rural Canada in Transition*, ed. M.A. Tremblay and W.J. Anderson (Ottawa: Agricultural Economics Research Council of Canada, 1966), 39.

48 A particularly useful source discussing these matters is Temblay and Anderson, *Rural Canada in Transition*.

49 Baillargeon, "'If You Had No Money,'" 228-29.

50 Slater, *Consumption Expenditures*, 112; Newman, "How Long Can the Boom Last?," 14.

51 Parr, *Domestic Goods*, 218-42; Shelley Nickles, "More Is Better: Mass Consumption, Gender, and Class Identity in Postwar America," *American Quarterly* 54, 4 (2002): 581-622.

52 John R. Seeley, R. Alexander Sim, and Elizabeth W. Loosley, *Crestwood Heights: A Study of the Culture of Suburban Life* (Toronto: University of Toronto Press, 1956), 43, 51.

53 Few data are available to indicate how these higher-level consumer goods were distributed. Porter, *Vertical Mosaic*, xlii, 4, 125-26, 132, estimated no more than 10 percent of all Canadian households on the basis of earned income alone.

54 S.D. Clark, *The Suburban Society* (Toronto: University of Toronto Press, 1966), 100-13, 120; S.D. Clark, "The Suburban Community," in *Urbanism and the Changing Canadian Society*, ed. S.D. Clark (Toronto: University of Toronto Press, 1961), 1-2, 20-21, 34-38.

55 Hutton, "Money," 11-13, 39.

56 John Clare, "The Scramble for the Teenage Dollar," *Maclean's*, 14 September 1957, 18-19, 106-12; Katharine Rollwagen, "Eaton's Goes to School: Youth Councils and the Commodification of the Teenaged Consumer," *Histoire sociale/Social History* 47, 95 (2014): 683-703; Doug Owram, *Born at the Right Time: A History of the Baby Boom Generation* (Toronto: University of Toronto Press, 1996), 84-110.

57 Rom Markin, *The Supermarket: An Analysis of Growth, Development and Change*, rev. ed. (Pullman: Washington State University Press, 1968), 43-44.

58 In most mass-media depictions, the "natural" position of husbands and fathers remained outside routine domesticity. Male contributions to domestic work tended to be classified as "help" rather than essential responsibilities, and those who ventured too far into realms regarded as feminine were gently mocked for their lack of skill in the kitchen and as hapless shoppers prone to impulse buying. Christopher Dummitt, "Finding a Place for Father: Selling the Barbecue in Postwar Canada," *Journal of the Canadian Historical Association* 9, 1 (1998): 209-23; Steven Gelber, "Do-It-Yourself:

Constructing, Repairing and Maintaining Domestic Masculinity," *American Quarterly* 49, 1 (1997): 66–112; Robert Rutherdale, "Fatherhood and Masculine Domesticity during the Baby Boom: Consumption and Leisure in Advertising and Life Stories," in *Family Matters: Papers in Post-Confederation Canadian Family History,* ed. Lori Chambers and Edgar-André Montigny (Toronto: Canadian Scholars' Press, 1998), 309–33. For a more nuanced appraisal with an emphasis on the money that could be saved by doing-it-yourself, see Mona Purser, "The Homemaker: Build It Yourself Plan Happy Way to Save Cash," *The Globe and Mail,* July 3, 1952, 11.

59 Joy Parr, "Household Choices as Politics and Pleasure in 1950s Canada," *International Labor and Working-Class History* 55 (1999): 122–24; Eichler, *Families in Canada Today,* 152–53.

60 Williams, "From Difference to Dominance to Domesticity," 1441–93.

61 Ruth Schwartz Cowan, *More Work for Mother: The Ironies of Household Technology from the Open Hearth to the Microwave* (New York: Basic Books, 1983), 100.

7

Racial Discrimination in "Uncle Tom's Town"

Media and the Americanization of Racism in Dresden, 1948–56

JENNIFER TUNNICLIFFE

On 5 December 1949, the small town of Dresden, Ontario, held a plebiscite on the matter of racial discrimination. Under pressure for unequal treatment of Black residents in the community, the town council asked citizens "do you approve of the Council passing a by-law licensing restaurants in Dresden and restraining the owner or owners from refusing service regardless of race, color or creed?"[1] The plebiscite was defeated by a vote of 517 to 108. The result generated widespread media attention to the town and local efforts to end discriminatory practices, contributing to a broader campaign to pressure the Ontario government to adopt and effectively enforce fair practices laws. In this chapter, I examine local and national newspaper coverage of the events in Dresden from 1948 to 1956, analyzing this coverage both as the major vehicle through which most Canadians learned about Dresden and what was happening in the town and as a reflection of social and cultural assumptions and understandings of discrimination, anti-Black racism, and rights and freedoms in 1940s and 1950s Canada.

The history of racial discrimination in Dresden and its connection to human rights activism have been recounted and analyzed by various scholars. James Walker argues that Dresden was used as "the practical example to humanize the problem of discrimination" in postwar Ontario, helping to create sufficient pressure to convince the provincial government to pass anti-discrimination laws that many policy makers saw as unnecessary but that had become politically expedient.[2] Ross Lambertson uses

Dresden to illustrate the contribution of trade unionists to the postwar human rights struggle by detailing how they supported the campaigns in Dresden.[3] John Cooper's *Season of Rage* focuses on the personalities involved, celebrating the work of the National Unity Association (NUA) and Hugh Burnett in the struggle for civil rights in Canada.[4] Burnett and the NUA have also been commemorated by the Ontario Heritage Trust,[5] and in 2019 Burnett was the subject of a play entitled "My Place Is Right Here: Hugh Burnett and the Fight for a Better Canada."[6]

Reflecting this volume's focus on the US impact on Canada, this chapter uses the case of Dresden to show how a campaign against racial discrimination in small-town Ontario was situated in a broader North American context and illustrates how concepts such as discrimination and anti-Black racism in Canada were influenced by Canadian understandings of the history and experiences of Black Americans, particularly in the southern United States.[7] In this regard, the media reporting of events in Dresden was heavily shaped by three themes: the town's history as a terminus of the Underground Railroad and therefore as a "safe haven" from slavery in the United States; the association of postwar racism and segregation as an American problem, particularly in the context of Jim Crow laws and the early American civil rights movement; and a sense that discrimination (especially violent discrimination) was alien or foreign to Canada. Although Canadians have long compared themselves with Americans, the tendency to do so on racial issues increased in the postwar era as the African American civil rights movement intensified, thereby drawing greater international scrutiny of the United States.[8] Canadian media coverage of Dresden illustrates how American images and examples were mobilized after the Second World War to perpetuate a narrative of Canada as anti-racist and of Dresden as an exception rather than the representation of deeper problems in Canada, thereby acting as a barrier to the acknowledgment of systemic forms of racism and to anti-racist activism generally.

DRESDEN IN POSTWAR ONTARIO

Dresden is a small agricultural town in southwestern Ontario, in the municipality of Chatham-Kent, close to the American border. Located on the traditional territories of the Anishinaabe, Attiwonderonk, and Mississauga, the town was "founded" when lumber merchants and farmers arrived from Britain, Germany, and the Netherlands in 1825. These European settlers pushed out most of the original Indigenous inhabitants, and by the 1850s Dresden was well established with a few hundred residents, mostly farmers.[9]

Without question, the town is best remembered as a terminus of the Underground Railroad. This secret network of abolitionists acted as a freedom movement from the late seventeenth century to the 1860s, helping African Americans in the southern states to escape slavery through routes to either the free northern states or Canada. In 1841, Josiah Henson, a former slave, used the network to flee north, crossing the Niagara River into Upper Canada (now Ontario) and eventually founding the Dawn Settlement near Dresden.[10] The settlement welcomed a combination of Black Loyalists who fought for the British in the American Revolution, Black American refugees from the War of 1812, and other Black migrants, including those fleeing slavery. Henson's life story became the loose inspiration for Harriet Beecher Stowe's *Uncle Tom's Cabin* in 1852, and the Dawn Settlement has since been commemorated as a "refuge" for fugitive slaves who escaped to Canada.[11] At its peak, the settlement had 500 residents, but by the late 1860s it was in decline, with some settlers returning to the United States after the abolition of slavery and others moving to the surrounding areas, including Dresden.[12]

The largest concentrations of the Black population in Upper Canada at this time were in rural farming communities like Dresden, and the Black presence in these areas remained strong into the twentieth century.[13] By the late 1940s, the total population of Dresden had grown to approximately 1,700, almost 20 percent of whom were Black residents.[14] Despite the long history of Black Canadians in the area, however, racial discrimination was prevalent in postwar Dresden. Two of the three local restaurants, Kay's Café and Emerson's Soda Bar Restaurant, would not serve Black customers. Local pool halls and the city's barbershops and beauty salons were also "whites only." Schools were inclusive, as were some clubs and recreational activities, but many of Dresden's churches did not welcome Black congregants. Black residents were also heavily restricted in their employment opportunities, and as a result they experienced racial discrimination in their everyday lives.[15]

The discrimination experienced in Dresden in the 1940s must be situated within Canada's longer history as a white settler society. Through the process of colonialism, European settlers established forms of white racial dominance in pre- and post-Confederation Canada. This dominance included the forced removal of and assimilationist policies toward Indigenous peoples as well as the development of systems of formal and informal governance that privileged white, British, middle-class, Protestant, heterosexual males above all others. From Confederation to the Second World War, governments in Canada used their legislative powers to pass laws that protected this group of subjects, regulating areas such as property ownership, employment, education, voting, and immigration to disadvantage women, lower classes, and religious and racialized minorities. Examples of legal discrimination in this period include explicitly racist immigration policies; laws banning racialized minorities from holding public office or serving on a jury; restrictive covenants against the presence of certain ethnic, racial, or religious groups within neighbourhoods; discriminatory enlistment policies during the First World War; segregated schooling; and restricted access to services based on gender, race, or religion.[16]

Although victims of prejudice fought these laws, the courts were of limited use in the day-to-day struggle for greater equality. There were virtually no laws in Canada prior to the Second World War to prohibit discrimination, and the courts themselves perpetuated systemic forms of discrimination.[17] For example, in 1940, the Supreme Court considered the case of Fred Christie, refused service in Montreal's York Tavern because it was the establishment's policy not to serve "Negroes." In its decision, the court stated that "any merchant is free to deal as he may choose with any individual member of the public. It is not a question of motives or reasons for deciding to deal or not to deal; he is free to do either."[18] In Nova Scotia, campaigns and legal challenges to racial discrimination and segregationist policies in the 1940s by women such as Pearleen Oliver, Carrie M. Best, and Viola Desmond were similarly unsuccessful because of Canada's lack of legal protection.

A limited form of rights activism developed in Canada in the 1930s, with members of ethnic, religious, libertarian, and other organizations pressuring the government for expanded rights protection.[19] It was not until 1944, however, that Ontario introduced the first law in Canada to prohibit discrimination explicitly. The Racial Discrimination Act prohibited the publication or public display of any sign or advertisement that discriminated on the basis of race or creed. Although Ontario MPPs had refused to support similar legislation a decade earlier, arguing that it gave the government too much power to interfere with individual freedom, a growing sensitivity toward discrimination in Canada after the war led to support for the new law.[20] Yet the law was very limited in scope. It was restricted to public acts, leaving discrimination that occurred within the private interactions of individuals or businesses acceptable.

As a result, Black Canadians continued to be treated as second-class citizens. Provincial laws and municipal bylaws, or more often a lack of legal protection, meant that in many places in Ontario, even after 1944, Black peoples were unwelcome in stores and restaurants and relegated to separate seating in movie theatres. Barrington Walker argues that Black Canadians were "caught between formal legal equality and deeply entrenched societal and economic inequality."[21] The legal segregation of public facilities and businesses common in the southern United States was not formalized in Canadian law, but nonetheless Black Canadians were extremely limited in their job and housing opportunities, which affected their socio-economic standing in Canadian society. "Despite the lack of legally codified Jim Crow laws in Canada," Walker argues, "social customs and court rulings that allowed individuals the freedom to act in a racially biased manner led many Black Canadians to identify Jim Crow as a continental rather than exclusively US phenomenon."[22] Again, this situation was supported by the courts. In 1948, a year before Dresden's plebiscite, the Supreme Court upheld a local law in the community of Grand Bend, Ontario, that forbade "Jews and Negroes" from owning property.[23] Racial discrimination in Dresden, therefore, though perhaps less concealed than in some other areas because of the large Black presence in the community, was representative of the experiences of Black Canadians and other racialized minorities in postwar Canada.

THE DRESDEN CAMPAIGN
TO END RACIAL DISCRIMINATION

The campaign to end racial discrimination in Dresden began in 1943 when Hugh Burnett,[24] a local Black man, wrote to the Canadian government to complain formally about racial discrimination that he experienced at a local restaurant. A Second World War veteran who was born and grew up in the Dresden area, Burnett settled in the town with his wife after his service, starting his own carpentry business. Tired of the racial discrimination that he experienced in Dresden, in his complaint Burnett informed the government that Kay's Café, owned by Morley McKay, refused to serve Black patrons.[25] When the government failed to take action, and in light of Canadian legal precedents in cases such as that of Fred Christie, rather than take to the courts, Burnett joined forces with other Black residents to found the National Unity Association. Comprised of farmers and tradespeople from Dresden and the surrounding area, the association had a mission to push for equal rights for the Black community through legislative change. One of its first actions was to approach the Dresden town council in 1948 to request that a non-discrimination policy be added as a condition for local businesses to receive licences. When the council denied this request, Burnett and the NUA widened their campaign, connecting with activists outside Dresden lobbying the Ontario government for fair practices laws to prohibit discrimination in the areas of employment, accommodation, and services.

Fair practices laws were anti-discrimination laws modelled on legislation first introduced in New York state in 1945 and adopted by numerous other American states throughout the 1950s.[26] Several scholars have written extensively about the close connection between civil liberties associations, minority groups (particularly Jewish Canadians), and labour groups during this period and their lobbying efforts to pressure Ontario's government to pass similar laws.[27] In 1949, the NUA joined a large delegation that lobbied the new Progressive Conservative premier, Leslie Frost, to adopt laws making it unlawful for employers to discriminate against a person in hiring, promotion, or termination, for trade unions to exclude members, or for landlords and business owners to deny accommodations, services, or facilities based on race, religion, colour, or nationality. Although the delegation did not specifically mention Dresden in its petition, it did call for municipalities to cancel licences for businesses that practised religious or racial discrimination.[28]

Frost and the Ontario government were reluctant initially, but the provincial campaign for fair practices laws was growing, and pressure was mounting. This pressure was felt by Dresden's town councillors, who decided that, rather than take direct action to adopt a municipal bylaw, they would hold a town-wide vote on the question of discrimination. Accordingly, in December 1949, they asked Dresden citizens whether or not they would support a new bylaw limiting business licensing to only those establishments that agreed not to discriminate on the basis of race, colour, or creed. News of the plebiscite captured media attention; the vote and the result were covered by local and national newspapers, and *Maclean's* Sidney Katz published an exposé entitled "Jim Crow Lives in Dresden."[29] This media attention raised the profile of the situation in Dresden, and following the defeat of the plebiscite human rights activists in Ontario used Dresden as an example of the urgent need for stronger anti-discrimination laws and pushed for another meeting with Frost. By 1950, the delegation lobbying the government had grown to several hundred activists, representing a wide variety of voluntary associations from across the province.[30] Their work was successful, and in 1951 Ontario passed Canada's first Fair Employment Practices Act and a Female Employees Fair Remuneration Act.[31] The province hesitated to adopt laws to prevent discrimination in services, facilities, and accommodations in public spaces, however, arguing that it did not have the jurisdiction to do so in cases in which municipal governments refused to pass bylaws.[32]

For Burnett and the NUA, the government's failure to adopt a fair accommodation act was significant because this type of law was needed to prohibit racial discrimination in the restaurants and barbershops of Dresden. With this in mind, they continued to work with the larger human rights community in Ontario, becoming a more central part of the activism to pressure Premier Frost for expanded legislative protection. The racial discrimination in the town, which by this point had been highlighted in media reports across the country, continued to be used to help convince the Frost government to take action.[33] Ultimately, the lobbying efforts were successful, and the Fair Accommodation Practices Act became law in Ontario on 6 April 1954.

Adoption of the act was not the end of the campaign for racial equality in Dresden, however. Not all businesses in the town complied with the new legislation, so from 1954 to 1956 the NUA was involved in efforts to test whether or not establishments would provide services to Black patrons and, in cases in which they would not, provided the evidence required to launch complaints to the Ontario Ministry of Labour, responsible for enforcing the new law. In total, eight complaints, a government commission, and several high-profile court cases were launched over the two-year period. The two businesses at the centre of the complaints were Kay's Café (the subject of Burnett's original complaint) and Emerson's Soda Bar Restaurant. The legal action generated much unrest in Dresden and continued to attract media attention. Tensions in the town were high, with white residents insisting that there was no problem, and that the laws were working, whereas the NUA and members of the Black community cited continuing patterns of racial discrimination. The situation garnered so much attention that the National Film Board of Canada filmed a documentary in 1954 entitled *The Dresden Story*.[34]

In January 1955, Morley McKay and Annie Emerson were found guilty of failing to uphold the standards of Ontario's Fair Accommodation Practices Act for their continued refusal to serve Black customers. These first convictions were appealed and overturned, leading to further complaints and a new prosecution against McKay, who was the most vocal opponent of the anti-discrimination laws and openly admitted that he would not serve Black customers.[35] In 1956, McKay was tried and convicted once again. This time the conviction was upheld on appeal, and he was forced to pay $100 in fines and more than $600 in court costs. No further appeals were launched, and the campaign that had started thirteen years earlier had finally succeeded; by the end of the year, Kay's Café had begun serving Black patrons. It is important to note, however, that the campaign took a significant toll on Hugh Burnett and other members of the NUA. Bromley Armstrong, a rights activist living in Toronto who became involved in the Dresden campaign, argued that Burnett was "ostracized" for his actions, eventually causing him to move to nearby Chatham.[36] And of course, though the fair practices laws helped to stem some of the overt forms of racial discrimination in Dresden, de facto forms of racial discrimination and systemic racism persisted.

THE ABSENCE OF BLACK HISTORY IN
THE CANADIAN NARRATIVE

Despite histories of prejudice and racial discrimination such as that in Dresden, narratives of Canadian history as raceless persist. This is the result in part of what Esmeralda Thornhill refers to as the "scarcely known and unknown story of Black people in Canada."[37] Her work contributes to a growing scholarship that exposes how Black peoples and their histories have been absent, and erased from, Canadian history.[38] This includes the very presence of Black peoples in Canada, their contributions, the reality of slavery in Canada's past, and the continued discrimination against Black Canadians and their exclusion from society. Although Black migrants have been arriving in Canada via Africa, Europe, the Caribbean, the United States, and beyond since the early seventeenth century, Afua Cooper argues that this history has been marginalized, "bulldozed and ploughed over," with the history of slavery in Canada particularly absent.[39]

When Canadians talk about slavery, most often it is from the perspective of Canada as a sanctuary for Black Americans escaping enslavement via the Underground Railroad. Yet slavery was a common practice in New France, with records revealing approximately 3,600 slaves having lived in the colony by the mid-1700s.[40] Slavery continued after the British conquest in 1763, with historians well documenting the sale and purchase of slaves in Upper and Lower Canada and the Maritimes.[41] That enslaved peoples made up a smaller proportion of the population, or that slavery was abolished earlier in British North America than in the United States, does not offset the brutality of the slave experience in colonial Canada. Rather, Cooper argues, "describing the Canadian form of enslavement as mild denies the humanity of the enslaved and further compounds their degradation."[42] It also allows for a misreading of Canadian history. As Abigail Bakan argues, "the absence of plantation slavery in Canada has been misread as an indication of Canada's race-neutral history," masking the reality that "far from being race-neutral, [Canada] was marked by a racialized culture of hegemonic whiteness."[43] Despite efforts to demonstrate the prevalence of slavery in Canada's past, and its historical impact on cultural attitudes and practices, most Canadians continue to avoid this history.

This is partly because of the historical centrality of stories of the Underground Railroad in school curriculums and in national commemorations of Black history in Canada. After the adoption of the Act to Limit Slavery, which stated that enslaved persons entering Upper Canada became free on arrival, over 30,000 slaves came to Canada via the Underground Railroad, settling mostly in what is now southern Ontario but also in Quebec and Nova Scotia.[44] In her research on the "usability" of the Underground Railroad narrative, Katherine McKittrick argues that this narrative has helped to position Canada as a refuge for Black bodies, which has been valuable in constructing Canada's self-image as a nation that welcomes and accepts non-whites.[45] In this way, the story of the Underground Railroad has obscured not only Canada's history of slavery but also the Canadian government's racist immigration policies, including steps taken to prevent Black migration in the early twentieth century, and the prevalence of rigid and widespread discrimination against Black Canadians (and other racialized minorities) in the post-slavery context. Instead, Canadians have long conceived of their country as one without a history of racism, a source of national pride.[46] This misconception of Canadian history, and the ignorance (wilful or not) of the Black experience in Canada, were certainly prevalent in much of the media coverage of events in Dresden. It was compounded by a tendency to place Canada's history of racial discrimination in contrast to that of the United States, encouraging the use of the United States as a foil to qualify practices in Canada in ways that prevented them from eroding the overall image of Canada as tolerant and welcoming.

DRESDEN AND THE TRANSNATIONAL LENS

Human rights scholars understand the importance of studying local and domestic aspects of Canada's history, recognizing that the lives of ordinary people are shaped by particular places and specific circumstances. James Walker argues that, by focusing on the Canadian experience, human rights historians find "not just an example of *what* happened, but lessons on *how* things happened."[47] He cautions that too great a focus on the influence of global or transnational trends can detract from our understanding of the distinctiveness of Canada's history of prejudice and discrimination, also subordinating the agency of Canadian activists, many of whom were members of marginalized groups. Although this is true, it is useful to consider the transnational lens as another layer to understand better how dominant ideologies, such as white supremacy, or the strategies of advocacy groups – many of whom operated transnationally – were influenced by events both inside and outside local, regional, or national contexts.

Ian Tyrell reminds us that all historical experiences are shaped by individuals, organizations, actions, and modes of thinking that extend beyond the nation; this does not render the nation or national context unimportant but reinforces that the "causes" or foundations of events or mindsets "operate simultaneously on different geographical and temporal scales, namely the local, regional, national, transnational, and global."[48] As the contributions to this collection remind us, Canadians in the postwar period were mindful of developments in the United States, and this awareness shaped developments in Canada. The preponderance of the United States and Canada's proximity to it meant that Canadians were particularly subject to its cultural influences. This was certainly the case in regard to ideologies of race and understandings of anti-Black racism. Both nations emerged from a white settler colonial process, under the influence of English customs and beliefs, and settlers brought ideas of race with them, setting the stage for a racial worldview. Over the past several hundred years, the migration of peoples (voluntary and forced), the sharing of ideas (those that perpetuated beliefs in racial hierarchies and those that challenged those beliefs), the modelling of policy, and exchanges through cross-border advocacy networks have all acted as forms of public diplomacy that have shaped the experiences of Canadians and Canada's self-image in relation to that of the United States. These experiences have shaped forms of Black consciousness as well; Wendell Adjetey points to major historical events such as the American Revolutionary War, the War of 1812, the Underground Railroad, twentieth-century cross-border migrations, immigration from the Caribbean, and social movements as contributing to a sense of shared consciousness between Black Americans and Canadians, as "diasporic peoples living in settler colonial societies with complicated racial histories."[49]

One of the most significant ways in which the United States has influenced Canada is in how it has been used as a foil to Canadian self-perception and identity. In terms of racial attitudes and understandings, this has led to what Rosanne Waters terms the "sanctimonious imagination": that is, "a lens through which many Canadians have viewed, and continue to view, their country as uniquely tolerant and free of racism" as a result of its comparison with the United States.[50] James Walker refers to this as the "North Star" myth, according to which "only south of the border were blacks subjected to violence, denied their citizenship rights, [and] forced into residential ghettos."[51] Such understandings of Canada were common in the postwar period, particularly as Canadians observed the growing racial tensions south of the border and the rise of the American civil rights movement. Historian Robin Winks argues that, during this period, "Canadians looked across the border with concern – and some air of superiority."[52] This greatly influenced how events in Dresden were framed within newspaper coverage.

PRINT MEDIA REPRESENTATIONS
OF THE DRESDEN STORY

A study of the newspaper coverage of the Dresden story reveals the types of information that most Canadians had access to about the town and the campaign to end its discriminatory practices and reflects some of the social and cultural assumptions that informed how many Canadians understood this discrimination and its place in postwar Canada. I looked specifically at English-language newspapers from across the country between 1948 and 1956, including newspapers in both rural and urban settings and with a variety of partisan leanings.[53] This cross-section of newspapers represents the mainstream news sources that would have been most commonly read by English Canadians at the time. Although newspaper articles, editorials, and letters to the editor offer only one lens through which to study historical events, these forms of print media were popularly consumed in 1940s and 1950s Canada and reveal how the events in Dresden were reported on, discussed, responded to, and framed within the broader context of anti-discrimination campaigns in Ontario and in relation to the United States.

Television broadcasting was in its infancy in the 1950s, and, despite the growth in popularity of radio broadcasts, newspapers remained one of the main vehicles for the dissemination of news and information in postwar Canada.[54] Daily newspapers attracted large readerships, one reason that Benedict Anderson argued that they were so essential to the development of "imagined communities" of the modern state.[55] But exactly whom these communities represented and served deserves attention. A study of the language and imagery used in news coverage can help us to uncover how power structures and social inequalities are produced, sustained, and operationalized in media communications.[56] Critical cultural studies scholars present the media as central to the construction and reconstruction of hegemonic ideologies such as capitalism, white supremacy, patriarchy, and heterosexuality by broadcasting hegemonic beliefs that serve to maintain a specific social order. American feminist Vivian Gornick has argued that the media not only reflect social and cultural assumptions about a phenomenon but also inform people about how issues are viewed or should be viewed.[57]

Mass-communication theories of "agenda setting" and "framing" are concerned with the extent to which news media can influence both the importance placed on certain topics or events in public discourse and how those topics or events are understood or interpreted.[58] One of the key elements of the influence of media is how they frame the content of the news that they provide, focusing attention on certain events and then placing them within particular fields of meaning.[59] They do so in the selection of which stories are told and which are not, how they are told and presented, the language and imagery used, and the themes invoked. Although this certainly does not have a universal effect on readers, and in fact is continually contested, it can have a common effect on larger portions of the readership, particularly when it reinforces ideologies held by readers.[60] Through agenda setting and framing, media can be a major instrument in shaping popular views and attitudes, in instituting change, or in helping to spread ideas that act as barriers to that change. Looking at newspaper reporting of anti-Black racism in Canada can provide a glimpse into how discrimination has been framed both abstractly and through the experiences of Black Canadians. It can also illustrate how Canadian institutions and citizens exercised power over Black Canadians, by controlling how stories were told, while maintaining a national and social narrative in which Canada was presented as a safe haven for Black peoples (particularly from the United States) and a country in which all people were treated fairly regardless of race, creed, or colour.

Rights abuses and racial discrimination became more frequent topics of concern in Canadian media in the 1940s. This can be attributed both to a growing rights movement in Canada, which worked to increase public awareness of discrimination and prejudice, and to increased sensitivity to questions of racism and discrimination in the context of the Second World War. For example, newspapers reported heavily on the internment and scheduled deportation of Canadians of Japanese ancestry, and increasingly after the war this was framed as a human rights issue.[61] The media also noted high-profile cases of discrimination against Black Canadians: the case of Fred Christie made headlines across the country as it moved through the courts,[62] as did Viola Desmond's challenge to segregationist policies in Nova Scotia.[63] However, anti-Black racism often was discussed through examples from the United States, including stories about racial violence and lynchings, Jim Crow laws, the tensions inspired by civil rights activism, and legislative reform. In her study of Canadian interactions with civil rights activism in the 1950s and 1960s, Rosanne Waters maintains that "scenes from the African American civil rights movement were regularly featured on the front pages of [Canadian] newspapers" in ways "frequently sympathetic" to the movement.[64] For example, in 1948, the year that the NUA was forming in Dresden, many newspapers across Canada reported on the growing opposition among Black Americans to segregation in schooling. On 20 January 1948, an article in the Regina *Leader-Post* reported on a US Supreme Court decision ordering Oklahoma to provide equal law school facilities for Black Americans despite the fact that Oklahoma's Constitution required separate schools.[65] The detail with which such issues were treated meant that the struggles of Black Americans in the postwar period would have been familiar to readers of Canadian newspapers, contributing to a sense that racial discrimination and violence were problems in the United States and in the American South specifically.

It was within this context that newspapers reported on the events in Dresden. Media coverage came in three waves between 1948 and 1956. The first reports came in 1948 as regional newspapers such as the *Windsor Star* and the *Chatham Daily News* commented on the complaints of racial discrimination coming out of Dresden. The town council's announcement of the plebiscite in April 1949 caught national attention, starting a second wave of reporting. Newspapers from Victoria to Halifax reported on the racial discrimination in Dresden, with coverage escalating in December in the days leading up to and following the voting and continuing with commentary on the results well into 1950. The final wave, which included the most extensive coverage, began shortly before the adoption of the Fair Accommodation Practices Act in 1954, focusing throughout 1955 and 1956 on the effectiveness of the law, the failure of some Dresden businesses to comply with it, and the subsequent court cases. The final article in the sample was printed on 25 December 1956, declaring a "happy ending" to the story when Morley McKay's restaurant finally began serving Black customers.[66]

Newspaper coverage of events in Dresden was diverse. Articles introduced readers to the town, detailed the racial discrimination experienced there by Black residents and visitors, described the campaign to end the discrimination and linked it to wider efforts to pressure the Ontario government to adopt fair practices laws, commented on the effectiveness of the Fair Accommodation Practices Act, reported on the failure of restaurants to comply with the new law, and traced the court cases to their conclusions. All the while, the journalists, editorialists, and citizens who wrote to the papers provided commentary on what was happening. The press coverage was overwhelmingly critical of the discrimination in the town, but individual columns or articles varied in how they presented and interpreted the issues at stake. In regard to how the discrimination was presented, three related themes stood out in the reporting. First, Dresden's history as a terminus of the Underground Railroad and its status as home to "Uncle Tom's Cabin" were heavily referenced in the newspaper reports.

This history was used to preface contemporary events in a way that depicted the racial discrimination of the period as new and at odds with Dresden's past. Second, there was widespread reference to the United States in the reports. It was common for the articles to characterize the racial discrimination in Dresden by evoking American images, locations, or events, thereby connecting Dresden to the American experience. Third, the Dresden story was often framed as unique in Canada, and the racial discrimination experienced by Black patrons in Dresden was "alien" or "strange" to the wider Canadian experience. Although these themes were not found in all articles or letters and at times were contested or contradicted by other reports, they appeared continually and consistently, and their repetition helped to frame how the Dresden story was reported generally by Canadian newspapers. A more detailed examination of these themes therefore can provide some insight into how newspaper reporting on Dresden reinforced the idea of Canada as raceless even while presenting an example of overt forms of racial discrimination against Black Canadians.

More than half of the articles published in the months leading up to the plebiscite in Dresden and in its immediate aftermath included references to the town's history as a terminus of the Underground Railroad. Dresden was commonly described as the "location of Uncle Tom's Cabin" or the home and burial site of "Uncle Tom" himself. It is worth noting that journalists rarely referred to Josiah Henson by his proper name or to the Dawn Settlement. This in itself reveals the extent to which the narrative of the Underground Railroad supplanted the true history of Black migrants to the areas surrounding Dresden. Prefacing reports of the upcoming plebiscite and the racial discrimination that inspired it were descriptions of Dresden's history as a "haven for runaway Negro slaves from the United States."[67] In several cases, more than half of an article was taken up with these descriptions, followed by only a brief account of the plebiscite and the contemporary complaints by Black residents. References to "Uncle Tom's Cabin" and the Underground Railroad persisted through the entire period of newspaper coverage under study, indicating to readers that this was an important aspect of the story.[68]

A key component of this reporting was the positioning of Dresden (and by extension Canada) as historical sanctuaries for Black peoples from the brutality of slavery in the southern United States. This component reinforced the "North Star" ideology in which slavery and violence against Black peoples was a feature of American, but not Canadian, history. For instance, the Toronto *Globe and Mail* reminded readers that Dresden had given "sanctuary to fugitive slaves a generation before American Negroes were emancipated."[69] A subsequent article in that paper claimed that "the entire town [had been] the escape centre for Negro slaves fleeing from the United States."[70] The authors make clear that Canada historically was a safer and more welcoming space for Black peoples than the United States and that the act of offering sanctuary was a communal experience, shared in this case by "the entire town" and, by inference, all Canadians.

The Underground Railroad is understood to be a defining moment for Canada. As Afua Cooper points out, "the image of Canada as 'freedom's land' has lodged itself in the national psyche and become part of our national identity."[71] The consequence of this, according to Katherine McKittrick, is that "many histories begin to disappear within the discursive celebratory confines of the Underground Railroad,"[72] including histories of discrimination and violence against Black Canadians. Although the reality of racial discrimination in Dresden in the 1940s and 1950s was never denied by newspaper reports, it was often qualified in the context of Dresden's longer history as a "safe haven," with this qualification at times taking up more space than reporting on the discrimination itself. References to "Uncle Tom" in particular were used to juxtapose this history with the contemporary "problem" that Dresden was having with racial discrimination. Headlines such as "Uncle Tom's Town Turns Down Negroes" and "Negro Discrimination Where Uncle Tom Is Buried" and comments that "Uncle Tom sleeps uneasily" exemplify how Dresden's historical connection to the Underground Railroad was used to make the refusal of restaurants and barbershops to serve Black customers all the more unexpected and out of step with the town's past.[73]

Instead, prejudice and segregation were presented as American problems. It was common for articles to characterize the racial discrimination in Dresden using terms and references that linked the town to the United States through a form of shared practice.[74] Barrington Walker argues that Dresden had become known popularly as the "Alabama of the North";[75]

this was reflected in the print media coverage from the beginning. The first article on Dresden, a *Windsor Star* editorial written in 1948, described the town as a place where "hard-working, respectable [Black] citizens are forced to buy their refreshments and carry them home to eat," remarking that "that's the same as the Deep South."[76] The discriminatory practices in Dresden were described as "Jim Crowism," and headlines such as "Jim Crow Lives in Dresden," "Jim Crow in Ontario Town," and "Jim Crow Line Drawn in Small Town Ontario" stressed the relationship between the racial discrimination in Dresden and the legalized system of racial segregation in parts of the United States.[77] Some of the articles were more explicit than others, with an article in the Montreal *Gazette* describing the unfair practices in Dresden as coming "by way of the 'Jim Crow' treatment in some American states."[78] It is worth noting that Black community newspapers in the 1940s also reflected this connection between Dresden and the southern United States. The *Clarion,* a newsletter in New Glasgow, Nova Scotia, printed an article outlining the discrimination in Dresden with the title "Canada or Dixie?" Similar headlines such as "Dresden or Dixie?" and "Mississippi – Dresden?" were also used by the *Canadian Negro* newspaper in Toronto.[79]

Although Black Canadians and the activists involved in the campaigns for fair practices laws might have recognized Jim Crow as well established in Canada, in the mainstream press coverage "Jim Crowism" was depicted as American.[80] This should be taken not as an argument that it was not a continental phenomenon but that it was not presented that way by the mainstream (white) press. Instead, it was presented as an American phenomenon manifesting itself in Dresden, a town that historically had been a "safe haven" for American slaves. This American influence was a real subject of concern, for contributors worried about its effect on Canada. John D. Bowley from Hamilton wrote a letter in 1951 urging the provincial government to deal quickly with the racial discrimination in Dresden, referring to it as a "shadow which has too closely allied us with outbreaks of racial intolerance as we have observed them in the United States."[81] A *Globe and Mail* article claimed that the people of Dresden had "failed the test" in not supporting the plebiscite to ban racial discrimination, thus bringing "shame" to the town and all of Ontario.[82] In voting to allow restaurant owners to discriminate based on race, colour, or creed, Dresden's citizens "approved a practice differing only in degree from the extreme Jim Crowism that is slowly becoming obsolete in the Deep South."[83] In a letter printed in the Victoria *Times Colonist,* one reader asked: "If discrimination is practiced in Dresden, what is to stop it from spreading to other Canadian cities and towns?"[84]

This argument relied on framing Dresden and its practices as an exception within Canada, a country relatively free from such racism. This was in line with a commonly held belief in the postwar period that any discrimination that did exist in Canada was the result of individual infractions rather than larger societal problems and that incidents of prejudice were isolated rather than indicative of systemic behaviours. Rights activists and members of minority groups resisted this understanding of discrimination, and the depiction of Canada as a country with no problem with racism or prejudice, but it was an uphill battle. It certainly appeared in the press coverage of Dresden. Some articles were more explicit than others. *Globe and Mail* columnist Frank Tumpane stated that "this is Canada, where everybody has equal rights, whether his skin is black, brown, or white. That tradition took a long time to establish. And it is a good tradition."[85] Others referred to Canada as "an example to the world" and a country "built on a cornerstone of tolerance to all races and creeds."[86] Many articles did acknowledge the reality of some racial and other forms of discrimination across the country but continued to present the practices in Dresden as out of line with Canadian values and traditions.[87] In speaking to Canada's track record, one reader wrote in to say that "Canadians in general have been inclined to consider the color bar as applied to negroes to be a particular anachronism of the United States. They will be surprised, therefore, to learn that the issue has been raised in the small Ontario town of Dresden." The author went on to claim that this was "a problem that should never arise in Canada."[88] Even local and regional newspapers presented Dresden as an exception to the "racial harmony" experienced in nearby towns. Chatham, only thirty kilometres from Dresden, was described as tolerant and harmonious, and the discrimination in Dresden was all the more "strange" because there were no such problems in cities such as Windsor or Toronto.[89] These stories were picked up by newspapers across the country.[90]

Adoption of the Fair Accommodation Practices Act had an interesting effect on the newspaper coverage of Dresden. Although reports shifted to cover and comment on the failure of businesses in Dresden to comply with the law, and to analyze its effectiveness, the idea that Ontario (and therefore Canada) had somehow righted themselves with the passage of such laws (even if it was thought that the laws were lacking) was clear in many of the articles. Newspapers quoted rights activists who claimed that "the new laws passed in [Ontario] have made Canada a world leader in the fight against racial intolerance."[91] McKay's prosecution, appeals, and final conviction were covered in great detail, acting as a bookend or conclusion to the story, often ignoring other forms of inequity or systemic racism that persisted. In its final article on Dresden in 1956, the *Globe and Mail* spoke of "a happy story about the town where the original Uncle Tom was buried." The article described Black customers entering Kay's Café in late 1956, being "served with a smile," and emerging with smiles themselves.[92] In total disregard of the eight years of strain that the campaign placed on Dresden, the article finished with a quotation from Morley McKay himself as he reflected on the relationship between himself and Black residents: "We get along fine."[93] Such reporting allowed the Dresden story to be reconciled with the broader narrative of Canada as a friendly and welcoming space for all people in contrast to the racial violence gripping the Deep South.

CONCLUSION

Other studies have analyzed in more detail than I have here the strategies used to lobby the provincial government to pass fair practices laws and how events in Dresden were tied to these campaigns. My purpose in this chapter has been to consider instead why, when Dresden could act successfully as an example for activists to push for stronger human rights laws, it could not erode the conventional wisdom of many Canadians in the postwar period that Canada was a raceless and tolerant nation that promoted equality for all. To do so, I have examined how the Dresden story was covered in English-language newspapers across the country to assess how racial discrimination was framed and to understand better the cultural attitudes toward and understandings of prejudice, anti-Black racism, and human rights in 1940s and 1950s Canada. What I have found is perplexing: the example of Dresden, though useful in pushing for expanded human rights protection, and significant in that it ended overt aspects of racial discrimination in the town, could also be used to reinforce and reproduce narratives of Canada as largely a "race-neutral" country and thus a "safe haven" for Black peoples.

How is that possible? The answer is complex, but in this chapter I have tackled one aspect by demonstrating the influence of American history and postwar developments in the United States on how Canadians conceptualized discrimination, supporting a view of racism and segregation as American problems and therefore un-Canadian. Newspapers framed racism in Dresden as out of step with its past as a sanctuary for enslaved Black Americans and mobilized American images and examples to connect the practices of business owners in Dresden with the Jim Crow laws of the Deep South and therefore as exceptional within Canada. Although there were voices that challenged these ideas, they were not amplified in the press, and the messaging was broad and consistent enough to allow the example of overt practices of racial discrimination in Dresden to coexist with, and even reinforce, beliefs in Canada as "freedom's land."

This story has relevance today. Canadians continue to use the United States, its history, and its contemporary developments as a foil to present Canada as a safer, kinder, and more tolerant place for Black and other racialized peoples. The media continue to contribute to this perception, as does how Canadians are educated on topics such as Black history, human rights history, and Canadian history generally. We continue to look across the border with concern – and some air of superiority. Until this view changes, it will be hard for us to acknowledge historical and systemic forms of discrimination and to challenge narratives of Canada as historically, and contemporarily, raceless.

NOTES

1 The question and the results were printed in newspaper reports across the country.
2 James W. St.G. Walker, "The 'Jewish Phase' in the Movement for Racial Equality in Canada," *Canadian Ethnic Studies* 34, 1 (2002): 14.
3 Ross Lambertson, "'The Dresden Story': Racism, Human Rights, and the Jewish Labour Committee of Canada," *Labour/Le travail* 47 (2001): 79. See also Ross Lambertson,

Repression and Resistance: Canadian Human Rights Activists, 1930–1960 (Toronto: University of Toronto Press, 2005), 281–317.

4 John Cooper, *Season of Rage: Hugh Burnett and the Struggle for Civil Rights* (Toronto: Tundra Books, 2005).

5 The plaque is located in Dresden at the intersection of St. George and St. John streets. The text can be found online at https://www.heritagetrust.on.ca/pages/programs/provincial-plaque-program/provincial-plaque-background-papers/hugh-burnett-and-the-nua.

6 The play was written by Aaron Haddad in 2019 and performed throughout the year by Flex We Talent, a theatre group made up of members of Caribbean heritage.

7 The terms "Black Canadian" and "African Canadian" are used interchangeably by some historians. In this chapter, I use the term "Black Canadian" to include those in postwar Canada who traced their heritage to Africa or the Caribbean. The term is capitalized to signify their history and racial identity. The term "Negro" was used commonly in postwar Canada to refer to people of African origin. This term is only used when quoted in its original context.

8 Mary Dudziak, *Cold War Civil Rights: Race and the Image of American Democracy* (Princeton, NJ: Princeton University Press, 2000); Brenda Gayle Plummer, ed., *Window on Freedom: Race, Civil Rights, and Foreign Affairs, 1945–1988* (Chapel Hill: University of North Carolina Press, 2003); Thomas Borstelmann, *The Cold War and the Color Line: American Race Relations in the Global Arena* (Cambridge, MA: Harvard University Press, 2001).

9 The community was first named Fairport, but the name changed to Dresden in the 1850s. Cooper, *Season of Rage*, 14.

10 Josiah Henson, *Life of Josiah Henson: Formerly a Slave* (Boston: Arthur D. Phelps, 1849).

11 Heritage Trust Ontario, "Josiah Henson Museum of African-Canadian History," https://www.heritagetrust.on.ca/properties/josiah-henson-museum.

12 Ibid.

13 Graham Reynolds, *Viola Desmond's Canada: A History of Blacks and Segregation in the Promised Land* (Black Point, NS: Fernwood, 2016), 54. For a thorough discussion of the geographic distribution of Blacks in Canada, see Joseph Mensah, *Black Canadians, History, Experience, Social Conditions*, 2nd ed. (Black Point, NS: Fernwood, 2010).

14 Lambertson, "Dresden Story," 61; Sidney Katz, "Jim Crow Lives in Dresden," *Maclean's*, 1 November 1949, 8.

15 Katz, "Jim Crow Lives in Dresden"; Walker, "The 'Jewish Phase,'" 12; Lambertson, "Dresden Story," 61.

16 For a discussion of early ideas of rights in Canadian society, see Dominique Clément, *Human Rights in Canada: A History* (Waterloo, ON: Wilfrid Laurier University Press, 2016).

17 James W. St.G. Walker, *"Race," Rights and the Law in the Supreme Court of Canada: Historical Case Studies* (Waterloo: Wilfrid Laurier University Press, 1997); Constance Backhouse, *Colour-Coded: A Legal History of Racism in Canada, 1900–1950* (Toronto: University of Toronto Press, 1999); Barrington Walker, *Race on Trial: Black Defendants in Ontario's Criminal Courts, 1858–1958* (Toronto: University of Toronto Press, 2010).

18 *Christie v York Corporation*, [1940] SCR 139, at 142.

19 Lambertson, *Repression and Resistance*, Chapter 1.

20 Statutes of Ontario, 1944, c 51; Brian R. Howe, "The Evolution of Human Rights Policy in Ontario," *Canadian Journal of Political Science* 24, 4 (1991): 788.

21 Walker, *Race on Trial*, 3.

22 Barrington Walker, "Finding Jim Crow in Canada, 1789–1967," in *A History of Human Rights in Canada: Essential Issues*, ed. Janet Miron (Toronto: Canadian Scholars' Press, 2009), 81.

23 Cooper, *Season of Rage*, 19.

24 In the period under study, Burnett signed his name "Burnette," and in the media coverage from the period it was always spelled that way. According to James Walker (who came to know Hugh personally) and Ross Lambertson, Burnett changed the spelling later in life after finding a family tombstone with the spelling "Burnett," so historians commonly use that spelling. See Lambertson, "Dresden Story," 62n55.

25 Cooper, *Season of Rage*, 26; Lambertson, "Dresden Story," 62.

26 Anthony S. Chen, "The Party of Lincoln and the Politics of State Fair Employment Practices Legislation in the North, 1945–1964," *American Journal of Sociology* 112, 6 (2007): 1713–74.

27 Walker, "The 'Jewish Phase'"; Carmela Patrias and Ruth A. Frager, "'This Is Our Country, These Are Our Rights': Minorities and the Origins of Ontario's Human Rights Campaigns," *Canadian Historical Review* 82, 1 (2001): 1–35; Lambertson, "Dresden Story."

28 Cooper, *Season of Rage*, 31.

29 Katz, "Jim Crow Lives in Dresden," 9.

30 Lambertson, "Dresden Story," 69.

31 For an outline of the development of provincial anti-discrimination laws, see Brian Howe, *Restraining Equality: Human Rights Commissions in Canada* (Toronto: University of Toronto Press, 2000), 8.

32 Lambertson, "Dresden Story," 69.

33 In the brief sent to the government, the delegation wrote that "the height of expression of Jim Crow in Canada is to be found in the town of Dresden, Ontario." Quoted in Lambertson, "Dresden Story," 69, 70n88.

34 Julian Biggs, dir., *The Dresden Story*, National Film Board of Canada, 1954, https://www.nfb.ca/film/dresden_story/.

35 The legal argument from McKay was that, though he did refuse to serve Black customers, he did so because the majority of his (white) clientele indicated that they would stop coming to the restaurant if he changed his policy. McKay used the arguments that had worked effectively in the case against Fred Christie only a decade earlier, that it was his "right of commerce" to serve, or not serve, whom he chose. This was heavily reported by the media at the time.

36 Armstrong expressed these sentiments in an interview in 2008. Kenneth Kidd, "Amid Sweeping Change, a Pivotal Anniversary Goes Unremarked," *Toronto Star*, 9 July 2008.

37 Esmeralda Thornhill, "So Seldom for Us, So Often against Us: Blacks and the Law in Canada," *Journal of Black Studies* 38, 3 (2008): 322.

38 See, for example, Afua Cooper, *The Hanging of Angélique: The Untold Story of Canadian Slavery and the Burning of Old Montreal* (Toronto: HarperCollins, 2005);

Harvey Amani Whitfield, *North to Bondage: Loyalist Slavery in the Maritimes* (Vancouver: UBC Press, 2016); Reynolds, *Viola Desmond's Canada;* Karen Flynn, *Moving beyond Borders: A History of Black Canadians and Caribbean Women in the Diaspora* (Toronto: University of Toronto Press, 2011); and David Austin, *Fear of a Black Nation: Race, Sex, and Security in Sixties Montreal* (Toronto: Between the Lines, 2013).

39 Cooper, *The Hanging of Angélique,* 7.

40 The majority of slaves in New France were Indigenous. Local records reveal 1,132 Black slaves in the colony. After the British conquest, the number of Black slaves increased significantly. Robin Winks, *The Blacks in Canada: A History,* 2nd ed. (Montreal and Kingston: McGill-Queen's University Press, 1997), 9.

41 Reynolds, *Viola Desmond's Canada,* 37. See also Whitfield, *North to Bondage;* and Cooper, *The Hanging of Angélique.*

42 Cooper, *The Hanging of Angélique,* 99.

43 Abigail B. Bakan, "Reconsidering the Underground Railroad: Slavery and Racialization in the Making of the Canadian State," *Social Studies* 4, 1 (2008): 5.

44 Many returned to the United States during and at the conclusion of the American Civil War. This number is quoted in numerous sources, including "Black History in Canada," Library and Archives Canada, https://www.bac-lac.gc.ca/eng/discover/immigration/history-ethnic-cultural/Pages/blacks.aspx.

45 Katherine McKittrick, "Freedom Is a Secret: The Future Usability of the Underground," in *Black Geographies and the Politics of Place,* ed. Katherine McKittrick and Clyde Woods (Toronto: Between the Lines, 2007), 98.

46 Backhouse, *Colour-Coded,* 13; Walker, *Race on Trial,* 4.

47 James W. St.G. Walker, "Decoding the Rights Revolution: Lessons from the Canadian Experience," in *Taking Liberties: A History of Human Rights in Canada,* ed. David Goutor and Stephen Heathorn (Don Mills, ON: Oxford University Press, 2013), 37.

48 Ian Tyrrell, "Reflections of the Transnational Turn in United States History: Theory and Practice," *Journal of Global History* 4, 3 (2009): 462.

49 Wendell Adjetey, "Policing Race: Rethinking the Myth of National Exceptionalism in a Canadian Context," Knowledge and Action, Humanity in Action, 2015, https://www.humanityinaction.org/knowledge_detail/policing-race-rethinking-the-myth-of-national-exceptionalism-in-a-canadian-context/.

50 Rosanne Waters, "A March from Selma to Canada: Canada and the Transnational Civil Rights Movement" (PhD diss., McMaster University, 2015), 11.

51 James W. St.G. Walker, *Racial Discrimination in Canada: The Black Experience,* Canadian Historical Association Booklets 41 (Ottawa: Canadian Historical Association, 1985), 6.

52 Winks, *The Blacks in Canada,* 448.

53 The time frame reflects the period between the first newspaper reports on complaints of racial discrimination in Dresden (1948) and the final court decision against Morley McKay and the opening of his restaurant to Black customers (1956). I analyzed 153 newspaper articles spread across twenty-three different newspapers, including newspapers in the areas surrounding Dresden (Windsor and Chatham), newspapers from Canada's largest cities (Vancouver, Calgary, Edmonton, Winnipeg, Toronto, Ottawa,

Montreal, and Halifax), as well as smaller cities and towns (Nanaimo, Victoria, Langley, Regina, Saskatoon, London, Brockville, and New Glasgow). To find articles, I screened hundreds of records retrieved from various online newspaper databases.

54 Gene Allen, *Making National News: A History of Canadian Press* (Toronto: University of Toronto Press, 2013); Gene Allen and Daniel J. Robinson, *Communicating in Canada's Past: Essays in Media History* (Toronto: University of Toronto Press, 2009); William J. Buxton and Catherine McKercher, "Newspapers, Magazines and Journalism in Canada: Towards a Critical Historiography," *Acadiensis* 28, 1 (1998): 103–26.

55 In his study of the role of print capitalism in twentieth-century Canada, Gerald Friesen agrees that newspapers could draw ordinary Canadians "into a *single* community." Gerald Friesen, *Citizens and Nation: An Essay on History, Communication, and Canada* (Toronto: University of Toronto Press, 2000), 162. Benedict Anderson discusses the power of print capitalism to awaken national imaginings in the second chapter of *Imagined Communities: Reflections on the Origin and Spread of Nationalism* (New York: Knopf Doubleday, 1983).

56 See, for example, Norman Fairclough, *Critical Discourse Analysis: The Critical Study of Language,* 2nd ed. (New York: Routledge, 2013).

57 Vivian Gornick, "Introduction," in *Gender Advertisements,* ed. Erving Goffman (Cambridge, MA: Harvard University Press, 1979), vii–ix.

58 Maxwell E. McCombs and Donald Shaw, "The Agenda-Setting Function of Mass Media," *Public Opinion Quarterly* 36, 2 (1972): 176–87.

59 Robert M. Entman, "Framing: Toward Clarification of a Fractured Paradigm," *Journal of Communications* 43, 4 (1993): 51–58.

60 Ibid., 52.

61 Stephanie Bangarth, *Voices Raised in Protest: Defending North American Citizens of Japanese Ancestry, 1942–49* (Vancouver: UBC Press, 2008), 101–7.

62 "Colored Men Sue Montreal Tavern," *Windsor Star,* 12 September 1936, 1; "Court Bars Color Line in Tavern; Awards $25 to Excluded Negro," Montreal *Gazette,* 25 March 1937, 1; "Can't Compel Serving of Beer to Negro," *Edmonton Journal,* 9 December 1939, 1.

63 "Halifax Woman to Take Action against New Glasgow Theatre Man," *Halifax Chronicle,* 30 November 1936, 2; "Theatre Sued over Ejection of Negress," *Vancouver Sun,* 20 November 1946, 11; "Desmond Appeal Decision Later," Saskatoon *Star-Phoenix,* 14 March 1947, 14.

64 Waters, "A March from Selma to Canada," 24.

65 "Negro Opposition to Separate School," Regina *Leader-Post,* 20 January 1948, 8.

66 "A Happy Ending: Two Taste of Town's Tolerance," *Globe and Mail,* 25 December 1956, 1.

67 See, for example, "Technicality Blocks Vote," *Calgary Herald,* 18 April 1949, 3; and "Dresden Puts Off Race Referendum on Technicality," *Globe and Mail,* 19 April 1949, 28.

68 These references appeared as late as 1955 in newspapers as close to Dresden as the *Windsor Star.* See "Dresden Cafe Man Faces Trial," *Windsor Star,* 24 November 1955, 1.

69 "Dresden Draws the Color Line," *Globe and Mail,* 8 December 1949, 6.

70 "Union Convention Raps Race Discrimination," *Globe and Mail,* 4 February 1953, 9.

71 Cooper, *The Hanging of Angélique,* 69.

72 McKittrick, "Freedom Is a Secret," 98.

73 "Uncle Tom's Town Turns Down Negroes," *Edmonton Journal,* 6 December 1949, 1; "Negro Discrimination Where Uncle Tom Is Buried," *Ottawa Journal,* 11 December 1943, 41; Katz, "Jim Crow Lives in Dresden," 8.

74 At times, Germany was also used as a reference, especially given that the town of Dresden was named after a town in Germany.

75 Walker, "Finding Jim Crow in Canada," 92.

76 R.M. Harrison, "Now," *Windsor Star,* 25 May 1948, 15.

77 Katz, "Jim Crow Lives in Dresden"; "Jim Crow in Ontario Town," *Vancouver Sun,* 6 December 1949, 6; "Jim Crow Line Drawn in Small Town Ontario," *Edmonton Journal,* 7 April 1949, 1.

78 "New Communism Endangers," Montreal *Gazette,* 17 January 1955, 13.

79 Carrie Best, "Canada or Dixie?," *Clarion* 2, 11 (1947): 1; "Dresden or Dixie?," *Canadian Negro* 2, 4 (1954): 2; John White, "Mississippi – Dresden?," *Canadian Negro* 3, 4 (1955): 1.

80 Walker, "Jim Crow in Canada," 81.

81 John D. Bowley, "Legislative Action Is Suggested," letter to the editor, *Globe and Mail,* 4 January 1950, 6.

82 "Dresden Draws the Color Line," *Globe and Mail,* 8 December 1949, 6.

83 Ibid.

84 "Super-Racism?," Victoria *Times Colonist,* 8 April 1949, 4.

85 Frank Tumpane, "It Isn't a Popularity Contest," *Globe and Mail,* 1 September 1954, 3.

86 See, for example, "Brief Urges Ontario Bar Intolerance," *Windsor Star,* 25 January 1950, 18.

87 "Dresden Electors to Vote on Race Issue," *Calgary Herald,* 7 April 1949, 1; "Dresden Delays Race Vote Owing to 'Bad Publicity,'" *Windsor Star,* 3 May 1949, 1.

88 "Super-Racism?," Victoria *Times Colonist,* 8 April 1949, 4.

89 "Racial Harmony, Tolerance Make Chathamites Proud," *Windsor Star,* 24 July 1948, 10.

90 For example, "Dresden Electors to Vote on Race Issue," *Calgary Herald,* 7 April 1949, 1.

91 Ron Haggart, "New TLC Leader Says Canada Leads World in Racial Intolerance," *Globe and Mail,* 27 August 1954, 10.

92 "A Happy Ending: Two Taste of Town's Tolerance," *Globe and Mail,* 25 December 1956, 1.

93 Ibid.

8

Between Distrust and Acceptance
The Influence of the United States
on Postwar Quebec

FRANÇOIS-OLIVIER DORAIS AND DANIEL POITRAS

The destiny of the United States is of supreme importance to us French Canadians. The American civilization represents a current of ideas, aspirations and sympathies by which we are strongly influenced and in which we will hardly be able to resist being drawn; this is why it is important for us to see clearly in its orientation, not to let ourselves be dazzled by false mirages and to put ourselves in a position to make a choice in what it offers to our imitation.

– EDMOND DE NEVERS, *L'ÂME AMÉRICAINE*, 1900

Readers for whom the idea that Quebec was marked by the "great darkness" (*grande noirceur*, 1860–1960), a period in Quebec history supposedly darkened by obscurantism, fear of the unknown, and isolation, might be surprised to read this quotation from Edmond de Nevers, which dates back to the beginning of the twentieth century. By breaking down the constructed category of the Quiet Revolution (1960–66) as the signifier of a great leap forward in Quebec's progress,[1] we see in this quotation several phenomena in a different light. Often associated with the dominant figure of Maurice Duplessis and the ascendancy of clerical nationalism, the decades prior to the 1960s in Quebec were not regressive or inward looking. Rather, these decades, in particular those of the immediate postwar period, show a society in constant and deep redefinition of itself, one searching for a way forward, re-examining its relationship to tradition, weighing its adherence to modernity, and re-evaluating the imprint of its external or foreign legacies. In this regard, the United States, which had become the new world power after the Second World War, had also acquired a new referential value in the Quebec imagination – one now more open to its influence.

Omnipresent in the history of cultural and material life of Quebec, nevertheless, in contrast to the abundant historiography on France-Quebec relations, the powerful neighbour to the south has not received sustained attention from historians. This blind spot can be explained by the tenacious tradition of anti-Americanism and anti-imperialism of nineteenth-century and twentieth-century Quebec, which painted the United States as a permanent threat to the identity and future of Francophones. However, the complexity of American influence on Quebec and its associated discourse tend to challenge this reduction. Indeed, Quebec's relationship with the United States suggests intertwined and ambivalent processes, which historian Yvan Lamonde ably summarizes as "neither with them nor without them."[2] The proximity of the two countries implied necessarily frequent relations that resulted in links – if not close ones, then at least real ones, always oscillating between distrust and acceptance. Thus, the postwar period in Quebec offers a privileged point of observation from which to probe the US-Quebec relationship, a time when American influence came to be perceived less as fate and more as opportunity. Moreover, during the postwar period, Quebec's relationship with the United States became a sign of its continental roots, torn constantly among an increasingly distant France, Great Britain, and Rome and a less and less contested American anchorage.

In this chapter, we provide an overview of the evolution of Quebec's perceptions of the United States and their effective influence on the economic, cultural, political, and intellectual life of Quebec in the particular context of the Second World War. After an overview of the preceding period (1900–39), when anti-Americanism was at its strongest, we highlight the importance of the war as a turning point. Highlighting the specificities of American influence in the years that followed, we demonstrate how this influence was exerted not only through several mediums – including radio and television – but also through visits by several Quebec artists and academics to the United States itself. These individuals, many of whom participated in the transformation of Quebec in the following decades, returned from the United States transformed by their experiences there.

THE SPECTRE OF AMERICANIZATION
(1900–39)

Quebec entered the twentieth century with questions about its future. The disenchanted promises of Confederation, the Riel affair of 1885, the allegiances shaken by the Boer War, and the succession of school crises in Manitoba (1890), Alberta (1905), Saskatchewan (1909), and Ontario (1912) served as breeding grounds for French Canadian nationalism. At the turn of the twentieth century, Quebec sought to define a specifically French and Catholic course of action in North America, in other words to form a French Canadian "reserve" within the constitutional arrangement of 1867. First fortified in the meetings of the Ligue nationaliste (1903), the columns of *Le Devoir* (1910), and the summaries of *L'Action française* (1917–28), this nationalist revival was based on a powerfully articulated critique of the two imperialisms – Yankee and British.[3] The old annexationist temptation promoted by a group of French-speaking liberals,[4] a possible and desired outcome in the nineteenth century, now had no more than a few supporters in Quebec. Thus, in the twentieth century, the consequences of American imperialism and its expansionist tendencies continued to be understood and feared. In *L'âme américaine* (1900), Nevers anticipated the need for a great perspective on the development of the United States and, according to him, the inevitable integration of North America into a single and vast republic. In this project, he emphasized, French Canada would have to make "its contribution to the intellectual progress, morality and variety of the union."[5] Meanwhile, Jules-Paul Tardivel, himself an American by birth, warned French Canadians against the prosperous image of their southern neighbour. In his journal, *La Vérité*, on 11 March 1899, Tardivel criticized American "Protestantism," "Liberalism," and "Masonism," those "modern errors" that "by diverting man's thoughts from the imperishable goods of heaven, tend necessarily to develop material prosperity."[6] Reacting to the stirrings of the annexationist scarecrow during the federal election campaign in 1911 – in which free trade with the United States was a defining issue – in *The Spectre of Annexation* (1912), the influential intellectual Henri Bourassa worried about "the universal contagion of American ideals, morals and mentality." According to him, the contagion had already introduced to Canada "party despotism, the abuse of political influence, the domination of finance, the venality of politicians and the corruption of public bodies."[7]

Thus, by the beginning of the century, the othering of the American republic, which certainly had been reinforced by Pope Leo XIII's condemnation of "Americanism" in 1899, had become part of the developing French Canadian nationalist discourse seeking to assert its national and religious specificity in relation to the outside world.[8] In a way, the French Canadian had become the opposite figure to the American. A reminder of an old *topos* inaugurated by Antoine Gérin-Lajoie and Henri-Raymond Casgrain in the nineteenth century, this figure was repeated in 1913 in Louis Hémon's famous novel *Maria Chapdelaine*, which made the crossing of the American border a social and cultural ban. This concern was also fuelled by the effective and increasingly visible economic and structural presence of the United States on Quebec territory at the beginning of the twentieth century. Very visible, this presence could be seen in the massive investment of Anglo-American capital in the exploitation of the province's natural resources, the establishment of international unions in Quebec factories, the increased presence of skyscrapers in Old Montreal modelled on the architectural program of American economic liberalism, or the attractiveness of New England factories to which Francophones had been emigrating massively since the middle of the nineteenth century.[9] The last phenomenon, in particular, despaired the French Canadian elites. According to some, this was a sign, among others, of a persistent social divide between the clerical elites and the francophone working class regarding the perception of the United States and Americanization.[10] In addition, American influence could be found in the pages of Quebec newspapers supplied with dispatches from the American Press Association as well as the circulation of American magazines in urban areas and the popularization of jazz clubs and burlesque cabarets. The craze for Hollywood movies in Quebec, tickets for which sold at very low prices, was accompanied by the increasingly widespread practice of certain American sports, such as baseball. On the other side of the border, however, Anglicization was taking a disturbing toll. This toll was felt especially by the new generations of Franco-Americans whose prospect of repatriation to Quebec as a result of a deteriorating economic climate was as worrying as the tourist frenzy at the resorts of Maine. The relatively popular acceptance of these American penetrations, which contrasted with the more pronounced rejection of the dangers and pitfalls of English Canadian contact, reinforced the anti-American discourse of a new cohort of nationalist thinkers. This cohort was led most notably by the clergy during the 1920s, and especially the 1930s, when the economic crisis was used as a convincing argument to illustrate the impasses of the Great Republic's materialism.

For historian Damien-Claude Bélanger, the anti-Americanism asserting itself in French Canada at the time converged with English Canadian imperialist thought. The former would come later to focus more on social, moral, and cultural issues, whereas the latter, especially vigorous between 1891 and 1911, was concerned more with the future of political institutions and the imperial bond and tended to focus on political and diplomatic themes. Both, however, proceeded from a similar distrust of liberal modernity, whose worst emanations were considered embodied by the United States: the obsolescence of traditional modes of production by industrial civilization; the replacement of faith by scientific and anthropocentric thinking; the erosion of traditional culture by the rise of mass consumer culture; and the triumph of revolutionary change over continuity, order, and deference.[11] Among the panoply of French Canadian intellectuals who denounced American influence, Victor Barbeau was certainly one of the most prominent: "They crush us with their national life. We seem to exist only to congratulate ourselves on having them as neighbors and to strive to resemble them as much as possible."[12] Canon Lionel Groulx, among the most influential intellectuals in interwar Quebec and then at the height of his career, was not to be outdone: "It seems that this people [the Americans] aims lower than God, which, for a Christian civilization, is the beginning of all disorder."[13] Criticism of Americanism reached its peak in 1936 in the pages of the *Revue dominicaine,* which devoted a special investigation to the facts and misdeeds of "our Americanization," that "long-standing encirclement" whose consequences were felt in all spheres of life. The first article in this issue stated that the American neighbour was feared for its "contagion of paganism" and, more particularly, its "naturalism," oriented, straight out of the cult of the "god-dollar," toward "material comfort" and "enjoyment egoism." This would translate in Quebec as "a weariness of the effort towards the supernatural and a search more and more disposed to be satisfied with the conquest of a corner of the earth: material ease, if not wealth."[14] To accentuate the fundamental irreconcilability of French Canadian and American cultures, these passages demonstrate how frequently anti-American rhetoric at the time relied on the analogy of an organism "contaminated" by a foreign agent.

The clerical elite in Quebec and its nationalist and traditionalist constellation had every interest in resisting American absorption in all its forms. First, what was at stake was the cultural survival of the French Canadian people, whose linguistic and religious integrity was clearly being threatened by migrants from the "little Canada" of the northeastern United States. Second, it is important to consider here the distant heritage, since the conquest of 1763, of the Catholic Church's tradition of loyalty, at least of its high dignitaries, toward the British Crown and power. This loyalty allowed the church and its elite to negotiate a relative margin of autonomy in Quebec in the management of parishes, schools, colleges, and universities. Just the prospect of having to cede these privileges was enough to make the clergy repel any idea of annexation with the United States, where a more liberal and egalitarian culture would threaten their ascendancy in society.

With the advent of the Second World War, anti-Americanism in Quebec would fade, giving way to a search for an original American inscription of French Canada. As we will see, a fundamental change in the modulation of the US-Quebec relationship would take place at this time. Although it would remain a structuring dimension of postwar traditionalist discourse, by the end of the 1960s, right-wing anti-Americanism would disappear almost completely in favour of a more pronounced left-wing critique of American militarism and conservatism[15] and Quebec youth's fascination with American counterculture.

THE SECOND WORLD WAR: A TURNING POINT

Just as the Hitlerization of Europe would prepare the Hitlerization of the globe, so an Americanization of Europe would prepare an Americanization of the globe. The second evil is less than the first, but in both cases, humanity would lose its past.

— SIMONE WEIL, *HISTORICAL AND POLITICAL WRITINGS*, 1943[16]

As elsewhere in the West, the Second World War brought about a number of changes in Quebec, among them a change in the representation of the United States, which had now acquired a new referential and strategic value. The outbreak of a global conflict and German domination of Europe shifted perspectives and encouraged Canadian political elites to follow a policy of increasingly close collaboration with the United States. This shift was sealed by the signing of joint trade and defence agreements.[17] Furthermore, between 1942 and 1944, in a lab on Mount Royal that later would become part of the Université de Montréal campus, the Canadian, American, and British governments sponsored research contributing to the development of the atomic bomb.[18] Moreover, the slow process of metropolitan disengagement from Great Britain – which had begun in 1918 and was authenticated by the Statute of Westminster (1931) – coupled with the fall of France in June 1940, an event experienced as an "intimate upheaval,"[19] precipitated a reflection among Québécois on the collective self and its external allegiances. This was especially evident in a major survey launched in November 1940 by *L'Action nationale*, the most influential journal of ideas in Quebec at the time. The journal called on the perspectives of more than fifty French Canadian intellectuals and artists regarding the future of

French Canadian culture. The diversity of responses reflected the recomposition of identity markers in action. Some called for a retreat to France and its heritage, others for a renewed association with English Canada, others still for a more forthright affirmation of Quebec's American destiny.[20] In the words of Pierre Popovic, at this time "America gradually went from being a threat to being evidence, a test and finally a risk to be taken."[21]

This (re)problematization of the US-Quebec relationship was most explicitly expressed perhaps in 1941 when various titles on the subject were published in the space of a few months. In his *Reflets d'Amérique*, Édouard Montpetit presented the United States as a nation of progress that, in the face of European totalitarianisms, would come to embody the new figure of the universal.[22] Under his pen, the American other took on the trappings of a renovating ideal whose "social dream of regeneration and happiness" likely would inspire the development of Quebec society.[23] Similarly, the immoderate American taste for money, advertising, and speculation, certainly reprehensible in many respects, had a positive impact on Quebec, for example by stimulating the development of its professional schools. For Montpetit, it was necessary that Quebec learn to "make use of American progress" while maintaining the right to "fortify [the] French attitude."[24] In other words, French Canada had to "hitch the wagon to the star," as he would write later.[25] For André Laurendeau, by trying too hard to warn against Americanism, the education system in Quebec kept French Canada in ignorance of the American fact. However, its increasingly visible presence now required a better knowledge of it in order to weigh the risks better. "The first concern must be to see clearly, and the fumes of anger or resentment have never helped in the analysis ... *Volens nolens,* we are linked to this great country. The United States cannot move without the whole of America trembling," wrote Laurendeau.[26] A similar observation was made by Gustave Lanctôt, who, in *Les Canadiens français et leurs voisins du sud,* deplored the fact that French Canadians "have never bothered to determine by methodical examination the place occupied by their own history in the vast historical perspectives of the continent."[27] Yet this American "beau risque" was far from being shared by the entire French Canadian intellectual class. In the same year, *L'Action nationale* devoted a dystopian dossier to "annexationism" and its potentially disastrous consequences for

French-speaking Canada. In the context of the war, the formation of new imperial blocs (the Japanese Empire, Soviet Republic, Rome-Berlin axis, proposed Franco-British union) was now feeding the fear of an eventual "American bloc" in which Quebec would drown.[28]

These simultaneous reflections on the future of French Canada in the shadow of the star-spangled banner point to an awareness, if not the beginning, of a form of "consent" to America, described by Lamonde as a major fact of the immediate postwar period. This consent was first and foremost an economic fact signalled by the increasing integration of North American markets, a consequence of the American economy's appreciable strengthening and its role as the world's leading power in the face of a disorganized Europe undergoing reconstruction. This reorientation toward economic continentalism would reinforce Quebec's dependence on the United States, which found in the province an important supplier of raw materials, particularly in the forestry and mining sectors.[29] The Unionist government of Maurice Duplessis not only desired but also encouraged this dependence on American monopoly capital, accentuated above all by the military needs of the Cold War and Korean War. Like several other provincial governments, simultaneously betting on the primacy of the market economy, the famous Quebec premier associated this dependence with work, progress, and prosperity, offering a way for French Canadians to achieve better socio-economic status.[30] Similarly, the United States saw Canada (and Quebec) as natural outlets for its own industrial production, which resulted in the establishment of production subsidiaries, stimulation of an import market, and massive investments in the manufacturing and advanced technology industries.[31] This continental economic integration, necessarily unequal, increasingly subjected Quebec to the forces of American society in the postwar period. The reality of such integration is that it would have repercussions beyond the economy and affect the cultural, political, and intellectual landscape of Quebec society.

Cultural Influence

During the postwar period, American cultural influence could be witnessed on two levels: popular and artistic culture. The former received the most attention from authorities, given the target audiences exposed to American cultural production: radio listeners, television viewers, film lovers, and readers. The authorities were concerned that this influence would contribute to the Americanization of Quebec life. The Royal Commission on National Development in the Arts, Letters and Sciences (known as the Massey Commission, 1949–51) affirmed it straightforwardly: "The American invasion by means of film, radio and periodicals is formidable." The commissioners added that "an exaggerated proportion of productions from a single foreign source can stifle rather than stimulate our own creative efforts."[32] In terms of artistic culture, during this time, what could be witnessed was the accentuation of cultural exchanges, notably thanks to the United States' and, in particular, New York's artistic renewal, which competed with Paris, in turn complicating Quebec artists' relationship with France and opening new horizons for thinking about art and its continental roots.

The influence of radio, which at the time reached a majority of the homes in Quebec and whose importance in terms of ideology and propaganda during the Second World War has been well documented, was of particular concern to the authorities. As early as 1929, a report by the Royal Commission on Broadcasting in Canada (the Aird Commission) called for federal government intervention to counterbalance American influence on the airwaves. The goal was to foster a Canadian identity. Twenty years later the Massey Commission made the same point. During the 1940s and part of the 1950s – the "golden age of radio" – most advertising revenues in Quebec came from American firms. There was also a marked influence of American advertising in program content such as *Théâtre Ford, La petite cigarettière,* and *La soirée au vieux moulin,* sponsored by Ford, tobacco distributor L.O. Grothe, and Purity Flour Mills, respectively. Although the language barrier prevented the broadcasting of purely American programs, "many of these programs were not only sponsored, but also produced by the advertiser or its agency."[33] Significantly, radio advertising was inserted into daytime programs reaching the female audience in particular, a clientele likely to purchase certain products. This is what Ernestine Pineault-Léveillé argued in 1936. Thanks to American "radio programs, he [the American] imposes on us an evil and expensive 'standard of living' that dangerously seduces French-Canadian women," who in turn are the vectors of Americanization in the home.[34] At the end of the 1950s, the influence of radio would be felt on another level: that of regulation. Canada would move from a British-inspired model – in which public service predominated – to an American-inspired model based on supervision and regulation.[35]

One of the most striking indications of American influence in Quebec during this period concerns the movie theatre, which Quebecers began to attend in increasing numbers. From 1945 to 1960, 64% of all feature films in Quebec cinemas came from the United States, compared with 20% from France.[36] The burgeoning American stardom worried many elites, who saw in it a mass culture gaining power and competing with traditional models of authority (including priests). In the mid-1950s, the vast proliferation of television sets in Quebec homes would again arouse the same fears. Some people saw television as an obstacle to the "difficult gestation of a Canadian civilization that was original in relation to that of the United States."[37] This influence was favoured by the geographic distribution of the Canadian population, a majority of which resided close to the southern border and within range of American channels (about 50% of Quebec households could receive American channels compared with 77% in Ontario).[38] However, the French Radio-Canada network broadcast only 10–20% of American programs, the lowest figure in the country. In terms of content, Dave Atkinson spoke of "children in the 1960s [who] were influenced by American cartoons on Saturday and Sunday morning shows. Television offered children Bugs Bunny, Disney's Wonderful World, Lassie, Rin Tin Tin, Batman." Nevertheless, it was mainly in terms of content that the American influence was increasingly felt. Quebec channels imitated US content, from variety shows to game shows to soap operas. According to Atkinson, the "very conception of television [was] becoming Americanized."[39]

The presence of American or Americanophile characters in Quebec culture dates back several decades. Most notably, that presence was embodied in figures of travellers and nomads such as Lorenzo Surprenant, who tried to convince Maria Chapdelaine to follow him to the United States, and in promoters of American culture or industrialization such as Jean-Charles Harvey's *Marcel Faure* (1922). During the postwar period, *La famille Plouffe,* a radio program and later soap opera broadcast from 1953 to 1959, would come to symbolize Quebec's tug-of-war over Americanization. Immensely popular, the show illustrated the rapid evolution of urban mores and was a good place to portray the tensions and promises of urbanization, modernization, mass consumption, and the American dream. Although some of the show's American characters represented the dangers of capitalist or even religious domination, indicated by the presence of Protestant pastor Brown, the show also included Quebec characters tempted by the appeals of the United States. This was the case with Guillaume Plouffe, a main character who pursued a baseball career in the United States. This temptation might have been nothing new, but it revealed a weakening of the clergy's authority, no longer able to hold its own against the appeal of American culture.[40]

Americans were not just characters on television or in movies. During this period, more and more Americans were coming to Quebec. Beginning in the interwar period, many American jazz musicians heeded the call of Billy Rose and Mort Dixon ("Goodbye Broadway, Hello Montreal") and fled prohibition-era United States for Quebec. These musicians transformed Montreal's cabaret and bar culture, contributing greatly to its reputation as a city of fun and vice in North America.[41] The entertainment industry reached its peak in the 1940s and 1950s when Montreal attracted millions of Americans, in turn becoming a hotbed of illegal and "immoral" mafia activity. Rural Quebec also attracted Americans. Presented as a folkloric and historical enclave largely preserved from modernization, as Nicole Neatby has shown, rural Quebec was seen by authorities not only as a source of revenue but also as a way to project and reinforce Quebec's distinctiveness in North America.[42] Tourism thus had become a tool for building the national imaginary. This was largely a consequence of the political class discovering, in the first half of the twentieth century, the early anglicization of Quebec's tourist structures, including largely English-speaking road signs, area inns named American House or New York Coffee, and meals imitating American food. During this time, the efforts of the French Canadian tourism board were aimed at sensitizing innkeepers and promoters to show the distinctive character of Quebec, even if it meant creating local legends and crafts and adopting "French-style" cuisine. The authorities wanted to involve the tourism sector in the campaign to re-Frenchify Quebec in order to showcase the province's European heritage to tourists. By the end of the 1950s, American tourists would be offered another image of Quebec, one less traditional and more dynamic, a kind of portal into an "original" francophone modernity.

American influence on Québécois literature and the arts was less of a concern to the authorities. Yet it did concern a limited number of people such as artists, intellectuals, and publishers. Nevertheless, thanks to a publishing boom during the war and in the years that followed, this influence would give rise to debates that revealed the increasingly inescapable reflection of Quebec's place in North America as well as the importance of the United States in reshaping Quebec's relationship with France. Until that point, France had long been the ultimate horizon for Quebecers in the artistic and intellectual fields. After all, it was fidelity to French tradition or spirit that anti-Americanists evoked to justify their distrust of the neighbour to the south. When the French reference point became more and more uncertain at the beginning of the 1940s, the United States started to be evoked in more favourable terms, beyond the polarities of materialism/spirit and low/high culture. From this point on, artists no longer wanted to "invoke the French mirage to fight the American mirage."[43] The imposing neighbour to the south now took on an important symbolic function. The United States allowed Quebecers to think in terms other than those related to France, the first step, for many writers and intellectuals at the time, toward the emergence of a distinctly Québécois culture.

This context explains why the Second World War led to great tensions between French and Quebec writers and publishers, accused of publishing fascist or collaborationist authors. Publisher Robert Charbonneau countered these accusations by defending the autonomy of Quebec literature. He called for a rapprochement with other literatures, including American and Russian, in order to counterbalance the French influence. According to him, "we are not French; our life in America, our cordial relations with our English-speaking compatriots and the Americans, our political independence, have made us different."[44] His goal was to transform Montreal into a cultural metropolis, like Paris or New York. Charbonneau's Americophilia also contained a certain "commercial opportunism" since the United

States was potentially an important market for Quebec books.[45] As early as the interwar period, several Quebec authors and translators became interested in American literature and, more broadly, in Americanness, such as Alfred Desrochers, Louis Dantin, Robert Choquette, and Rosaire Dion-Lévesque. A Franco-American born in New Hampshire, Dion-Lévesque translated American poet Walt Whitman in 1933. As a sign of the times, he insisted on the spiritual renewal staged by Whitman in his presentation of the work – unlike the French translators, who had emphasized the political and homosexual dimensions of the work.[46]

After the Second World War, Quebec poetry framed the territory of North America in a new light; the United States, as a reference or horizon, symbolized a continentalism fed by fantasy. In Quebec, the theme of decadence (individual and collective) at the heart of American intellectual culture echoed the theme of the degradation of the colonized and increasing distinction from the European French. This echo opened the way for the reappropriation of the conquered territory's imaginary, as the poetics around the great hydroelectric projects of the early 1960s would attest. For Pierre Nepveu, "expansion and degradation, or vice versa, this complementary couple provides the two key images of our relationship to American culture, images where a flourishing exteriority and an interiority eaten away by death and nothingness cohabit."[47] In Quebec, where artistic censorship was rampant at the time, this paradox between the call for a "flourishing exteriority" and the torments of a "gnawed interiority" was heard particularly by avant-garde artists. The end of Parisian supremacy and the emergence of New York as the capital of modernity and creativity meant that more and more Quebecers were paying attention to New York or going there.

Paul-Émile Borduas, possibly Quebec's most famous painter, stayed in New York from 1953 to 1955. Author of *Refus global* (1948), Borduas was a somewhat mythical figure of the Quebec avant-garde scene during the 1940s and 1950s and had become the symbol of the unfairly treated artist in his home province. It was in New York that he was able to "experience his perception of the North American imaginary of space" and to flourish in an environment in which the "divide between scholarly culture and popular culture is attenuated."[48] Another painter, Jean-Paul Riopelle, also discovered American painting, this time in Paris, in the company of other American painters living there, such as Al Held, Shirley Jaffe, and Kimber Smith. These visits and encounters contributed to the American influence on painting in Quebec. In particular, this influence could be felt through themes such as "the poetry of the non-poetic, that is to say, the tendency to push the boundary between art and non-art in a new direction [and] the revolt against depersonalization."[49] Moreover, Borduas's main styles are reminiscent of those of American painter Jackson Pollock and writer Jack Kerouac, both apostles of spontaneous art.

Political Influence

The strongly articulated risk of "moral annexation" with the United States in Quebec did not prevent American political influence from being felt, directly or indirectly. For Quebec elites, the United States served primarily as a vehicle for thinking about the development of Quebec's political personality (in relation to Canada and the rest of the world), first as an interlocutor with its southern neighbour and then, during the 1960s, as a political entity seeking autonomy.

The United States played a key role in reconfiguring the relationship between Quebec and Canada in the postwar period. Fearing assimilation, many English Canadians aspired to a Canadian nation largely emancipated from British influence. Quebec and its distinct culture, impervious to foreign acculturation, appeared to be a valuable bulwark against Americanization. This would become even more true in the 1960s, when the merits of a bicultural Canada were extolled.[50] In 1939, French sociologist and historian André Siegfried, an astute commentator on the Canadian scene, believed that a Canada in progressive detachment from its British heritage would be possible only insofar as its culture was "Anglo-French in its origins and institutions, but American in its geographical atmosphere, with the poetic and prestigious nuance of the Great North."[51] Quebecers would not fail to use their distinct culture to assert their place and symbolic usefulness in the federation. Influenced by this argument, Toronto journalist Doug Hubley put it this way: "Canada's Future: Materialism or Culture?"[52] In so doing, he revived an old anxiety about the distinction between the English Canadian and the American. This crisis of identity led many to exacerbate the representation of a distinct but "tightly woven" Quebec that contrasted with both the emerging Canadian mosaic and American "melting pot" representations.

One of the indirect American political influences on Quebec was the use of the "melting pot" to reinforce, in contrast, a vision of a more or less homogeneous Quebec, united around its language, religion, and political and cultural aspirations as a distinct people. The United States was wilfully used as a scarecrow by those who feared the loss of Quebec's political weight and who saw in a "united" multicultural Canada "a reissue of the American 'melting pot' of which we know well who would pay the price."[53] This fear actualized the danger of assimilation into the great North American whole. "Do we not already have difficulty," wrote J.-H. Bender, "in obtaining justice from our compatriots [Canadians]?" "What would it be like if we fell into the American 'melting pot' where we would be one against twenty?"[54] Evocations of this melting pot – which was known from afar – also served to reiterate Quebec's distinct character. During a weekend of student exchange between the Université de Montréal and the University of Toronto in December 1955, the United States was at the heart of the discussions, either as a subject or as an inescapable reference point for thinking about the future of Quebec and Canada. In their report on the event, the Quebec students noted that many English Canadians "did not understand that there was no question of having an American melting pot in Canada." They also noted that "as much as we distrust the federal government, our English-speaking compatriots distrust the Americans. There is a curious similarity of problems."[55] Certainly, the American reference was a key issue around which English Canadians and Quebecers could talk to each other and, more importantly, think about the future of their communities.

The issue of diversity had been debated two years earlier at the Université de Montréal around an ambitious and pioneering theme, "the preservation of ethnic cultures within a Nation of heterogeneous nationalities." Three speakers were invited to represent the views of French Canada, English Canada, and the United States, respectively: historian Guy Frégault of the Université de Montréal, Frank Scott of McGill University, and Richard Bliss of Cornell University. Bliss spoke about the situation in the United States, where the challenge was "to integrate and assimilate the various national groups that have not yet melted into the 'melting pot.'" Scott argued for a plural society and cultural and ethnic diversity, whereas Frégault was "darkly pessimistic and somewhat discouraging" in predicting an increasingly insignificant place for Quebec in North America.[56]

In some cases, the American "melting pot" served not to actualize the old fear of assimilation but to project the idea of a strong, dynamic, and assimilative community. In a series of articles written in New York, where political scientist Gérard Bergeron spent some time studying, he spoke with admiration of the "multiple, multicoloured, omnipresent people [of New York]." He saw in New York's diversity and audacity not only the ultimate in the modern metropolis but also a bridge between continents and even "the capital [of] peaceful organization."[57] Would it be possible to transpose this model to Quebec? It was this question that struck French Canadian historian Michel Brunet, one of the most influential intellectuals of the 1950s and 1960s in Quebec, during a study visit to Clark University in Massachusetts. When asked by a "Jewish professor" (author's words) whether Quebec was anti-Semitic, Brunet replied that "we are perhaps the least anti-Semitic people in existence, and if we were strong enough to assimilate the Jew, anti-Semitism would hardly exist here. Unfortunately, this inability to assimilate immigrants proves our weakness."[58]

With the opening of the Quebec General Agency in New York in 1943 – the province's first representation in the United States – rapprochement with the United States took place at the official level. For the occasion, Charles Chartier was appointed as the general agent, a role that followed the adoption of the provincial law (1940) on general agents. These agents had a fairly limited mandate in the economic sphere. Their work was aimed primarily at "developing the foreign trade of the province, provoking the establishment of new industries, promoting tourism, and for all other purposes under provincial jurisdiction."[59] The New York agency, located in the Rockefeller Center building in Manhattan, eventually took the official name of Commercial and Tourist Bureau. It was largely underfunded, however, before the Quiet Revolution, when it was finally promoted to the status of a general delegation. This promotion embodied the Quebec government's ambition to establish a relationship with the United States as structured and special as that with France.

Despite his lack of interest in the bureau, as noted earlier, Duplessis was very supportive of American capital and investment.[60] He was also sensitive to American political campaigns. The Union Nationale's election campaign practices of 1948, 1952, and 1956 resembled commercial marketing and advertising methods, used considerable financial resources, and favoured a highly personalized method of communication. In that regard, they were very reminiscent of those organized in the United States during the same period. As Alain Lavigne and Andréanne Cantin have shown, in the 1940s the Union Nationale transposed American-style political marketing methods to Quebec well before they were transposed to the Canadian federal level or to Europe.[61] Above all, this avant-gardism would be the result of singular conditions within the Union Nationale, namely the presence of a chief organizer, the massive use of all available media, and effective advertising techniques. As premier, Jean Lesage followed suit in 1960 with a campaign even more clearly indexed to American strategies.

Intellectual Influence

> *Let's look to New York when it comes to finance and*
> *to Chicago when it comes to pigs. But when it comes to*
> *literature, art, science, culture, let us remember that the*
> *Gods have not yet crossed the Atlantic.*[62]
>
> – VICTOR BARBEAU, "LA POLITIQUE," 1922[63]

Since Victor Barbeau's lapidary judgment of the United States in 1922 and the postwar period's version of America as a "beautiful risk," a lot of water had flowed under the bridge. We do not know whether "the Gods ... crossed the Atlantic," but many Quebecers certainly crossed the US border as travellers or for stays of varying lengths. Their experiences there were not only decisive in facilitating the US influence on Quebec but also served as a reflection on Americanness: that is, the fact of a cultural identity belonging to the North American continent. During the postwar period in particular, both the United States and Quebec – which had long seen itself as a society of old European ancestry – were being viewed increasingly as new communities.[64] This representation encouraged these communities to explore their identities for themselves rather than in terms of an often negative comparison with European societies.

Some conducted this exploration through the readings of American authors. This was the case of Jean Le Moyne, credited with the first literary assertions of Québécois Americanness. To evoke the relationship to the land, in *Convergences* Le Moyne posits that Indigenous peoples – "too primitive and too weak," whose cultures were "mummified in harmless folklore and cloistered in reserves" – stood in opposition to the Americans, who were "always in the process of becoming."[65] And what about Quebecers? Rather than approach them separately, Le Moyne links their fate with that of Americans: "Now, we Canadians, Americans ... Our total reality is this: the duplication inherent in our situation in the world, the tearing apart that our evolution entails, the lack of coincidence and contemporaneity with ourselves."[66] Out of step with the present, Le Moyne's passage demonstrates that, by the 1960s, Quebec still had not come into itself. In other words, its attachment to America was still seen, in fact, as the condition for a more successful correspondence between the reality of a changing Quebec (the place) and the desire to achieve a clearer sense of self (the culture). This approach was in contrast to the "our master is the past" ("*notre maître, le passé*") axiom, by which Quebec had to be kept as it was. However, at that time, the question was not whether to reject European heritage. Rather, as Le Moyne vowed, "we would insert ourselves into European continuity and our American originality would make its first act of full creative consciousness."[67]

Some sought this creative consciousness by making connections with American literature. This was the case of Jean Pivcevich, who used a quotation from Walt Whitman as an exergue in an article on American literature ("my heart is with all you rebels – all of you today, always, wherever; your flag is my flag"). He added that "American literature has had to go through the same trance that we are going through now. It, too, has had to start anew with an old legacy ... We present this study as a suggestive parallel."[68] The connection between the two trajectories of the new communities drew from the "myth of starting over," often used to describe the relationship to space and time on the continent.[69] For Pivcevich, however, the superiority of American literature compared with French Canadian literature was not a natural given; rather, it was the result of the United States' accelerated evolution and Quebec's impeded growth. This aspiration to the "becoming mode" was also evident with Borduas, who saw in the United States the condition of a universal and post-national society in phase with the postwar period. In 1959, he wrote to Claude Gauvreau: "Let us forget, if necessary, the beautiful stories of our grandmothers and let us contribute in all sincerity, with all our weight to the extraordinary North American adventure. An unlimited, exceptional future awaits us that is worth more than all the pasts of history."[70] This groping and sometimes exalted search for Quebec's originality would have several repercussions during the Quiet Revolution and the countercultural period at the turn of the 1970s when Quebec would be referred to as a laboratory of modernity.

Among the groups and individuals who had the privilege of immersing themselves in American culture were university students. During the 1940s and 1950s, many students from the Université de Montréal were able to travel to Europe and the United States, allowing them to appreciate more clearly Quebec's place between the Old World and the New World. Pierre Perrault, a future pioneer in Quebec documentary film, returned from an international seminar in the Netherlands to declare, using a very Tocquevillian formula, that "one thing is certain: Europe ends the journey that America begins."[71] Hubert Aquin, a future writer, wrote in the same vein: "European civilization is dying, American civilization is gaining momentum," adding that Quebec should "take advantage of this split."[72] Others participated in the International Relations Clubs that brought together dozens of universities in the United States and Canada and allowed many Quebec students to debate with American students.[73] They were not alone. Hundreds of scholarship recipients also travelled to the United States at the same time. Upon their return to Quebec, they were dubbed the "returns from America" ("*retours d'Amérique*").

In Quebec's transnational imaginary, the figure of the "returns from Europe" ("*retours d'Europe*") – which refers to individuals, mostly artists, who went to Europe, and especially Paris, during the years 1900–40 to experience a culture shock – is much better known than the figure of the "returns from America." The "returns from Europe" were a tenacious link between Quebec and France, despite an increasingly tangible – and painfully experienced – gap.[74] The "returns from America" would appear more during the Second World War following the occupation of France, a situation that forced many young Quebec researchers to complete their university training in the United States. The multiplication of these study stays, encouraged by a provincial scholarship program,[75] or by large philanthropic foundations such as Carnegie and Rockefeller, reflected a growing willingness among Quebec universities to adopt North American conditions of higher education and open up to the rational doctrines of civic, social, and economic sciences.

Anxious to mitigate the effects of the crisis of the 1930s, university authorities increasingly considered how positive science could contribute to the social and industrial well-being of Quebec society (insofar as this science could accommodate the dogma of the Catholic faith). The leader of this movement, Brother Marie-Victorin, for example, considered science as having the ability to impose itself as "the instrument of economic conquests" in Quebec. To do so, it had to move away from "platonic equivalences with the degrees of the University of Paris" and instead favour "real equivalences between our degrees and those awarded by universities in Canada and the United States."[76] This alignment with the university standards in the United States was also reflected in architecture. The architect of the Université de Montréal, Ernest Cormier, toured the United States thanks to the Rockefeller Foundation in order to draw inspiration for the construction of the university's main building, completed on Mount Royal in 1943. The design reflected his visits to New York, Cincinnati, St. Louis, and Chicago. The tour had confirmed for Cormier the obsolescence of the regionalist approach and confronted him with the fact that "the differences are diminishing between countries, thanks to the rapidity of exchanges and our present means of locomotion." For him, this connection implied that "our mentality is indeed American."[77]

Quebec's alignment with Anglo-Saxon university standards of North America was revealed further at the level of university governance structures following American inspector Irwin Conroe's investigation of the

Université de Montréal. In the Conroe Report (1947), using the American university models, he suggested the creation of a board of governors, the systematization of the status of professors, and the rational planning of resources. At Laval University, Father Georges-Henri Lévesque, the founder of the then-nascent Faculty of Social Sciences, made an overture to the American social sciences. One of the structuring elements of his disciplinary project was the orientation toward a link among modern science, theology, and social intervention. This disciplinary project was made possible notably through the University of Chicago sociologist Everett C. Hughes, who had a significant influence on the first years of the Faculty of Social Sciences at Laval,[78] and through the support of the Carnegie Foundation. Lévesque had even sent his first graduate student cohort to acquire specialized training in the social sciences in the United States.[79]

Moreover, between 1940 and 1949, the "returns from America" – nearly 150 of them[80] – favoured numerous cultural and intellectual transfers between Quebec and the United States during the postwar period, a phenomenon still not well documented. The rise in American universities' reputations was commensurate with their internationalization, particularly as a result of the favourable reception that they had given to many scholars and intellectuals exiled from Europe. This fact had not escaped the notice of the Massey Commission, whose final report deplored the brain drain from Canada to the United States. In the humanities and social sciences, these cross-border scholarly migrations had a lasting impact on the careers of young Quebecers later called on to shape the Quebec of the Quiet Revolution. This was the case, for example, with sociologist Jean-Charles Falardeau, who completed a doctorate in sociology at the University of Chicago in the early 1940s; historian Marcel Trudel, who went to Harvard University in 1945 as a visiting professor for two years;[81] historian Michel Brunet, who stayed at Clark University at the end of the 1940s in order to complete a doctoral thesis in American history; sociologist Guy Rocher, who moved to Harvard in 1950 to complete a doctorate in sociology under the supervision of Talcott Parson; and anthropologist Marc-Adélard Tremblay, who trained in anthropology at Cornell University from 1950 to 1956 under the supervision of Alec Leighton and where he directed an anthropological team and conducted research among the Navajo. All of these students, and many others, returned to Quebec afterward, were hired in the first cohorts of lay professors, and worked on the development of universities in Quebec.

Often, these stays in the United States offered unusual experiences and provided changes of scenery. They allowed students to breathe the climate of a cultural and intellectual life different from the Quebec of their youth, meet new people, discover new authors, and acquire new knowledge and practices. For many, a visit to the vast American campuses was an opportunity to become aware of the inadequacies and "backwardness" of Quebec, particularly in the field of higher education. From a scientific point of view, and for those who experienced them, these visits favoured the development of a new scholarly "ethos" indexed to the model of the large liberal research university. In this model, the pedagogical approach of the seminar, the duality of teaching and research, the practice of an institutionalized, autonomous, and specialized science, as well as the separation of scientific theory and religion were particularly valued. Finally, on a cultural level, these stays inaugurated, in many cases, contact with a certain moral, cultural, and intellectual relativism. A consequence of the multi-faith environment of the American campuses, this contact contrasted with the normative Catholic science of Quebec universities to the point of shaking, in Guy Rocher's case, one's religious faith.[82]

CONCLUSION

The American incursion into Quebec in the twentieth century presented itself less as a political annexation project and more as an economic and cultural one. Because of its subtlety and fluidity, American influence was undoubtedly more effective. For French-speaking Quebec, undergoing rapid industrialization and urbanization and eager to catch up economically and socially, proximity to an economic and military superpower such as the United States certainly brought advantages. Among others, they included the guarantee of a higher standard of living, greater comfort, and the possibility of integration into consumer society. This material appetite was also coupled with the desire among a good number of Quebecers, already distanced from their clerical and traditional past, to participate in the great march of progress embodied by postwar America. As Édouard Montpetit wrote in 1941, the rise of "Americanism" appeared as a "universal fact generated by Europe" and the new incarnation of "modern progress."[83] If yesterday's Anglo-Protestant America appeared as the encouraged antithesis of the Catholic vocation of French Canada, then by the 1940s it had become a destination full of possibilities.

This cultural and intellectual confluence with the United States after the Second World War was by no means spontaneous. Accompanying the wider movement of transformation of the traditional identity referents in Quebec, this confluence included the metropolitan disengagement from France. It also heeded the multiplication of calls for a new understanding of freedom, one no longer consenting to the Catholic creative plan but rising to a philosophical claim of freedom of conscience.[84] This connection with America also proceeded from a natural endosmosis, conditioned in part by the geography of Quebec, which placed it historically in the republic's privileged circle of influence. In other words, Americanization was not so much a choice as a given of history, the effects of which were reflected in several spheres of Quebec life, whether in popular culture or in the persistence of a liberal political tradition,[85] the entrepreneurial spirit of the francophone bourgeoisie,[86] the economic rationality of the peasantry,[87] and even the novels of the land that, according to some, supported a form of adherence to the values of progress and the American myth.[88] In his work on Saguenayan society, historian Gérard Bouchard emphasized the similarities between French Canadian and US rural societies, which shared "rudeness of manner, refusal of formalism, spirit of independence, pragmatism, taste for adventure, disrespect for hierarchies, distrust of all forms of interference in local affairs, a mixture of individualism and communitarianism."[89] In the same vein, Yvan Lamonde went as far as to make *américanité* not only the fact of continental belonging but also, to a large extent, the reference to the Anglo-American world, a determining factor in the making of Quebec's history. For Lamonde, this *américanité* supplanted the importance of the link with France and the Catholic Church. This observation was reflected in his formula "Quebec identity = – (F) + (GB) + (USA)^2 – (R),"[90] that is less France, more Great Britain, more United States squared, less Rome. For Bouchard, as for Lamonde, the recognition of Quebec's Americanness was seen as a truth of Quebecers' relationship with themselves, as "a more accurate perception of oneself and of others" than the world vision proposed by clerical nationalism.[91] The latter, anxious to maintain its foundations and its power, had long suppressed the American anchorage of French Canada in favour of a cult of Europeanism, the culture of French importation, and its ancient attributes, such as Catholicism and agriculturalism.

This overdetermined reading of the United States in Quebec's historical trajectory gave rise to heated historiographical debates in the 1990s and 2000s. A significant qualitative leap can be observed between the documentation of the many objective vectors of US influence on Quebec's history and the postulation that the Quebecer, effectively, is an *American being*. In his masterful critique of Americanness, sociologist Joseph Yvon Thériault warned against this shift by showing that the similarity of the socioeconomic processes at work in the development of Quebec and US societies, or the simple territorial insertion of Quebec, did not necessarily translate into a subsuming cultural fact. For him, the promoters of Americanness such as Bouchard and Lamonde had another agenda in mind: that of accrediting modern Quebec's break with traditional French Canadian culture and "normalizing" its historical course by showing that modernity in fact had entered in a Chevrolet (to use Gilles Gagné's expression[92]). In doing so, the Americanness thesis would lead us to overlook what remains of the history, culture, and memory of French Canada, whose specificity is to be seen not only in the fact of a belonging shared with all of North America. Rather, as Thériault has emphasized, it is more on the ground of a "refusal" of *américanité* that the singular "national intention" of French Canada was built historically, which refers to the old historical aspiration to constitute a French model of societal integration distinct from that of the rest of Anglo-America.[93] It is certainly not wrong to say that there remains, in the history of Quebec, a negation or at least an ambiguity to its rooting in America. This, however, does not prevent us from understanding the collective representations of French Canada – shaped at first by language and religion, as deployed in relation to currents similar to other North American societies.

NOTES

Epigraph: Edmond de Nevers, *L'âme américaine, tome II: L'évolution – À travers la vie américaine – Vers l'avenir* (Paris: Jouve and Royer, Éditeurs, 1900), 223.

1 E.-Martin Meunier, "La Grande Noirceur canadienne-française dans l'historiographie et la mémoire québécoises: Revisiter une interprétation convenue," *Vingtième Siècle: Revue d'histoire* 1, 129 (2016): 43–59.

2 Yvan Lamonde, *Ni avec eux ni sans eux: Le Québec et les États-Unis* (Montreal: Nuit blanche éditeur, 1996).

3 Ibid., 51–52.

4 The annexationist movement in French Canada was driven essentially by the intellectual and political faction of the "reds," who shared a common democratic conception of the people. This current was embodied in the activities of the Institut canadien de Montréal, but also in certain influential figures, such as Louis-Joseph Papineau and his nephew, Louis-Antoine Dessaulles. See Jean-Paul Bernard, *Les Rouges: Libéralisme, nationalisme et anticléricalisme au milieu du XIXe siècle* (Montreal: Les Presses de l'Université du Québec, 1971).

5 De Nevers, *L'âme américaine,* 223.

6 Quoted in Pierre Savard, *Jules-Paul Tardivel, la France et les États-Unis (1851–1905)* (Quebec: Les Presses de l'Université Laval, 1967), 206.

7 Henri Bourassa, *The Spectre of Annexation and the Real Danger of National Disintegration* (Montreal: Le Devoir, 1912), 24.

8 Of course, this discourse also implied a desire for cultural distancing from elements endogenous to the Canadian territory, starting with the Indigenous peoples. See Claude Gélinas, "Les autochtones dans la trajectoire historique du Québec," in *Les autochtones dans le Québec post-confédéral (1867–1960)* (Québec: Septentrion, 2007), 58–89.

9 According to the statistics compiled by Yolande Lavoie, between 1840 and 1940, the net emigration from Quebec to the United States amounted to approximately 925,000 people. See Paul-André Linteau, René Durocher, Jean-Claude Robert, and François Ricard, *Histoire du Québec contemporain, tome 2, le Québec depuis 1930* (Montreal: Boréal, 1989), 36.

10 Gérard Bouchard and Yvan Lamonde, eds., *Québécois et Américains: La culture québécoise aux XIXe et XXe siècles* (Montreal: Fides, 1995).

11 Damien-Claude Bélanger, "L'antiaméricanisme et l'antimodernisme dans le discours de la droite intellectuelle du Canada, 1891–1945," *Revue d'histoire de l'Amérique française* 61, 3–4 (2008): 501–30.

12 Victor Barbeau, "La politique: La méthode américaine," *Les Cahiers de Turc* (5) (Montreal: Roger Maillet, 1922): 31, 34.

13 Lionel Groulx, *Nos responsabilités intellectuelles: Conférence prononcée le 9 février 1928, à la Salle Saint-Sulpice* (Montreal, 1928), 28.

14 Raymond-M. Voyer, "L'américanisme et notre vie religieuse," *Revue dominicaine* 42 (1936): 9–11.

15 Bélanger, "L'antiaméricanisme et l'antimodernisme," 506.

16 Simone Weil, *Oeuvres* (Paris: Gallimard, 1999), 436–37.

17 In this regard, it is worth noting the signing of an important tripartite London-Ottawa-Washington trade agreement in 1938. Worth mentioning also is the Ogdensburg Agreement (August 1940), the Hyde Park Agreement (April 1941), and the Canada-US Agreement that concluded at about the same time as the canalization of the St. Lawrence River (1941) and aimed at multiplying the links between the American and Canadian economies.

18 Gilles Sabourin, *Montréal et la bombe* (Québec: Les Éditions du Septentrion, 2020).

19 Gilles Gallichan, "Le 'bouleversement intime': Le Québec et la France vaincue de juin 1940," *Les Cahiers des Dix* 59 (2005): 239–83.

20 Marie-Thérèse Lefebvre, "D'où venon-nous? Qui sommes-nous? Où allons-nous? Enquête sur la culture canadienne-française durant la Seconde Guerre mondiale," *Les Cahiers des Dix* 66 (2012): 167–99.

21 Pierre Popovic, "Retour d'Amérique," *Études françaises* 27, 1 (1991): 92.

22 Gérard Fabre, "La tentation américaine d'Édouard Montpetit," *Histoire, économie et société* 4 (2017): 54–71.

23 Édouard Montpetit, *Reflets d'Amérique* (Montreal: Éditions Bernard Valiquette, 1941), 252.

24 Ibid., 253.

25 Édouard Montpetit, "Le char à l'étoile," in *Souvenirs II: Vous avez la parole* (Montreal: Les Éditions de l'Arbre, 1949), 155.

26 "Le premier souci doit être de voir clair, et les fumées de la colère ou du ressentiment n'ont jamais aidé à l'analyse ... *Volens nolens,* nous sommes liés à ce grand pays. Les États-Unis ne sauraient bouger sans que toute l'Amérique tremble." André Laurendeau, "Connaissance des États-Unis," *L'Enseignement secondaire* 21 (1941): 207.

27 "[N]e se sont jamais souciés eux-mêmes de déterminer par un examen méthodique la place qu'occupe leur propre histoire dans les vastes perspectives historiques du continent." Gustave Lanctôt, *Les Canadiens français et leurs voisins du sud* (Montréal: Éditions Bernard Valiquette, 1941), v.

28 Jacques Perrault, "Un aspect favorable de l'annexionnisme," *L'Action nationale* 17, 6 (1941): 456.

29 John A. Dickinson and Brian Young, *Brève histoire socio-économique du Québec* (Sillery: Le Septentrion, 1992), 293.

30 Gilles Bourque, Jules Duchastel and Jacques Beauchemin, *La société libérale duplessiste* (Montreal: Presses de l'Université de Montréal, 1994), 192.

31 Linteau et al., *Histoire du Québec contemporain,* 225–35.

32 Royal Commission on National Development in the Arts, Letters and Sciences, Chapter 2: "The forces of geography" (Ottawa: King's Printer, 1951), 21.

33 Michel Filion, "La publicité américaine à la radio canadienne: Le cas du réseau français de Radio-Canada, 1938–1958," *Revue d'histoire de l'Amérique française* 50, 1 (1997) : 86.

34 Ernestine Pineault-Léveillé, "Notre américanisation par la femme," *Revue dominicaine* 42 (1936) : 131.

35 Pierre Trudel, "L'influence des modèles américains dans la réglementation des industries culturelles – Quelques intuitions," in *Variations sur l'influence culturelle américaine,* ed. Florian Sauvageau (Québec: Les Presses de l'Université Laval, 1999), 21.

36 Lamonde, *Ni avec eux ni sans eux,* 67.

37 Gilbert Maistre, "L'influence de la radio et de la télévision américaines au Canada," *Recherches sociographiques* 12, 1 (1971): 51.

38 Ibid., 52.

39 Dave Atkinson, "L'américanisation de la télévision: Qu'est-ce à dire?," in *Variations sur l'influence culturelle américaine,* ed. Florian Sauvageau (Québec: Les Presses de l'Université Laval, 1999), 67.

40 Jonathan Weiss, "Les Plouffe et l'Américanisme au Québec," *Revue canadienne des études sur le nationalisme* 3, 2 (1976) : 226–30.

41 Michael Hawrysh, "Une ville bien arrosée: Montréal durant l'ère de la prohibition (1920–1933)" (MA thesis, Université de Montréal, 2015).

42 Nicole Neatby, *From Old Quebec to La Belle Province: Tourism Promotion, Travel Writing, and National Identities, 1920–1967* (Montreal and Kingston: McGill-Queen's University Press, 2018).

43 Jacques Cotnam, "La prise de conscience d'une identité nord-américaine au Canada français (1930–1939)," in *Les grands voisins,* ed. Gilles Dorion and Marcel Voisin (Bruxelles: Éditions de l'Université libre de Bruxelles, 1984), 79.

44 Robert Charbonneau, *La France et nous: Journal d'une querelle* (Montreal: Éditions de l'Arbre, 1947), 23.

45 Robert Dion, "La France et nous après la Seconde Guerre mondiale: Analyse d'une crise," *Voix et Images* 12, 2 (1988): 299.

46 Delphine Rumeau, "La traduction de Walt Whitman par Rosaire Dion-Lévesque: Les ambiguïtés d'une appropriation," *Globe* 16, 1 (2013): 159–79.

47 Pierre Nepveu, "Le poème québécois de l'Amérique," *Études françaises* 26, 2 (1990): 12.

48 Louise Vigneault, "Peinture et territoire en dialogue: Regards de Paul-Émile Borduas sur l'Amérique," *Mens: Revue d'histoire intellectuelle et culturelle* 10, 1 (2009): 52, 76.

49 François-Marc Gagnon, "La première expérience québécoise de la peinture abstraite américaine (les années 1950)," in *Québécois et Américains: La culture québécoise aux XIXe et XXe siècles,* ed. Gérard Bouchard and Yvan Lamonde (Montreal: Fides, 1995), 264.

50 José E. Igartua, *The Other Quiet Revolution: National Identities in English Canada, 1945–71* (Toronto: University of Toronto Press, 2006).

51 André Siegfried, *Le Canada, puissance internationale,* 3rd ed.(Paris: Librairie Armand Colin, 1939), 201.

52 Doug Hubley, "Canada's Future: Materialism or Culture?," *Varsity,* 1 December 1955.

53 J.M.L., "Faut-il boycotter le recensement?," *Le Devoir,* 20 December 1960.

54 J.-H. Bender, "À la veille de la convention de Winnipeg," *Le Devoir,* 24 October 1942.

55 André Paquette, "A Terrific Week-End," *Quartier latin,* 15 December 1955.

56 Jacques Brossard, "Canada, États-Unis, et préservation des cultures ethniques," *Quartier latin,* 26 February 1953.

57 Gérard Bergeron, "Le corps et l'âme de New-York," *Notre temps,* 14 September 1946, 1.

58 "Entrée du 17 mai 1949 – Journal de tournée américaine de Michel Brunet," Archives de l'Université de Montréal, Fonds Michel Brunet, P136/J 2, 22.

59 Stéphane Paquin, "La politique internationale du Québec envers les États-Unis: Un essai de périodisation (note de recherche)," *Études internationales* 45, 2 (2014): 261–84.

60 Gilles Bourques, Jules Duchastel, and Jacques Beauchemin, *La société libérale duplessiste* (Montreal: Presses de l'Université de Montréal, 1994).

61 Alain Lavigne and Andréanne Cantin, "Des campagnes électorales à l'américaine sous Duplessis," *Bulletin d'histoire politique* 24, 1 (2015): 38.

62 "Regardons vers New York lorsqu'il s'agit de finances et vers Chicago lorsqu'il s'agit de cochons. Mais lorsqu'il y va de littérature, d'art, de science, de culture, rappelons-nous que les Dieux n'ont pas encore traversé l'Atlantique."

63 Barbeau, "La politique," 34.

64 Gérard Bouchard, "Populations neuves, cultures fondatrices et conscience nationale en Amérique latine et au Québec," in *La nation dans tous ses états: Le Québec en comparaison,* ed. Gérard Bouchard and Yvan Lamonde (Montreal: Harmattan, 1997), 15–54.

65 Jean Le Moyne, *Convergences* (1951; reprinted, Montreal: HMH, 1962), 198–200.

66 "Or, nous autres, Canadiens, Américains ... Notre réalité totale, c'est ceci: le dédoublement inhérent à notre situation dans le monde, le déchirement que comporte notre évolution, le défaut de coïncidence et de contemporanéité avec nous-mêmes." Ibid., 211.

67 Ibid., 211.

68 Jean Pivcevich, "Les révoltés de la littérature américaine," *Quartier latin,* 16 March 1951.

69 Jean Morency, *Le mythe américain dans les fictions d'Amérique de Washington Irving à Jacques Poulin* (Montreal: Nuit blanche éditeur, 1994).

70 "Oublions, si nécessaire, les belles histoires de nos grands-mères et contribuons en toute sincérité, de tout notre poids à l'extraordinaire aventure nord-américaine. Un avenir illimité, exceptionnel, nous attend qui vaut mieux que tous les passés de l'histoire." Cited in Étienne Beaulieu, *La pomme et l'étoile* (Québec: Groupe Nota bene, 2019), 139.

71 Pierre Perreault, "Opinion," *Quartier latin,* 7 October 1949.

72 Hubert Aquin, "Les miracles se font lentement," *Quartier latin,* 16 March 1951.

73 Daniel Poitras, "Relations internationales et expérience américaine: Le voyage au bout de la nuit des étudiants montréalais aux États-Unis (1947–1955)," *Mens: Revue d'histoire intellectuelle et culturelle* 20, 1–2 (2019–20): 69–105.

74 Michel Lacroix, *L'invention du retour d'Europe: Réseaux transatlantiques et transferts culturels au début du XXe siècle* (Québec: Les Presses de l'Université Laval, 2014).

75 Robert Gagnon and Denis Goulet, *La formation d'une élite: Les bourses d'études à l'étranger du gouvernement québécois (1920–1959)* (Montreal: Boréal, 2020).

76 Marie-Victorin, "Les sciences naturelles dans l'enseignement supérieur," in *Frère Marie-Victorin: Science, culture et nation: Textes choisis et présentés par Yves Gingras* (Montreal: Boréal, 1996), 91.

77 Isabelle Gournay, "La formation et les premières œuvres d'Ernest Cormier," in *Ernest Cormier et l'Université de Montréal*, ed. Isabelle Gournay (Montreal: Centre canadien d'architecture and Éditions du Méridien, 1990), 37.

78 Jean-Philippe Warren, *L'engagement sociologique: La tradition sociologique du Québec francophone (1886–1955)* (Montreal: Boréal, 2003).

79 Jules Racine St-Jacques, "Un virage américain? L'acculturation disciplinaire des premiers diplômés de la Faculté des sciences sociales de l'Université Laval," *Mens: Revue d'histoire intellectuelle et culturelle* 20, 1–2 (2019–20): 45–68.

80 Gagnon and Goulet, *La Formation d'une élite*.

81 François-Olivier Dorais, "Marcel Trudel à Harvard: Trajectoire d'un 'retour d'Amérique,'" *Mens: Revue d'histoire intellectuelle et culturelle* 20, 1–2 (2019–20): 135–72.

82 Interview with Guy Rocher, Montreal, 3 March 2020.

83 Édouard Montpetit, *Reflets d'Amérique* (Montreal: Éditions Bernard Valiquette, 1941).

84 Yvan Lamonde, *La modernité au Québec – Tome II: La victoire différée du présent sur le passé (1939–1965)* (Montreal: Fides, 2016), 330.

85 Bernard, *Les Rouges*.

86 Fernande Roy, *Progrès, harmonie, liberté: Le libéralisme des milieux d'affaires francophones de Montréal au tournant du siècle* (Montreal: Boréal, 1988).

87 Gilles Paquet and Jean-Pierre Wallot, *Patronage et pouvoir dans le Bas-Canada* (Montreal: Les Presses de l'Université du Québec, 1973).

88 Robert Major, *Jean Rivard ou l'art de réussir: Idéologies et utopie dans l'œuvre d'Antoine Gérin-Lajoie*, *Vie des lettres québécoises* (Sainte-Foy: Les Presses de l'Université Laval, 1991).

89 "Rudesse de manières, refus du formalisme, esprit d'indépendance, pragmatisme, goût de l'aventure, irrespect des hiérarchies, méfiance à l'endroit de toutes les formes d'ingérence dans les affaires locales, mélange d'individualisme et de communautarisme." Bouchard, "Populations neuves," 37.

90 Yvan Lamonde, *Allégeances et dépendances: L'histoire d'une ambivalence identitaire* (Québec: Nota Bene, 2001), 266.

91 Bouchard, "Populations neuves," 16.

92 Gilles Gagné, cited in Jean-Philippe Warren, "Entrer dans la modernité en Chevrolet?," *Histoire Canada*, 17 May 2019 [online] https://www.histoirecanada.ca/consulter/canada-francais/entrer-dans-la-modernite-en-chevrolet.

93 Joseph Yvon Thériault, *Critique de l'Américanité: Mémoire et démocratie au Québec* (Montreal: Québec Amériques, 2002).

Part 3

CULTURAL CONUNDRUMS IN AN AGE OF PROSPERITY

9

Living the Good Life?

Canadians and the
Paradox of American Prosperity

STEPHEN AZZI

I don't know why I can't get enthusiastic about American
civilization. Certainly, on the whole, everybody is better
fed and housed and clothed than in Britain or in Europe.
Infinitely more chances to get ahead, too ... What's really
blocking me, I suppose, is a congenital inability to believe
that hot-water taps and superior plumbing and Mixmasters
and skyscrapers represent the essence of civilization or the
good life.

– GREGORY ROLPH, IN W.G. HARDY,
THE UNFULFILLED

Dwight Eisenhower spoke twice before joint sessions of the Canadian Parliament. The US president's first address, on 14 November 1953, was unremarkable, characterized by the bland platitudes that the situation usually required. "Our common frontier grows stronger every day, defended only by friendship," he told his audience. "Its strength wells from indestructible and enduring sources – identical ideas of family and school and church, and traditions which come to us from a common past." From this partnership, "a progressive prosperity and a general well-being" had evolved. It was "mutually beneficial" and "without parallel on earth." To be sure, Eisenhower did not shy away from substantive issues. He urged the joint Canada-US development of the St. Lawrence Seaway, freer trade between the two countries, and greater defence cooperation to counter the threat of a Soviet attack. Still, optimism pervaded the speech: "Beyond the shadow of the atomic cloud, the horizon is bright with promise. No shadow can halt our advance together."[1] With his bromides about bilateral harmony, the president's comments were typical of the comfortable rhetorical relationship between the North American neighbours in that period.

In his second address, on 9 July 1958, Eisenhower's tone changed from celebration to rebuttal. Eisenhower arrived in Ottawa at a time when English-speaking Canadians had grown critical of American investment in Canada, Canada-US trade relations, and the American practice of selling surplus wheat abroad at below market price. He went through each of these issues, defending his country, arguing that Canadians frequently benefited from US policies, and challenging the positions of Canada's Conservative government. He specifically objected to Prime Minister John Diefenbaker's proposal to divert 15 percent of Canada's trade from the United States to Britain: "I assume that Canada is as interested as we are in the expansion of world trade rather than in its artificial redirection."[2] Canadians did not welcome these remarks. A Conservative senator thought the address a "kick in the teeth."[3] The *Ottawa Citizen* characterized it as a "tough speech" and noted that Minister of Finance Donald Fleming "stared sullenly into space" when Eisenhower appeared to rebuke Canadian fiscal policy.[4] "On every single point at issue between the two nations," reported the *Vancouver Sun*, "the president slapped down the Canadian complaint with a spirited defence." The president had, "in effect, told Canada to stop quibbling, that the United States knew best."[5]

In the five years between his two speeches to Canada's Parliament, Eisenhower and his policies had not changed. Canadians and their government had. Throughout the 1950s, Canadians benefited from living next door to the world's most dynamic economy. Yet they became increasingly anxious about American influences on Canadian life as the decade progressed. By 1958, criticisms of the United States were common in English Canadian public life. They had less to do with the specific issues that

Eisenhower addressed than with a general disquiet about the values of American society and Canada's intimate ties to the United States.

Historians have tended to view the 1950s as a time of consensus, when Canadians and Americans shared similar views on social, economic, political, and international issues, a period of calm before the anti-American storm of the 1960s and 1970s.[6] A closer examination of the 1950s reveals a growing skepticism about the impact of the United States on Canadian society, beginning in the middle of the decade. This uncertainty was linked directly to the prosperity of the era and to a paradox. How were Canadians to enjoy the good life that came bubbling up from the United States without themselves becoming too much like Americans?

Often viewed as a staid decade, the 1950s in fact were a period of dramatic change. Canada's gross national product (GNP) doubled between 1950 and 1960, resulting in a higher standard of living for nearly all Canadians (see Figure 9.1). Wages and working conditions improved, in part because union membership rose rapidly, doubling from 1945 to 1960.[7] For workers in manufacturing, average hourly earnings increased by almost 60 percent.[8]

FIGURE 9.1

Gross national product of Canada, 1945–65

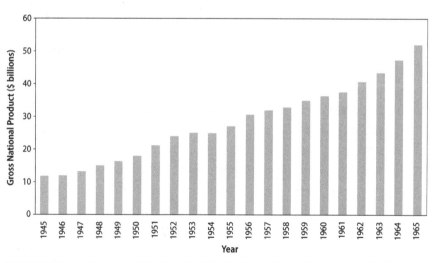

Source: Dominion Bureau of Statistics, *Canada One Hundred, 1867–1967* (Ottawa: Dominion Bureau of Statistics, 1967), 324.

Until 1958, the unemployment rate remained below 5 percent. The average family income in constant dollars rose 35 percent from 1951 to 1961.[9] Poverty still existed, especially among Indigenous peoples, non-unionized workers, recent immigrants, and Canadians who lived in the Atlantic provinces or in rural areas. Yet most Canadians benefited from a thriving economy that became more equitable, as the gap between rich and poor narrowed.

The growth in Canadian prosperity was aided by government policy, which helped to maintain a stable, expanding economy. In 1950, Canada became the first country to leave the Bretton Woods system, the agreement that fixed international exchange rates for all major currencies by requiring each advanced economy to base the value of its currency on a specific quantity of gold. Although the International Monetary Fund criticized Canada for floating its currency, the move meant that the Canadian economy was well equipped to adjust to global economic volatility. As a result, inflation was consistently low in the 1950s, with the consumer price index (CPI) rising less than 1.5 percent in most years.[10]

Affluence transformed the Canadian way of life. The biggest change was the remarkable number of women who entered the paid workforce. The percentage of married women working outside the home quadrupled between 1941 and 1961.[11] And prosperity meant that they were more willing to have children, as seen in the fertility rate, which rose 75 percent for women aged twenty to twenty-four between 1940 and 1957.[12] By 1958, Canada's birth rate was greater than that of Japan, the United States, France, West Germany, Italy, and Scotland. It was 65 percent higher than that of England and Wales.[13] That higher birth rate, more than immigration, accounted for the rapid growth of Canada's population from 11.5 million at the end of the Second World War to 18.2 million in 1961.[14] The birth rate also explains why the population was young, with 42 percent of Canadians under the age of nineteen in 1959.[15] The many young people in the population and greater expectations for education led to increased enrolment in universities. The number of full-time university students in Canada rose 30 percent in just three years from the 1956–57 to the 1959–60 academic years.[16] With the founding of new postsecondary institutions and the rapid expansion of existing ones, university education became an option for more Canadians than ever before.

The middle class grew as white-collar work increasingly took over from blue-collar work. More Canadians moved to the suburbs, where they could own a home with a large yard, shop in supermarkets, purchase the latest home appliances, and send their children to new schools. More than one million housing units were constructed over the course of the 1950s, most of them in the suburbs.[17] Canadians, particularly those in the more prosperous regions, became highly mobile. Researchers at the University of Toronto's School of Social Work interviewed 700 Ontario families in 1957 and discovered that 60 percent had lived in their homes for less than four years. Only 15 percent were still in the same dwelling that they had occupied 12 years earlier.[18]

Canadian homes showcased the country's rising standard of living. The proportion of dwellings that lacked piped running water dropped from 40% in 1941 to 11% in 1961.[19] Homes that did without a bath or shower dropped from 51% to 20% in the same period.[20] Those that lacked a flush toilet dropped from 44% to 15%.[21] The number of residential telephones more than doubled between 1950 and 1960.[22] The production of household appliances had been limited during the Second World War, when metals were needed to produce military equipment. After the war, personal expenditures on durable goods soared, more than doubling between 1947 and 1960.[23] In most Canadian homes, iceboxes made way for electric refrigerators, both because they were now widely available and because their cost dropped substantially in the 1950s.[24] Central furnaces replaced stoves as the main source of heat in Canadian homes.[25] One sign of the changing times was the catalogue for the Simpson's department store, which included one lawnmower in 1951 but eight in 1954.[26] Canadians witnessed nothing short of a revolution in their homes.

The automobile also fundamentally altered Canada. In the war years, Canadians had found it difficult to purchase and maintain a car. No passenger automobiles were manufactured in 1943 and 1944 and fewer than 2,000 in 1945.[27] Tires were difficult to find, replacement parts scarce, and gasoline rationed. After the war, car ownership became common, with the number of passenger cars on Canadian roads more than doubling between 1950 and 1960 (see Figure 9.2). The style of cars reflected the affluence of the day. Canadians drove the enormous automobiles produced

FIGURE 9.2

Registered passenger cars in Canada, 1945–65

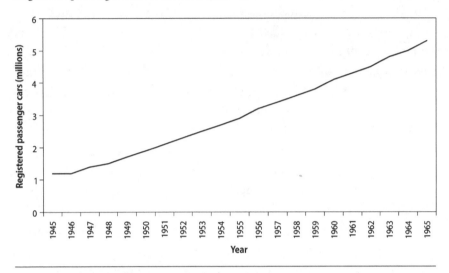

Source: Dominion Bureau of Statistics, *Canada Year Book* (Ottawa: Dominion Bureau of Statistics, 1947–67).

in Detroit, ostentatious vehicles with glistening chrome bumpers and huge tail fins, often equipped with power steering and potent V8 engines. According to one observer, "the Canadian who has 'arrived' drives a Cadillac," the leading American luxury car.[28] By 1955, there were more Cadillacs in Toronto than in any other North American city except Detroit and Los Angeles.[29] Suburbs were designed around the automobile. Rather than walk to a nearby grocery store, suburbanites drove to large supermarkets. Drive-in cinemas and restaurants appeared. Vancouver opened a drive-in bank in 1950, the same year that Ottawa held the country's first drive-in church service.[30] Shopping centres popped up in cities across Canada, beginning with Park Royal in West Vancouver in 1950. Increased automobile ownership also meant growing demand for petroleum and rubber. By the end of the 1950s, Polymer Corporation in Sarnia, Ontario, was producing one-tenth of the world's synthetic rubber.[31]

American-owned retail stores appeared across Canada. In 1952, the Canadian chain Simpson's reached an agreement with the American retail powerhouse Sears, leading to the opening of Simpson-Sears stores in the country's urban centres. Two American discount retailers, Kresge and Woolworth's, were well established in Canada before the Second World War, but they expanded their presence in the country by opening many new outlets in the 1950s. By 1960, Woolworth's owned 247 stores in Canada and Kresge 96.[32] The discount chains forced many smaller Canadian retailers out of business, while Simpson Sears challenged the dominance of Canadian powerhouses Eaton's and the Hudson's Bay Company.

Canadians were eager to travel to the United States to shop.[33] Vancouverites often made purchases in Bellingham, Washington; Winnipeggers in Grand Forks, North Dakota; Torontonians in Buffalo, New York; and Montrealers in Plattsburgh, New York. The newspapers in those Canadian centres ran ads from American businesses across the border. *Globe and Mail* columnist Joanne Strong spoke highly of shopping in Buffalo: "You can buy items there you won't find in Toronto. Some things – children's clothes, dry goods, nylons – are cheaper. The US sales girls are twice as courteous, helpful and cheerful as their Canadian counterparts."[34] Journalist Peter Gzowski gushed in the pages of *Maclean's* about a three-day weekend trip that he and his wife made to New York City. At Klein's department store, Jennie Gzowski purchased "an Arnel-and-Dacron tweed coat and dress ensemble and a black silk shantung cocktail dress for $9.98." According to Gzowski, his wife said that "she couldn't buy them in Toronto for eighty dollars." They found that liqueurs were also cheaper there than in Canada, and they were able to buy cookbooks that they could not find at home. In New York, the Gzowskis ate the best steaks that they had ever eaten and lasagne "as light as crêpes suzette."[35]

The 1950s were a period of rapid technological change. Television receivers were widely available in the decade's early years. The transistor radio was released commercially in 1954, around the same time that high-fidelity stereo systems were introduced. The United States was the source of most of this new technology, as radio receivers and television sets sold in Canada were usually produced by branch plants of American firms or by Canadian firms with licensing arrangements to manufacture American products for the Canadian market. Television, likely the most significant technological advance, rearranged lifestyles. Canadians near the US border had been receiving TV signals from the United States as early as the late 1940s. The Canadian Broadcasting Corporation (CBC) began the first television broadcasts in Canada, opening stations in Montreal and Toronto in 1952. Soon there were CBC or private stations in all of Canada's large and mid-sized cities. By 1961, 82.5 percent of homes owned a television set, and 5.1 percent owned two or more.[36] Canadians became much more likely to stay at home in the evening, many of them eating reheated TV dinners on TV tables in front of TV sets. Cinema receipts plunged, forcing more than 40 percent of Canadian movie theatres to close over the last six years of the decade.[37] Newspaper circulation slowly declined as people came to rely increasingly on television for daily news.[38]

Prosperity shook up governments, creating new expectations in the areas of health care, pensions, and education.[39] New social programs were introduced, and old programs became more generous. Unemployment Insurance had been created in 1941, but the program originally covered only a small portion of Canada's working population. More and more Canadians were brought into the system, so that four-fifths of Canadians in non-agricultural jobs were covered by 1960.[40] Unemployment benefits increased, with the average weekly payment rising from $14.12 in 1950 to $22.39 in 1960.[41] Saskatchewan inaugurated the country's first government-run hospital insurance program in 1947, quickly followed by British Columbia and Alberta. The federal Liberal government of Prime Minister Louis St. Laurent introduced a national hospital insurance plan in 1957. The government also overhauled the pension system. Created in 1927, Old Age Pension had been paid only to those in need over the age of seventy. That program was replaced in 1951 with two new pension programs. Old Age Security was provided to all Canadians seventy and older. Old Age Assistance was given to those in need aged sixty-five to sixty-nine. As a result of these and other initiatives, government expenditures rose rapidly. By 1960, the total expenditures of all levels of government in Canada had doubled from 1945 and grown tenfold since 1936.[42]

These changes were accompanied by optimism. When pollsters asked Canadians in 1956 if they saw their country entering a period of extensive development in the next ten to twenty years, 85 percent of respondents answered in the affirmative.[43] Canadians displayed their confidence in how they handled their money, spending substantially more and saving less as

FIGURE 9.3

Savings rate among Canadians (personal savings divided by personal disposable income), 1951–60

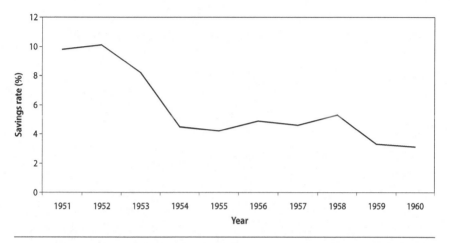

Source: Department of Finance, *Economic Reference Tables, August 1996*, 25, Table 14.

the 1950s wore on (see Figure 9.3). Canadian writers frequently noted that the country enjoyed the second-highest standard of living in the world.[44] "It is as though Canada's place in the future had been assured and her title to it made effective in this century," wrote journalist and lawyer John Fisher, who described Canada's mood in 1957 as one of "burgeoning virility."[45] Another writer, D.M. LeBourdais, proclaimed in 1956 that Canada stood "at the threshold of what might easily prove to be a marvelous future." As Canada pushed north and developed further resources, the country would "take her place among the great nations of the earth."[46] A group of prominent Canadians, including Lester B. Pearson, the secretary of state for external affairs, contributed to a book in 1953, *Canada: Nation on the March*, which contained its message in its title.[47] A leading journalist, Bruce Hutchison, published a similarly buoyant volume titled *Canada: Tomorrow's Giant*, in which he predicted that Canada was "destined to be a leading power not long hence."[48]

For the most part, Canadians seemed to be satisfied with their lot in the 1950s. A Gallup Poll in 1956 showed that 42 percent of Canadians were happier than they had been five years earlier, while only 10 percent were less happy. This mood was clearly linked to growing prosperity. Those who thought that Canada's standard of living was higher than five years earlier were the most likely to declare that they were happier.[49] But there were limits. In the late 1940s and early 1950s, sociologists conducted a five-year examination of the affluent Toronto neighbourhood of Forest Hill. They found no evidence that the mental health of Forest Hill's residents was better than that of those who lived in less affluent areas.[50] Instead, they frequently discovered an odd combination, "a sense of optimistic wellbeing and a vague malaise."[51] Canadians were not unique in these feelings, which were also common in the United States.[52]

Economic progress had brought with it both sweeping socio-economic changes and closer ties to the United States. Modernization had been transforming Canadian society since at least the mid-nineteenth century, but that process seemed to accelerate in the 1950s. Mass culture, technology, modern advertising, secularism, changing morals, the move to the suburbs – all signalled a move toward American materialism, which many Canadians found troubling.

Across Canada, a significant minority sought to resist these trends. Debate erupted in Ontario after the provincial legislature allowed municipalities to decide, by plebiscite, whether to permit spectator sports and movies on Sunday afternoons. By 1955, sixty-nine municipalities had voted on Sunday sports, with forty-two opting in favour. Notably, twenty-seven municipalities voted against, including Hamilton and Ottawa. Some saw the change as a product of the dangerous influence of the United States. In 1952, the minister at Ottawa's Westboro United Church, D.B. Macdonald, complained about the "Americanization of our Sunday." "That is why some of us are living in Canada," he explained, "because we don't want that kind of thing."[53] Comparable votes took place in municipalities in other provinces. An editorial in the *Lethbridge Herald* praised Vancouverites for rejecting "wide-open Sundays," saying that the decision proved "that Canadians aren't as Americanized as some people like to think we are."[54] Similar arguments broke out in several cities over whether shops should be permitted to open in the evening, as many jurisdictions required stores (including grocery stores) to close at 6 p.m.[55]

Disagreements raged over more banal matters, such as whether margarine should be the same colour as butter. To protect dairy farmers from competition, Quebec banned the sale of margarine, while other provinces, seeming to believe that shoppers could not read labels or taste the difference, required that margarine be white or bright yellow so that consumers would not confuse it with butter. This was more than just the dairy industry protecting its own interests. In 1955, 31 percent of respondents to the Gallup Poll thought that the law should prevent margarine from being the same colour as butter.[56]

Intellectuals articulated the otherwise inchoate concerns of many Canadians, above all their gnawing sense of unease over the modernization and Americanization of their society. Philosopher George Grant warned that "a terrible price is being paid all over North America for the benefits of the mass society." According to him, there was "nothing wrong with automobiles and washing machines, but they must be known as simply means – means of richness of life for individuals and societies." The expanding economy was "no longer a means to us – a means for the liberation of the spirit – it has become an end in itself and as such is enslaving us."[57] Sociologist Murray G. Ross recognized the "many rewards" of technological progress, including "unprecedented prosperity, leisure, and material goods for the common man." Yet modern urban life had "little meaning ... [and] human relationships little depth or significance." Tobacco, alcohol, and mass culture had become little more than a cover for "loneliness" and a "feeling of insignificance."[58]

The United States was a ready scapegoat for all that was wrong with Canada, from gambling, alcohol abuse, and rising divorce rates to the drabness of Canadian suburbs.[59] Peter Plow, a Montreal writer for *Canadian Commentator* magazine, noted that anti-Americanism seemed to be in fashion among the country's educated elite in the late 1950s. "It has almost become a matter of faith," he wrote, "to deplore the degrading influence ... of American materialism, commercialism, and low grade mass entertainment."[60] Giving voice to this tendency, historian J.M.S. Careless argued that Canadians were immature, striving "to make this nation a second-best United States in terms of bath-tubs and Buicks, with little awareness of the cultural growth which gives that country bone, fibre, and a vigorous national life of its own."[61]

The critics were particularly troubled by modern advertising techniques, developed in the United States and beginning to infiltrate Canada. One writer complained about the "miles and miles of fatuous smiles and imbecilic grins perpetrated on the reading public by the characters in virtually every type of American advertising."[62] For economist Harold Innis, American commercialism and advertising had "disastrous" effects on Canadian culture: "The cultural life of English-speaking Canadians" was being "subjected to constant hammering from American commercialism." Canadians were "fighting for their lives." Canada's traditional tie to Britain, it seemed, was being replaced by a closer tie to the United States: "The jackals of communications systems are constantly on the alert to destroy every vestige of sentiment toward Great Britain, holding it of no advantage if it threatens the omnipotence of American commercialism."[63] The use of American advertising techniques in the political sphere was especially troubling, leading Canada to adopt the worst traits of mass democracy in the United States. "The new politics emphasizes personalities at the expense of policies, it concentrates on projecting images rather than on stimulating rational discussion," wrote historian Frank Underhill in 1961. The House of Commons was threatened with obsolescence – as were voters. Instead of an engaged citizen, the voter had "become a passive consumer of well-advertised motor cars and detergents."[64]

These views were not limited to the elite. When the Gallup Poll asked in 1961 if the Canadian way of life was influenced too much by the United States, 38 percent of respondents said yes. When asked for examples, respondents pointed to the role of American investors in controlling Canadian industry, the tendency of Canadians to copy the American way of life (including American materialism), and American advertising in Canadian periodicals and on Canadian radio and television stations.[65]

While many Canadians were worrying about the influence of American commercialism, the United States was playing a key role in the rise of Canadian affluence and in the reshaping of Canadian society. American demand for Canadian raw materials fuelled the Canadian economic boom. By 1957, the United States was purchasing almost 60 percent of Canadian exports, up from 41 percent in 1939.[66] The United States also provided many of the consumer goods that Canadians craved. In 1957, it was the source of 71 percent of Canadian imports.[67] US capital and technology had undertaken the expensive and risky development of Canada's oil, natural gas, and iron ore industries. Imperial Oil, a subsidiary of Standard Oil of New Jersey, spent $23 million drilling 133 dry wells in Alberta before striking oil at Leduc in 1947.[68] As a result, Canadian crude oil production rose from 7.7 million barrels in 1947 to 189.5 million barrels in 1960.[69] The royalties to the Alberta government allowed it to pay off the province's debt and build highways, hospitals, schools, and other infrastructure. In 1950, the Interprovincial Pipe Line was built from Edmonton to Superior, Wisconsin, where oil could be taken by lake tanker to Sarnia, Ontario, for refining. In 1953, the pipeline was extended all the way to Sarnia. The Trans Mountain Oil Pipe Line was built from Edmonton to Vancouver in 1952–53. American capital developed iron ore in the Ungava region of northern Quebec and Labrador, allowing for a fifteen-fold increase in shipments of the ore from 1948 to 1960.[70] A joint Canada-US project, the St. Lawrence Seaway opened in 1959, providing hydroelectric power and allowing ore from Quebec and Labrador to be transported to steel mills in the American Midwest. This resource boom meant that unemployment remained low for most of the 1950s.

As the decade marched on, the substantial role of American capital in Canada's economic development became a topic of national debate. For generations, Canadians had sought American capital.[71] The National Policy of Prime Minister John A. Macdonald in 1879 raised Canadian tariffs for the explicit purpose of forcing American manufacturers to set up factories in Canada. High tariffs remained in place until the mid-1930s, when they slowly began to drop, but successive governments remained committed to luring foreign investment to Canada. But by the mid-1950s, the public mood had changed. Opinion leaders increasingly balked at the growth of foreign capital in Canada and at its concentration in certain sectors. In fact, foreign capital had long maintained a strong presence in Canadian manufacturing and had been higher in the 1920s than it was in the 1950s (see Figure 9.4). What changed in the 1950s was not so much the level of foreign investment as the growing role of foreign capital in resource

FIGURE 9.4

Foreign investment in Canada in non-financial industries, 1926–61

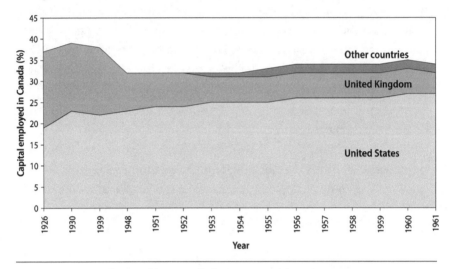

Source: Statistics Canada, *Canada's International Investment Position*, 232.

extraction. From 1946 to 1955, about 70 percent of new American direct investment in Canada went into the petroleum, mining, and pulp and paper industries.[72] The result was that, by 1955, 79 percent of Canada's petroleum and natural gas sector and 58 percent of Canada's mining and smelting sector were controlled by foreigners.[73] Increasingly, opposition politicians and media commentators complained that Canadians were being reduced to "hewers of wood and drawers of water" for Americans, and Canada was becoming a colonial backwater for the rapacious United States.[74]

The unease about modernity and the influence of the United States on Canadian life was constant throughout this period, but little was said in the early 1950s about American economic control. The key voices of economic nationalism of the late 1950s were largely silent at the beginning of the decade. Beland Honderich, the *Toronto Star*'s financial editor, recognized in 1950 that it was unrealistic to expect Canadian resources to be developed solely with Canadian money. The country lacked the necessary capital, and local investors tended to be cautious. The choice for Canada was clear, "foreign investment or a slower rate of development." Without

American investment, "we would probably not have an oil boom in the West, and we might be years away from exploiting the rich iron ore deposits in Ungava."[75] In 1952, Honderich warned readers not to be "too alarmed by the millions of investment dollars pouring into Canada from the US," pointing out that Americans owned a smaller share of Canadian business than they had in 1939.[76] James Coyne, the deputy governor of the Bank of Canada, was concerned in 1950 that Canadian resources were being developed by foreigners, but he seldom spoke publicly about the issue. When he did, he employed the tedious prose of a central banker, drawing little media attention.[77] Before 1954, Michael Barkway, the Ottawa correspondent for the *Financial Post,* published nothing negative about foreign investment in Canada. Walter Gordon, a senior partner in the country's largest accounting firm, Clarkson, Gordon, and Company, and the president of the management consulting firm J.D. Woods and Gordon, wrote and spoke on a range of issues – taxation, wage and price controls, the level of government expenditures – but did not address the issue of American economic influence in Canada.

All this began to change, gradually, in the middle of the decade. In 1955, several observers noted growing alarm about American control of Canada's economy.[78] In October, the Royal Commission on Canada's Economic Prospects, chaired by Gordon, began public hearings. Over the next five months, the commission heard arguments against foreign investment from professional organizations, investment dealers, and organized labour. By early 1956, journalists and politicians from across the political spectrum objected frequently to American economic influence. "Canada is paying for its lush prosperity by selling the ownership of its productive enterprises to Americans," Barkway wrote.[79] Liberal Senator David Croll argued that Canada was experiencing "economic colonialism." He said that Canadians were concerned "over our being mortgaged to US corporations who are beginning to control our economic future." "We must call a halt," he insisted.[80] George Drew, the Conservative leader of the opposition, was more dramatic. "Canadians should declare their economic independence of the United States," he insisted. Canadians were "not going to be treated as though we were the 50th state of the United States." They were "not going to be hewers of wood, drawers of water, and diggers of holes for any country, no matter how friendly that country may be."[81] According to M.J. Coldwell, the leader of the social-democratic Cooperative Commonwealth Federation (CCF), then the third party in the House of Commons, "the domination of our economic life by these foreign corporations is threatening the independence of this country."[82]

In April 1956, the routine release of foreign investment numbers by the Dominion Bureau of Statistics fuelled complaints about American influence. Léon Balcer, MP and president of the Progressive Conservative Party, warned of an "invasion of American capital" that would become "a serious threat to Canada's economic independence."[83] Conservative MP E. Davie Fulton anticipated the "complete outside domination, certainly of the more important segments of our economy, and probably of all the important segments of our economy."[84] Another Conservative MP, John Diefenbaker, accused the Liberal government of selling out Canada to the United States and warned that Canada would be annexed to the United States if the Liberals were re-elected.[85]

Into this kindling, the Liberal government threw a match. The government proposed the construction of a pipeline, funded largely by American capital, to transport natural gas from Alberta to Ontario. During the raucous pipeline debate in the spring of 1956, opposition MPs used inflammatory rhetoric to attack foreign investment in Canada. Coldwell predicted that Canada's "political independence one day will disappear" if the trend continued toward American control of Canadian industries and resources.[86] Conservative Donald Fleming denounced C.D. Howe, the minister of trade and commerce who was responsible for the pipeline proposal, as being "indifferent to the fact that we are buying from the United States nearly $1 billion worth of goods every year more than we sell to that country." Howe would "not lift a finger in the face of the growing concentration of Canadian trade in the American basket." He viewed "with equanimity and indifference the growing United States economic influence over Canada" and wanted "to play fast and loose with a great national heritage." From Fleming's dark perspective, it was "the duty of free men in a free Canadian parliament to assert Canada's independence of United States economic domination."[87]

Public opinion shifted, becoming more hostile to foreign investment. A survey in 1955 had shown that 27 percent disapproved of the use of foreign capital to develop Canadian resources, while 49 percent approved.[88] But the next year the *Economist* magazine commented on a new tone in Canada: "Every reference to United States influence ... is greeted resentfully; and Canadians' comments on their overshadowing neighbour contain an element of derisive envy."[89] In 1956, 43 percent of respondents were against the influx of more US capital into Canada, rising to 53 percent in 1961.[90]

The Gordon Commission's preliminary report, released in January 1957, legitimized anxieties about the role of American capital in Canada's development. Although the commissioners recognized the benefits of foreign investment, they worried about its concentration in certain sectors and warned that the growth in foreign control would create problems in the future.[91] In the days after the release of the report, a debate over foreign investment erupted in Canada. "Because of the nationalistic tone of their *Preliminary Report*," observed economist George Mowbray, "it is difficult to resist the conclusion that the commissioners knew they were starting a brushfire."[92] Fanned by the opposition parties, those flames would scorch the federal Liberals.

In the federal elections of 1957 and 1958, John Diefenbaker, who had become the Tory leader in December 1956, capitalized on growing doubts about the value of American capital. He accused the Liberals of arrogance and of selling out Canada, never specifying how they were doing so and never explaining what he would do differently. In Courtenay, British Columbia, he condemned the government for "permitting Canada to go along the road to ultimate economic serfdom."[93] In Quebec City, he suggested that Canada was losing control of its economy to foreigners.[94] Diefenbaker declared his party's position in a letter to a young couple, later published in *Maclean's*: "We Conservatives believe this dependency upon the US has gone too far, that Canadian well-being, the Canadian economy are far too vulnerable to American whims and American reversals."[95] Diefenbaker's Conservatives won a plurality of seats in the June 1957 election and formed a minority government, ending twenty-two years of Liberal rule. They went on in the March 1958 election to win the largest majority in Canadian history. According to the *Atlantic* magazine, there "were no real issues" in the 1958 campaign. "There was only a quiet but growing

Canadian nationalism, which has become apparent since the American ownership of so large a share of Canadian industry was brought out into the open."[96]

Although the Conservatives had made the most of public anxieties and their leader had declared that American capital threatened Canada's well-being, they did not in fact oppose foreign investment. In September 1957, Minister of Finance Donald Fleming assured an audience in Washington, DC, that the government welcomed American capital. He was surprised, he claimed, to discover that many Americans believed that the Tory government was hostile to American investment, a view that he described as a "complete misapprehension."[97] The Diefenbaker government introduced legislation to restrict foreign control of insurance companies, broadcast outlets, and firms applying for oil and gas leases in the Canadian north and offshore but did nothing else to limit or regulate foreign investors. Diefenbaker had hinted in the election campaign of 1957 that he would impose a surtax on the exports of unprocessed iron ore, but nothing came of that.[98] The government ignored the final report of the Gordon Commission, which fretted about the operations of foreign-owned firms in Canada. In early 1960, the governor of the Bank of Canada, James Coyne, began voicing apprehensions about Canada's reliance on foreign capital.[99] Partly because of this concern, the bank began pursuing a tight monetary policy. Alarmed about its effect on employment, the government denounced Coyne and forced him from office. By the early 1960s, the task for the Bank of Canada and the Diefenbaker government was to live with American prosperity without getting too close to the United States.

Well before the 1960s, the desire to distinguish Canada from the United States had moved to the foreground. Canadians embraced affluence: they delighted in driving large automobiles, living in modern suburbs, and eating in front of the television set. But by the mid-1950s, a substantial number felt Gregory Rolph's sense of dislocation and unease, both with the changes brought about by American prosperity and with its source. A minority of Canadians sought to stop or stall the process of modernization. Others worried about American power, condemning American trade policies or the practices of American-owned firms in Canada. For English Canadians in the age of Eisenhower, the challenge was how to enjoy the good life without becoming American.

NOTES

Acknowledgments: I am grateful to Norman Hillmer for reading and commenting on an early draft of this chapter, Bettina Liverant for providing helpful advice, and Jessica Brandon-Jepp for assisting with the graphs.

Epigraph: W.G. Hardy, *The Unfulfilled* (Toronto: McClelland and Stewart, 1951), 233.

1 Dwight Eisenhower, speech, 14 November 1953, *House of Commons Debates,* 22nd Parliament, 1st Session, vol. 1, 23–28.

2 Dwight Eisenhower, speech, 9 July 1958, *House of Commons Debates,* 24th Parliament, 1st Session, vol. 2, 2084. On relations in 1958 between Diefenbaker's Canada and Eisenhower's United States, see Asa McKercher, "Dealing with Diefenbaker: Canada-US Relations in 1958," *International Journal* 66, 4 (2011): 1043–60.

3 Tom Gould, "Ike's Call 'Fiasco,'" *Vancouver Sun,* 10 July 1958, 1, 2.

4 Austin F. Cross, "Tough Speech by 'Ike,'" *Ottawa Citizen,* 9 July 1958, 8.

5 Gould, "Ike's Call 'Fiasco,'" 1, 2.

6 See, for example, John Herd Thompson and Stephen J. Randall, *Canada and the United States: Ambivalent Allies,* 4th ed. (Montreal and Kingston: McGill-Queen's University Press, 2008), 7, 199. Thompson and Randall see the 1950s as a period when the two countries were united in "a cold war alliance based on economic interest and shared assumptions about the nature of the world and their responsibilities within it." This "binational consensus" fragmented only in the 1960s, with 1961 as the turning point, the beginning of a period in which the "moose ... roared."

7 From 711,000 in 1945 to 1.46 million in 1960. Dominion Bureau of Statistics, *Canada Year Book, 1961* (Ottawa: Dominion Bureau of Statistics, 1961), 768.

8 Ibid., 742.

9 Dominion Bureau of Statistics, *Income Distributions: Incomes of Nonfarm Families and Individuals in Canada, Selected Years 1951–1965* (Ottawa: Dominion Bureau of Statistics, 1969). The calculation comes from using average median family income in Table 1, 14–16, adjusted by the CPI figures on 39.

10 The peak was in 1957, when consumer prices rose 3.22 percent. This was an anomaly. Dominion Bureau of Statistics, *Canada Year Book, 1957–58* (Ottawa: Dominion Bureau of Statistics, 1958), 1079; Dominion Bureau of Statistics, *Canada Year Book, 1961,* 946.

11 In 1941, only 4.5 percent of married women were part of the paid labour force. By 1961, this number was 22 percent. Byron G. Spencer and Dennis C. Featherstone, *Married Female Labour Force Participation: A Micro Study* (Ottawa: Dominion Bureau of Statistics, 1970), 12, Table 1.

12 The fertility rate rose from 130 births per 1,000 women in 1940 to 227 per 1,000 women in 1957. A. Romaniuc, *Current Demographic Analysis, Fertility in Canada: From Baby-Boom to Baby-Bust* (Ottawa: Statistics Canada, 1984), 133, Table 2.1.

13 Dominion Bureau of Statistics, *Canada Year Book, 1960* (Ottawa: Dominion Bureau of Statistics, 1960), 268.

14 Dominion Bureau of Statistics, *Canada Year Book, 1962* (Ottawa: Dominion Bureau of Statistics, 1962), 1196.

15 Dominion Bureau of Statistics, *Canada Year Book, 1960*, 198.

16 The number of full-time university students grew from 78,100 in 1956–57 to 102,000 in 1959–60. Ibid., 393.

17 Canada, Department of Finance, *Economic Reference Tables, August 1996* (Ottawa: Department of Finance, 1996), 52, Table 26.

18 Albert Rose, "Canada: The Design of Social Change," *Business Quarterly* 23, 4 (1958): 208.

19 Dominion Bureau of Statistics, *Eighth Census of Canada, 1941*, vol. 9, *Housing* (Ottawa: Dominion Bureau of Statistics, 1949), 66, Table 14; Dominion Bureau of Statistics, *Housing in Canada*, 1961 Census of Canada, Series 7.2 (Ottawa: Dominion Bureau of Statistics, 1966), 4–32, Table XXVI.

20 Dominion Bureau of Statistics, *Eighth Census of Canada, 1941*, vol. 9, 69, Table 15; Dominion Bureau of Statistics, *Housing in Canada*, 4–35, Table XXVII.

21 Dominion Bureau of Statistics, *Eighth Census of Canada, 1941*, vol. 9, 73, Table 16; Dominion Bureau of Statistics, *Housing in Canada*, 4–35, Table XXVII.

22 The number of telephones increased in this period from 1.6 million to 3.5 million. Dominion Bureau of Statistics, *Canada Year Book, 1961*, 858; Dominion Bureau of Statistics, *Canada Year Book, 1962*, 841.

23 Personal expenditures on durable goods rose from $841 million in 1947 to $2.7 billion in 1960. Dominion Bureau of Statistics, *National Accounts: Income and Expenditure by Quarters, 1947–1961* (Ottawa: Dominion Bureau of Statistics, 1962), 20–23, Table 4.

24 In 1941, only 20.9 percent of Canadian homes were equipped with an electric or gas-powered refrigerator, 30 percent relied on an icebox or other form of refrigeration, while 49.1 percent had no refrigeration facilities. Dominion Bureau of Statistics, *Eighth Census of Canada, 1941*, vol. 9, 77, Table 17. By 1961, 91 percent of Canadian homes had a refrigerator. Dominion Bureau of Statistics, *1961 Census of Canada*, Series 2.2, *Housing: Living Conveniences*, Bulletin 2.2-5, vol. 2, part 2 (Ottawa: Dominion Bureau of Statistics, 1963), Introduction, n.p. The cost of refrigerators fell 32 percent from 1951 to 1956. Clarence L. Barber, *Canadian Electrical Manufacturing Industry* (Ottawa: Royal Commission on Canada's Economic Prospects, 1956), 15.

25 In 1941, 61.2 percent of homes were heated by a stove. Dominion Bureau of Statistics, *Eighth Census of Canada, 1941*, vol. 9, 51, Table 10. By 1961, 67.5 percent used a central furnace; only 29.1 percent relied on a stove or space heater. Dominion Bureau of Statistics, *Housing in Canada*, 4–30, Table XXIV.

26 John Gray, "Why Live in the Suburbs?," *Maclean's*, 1 September 1954, 10.

27 Dominion Bureau of Statistics, *The Canada Year Book, 1951* (Ottawa: Dominion Bureau of Statistics, 1951), 745.

28 Otto Butz, "Canada's Besieged Culture," *Antioch Review* 16, 1 (1956): 93. Butz, a German Canadian, was an assistant professor of politics at Princeton University.

29 "Cadillacs Prosperity Yardstick," *Vancouver Sun*, 11 June 1955, 16.

30 "'Drive-In' Bank First in Canada," *Vancouver Province*, 23 June 1950, 17; Betty Cameron, "1st Service at Drive-In Church Held," *Ottawa Citizen*, 8 May 1950, 6.

31 Matthew J. Bellamy, *Profiting the Crown: Canada's Polymer Corporation, 1942–1990* (Montreal and Kingston: McGill-Queen's University Press, 2005), 89.

32 Canadian Press, "More Stores for Woolworth," *Vancouver Province,* 13 December 1960, 8; Ray Magladry, "Trend to Watch: 'Discount House' Invading Canada," *Financial Post,* 29 October 1960, 1, 2.

33 Sarah Elvins, "'A River of Money Flowing South': Cross-Border Shopping in North Dakota and the Insatiable Canadian Desire for American Goods, 1900–2001," *History of Retailing and Consumption* 1, 3 (2015): 230–45. I am grateful to Bettina Liverant for recommending this source. In 1957, the Montreal *Gazette* reported that 10,000 Canadians had crossed into Plattsburgh on one March weekend. "10,000 Prove Winter's Over," Montreal *Gazette,* 20 March 1957, 28.

34 Joanne Strong, "Trip to Buffalo Can Cure Wife's Blues," *Globe and Mail,* 6 October 1960, 23.

35 Peter Gzowski, "Holiday Weekend in New York," *Maclean's,* 2 July 1960, 34, 36.

36 Dominion Bureau of Statistics, *Housing in Canada,* 4–39, Table XXIX.

37 In 1953, cinema receipts peaked at $108.6 million before dropping to $72.3 million by 1960. Dominion Bureau of Statistics, *Canada Year Book, 1960,* 930; Dominion Bureau of Statistics, *Canada Year Book, 1962,* 876. The number of cinemas in Canada dropped from 2,813 in 1954 to 1,659 in 1960. Dominion Bureau of Statistics, *Canada Year Book, 1957–58,* 945; Dominion Bureau of Statistics, *Canada Year Book, 1962,* 876.

38 Dominion Bureau of Statistics, *Canada Year Book, 1960,* 917.

39 The *Ottawa Citizen* argued for a national health insurance plan, pointing out that Canada enjoyed the second-highest standard of living in the world but ranked twelfth in infant mortality. "Next Step in Social Security," *Ottawa Citizen,* 7 January 1952, 26. Liberal MP David Croll made the same argument later in 1952. "Croll Calls on Parliament to Pave Way for Health Insurance," *Windsor Star,* 5 December 1952, 25. The National Federation of University Students pointed out that, despite the country's prosperity, Canada provided much less assistance to university students than other countries. "Strike Plan Rejected by Students Here," Saskatoon *Star-Phoenix,* 18 October 1956, 3.

40 Dominion Bureau of Statistics, *Canada Year Book, 1960,* 784.

41 Statistics Canada, *Canadian Economic Observer: Historical Statistical Supplement, 1993/94* (Ottawa: Statistics Canada, 1994), 43, Table 10.

42 Statistics Canada, *Canadian Economic Observer,* 15, Table 3.

43 Canadian Institute of Public Opinion, "Canadians Optimistic about Nation's Future," *Edmonton Journal,* 7 July 1956, 38.

44 See, for example, John Fisher, "Canada: Proving Its Claim on a Century," *Rotarian,* August 1957, 8; "Winspear Urges Meet Obligations," *Edmonton Journal,* 17 June 1952, 2; "Canada's Industrial Boom Said to Be without Parallel," Montreal *Gazette,* 22 October 1952, 10. In 1962, F.E. Cleyn, the president of the textile firm Cleyn and Tinker, wrote that Canadians had come to regard the second-highest standard of living "as something sacred and timeless." F.E. Cleyn, "A Manufacturer's View," in *Canada, the Commonwealth, and the Common Market: Report of the 1962 Summer Institute, Mount Allison University* (Montreal: McGill University Press, 1962), 57. "Banquet speeches at business conventions often proclaim lustily that Canada has 'the second-highest standard of living in the world,'" according to *Saturday Night* magazine in 1961. "Enterprise v. Socialism," *Saturday Night,* 30 September 1961, 6.

45 Fisher, "Canada," 9.

46 D.M. LeBourdais, *Canada's Century* (Toronto: McClelland and Stewart, 1956), 1, 195.

47 Lester B. Pearson et al., *Canada: Nation on the March* (Toronto: Clarke Irwin, 1953).

48 Bruce Hutchison, *Canada: Tomorrow's Giant* (Toronto: Longmans, Green, 1957), Foreword.

49 Canadian Institute of Public Opinion, "Gallup Poll of Canada: 42 p.c. Happier, 10 less, 47 p.c. Just about the Same," *Toronto Star,* 28 March 1956, 22.

50 John R. Seeley, Alexander Sim, and Elizabeth W. Loosley, *Crestwood Heights: A Study in the Culture of Suburban Life* (New York: Basic Books, 1956), 410.

51 Ibid., 124–25.

52 See, for example, C. Wright Mills, *White Collar: The American Middle Classes* (New York: Oxford University Press, 1951).

53 "Church Plans Car Pool to Combat Sunday Sport," *Ottawa Citizen,* 7 October 1952, 20.

54 "The Vancouver Vote," *Lethbridge Herald,* 15 December 1951, 4.

55 See Michael Dawson, *Selling Out or Buying In? Debating Consumerism in Vancouver and Victoria, 1945–1985* (Toronto: University of Toronto Press, 2018).

56 Canadian Institute of Public Opinion, "Women Still Vote 2 to 1 for Colored Margarine," *Edmonton Journal,* 2 July 1955, 22.

57 George Grant, "The Minds of Men in the Atomic Age," in *Collected Works of George Grant,* vol. 2, *1951–1959,* ed. Arthur Davis (Toronto: University of Toronto Press, 2002), 158–59.

58 Murray G. Ross, "Man and His Lack of Community," in *The Light and the Flame: Modern Knowledge and Religion,* ed. R.C. Chambers and John A. Irving (Toronto: The Ryerson Press, 1956), 65–66.

59 Carl T. Rowan, "Americans Are in Cultural War with Canada – and Don't Know It," *Toronto Star,* 14 April 1960, 7.

60 Peter Plow, "Anti-America Fad Spreads among Spoiled Canadians," *Vancouver Sun,* 11 August 1959, 5.

61 J.M.S. Careless, "Canadian Nationalism: Immature or Obsolete?," *Report of the Annual Meeting,* Canadian Historical Association (1954), 13.

62 John Gardiner, "Those Perpetual Grinners Who Act Consumer Roles!," *Windsor Star,* 28 July 1952, 4.

63 Harold A. Innis, "The Strategy of Culture," in *Changing Concepts of Time* (Toronto: University of Toronto Press, 1952), 18–19.

64 Frank H. Underhill, in *The Price of Being Canadian: 7th Winter Conference,* ed. D.L.B. Hamlin (Toronto: University of Toronto Press, 1961), 9.

65 "Big Increase in Opinion U.S. Too Influential Here," Canadian Institute of Public Opinion, Gallup Poll of Canada, 2 December 1961.

66 F.H. Leacy, ed., *Historical Statistics of Canada,* 2nd ed. (Ottawa: Statistics Canada, 1983), Series G389, G393, and G401–7.

67 Ibid., Series G408–14.

68 Peter C. Newman, "Who *Really* Owns Canada?," *Maclean's Magazine,* 9 June 1956, 92.

69 Dominion Bureau of Statistics, *Canada One Hundred,* 218.

70 Statistics Canada, *Canadian Economic Observer*, 85, Table 27.

71 On the debate over American capital in Canada, see Stephen Azzi, "Foreign Investment and the Paradox of Economic Nationalism," in *Canadas of the Mind: The Making and Unmaking of Canadian Nationalisms in the Twentieth Century*, ed. Norman Hillmer and Adam Chapnick (Montreal and Kingston: McGill-Queen's University Press, 2007), 63–88.

72 Irving Brecher and S.S. Reisman, *Canada–United States Economic Relations* (Ottawa: Royal Commission on Canada's Economic Prospects, 1957), 95.

73 Statistics Canada, *Canada's International Investment Position: Historical Statistics, 1926 to 1992* (Ottawa: Statistics Canada, 1993), 227, 228.

74 See, for example, "Why Just Hewers of Wood?," *Star Weekly*, 11 February 1956, Section 1, 11; "Sharp Blast at Loan Companies Features Senate Debate on Bill," *Ottawa Journal*, 7 March 1956, 7; "Unless U.S. Economic Ties Shattered Canada's Future Lost, Drew Warns," *Hamilton Spectator*, 20 March 1956, 7.

75 Beland Honderich, "Americans Developing Our Natural Resources: Is This Good or Bad?," *Toronto Star*, 3 August 1950, 18.

76 Beland Honderich, "U.S. Own Smaller Part of Canadian Business than It Did in 1939," *Toronto Star*, 16 April 1952, 22.

77 See, for example, "The Lag in Canadian Investment," *Ottawa Citizen*, 19 May 1950, 40.

78 See, for example, "U.S. Students Are Surprised by Antagonism," *Globe and Mail*, 16 April 1955, 3; G.E. Hall, "Here's a Tip to U.S. Firms in Canada," *Financial Post*, 22 October 1955, 25; "Certain Matters of Hard Economic Fact," Saskatoon *Star-Phoenix*, 16 December 1955, 19.

79 Michael Barkway, "How We Are Paying for Our Prosperity," *Financial Post*, 17 March 1956, 25.

80 Canadian Press, "Croll Raps Economic 'Invasion,'" Montreal *Gazette*, 7 March 1956, 1.

81 George Drew, "Time for Decision," speech to the Junior Chamber of Commerce of Hamilton, 19 March 1956, Library and Archives Canada, George Alexander Drew Fonds, MG32 C 3, vol. 316, file 375.

82 M.J. Coldwell, speech, 15 March 1956, *House of Commons Debates*, 22nd Parliament, 3rd Session, vol. 2, 2184.

83 Léon Balcer, speech, 11 April 1956, *House of Commons Debates*, 22nd Parliament, 3rd Session, vol. 3, 2826.

84 E. Davie Fulton, speech, 17 April 1956, *House of Commons Debates*, 22nd Parliament, 3rd Session, vol. 3, 2995.

85 Canadian Press, "Diefenbaker Raps 'Sell-Out' to U.S. Firms," *Ottawa Citizen*, 9 April 1956, 9.

86 M.J. Coldwell, speech, 14 May 1956, *House of Commons Debates*, 22nd Parliament, 3rd Session, vol. 4, 3885.

87 Donald Fleming, speech, 15 May 1956, *House of Commons Debates*, 22nd Parliament, 3rd Session, vol. 4, 3935.

88 Robert M. Campbell, "News and Views on Market Research," *Canadian Business*, April 1955, 78.

89 "Growing Pains of a Young Giant," *Economist,* 15 December 1956, 981.

90 "Public Divided on View towards More U.S. Capital," *Montreal Star,* 21 July 1956, 7; "Majority Hold View Enough U.S. Investment in Canada," Canadian Institute of Public Opinion, Gallup Poll of Canada, 12 April 1961. In 1956, 17 percent of respondents disapproved of US investment, both past and present, while 26 percent approved of past US investment but believed that there was now enough US capital in Canada.

91 Canada, Royal Commission on Canada's Economic Prospects, *Preliminary Report* (Ottawa: Royal Commission on Canada's Economic Prospects, 1956), 86–89; Stephen Azzi, *Walter Gordon and the Rise of Canadian Nationalism* (Montreal and Kingston: McGill-Queen's University Press, 1999), 34–65.

92 George Mowbray, "'Little Canadianism' and American Capital," *Queen's Quarterly* 65 (1958): 18.

93 "Diefenbaker Keeps Drawing Big Crowd," *Vancouver Sun,* 23 May 1957, 22. I am grateful to Steven Schumann for this reference.

94 Wilbur Arkison, "PC Leader Opens Provincial Appeal," Montreal *Gazette,* 29 April 1957, 1.

95 "Why Should We Vote for You?," *Maclean's,* 8 June 1957, 68.

96 "Atlantic Report: Canada," *Atlantic Monthly,* June 1958, 20.

97 Harold Greer, "Not Antagonistic to U.S. Capital Here – Fleming," *Toronto Star,* 27 September 1957, 21.

98 Peter C. Newman, "Can We Get along without U.S. Dollars?," *Maclean's,* 23 April 1960, 2.

99 Bank of Canada, *Annual Report of the Governor to the Minister of Finance and Statement of Accounts for the Year 1959* (Ottawa: Bank of Canada, 1960).

10

Make Room for (Canadian) TV

Print Media Cover the Arrival of Television
in the Shadow of American
Cultural Imperialism, 1930–52

EMILY LeDUC

In March 1951, eighteen months before the inaugural broadcast of the television arm of the Canadian Broadcasting Corporation (CBC), *Maclean's* magazine published a three-page feature titled "What TV Will Do to You."[1] Alongside a series of humorous cartoons about the impending arrival of television sets in modern Canadian homes, the article gave a sweeping account of the various ways in which the new medium would shape postwar lives and identities for the general public. Drawing from experiences in Britain and America, where television first premiered in 1936 and 1941, respectively, author Don Magill examined the impact of the new broadcasting medium on the economy, national politics, and international relations. He also assessed television's role in reshaping various cultural industries, including sports, film, advertising, and consumer goods. According to Magill, however, television's "greatest effect" would be in the social and cultural realm. He speculated about what the power of television could do to marriages, childrearing, children's intellectual capacity ("will we all be televidiots?"), formal education, and even one's relationship with neighbours. Television's potential effects on societal beliefs about violence, gender roles, class, and the pace of everyday life were touched on in a tone neither wholly celebratory nor cautionary but completely transfixed with the power and possibility of this revolutionary technology.

In the years since the dawn of television, historians and cultural critics have produced volumes considering these very themes and questions.

Anywhere that television has achieved prominence, which truly is just about everywhere, scholars have worked to understand its appeal, impact, and legacy for modern societies. Although most prominent television scholarship focuses on more recent developments in the medium or on wholly abstract cultural theories about communication at large, there does exist a small but influential body of work that focuses on television's formative years.

One of the earliest and most significant studies in the North American context is Lynn Spigel's *Make Room for TV: Television and the Family Ideal in Postwar America* (1992). Like Magill's piece in *Maclean's,* Spigel's monograph positioned television, both figuratively and literally, within the private and semi-public spaces of American postwar communities. Within her study, Spigel addressed important questions about early TV, such as "how over the course of a decade did television become part of people's daily routines? How did people experience the arrival of television in their homes and what were the expectations for this new mass medium?"[2] She also focused on how the American public first learned about television through other forms of popular media in the late 1940s and 1950s. But what about the history of Canadian television?

Like so much cultural history, the field and the mediums that it covers are dominated by the stories and experiences of American industry. Although there are important parallels between television's emergence in Canada and the United States, and though the US cultural impact in Canada is immense, the history of Canadian television deserves its own study. However, few works examine early television history in Canada. The most comprehensive and often cited is Paul Rutherford's *When Television Was Young: Primetime Canada, 1952–1967.* It serves as one part procedural history of the establishment of public and private television broadcasting in Canada, one part examination of the various genres of programming available in the first fifteen years on air, and one part analytical response to communication theories such as those of Marshall McLuhan and Harold Innis.[3] Beyond Rutherford, Mark Raboy's *Missed Opportunity: The Story of Canadian Broadcasting Policy* detailed twentieth-century broadcasting policy and its politics. Building on Raboy's work, in 2008 Ryan Edwardson expanded the temporal borders of the project and looked at the effort to connect cultural industry to national identity at various points from the late colonial period onward.[4] Collectively, these works have laid the foundation for the study of the early television era in Canada. Yet important gaps remain in understanding the arrival of television in the Canadian context.

One issue with the extant historiography is its focus on American content's influence on Canadian values, so that the story of Canadian television as a whole is often popularly characterized as an international struggle between two forms of the same medium – of Canadian versus American television content. Departing from this singular focus, in this chapter I adapt Spigel's methodology to show how other Canadian cultural industries, in this case various forms of print media, covered, considered, criticized, and ultimately represented the introduction of television as a new medium in the Canadian cultural scene. In doing so, I build on previous works by communications scholars Gene Allen and John Nerone and their arguments for the existence of an ecology of cultural mediums. More specifically, Nerone shows that mediums cannot be wholly singular, nor do they exist within a vacuum. Rather, he writes, cultural mediums are "exactly what the word suggests: Something between other things ... a set of relationships within a social and cultural ecology."[5] Allen's work posits further that larger shifts in socio-cultural attitudes of a period cannot be wholly understood without recognition of this interplay between mediums.[6] Together their work cautions the historian against approaching cultural mediums as monoliths and demonstrates that any analytical record that fails to explore the relationships between cultural productions is ultimately incomplete. In building on these positions, I challenge a previous tradition of narrating and evaluating the histories of Canadian cultural industries within themselves or juxtaposing them solely against the threat of American cultural imperialism. Instead, I use print media's early coverage of TV to demonstrate that, in addition to external threats in the form of American content, Canadian cultural industries grappled with an equally salient awareness of internal sources of competition by way of other Canadian cultural mediums. The arrival of television specifically served as a point of meditation for Canadian cultural industries at large, and as such these industries often used their own mediums as vehicles to have conversations about the purpose, utility, economy, and overall impact of cultural production on both society and statecraft.

Through the approach described above, I answer three interrelated questions. First, as a matter of context, how were other cultural mediums faring with the realities of American influence prior to the introduction of the new medium of television? Second, how was television covered in print media, which angles and issues were explored, and did that change over the first two decades of broadcasting? Third, and perhaps most critically, how can we characterize the relationship between cultural mediums in Canada, particularly between 1930 and 1952 as television became a technological reality within the nation?

To address these questions, I offer a brief contextual review of the story of and barriers to early television broadcasting in Canada, followed by a close analysis of print media's coverage of early television published in the years before Canadian television's inaugural season in 1952. The coverage in this period is characterized by a heightened sense of anticipation that invoked both curiosity and anxiety. When it came to the arrival of this new technology, print media most often focused on one of four key questions. What will television be like when it comes to Canada? Who should control television, and how should it be administered? What will television "do" to Canadian audiences? What will television do to other cultural mediums in Canada? Together these documents reveal the importance of studying the success of early TV, both as a cultural industry and as an instrument of nationalism, within a larger conversation about the overall evolution of cultural production in Canada during the twentieth century.[7] If a hallmark of Canadian history is how it has lived in the shadow of American exceptionalism, the birth of the age of television must be understood both in relation to that shadow and in spite of it. That is, the challenges of early television in Canada cannot be separated from a larger conversation about continentalism and American cultural imperialism. Yet these challenges must also be explored *within* the shade in which the Canadian cultural landscape has been sown, for charting the intricacies between overshadowed mediums is integral to understanding the composite whole of the Canadian cultural scene and its response to burgeoning American hegemonies.

THE DEVELOPMENT OF EARLY POSTWAR
TELEVISION IN CANADA

Arguments over which country produced the first television program depend on what constitutes the meaning of "program." The ability to send and receive images wirelessly first occurred in Britain in the late 1920s.[8] These early days of the medium were mostly various forms of broadcasting experimentation, including single images, test patterns, and rudimentary title cards, followed later by simple visualizations, physical objects, one-act plays, and other basic presentations. In 1925, Selfridges department stores in Britain invited John Logie Baird, a Scottish electrical engineer often regarded as the "Father of Television," for a series of demonstrations of his "televisor."[9] Three years later one of the earliest known examples of a television broadcast came from the United States in the form of a daily experimental broadcast that captured a papier-mâché figure of the cartoon *Felix the Cat* on a rotating platform for two hours at a time.[10] In Canada, there is some evidence of early television experimentation as well, primarily at Montreal's École Polytechnique in the early 1930s. Early broadcasting efforts grew rapidly in the 1930s, and the United States produced twenty-three limited-range television stations by the outbreak of the Second World War.[11] Following the war, television resumed its rapid growth in America, with the National Broadcasting Company (NBC) becoming the first regular national television service in the country in 1945.

In Canada, households with a television set within range of American signals were able to receive American programming options as early as 1948.[12] By April 1950, Canadians had purchased approximately 13,500 television sets, and by 1952 an estimated 100,000 Canadians received American programming signals from across the border.[13] Although much slower to develop a television industry, the first two CBC stations premiered a regular broadcasting service in September 1952. Within a year, Canadian television stations served 25 percent of the population, and approximately a third of households owned a set.

The story of how Canadian television came to be under a hybrid public-private ownership model deserves far more space than this chapter allows. However, it is important to summarize the barriers that an independent

Canadian television service faced in its early years. National goals of forming a distinctly Canadian television culture were drastically limited by six key, interrelated factors: timing, demography, geography, finances, utility, and diverse actor interests.

If domestic television was to be the product of an experiment in cultural nationalism, then the Canadian public served as the consumers. For television to become a successful medium through which to convey a message, a robust – and ideally homogeneous – audience would have to be secured. Thus, Canada's demography provided the television experiment with one of its key ingredients as well as one of its first problems. The Canadian population effectively doubled from the time of Baird's television demonstrations in 1925 (est. 9,294,000) to the end of the first decade of Canadian television in 1961 (est. 18,238,000), providing a ripe market of cultural consumers.[14] That said, this growing population also posed two important challenges for television pioneers. First, though the majority of the population lived in either Ontario (3,787,655 in 1941; 6,236,092 in 1961) or Quebec (3,331,882 in 1941; 5,259,211 in 1961), approximately 40% of the country lived in one of the remaining eight provinces or two northern territories.[15] Similarly, though a small majority of Canadians lived in urban centres across Canada (6,252,416 in 1941; 11,068,848 in 1961), rural populations accounted for approximately 46% of the total in 1941.[16] Thus, the Canadian television audience was spread across the country in uneven pockets of distribution.

Canada faced a second barrier in developing a homogeneous television system because of a significant number of francophone Canadians. According to the census in 1941, 3,354,753 respondents, or 29%, identified French as their mother tongue compared with 6,448,190 respondents, or 56%, who selected English.[17] As such, French programming and translation services would be required to achieve a national network.

Another limitation was geographic. With a total area of 9,984,670 square kilometres, Canada is Earth's second largest country.[18] Combined with a low population density of 3.32 people per square mile in 1941, it is clear that early television consumers were not just spread widely across the country but also lived in vastly different terrains and climates.[19] Since the CBC was limited by the physical range of the television signals of the era, it was clear early on that any plan for a network reaching audiences across Canada would require the construction of potentially dozens of television stations and various other signals infrastructure, all at an immense cost. Moreover, sharing the world's longest international border with the United States further emphasized the geographic barriers within Canada, because signals from American stations along the border could be received by Canadian homes within their ranges.

Overall, the single most important barrier to an autonomous Canadian television service was, perhaps unsurprisingly, financing. The capital needed to fund a national network producing original content for the majority of its schedule proved to be even greater than the most extravagant estimates. Expenditures associated with the early years of television fall into two categories. In addition to the upfront costs of network construction, annual operating costs presented the largest financial burden because of the production of original programming, which required a robust technical staff to film and edit shows, writers to create content, talent to be featured onscreen, and various other departments, including hair and makeup, set dressings, and sound and effects. In one report from 1949 submitted to the Royal Commission on National Development in the Arts, Letters and Sciences, or Massey Commission (a formal investigation of the state of cultural affairs in Canada commissioned by the federal government), the estimated cost of construction of a new station in 1951 amounted to $500,000, with operating costs running an additional $500,000.[20]

The funding issue brought forward the fourth and fifth obstacles in negotiating a future for Canadian television: its purpose or utility and the diversity of actor interests involved. In asking who should pay for Canadian television, there emerged a larger question: who would benefit from it? In considering the utility of the medium in Canada, two central schools of thought existed, each with its proponents and detractors, and all of them heavily debated and documented during the Massey Commission hearings in 1949 and 1950.[21]

First was the argument that any pursuit of a national network in Canada should be driven by the desire for a stronger patriotic nationalism in the face of American cultural imperialism. Upper-class cultural elites overwhelmingly regarded American cultural offerings as dangerous, venal, and "lowbrow." They argued further that it was the imperative of the federal government to act swiftly to develop a national television service that could stand in opposition to American values by promoting programming of a more "refined" and distinctly Canadian quality.[22] For these Canadians, the greatest potential of television was as a soft-power vehicle to promote unity, patriotism, and trust in the nation-state.

Second was the opposing argument that television should be a cultural commodity for entertainment and information, around which a private enterprise could be built. Among the biggest proponents of this view were leaders in the communications industry and everyday Canadians with previous exposure to American programming. Industry leaders argued that Canadian television should avoid the British model of public broadcasting and instead follow the wildly successful private networking approach adopted by the United States, in turn developing a strong communications industry in Canada without having to rely on Hollywood for resources. Their arguments leaned heavily on economics, employment rates, and the importance of free enterprise. Advertisers also wished to capitalize on television's power as a new economic avenue. In their comments to the Massey Commission and in other news outlets of the period, a significant number of working- and middle-class Canadians rejected the "highbrow" arguments of cultural elites and expressed their desire for family-friendly entertainment without having much concern about or need for a homogenized national culture. One respondent to the Massey Commission put it plainly: "I am an ordinary citizen and taxpayer. I have no culture and as I seldom listen to the CBC, I'm afraid I will never have any."[23] For many Canadian citizens, the threat of Americanization simply was not an issue, with some going so far as to welcome American cultural production with open arms.

The sixth and most significant barrier faced by an early Canadian television service was timing. Television in Canada, from the outset, was a race against time or, more precisely, a race against America. Most of the obstacles encountered in the Canadian context were simply not problems for the United States, where there was an exponentially larger consumer base as well as an existing communications and film industry. In essence, the United States had more money, more human resources, more resource pools to consult and utilize, a more cohesive vision, and no language barrier with which to contend. Canada was late to the party, started out with less, and tried to develop a television service that would please everyone – ensuring in fact that it would please virtually no one.

The first decade of television broadcasting in Canada, and the years that preceded it, were rife with obstacles, debates, and conflicts over the scope, purpose, and potential of the new medium. To understand properly the rocky and contested nature of this formative decade for the medium, it is useful to consider how other forms of Canadian cultural production sought to make sense of the new, suddenly unavoidable, phenomenon of television.

"MAKE WAY FOR THE ONE-EYED MONSTER"

Described as "the power of seeing across great distances," television was first covered in *Maclean's* in 1924 in an article titled "Will We See around a Corner?" The author, physicist Oliver Lodge, detailed the technology of the earliest British broadcasting experiments while offering a pessimistic meditation on modernity: "I am not sanguine of anything that can be properly called television for a good many years yet, perhaps not a century, though any invention humanity wants to devise will probably be sooner or later accomplished." He continued that "there is no use enlarging our powers of communication if we have nothing worthwhile to say."[24] Other early commentators also wondered about how and when television would be realized, though generally with a less dour appraisal of the medium as a marker of progress and modernity. In 1929, *Maclean's* again covered the march of television, remarking that "we are now approaching one of the most fantastic of all the scientific miracles." Described as "charming," "tremendous," and "instructional," the awesome potential of television was characterized as an imminent shock to the socio-cultural norms of the average Canadian family.[25] A year later another piece explained the recent advances made by Baird, engaging with visions of global grandeur and highlighting television's future ability to shrink the map and bring international news and culture directly to viewers in their homes.[26] Similar examples married the technological explanations of television with larger musings about humanity's artistic and humanistic achievements as well as a romantic view of the near future.

By 1937, *Maclean's* was running multi-page features on early British and American broadcasting. In one such article, journalist Thomas Wayling devoted half a page to every detail of his mesmerizing first experience viewing television while repeating the mantra "television has arrived."[27] Articles written in this vein continued to feature in magazines and newspapers with increasing frequency right up to the debut of Canadian television. In 1949, four years after the launch of NBC's television service, the word *television* appeared in at least 630 unique iterations in the *Globe and Mail.* Among them was an opinion piece that described the author's first viewing experience as a "pleasure" that would make radio "dull and unilluminating." The author then called on the CBC to expedite its television plans, noting that "you cannot have progress unless you progress."[28] That year *Maclean's* ran a full-page pictorial featuring seven photographs of men, women, and children with faces of wonderment, curiosity, awe, and confusion. The title asked readers "What Are They Looking At?" and two pages later revealed that the subjects were looking at themselves broadcasted live on television screens at the Marconi television booth at the Canadian National Exhibition.[29]

Although clearly captivating, early brushes with television raised important issues. In his article in 1951 "What TV Will Do to You," Don Magill raised one of the most common themes in early print coverage of television: the question of how the act of watching television would affect an individual and Canadian domestic life. Although authors who pondered the television experience often evoked an excited futurism, discussion of the long-term effects of viewership was more cautious, at times panicked, and almost always prescriptive in some way. Because of the global timeline of television, journalists often employed the American experience of TV as a kind of case study of what could happen in Canada. Magill claimed that there was "no doubt" television would change Canadian lives and argued that the impact would fall somewhere between the "moderate" influence of British television and the "social Revolution" that it engendered in the United States. Magill noted that television would bring "the family together in the home" but stymie interpersonal communication in favour of passive viewing.[30] An article in 1949 in the *Globe and Mail* agreed, citing surveys conducted by the *New York Times* television editor Jack Gould. Those results indicated that the average set was in use for three to five hours per day but dispelled notions that "this companionship would make for a united front" since respondents often noted a one-way flow of information between the television set and the viewer but not much among viewers themselves.[31]

Another common concern was television's impact on children. Gould's surveys revealed that having sets in the home exposed children to various types of entertainment at younger ages than had occurred previously. Gould wondered whether television would "ruin" other forms of entertainment for the next generation given its omnipresence in the home at such a formative age.[32] Magill also considered the place of television in young Canadians' lives. Highlighting concerns about violent content and adult themes, he focused on a number of American teachers who spoke out about television making students "jaded" and concerned with topics not typical for their age group. Still, Magill observed, others noted the convenience of television for childrearing, allowing mothers to occupy their kids while homemaking, but the question of "at what cost?" often followed.[33] It is also worth noting that, though these articles generally had a cautionary tone when it came to television's impact on children, proponents of television argued that programming provided excellent educational opportunities and that its accessibility would create better-informed youth and eventually "make them better citizens."[34]

As the seminal voice of Canadiana for a generation, Pierre Berton also wrote on the inevitable influence of television in a *Maclean's* article in 1949, "Make Way for the One-Eyed Monster." He detailed his experience of being a Canadian visiting a television-obsessed Manhattan and the unexpected culture shock that he encountered there. Likening television viewing to a new kind of addiction, Berton remarked on how owning a television set was a new form of social capital allowing average Americans to become suddenly popular members of their neighbourhoods. According to him, Americans with a television set would often find that their homes became sites of social gatherings for viewing nightly programming. That said, Berton reported that this new form of cultural power was tenuous, for previously popular residents could be ostracized quickly if another neighbour purchased a larger or more elaborate television set. By his account, few were able to rebuke television's warm glow, and – even among his friends who labelled the medium a "monster who will devour us all unless we resisted" – the new phenomenon was often impossible to avoid. Calling it a "televirus," Berton mapped the shift in public leisure spaces, writing about how television sets quickly became fixtures of Manhattan bars, department stores, and even local indoor swimming pools, as well as the consumer goods industries that sprang up around television's most popular programs. On describing a set, he wrote of a "monster, its great polyphemus eye returning the unblinking gaze of the youngsters. From its flat cranium there protruded two great beetle-like feelers, knobbed at the end. Later I learned this was a built-in antennae, but at the moment the whole machine bore an uncanny resemblance to one of the Insect Men of Mars."[35] Despite his later success on television, evidently Berton had grave doubts about the emerging medium.

Perhaps most interesting in these three articles is not the cautionary tone of alarm or the concern about changes to social structure but the perceived inevitability of television's impact. All three articles are resolute in their assertion that television would permanently change the course of everyday life in Canada. Although there was some debate about the extent of change, print articles about television published before 1952 almost unanimously emphasized the medium's inexorable power. Moreover, these articles implicitly blamed this inevitability on a growing twentieth-century obsession with leisure and entertainment. This is noteworthy given that doing so simultaneously limited a consumer's agency and an individual's power to control the proliferation of technological advances and by extension one's ability to control modernity or the path of societal progress.

However, not all early commentators on television agreed with this line of thinking. In 1944, playwright Merrill Denison wrote that only "one person" could answer the question of what television would become: the viewer. "From you and you alone," Denison wrote, "will come the answer as to whether television is a potent medium of entertainment, with revolutionary social, cultural and industrial potentialities, or whether it is something else again."[36] That said, concerns about the influence of new cultural technologies were not unique to the era of television. Earlier articles published in both news and magazine outlets postulated about the possible ill effects of film and radio. For example, a *Chatelaine* article in 1934 warned of "Radioitis" – the possibility that too much exposure to radio could make children struggle at school or, worse, suffer hearing loss.[37] Thus, though this early trend in coverage of television's potential impact is instructive, it was not born of the era but demonstrates a cultural awareness of the coming medium's power in shaping postwar society and values.

A third theme in the print coverage of television's inception was the question of who should possess regulatory control over the new Canadian technology and, by extension, who was best qualified to make that determination. Unlike the previous two themes, this type of press coverage was markedly less speculative or visionary, opting instead for procedural reporting that highlighted the three sides of an emerging debate over public or private control. That said, neither newspapers nor magazines shied away from making their opinions known, each with its own reasons for support or not for the public, private, or hybrid model. Articles in this group began appearing in 1948, following the formation of the CBC Board of Governors and their declaration of intent to "extend [their] control of radio broadcasting to the field of television," and with increasing frequency featured regularly in print media until publication of the Massey Commission's report in 1951.[38]

The federal government announced the formation of the Massey Commission in January 1949. Its goal was to examine activities of federal agencies related to "radio, films, television, the encouragement of arts and sciences, research, the preservation of our national records, a national library, museums, exhibitions, relations in these fields with international organizations, and activities generally which are designed to enrich our national life, and to increase our own consciousness of our national heritage and knowledge of Canada abroad."[39] Prime Minister Louis St. Laurent officially appointed the commission three months later under the direction of former diplomat and University of Toronto Chancellor Vincent Massey. As the first royal commission to consider broadcasting since the Aird Report on radio in 1929, the Massey Commission evolved from a growing concern among nationalists about the impact of continentalism. Canada had developed greater international recognition during the Second World War, and the continued global progress of industrial development led to a desire for a strong cultural identity in Canada. Also, the omnipresence of the American cultural juggernaut, whose depth and breadth of offerings would always overshadow Canadian potential, added to an emerging sense of alarm about Americanization in Canada. Cultural nationalists hoped that cultivating a strong and unified cultural identity would translate into a tangible feeling of social solidarity and thus a resilient nation capable of resisting American cultural imperialism. The commission held its first public hearing on 6 September 1949, three years to the day before the first CBC-TV broadcast. In total, Massey and his team held 114 meetings in sixteen cities covering all ten provinces, hearing from 1,200 witnesses and receiving 450 briefs on the state of culture in Canada.[40]

Print media coverage of television in this period is best organized around the stages of the Massey Commission: before its inception, following its announcement, and during public hearings. Although there was a noted increase in articles denoting frustration at the slow pace of building Canada's television service, both supporters and detractors could be found throughout the period 1948–51.

The debate over regulatory control began to pick up steam following the publication of a prepared statement by the CBC Board of Governors on 18 May 1948. Regarding their intention to develop a national television service, the board promised to "exercise great care" when considering applications for private licences but noted that "frequencies will probably be limited." Asserting that Canada should not "lag behind" in television development, but that channels should be of "use in the public interest," the board asserted that they would "follow a policy of not granting permission for individual private [TV] stations to become outlets for non-Canadian programs." The statement closed by reiterating that the CBC expected to extend Canadian television broadcasting in much the same way that it administered the national radio service, "so as to benefit the greatest possible number of people [and be] of great benefit to Canada."[41]

Two months later the *Globe and Mail* reported on a major development in the CBC's efforts to get Canadian television off the ground: bilateral negotiations between Canada and the United States over usage rights for available broadcasting channels. Because of its recent naissance, television technology was limited by a small number of existing frequencies. Each station had to be assigned its own channel in order to avoid signal scrambling within a given geographic range. Given the length of the shared border between the two nations, an agreement was required to divvy up the available channels. These negotiations, the *Globe and Mail* confirmed, "would prevent the growing American industry from grabbing all [the channels] before the Canadian industry is even born." That said, the article noted that private communications entrepreneurs on both sides of the border accused the CBC of being a "dog in the manger" as it aggressively fought to claim television channels that it had neither the physical stations nor the programming to operate yet, thus preventing those with the available resources from doing so. Ultimately, the article argued that this panic over available frequencies was somewhat overstated – even though only twelve unique frequencies were available at the time, almost all television stations were limited by short-wave broadcasting. This meant that, with proper planning and enough geographic distance among them, multiple stations could use the same channels, and this issue would really affect only densely populated areas that sought to build multiple stations.[42]

By November 1948, print media were regularly reporting on the largest stumbling block for the CBC's plans: finances. Despite earlier promises to begin considering applications for partnerships with private investors who had the capital necessary to build network infrastructure, the lack of funds had "indefinitely postponed the establishment of private or publicly owned stations in Canada." Moreover, the CBC had rejected all previous applications for private stations, including four in Toronto and two in Montreal. The article noted that the CBC halted further development plans until a collaborative partnership between public and private broadcasters was established and further funding was acquired. Observing that the CBC's plan was predicated on instituting an annual licensing fee of ten dollars for all Canadian television sets, author Harvey Hickey questioned whether this approach was sustainable given its high price. He pointed out that Britain's licensing fee was less than half at four dollars per year, and the United States had no fee because of its private enterprise model.[43]

In a feature article published in *Maclean's* one week before the announcement of the Massey Commission, the magazine's Ottawa editor, Blair Fraser, explained "Why They Won't Let You Have TV," pinning the blame on the CBC's monopoly. As he put it, the problem was that "Ottawa balks the CBC and the CBC balks private showmen," and all the while "we are falling so far behind on TV we may never catch up." In Fraser's view, the most exposure that Canadians could manage at the time was for "southern Ontario barflies to occasionally catch the new culture on the Buffalo channel." Although critical of the CBC's approach, Fraser was a strong proponent of the medium itself, writing of it as "a tremendous social force" and predicting that "its potential impact" would be "greater than radio, telephone, or film." According to him, the CBC had "not yet given up hope of getting into TV's ground floor" and "doesn't want private TV to be too far ahead or too deeply entrenched" because "the overall aim [was] to stimulate Canadian national life and not merely provide [a] means of broadcasting non-Canadian visual material in this country." Without significant sums of money, however, those goals were all but impossible to achieve, and it was clear, Fraser argued, that the federal government was going to drag its feet on funding the CBC as long as possible. "I don't know anything about television," one government minister told him, "but it costs money so my instinctive reaction was against it. We are in too many things already." That said, Fraser was not blind to the delicate balance required in the debate over the public versus the private model. He recognized that the "primary motive of US-TV [was] to sell" consumer goods and services through advertising and product placement, and that calling on the federal government to allow private investors to circumvent the CBC's plans would deliver "a final log-sized straw to the burden of Americanization that's borne already in the cultural life of Canada." Still, Fraser argued that Canada was "missing [out on] the greatest instrument of mass communication ever devised" and queried whether the federal government could "not only refuse to do anything [about television] itself, but refuse to let private companies do it at their own expense either." In his assessment, there were three possible solutions to the problem of Canadian TV: stay the CBC's course and continue to fall behind, grant private licences immediately and allow public television to grow "slowly" with a more limited role, or fully and immediately fund the CBC's development plans.[44]

The CBC was also the target of a *Globe and Mail* editorial titled "In the Public Interest." As the editorialist put it, "in its anxiety to protect the public from 'monopolistic' abuse by private stations, CBC has succeeded only in delaying the development even beyond the horizon of time." In the newspaper's view, the CBC's "whole record on this matter" was "one of repression, procrastination, and frustration," as well as "bureaucratic over-zealousness," whereby, "as always, the Canadian people are the losers." Even taking issue with the CBC's stated purpose of trying to make television "basically Canadian," the editorialist pointed to the growing availability of American signals in border towns and cities, concluding that, with Canadians living near the border buying televisions to tune in to US stations, "the CBC's policy of obstruction has defeated itself."[45]

Reactions to the announcement of the Massey Commission were not much kinder. The conservative *Globe and Mail* heavily criticized the Liberal government's move, contending that there was ample evidence for the government to take a stand on the issue of the regulatory control of television. Labelling the idea of a royal commission on culture "redundant," the editors called out the federal government's indecisiveness and asserted that the establishment of an independent regulatory body open to approving private licensing applications was the only appropriate solution, deeming the commission wholly unnecessary.[46] *Globe and Mail* coverage also agreed with the assertion that a commission would serve only to drag out an already elongated process. For instance, Senator Rupert Davies, the former publisher of the *Kingston Whig-Standard,* was quoted as appraising the commission announcement as "a downer" and "much too sweeping" to solicit real results. His fear was that Canada had made no strides on the television problem and that earlier negotiations with the United States over broadcasting frequencies would be harder to enforce the longer Canada failed to make any progress.[47] The newspaper also featured an opinion piece by P.W. Cook, who called for a national plebiscite on broadcasting to be conducted prior to the formal appointment of a royal commission. As Cook put it, "the people of Canada own the CBC. Since it is a daily and intimate part of their lives they have the fullest right to determine its disposition," and it was clear that many Canadians were dissatisfied with the organization. "Let the people speak," Cook asserted, suggesting that Canadians be asked to choose from among three options regarding CBC television operations: the status quo, increased federal funding to the organization but with independent operators in charge of commercial broadcasting, and the liquidation of the CBC's control of television, albeit with "adequate safeguards" for high-level sustaining programs and for public and government airtime requirements."[48] Cook's suggestion represents a body of evidence emphasizing strong public opinion on the matter of broadcasting politics. Although the average Canadian's perspective might have been less refined by the standards of cultural elites, Canadians possessed strongly held ideas about their country's cultural products. Vincent Massey made explicit efforts to prevent the commission from being overrun by "highbrow" elitism, but many Canadians clearly wished to cut through bureaucratic entanglements and focus on securing the future of broadcasting, regardless of whether they believed in a public or private approach.

Beginning in the summer of 1949, print media published a series of reports on the public hearings and meetings of the Massey Commission. Although most were procedural in content, a significant number included editorial opinions. Most of the witnesses or briefs presented to the commission dispensed arguments, suggestions, and perspectives that would benefit directly the individual or organization in question. One of the more popular testimonies was that of Jack Kent Cook, a radio and print executive. According to one article, he contended that, rather than seek investment from exterior private investors, licences should be given to existing radio operators in Canada. Furthermore, he advocated the creation of an independent regulatory body and suggested that the CBC focus on producing programming for a national audience that would be distributed to privately owned stations tasked with transmitting it since they already held the necessary capital for construction and administration. A number of associations had concerns about giving control to private investors, however, and its impact on the medium's potential to build a stronger cultural economy in Canada. The Federation of Musicians of America and Canada warned that independent stations were "primarily interested in a profitable operation and not too greatly, if at all, concerned with the development or employment of Canadian artists." Similarly, the Canadian Association for Adult Education stated that it wanted to see television development "in the hands of the public," rather than an entity of private enterprise, since "the American experience of private management was far from reassuring," but still "not necessarily in government control."[49]

There were also advocates of public ownership. In April 1950, the Liberal-friendly *Toronto Daily Star* – which tended to assert a strident Canadian nationalism – pleaded against turning Canadian television over to private enterprise in a "monopoly of telecasting." The newspaper's editors cautioned against repeating history as it pertained to radio, pointing out that "neither the federal authorities [n]or the Canadian people are likely to be satisfied at the prospect of extending the commercially dominated program output of private radio into the field of TV." In the view of the editors, "the best interest of the public and the nation" must take precedence, adding that there could "be little question that television should be controlled and mainly operated by the CBC. Television is too potent an instrument of entertainment, education and propaganda, and too important to national defence too."[50] Later that year Pierre Berton took a similarly sympathetic stance toward the CBC in *Maclean's,* observing that it was simply impossible to please everyone. With a litany of adjectives, he wrote that the CBC had been called "bullheaded, autocratic, dictatorial, spineless, weak, pathetic, cheap, high-handed, bumbling, non-sensical, dishonest, power crazy, idiotic, and absurd," as well as "a milch cow, a centaur, and a dog in the manger," even "the worst broadcasting service in the world." But as Berton put it, whereas "unlike the big US networks, which try to please most of the people, most of the time, the CBC's job is to please *all* of the people, part of the time." Berton did not provide a strong case for whether Canada should go the route of public or private broadcasting. Instead, he predicted that Canada would "end up, in television as in radio, with a saw off between public and private ownership," which he believed would only continue to generate bad favour for the CBC until a better solution could be determined. Until then, he argued, the corporation would continue to expand and operate with the same "curious brew of corn, culture, and Canadianism which like so many other facets of life above the 49th parallel, l[ay] somewhere between the British and the American way of doing things." Some readers objected to Berton's analysis, with one letter writer, a Saskatchewan resident, asking "how can it be said that the CBC is impeccably impartial when public funds are used to build a multimillion dollar television outlet that very few Canadians will be able to use?" "The CBC can please me very easily," the reader continued, by "just disintegrat[ing]." A second correspondent, a man in Toronto, pushed further: "Unless you are a farmer, an Eskimo, or an opera fan, the CBC probably holds no interest to you. It may be likened to a virile mother giving her protesting children what she thinks they need instead of what they want."[51]

It is clear, then, that opinions about whether television should be a public or private endeavour in Canada were as varied as they were passionate. The Massey Commission served as a kind of central point around which a debate without a good solution could be organized. Despite both the plethora of different evidence presented to the commission and a flurry of detailed press coverage, ultimately Berton was right – Canada ended up with a hybrid public and private model suggested before the Massey Commission was even appointed.

The final theme in print media coverage of the arrival of television surrounds the question of television's impact on other cultural mediums in Canada. If anxieties about how television might change culture were frequent topics of print media in the 1940s, then it is logical to assume that corporate executives in other Canadian cultural mediums had conversations about what the arrival of television would mean for their businesses. By examining print media content from this era, historians can ascertain how these industries regarded the prospect of television both as an avenue of creative opportunity and as a direct threat to their bottom lines. In reviewing the source base, it becomes clear that early industry opinions on television were mixed. Commentators and businesspeople with interest in newspapers, magazines, radio, film, and theatre had a range of perspectives that can be characterized as ranging from cautiously optimistic, to deeply concerned, to openly hostile. That said, print media sources reveal that the radio industry in particular held the strongest and most alarmist positions on the new medium, whereas the print industry often had more neutral or even positive perspectives. As revealed in the editorials on the public versus private debate seen above, newspapers and magazines more easily welcomed television. Whereas conservative, pro–private enterprise voices pushed for the introduction of television sooner than later, and more liberal voices regarded a national television service as necessary for the development of a unified Canadian cultural identity, there was a general acceptance of the new medium among print industries. It is possible, even likely, that the difference in attitude between mediums can be attributed to the fact that print media had already survived a major innovation in cultural communication after the introduction of radio broadcasting in the 1920s.[52] In weathering radio's early years and adapting their business models to account for the subsequent losses in advertising, perhaps print media were less concerned than their radio counterparts about television as a direct threat.

To be sure, the radio industry had good reason to be concerned. A Duane Jones survey in 1949 republished in the Canadian press reported results from 1,580 American respondents on how much family life in America had changed following the introduction of broadcast television. More than 90% of respondents reported listening to radio less after purchasing a television set, 80% went to the movies less, 58% read fewer books, 48% read fewer magazines, and 23% read newspapers less.[53] Alongside the wide-eyed speculation regarding television's potential effects on society, Canadian cultural industries regularly looked to the United States to form opinions on the impending economic impact of the new technology. Briefs submitted to the Massey Commission by radio officials regularly leaned on these figures, often describing a "gloomy" view of the future of radio: it was "only a matter of time" before radio took a "backseat to the newer medium."[54] As early as 1939, however, journalists pointed out the problem that television's popularity could pose for radio set sales. One article claimed that "television had the limelight of public interest" but that "the headlines given to the official debut of sight broadcasting ... turned to headaches for some [radio] dealers" as customers avoided upgrading to the newest or most advanced radio set in favour of saving for a new television.[55]

The same year a *Maclean's* editorial pushed back against the anxieties of radio producers and fans. "A radio enthusiast informs us," the piece began, that "within a few years broadcasting development and television will knock all printed matters into a cocked hat and that in time few people will have the habit of reading." The editorial board responded by quoting the archbishop of Liverpool: "I am one of those who think that listening in will never oust the habit of reading, and that only in the harmonious blending of the spoken and written word is the power of the publicist at its highest." They continued that "the spoken word is fleeting, [whereas] the printed word remains and tends to anchor itself to the mind."[56] The enthusiastic sentiment here – the notions that radio was the primary communications medium, that print media were secondary, and that the introduction of television would usurp them both – represented a trend in opinions and editorials by radio personnel throughout the 1940s. On the contrary, print media established a more comfortable and less anxious position by promoting itself as being a wholly different experience and as having a unique utility compared with radio or television.

A decade later radio's position of concern had only worsened. One *Globe and Mail* article on shrinking film and radio audiences painted a bleak picture claiming that radio "is aware of the grim spectre of television over its shoulder." Again pointing to trends in America, journalist John Verner McAree noted that "top-ranking [radio] programs lose half their pulling power if there is a television set in the home." McAree, however, saw the inevitable losses to the radio industry as at least partly its own fault. The radio and film industries had erred, he contended, in being "deluded by what they [thought] of as a mass medium," whereby the assumption is that the "mass" is a singular, dense, unchanging body rather than a "plurality" made up of "many other masses." He argued that, though novelty played a role, radio and film "entrench[ed] themselves" by seeking the kind of audience that they desired, "which does not grow, makes no demands, is dumbly grateful," whereas television catered more effectively to different audiences and their varied interests. The piece closed on a sombre note: "Programs are living things, and when the dying competes with the living ... we know which survives."[57] In another article a year later, McAree reported that 75–90 percent of television owners listened to radio less often than before. He sourly related that these findings were unfortunate since television required more active viewing than radio and thus, he concluded, would result in less productivity in the home.[58]

Television's impact was keenly felt. A 1948 *Globe and Mail* article penned by film actor Peter Whitney put it plainly: the entertainment industry "is at the beginning of a technological revolution perhaps more profound than the introduction of broadcasting if not of the movie." Whitney argued that in this new era, in which some had begun referring to radio as the "blind" medium, its leading voices "thought television will all but drive nearly all audible broadcasting out of existence." Expressing an opinion commonly held at the time, Whitney emphasized that "advertisers rule" and will go wherever audiences are most likely to follow. In the case of movies, he quipped that viewers would happily choose "mediocrity" on television over "excellence" on film if they can keep their "carpet slippers and comfort by their own hearth."[59] This apparent dichotomy between film and television continues to exist in the minds of many cultural critics.

As for radio, emphasizing the parallels between its emergence and that of television, in 1953 *Maclean's* featured a six-page retrospective on the first days of broadcast radio in Canada in 1922, underscoring the impact of novelty. Editor Robert Collins waxed poetic in his narrative of early radio, and his tone was similar to that of Berton in his pieces on the awesome future of television, demonstrating Whitney's point that culture in some ways is simultaneously cyclical and evolving. Collins wrote that he wanted to pen the feature "before television shoves radio into the limbo," and his words read like a love letter harkening back to the medium's youth before corporate considerations, government mandates, and fears of the future sullied a more "genuine" experience of radio listening.[60]

Radio and its supporters in the press viewed television as a direct threat, but print media were more receptive. In addition to opinions expressed during the regulatory debates, a number of print outlets explicitly engaged with how television might affect their own medium. Similar to radio, print media looked to America to form their opinions about television's arrival. In 1943, a *Globe and Mail* article described a cooperative effort by the television and newspaper industries to demonstrate how the two mediums could work together to enhance or augment news support. Described as "supplement[ation]," the demonstration showed how television could report the news after the Second World War. A television station in New York broadcast an hour-long program in which it combined the projection of images of the *New York Times* with "re-enactments" of various "stories, want ads, display advertisements, [and] comic cartoons" contained therein. This type of article in the Canadian press was common in the early years of American broadcasting, and the tone regularly emphasized innovation, possibility, and growth as opposed to characterizing TV as a threat. Print media, it seems, accepted the inevitability of television early on and, unlike radio, were more interested in understanding how it added to the Canadian cultural landscape rather than focusing their efforts on trying to limit its potential.[61]

This conciliatory approach perhaps resulted from the fact that early reports and surveys in the United States did not position television as a medium-killing threat in the way that they did for radio. A *Globe and Mail* article in 1951 by American television columnist Jack Gould concluded that "the printed word, at present, is not seriously endangered by the visual medium's invasion of the home." Gould reported that, though sales of books for adults had decreased, the use of public libraries was trending upward. Moreover, newspaper circulation was steadily increasing in cities with television, and a "major surprise" was the "refutation of the persistent assumption that the young book reader would be lost to television." Instead, children were reading more books, not fewer, and Gould argued that exposure to television was increasing students' interest in a variety of topics, which those students were then turning to literature to explore further. McAree's earlier article corroborated this finding, calling it an "oddity" that television owners tended to read more morning newspapers.[62] Television's impact on the media landscape was more complicated than alarmist coverage had predicted.

Another reason for the lack of concern about television could have come from the number of newspaper articles that questioned the medium's potential to emulate successfully the role of news media. In 1952, the assistant executive editor of the *Minneapolis Star and Tribune* told the Canadian Managing Editors' Conference that television "had not yet learned to be an effective news medium." In doubting television's ability to replace print media ever, W.P. Stevens remarked that "the printed word provided a permanent record which could be read at a person's own speed" and noted that surveys of American respondents still heavily favoured newspapers as their preferred source of information.[63] Similarly, Alan Harvey observed that public officials had little love for the new medium. Politicians, he wrote, were wary of television as a vehicle for disseminating party platforms during election seasons, and often they cited a discomfort with the idea of appearing on television in any kind of live capacity.[64] This attitude among politicians clearly did not last.

Although less concerned about a threat from television, a number of print outlets were less enthusiastic about the CBC's continued regulatory control over television since the challenge of monopolies was a regular concern for the print industry. An editorial in 1951 in *Maclean's* expressed that the magazine's editors had little fear that television would "divide or destroy" Canadian radio regardless of a private or public structure, but it found monopolies "particularly distasteful in the field of communication and information." The editorial board was happy to see that the Massey Commission would bring the reality of Canadian television closer but lamented its decision not to adopt an independent regulatory body or offer more freedoms and protections for private television interests. Thus, though little evidence exists to suggest that newspaper and magazine editors held the same alarmist and negative viewpoints as executives in the radio industry, it should not be mistaken for a complete lack of interest in or opinion about the politics of television's arrival in the Canadian cultural scene, its own unique media environment shaped by Canada's economy, society, and geography, including proximity to the United States.[65]

To conclude, the Massey Commission's formal report, published in 1951, argued that in the case of Canadian culture "influences from across the border [are] as pervasive as they are friendly" and that it would be in the "national interest to give encouragement to institutions which express national feeling, promote common understanding and add to the variety and richness of Canadian life." Its recommendations revolved around funding and supporting as much original Canadian cultural content as possible through the growth and promotion of both amateur projects and professional industries. Much of what has been published about the commission's legacy and the conversations that surrounded it seeks to answer whether the cultural policies of Canada have done enough to ward off an overgrowth of American influence. Most of these studies recognize the reality of Canadian culture's inescapable place within an American shadow, but not nearly enough attention has been paid to the relationships fostered *within* that shadow.

Too often the cultural industries of Canada have been characterized as a monolith in opposition to those of the United States. As print media coverage of early television demonstrates, it is far more accurate to envision the Canadian cultural scene as a network of mediums and their communities situated within a valley perpetually shaded by the American mountain. The need, then, is to understand how each of these mediums and their communities have aligned in partnership, competed for resources, and struggled alongside each other all while combatting the reality of American influence. As Massey wrote, "good will alone can do little for a starving plant; if the cultural life of Canada is anaemic [sic], it must be nourished."[66] If historians of Canadian culture have any hope of nourishing and protecting it from further Americanization, then they must understand better the relationships among cultural industries within Canada.

NOTES

1 Don Magill, "What TV Will Do to You," *Maclean's*, 1 March 1951, 24.

2 Lynn Spigel, *Make Room for TV: Television and the Family Ideal in Postwar America* (Chicago: University of Chicago Press, 1992), 2.

3 Paul Rutherford, *When Television Was Young: Primetime Canada, 1952–1967* (Toronto: University of Toronto Press, 1990). Some of the key theories to which Rutherford responds can be found in Marshall McLuhan, *Understanding Media: The Extensions of Man* (New York: Signet Books, 1964); Harold Innis, *Empire and Communications* (Oxford: Clarendon Press, 1950); Harold Innis, *The Bias of Communication* (Toronto: University of Toronto Press, 1951); and Harold Innis, *The Strategy of Culture* (Toronto: University of Toronto Press, 1952).

4 Mark Raboy, *Missed Opportunity: The Story of Canadian Broadcasting Policy* (Montreal and Kingston: McGill-Queen's University Press, 1990); Ryan Edwardson, *Canadian Content: Culture and the Quest for Nationhood* (Toronto: University of Toronto Press, 2008). Other studies include William H. Melody, "The Canadian Broadcasting Corporation's Contribution to Canadian Culture," *Journal of the Royal Society of Arts* 135, 5368 (1987): 286–97; Margaret Prang, "The Origins of Public Broadcasting in Canada," *Canadian Historical Review* 46, 1 (1965): 1–28; and Mary Vipond, "Whence and Whither: The Historiography of Canadian Broadcasting," in *Communicating in Canada's Past: Essays in Media History*, ed. Gene Allen and Daniel J. Robinson

(Toronto: University of Toronto Press, 2009), 233–56. Also of use is Stephen Cole, *Here's Looking at Us: Celebrating Fifty Years of CBC-TV* (Toronto: McClelland and Stewart, 2002).

5 John C. Nerone, "A Local History of the U.S. Press: Cincinnati, 1793–1858," in *Ruthless Criticism: New Perspectives in U.S. Communication History*, ed. William S. Solomon and Robert W. McChesney (Minneapolis: University of Minnesota Press, 1993), 39.

6 Gene Allen, "Old Media, New Media, and Competition: Canadian Press and the Emergence of Radio News," in *Communicating in Canada's Past: Essays in Media History*, ed. Gene Allen and Daniel J. Robinson (Toronto: University of Toronto Press, 2009), 47–49.

7 A brief note on the limitations of this type of study: the source base was produced primarily for and by an audience that in most cases was white, middle-class, English-speaking Ontarians. Although scholars have begun to analyze issues and realities of diversity in postwar history, further study specifically on representation in early media will be necessary as it applies to the advent and growth of television in Canada.

8 Mary Vipond, *The Mass Media in Canada* (Toronto: Lorimer, 1992), 47.

9 Gary Edgerton, *The Columbia History of American Television* (New York: Columbia University Press, 2007), 19.

10 *Felix the Cat*, MZTV Museum of Television, Toronto. See also Edgerton, *The Columbia History of American Television*, 51.

11 Doug Owram, *Born at the Right Time: A History of the Baby Boom Generation* (Toronto: University of Toronto Press, 2018), 88.

12 Edwardson, *Canadian Content*, 69.

13 Ibid. See also Rutherford, *When Television Was Young*, 49.

14 Statistics Canada, "Series A1 – Estimated Population of Canada 1867 to 1977," table, 7, https://www150.statcan.gc.ca/n1/en/pub/11–516-x/pdf/5500092-eng.pdf?st=G1SrI1c3.

15 Statistics Canada, "Series A2–14 – Population of Canada, by Province, Census Dates, 1851 to 1976," table, 8, https://www150.statcan.gc.ca/n1/en/pub/11–516-x/pdf/5500092-eng.pdf?st=G1SrI1c3.

16 Statistics Canada, "Series A67–69 – Populations, Rural and Urban, Census Dates 1871 to 1976," table, 11, https://www150.statcan.gc.ca/n1/en/pub/11–516-x/pdf/5500092-eng.pdf?st=G1SrI1c3.

17 Statistics Canada, "Series A185–237 – Mother Tongues of the Population, Census Years, 1931 to 1976," table, 19, https://www150.statcan.gc.ca/n1/en/pub/11–516-x/pdf/5500092-eng.pdf?st=G1SrI1c3.

18 Statistics Canada, "Geography," https://www150.statcan.gc.ca/n1/pub/11–402-x/2012000/chap/geo/geo-eng.htm.

19 Statistics Canada, "Series A54–66 – Population Density per Square Mile, Canada and Provinces, 1871 to 1976," table, 10, https://www150.statcan.gc.ca/n1/en/pub/11–516-x/pdf/5500092-eng.pdf?st=G1SrI1c3.

20 Paul Litt, *The Muses, the Masses, and the Massey Commission* (Toronto: University of Toronto Press, 1992), 141.

21 See ibid.

22 Ibid., 380.

23 Quoted in Royal Commission on National Development in the Arts, Letters and Sciences, *Report of the Royal Commission on National Development in the Arts, Letters and Sciences, 1949–1951* (Ottawa: Edmond Cloutier, 1951), vol 21, 264, 1–2. https://www.collectionscanada.gc.ca/massey/h5–406-e.html.

24 Oliver Lodge, "Will We See round a Corner?," *Maclean's*, 1 March 1924, 43.

25 R.E. Sherwood, "And the Next Is Television," *Maclean's*, 15 September 1929, 28.

26 "Tele-Talkies May Come," *Maclean's*, 1 September 1930, 26.

27 Thomas Wayling, "Television Broadcast," *Maclean's*, 15 August 1937, 8.

28 Terence Cronyn, "Television Difference Emphasized," *Globe and Mail*, 13 October 1949, 6.

29 "What Are They Looking At?," *Maclean's*, 15 November 1949, 60–62.

30 Magill, "What TV Will Do to You," 24.

31 J.V. McAree, "What Television Is Doing to Homes," *Globe and Mail*, 24 June 1949, 6.

32 Ibid.

33 Magill, "What TV Will Do to You," 24.

34 Ibid, 26.

35 Pierre Berton, "Make Way for the One-Eyed Monster," *Maclean's*, 1 June 1949, 8, 56–57.

36 Merrill Denison, "What about Television?," *Maclean's*, 15 December 1944, 17, 38–41.

37 Harry Hill, "'Radioitis' – Is It Making Our Children Deaf?," *Chatelaine*, April 1934, 14, 50.

38 "CBC Bans Private Station Outlets for U.S. Television," *Globe and Mail*, 18 May 1948, 1.

39 Throne Speech, 26 January 1949, 9, https://www.poltext.org/sites/poltext.org/files/discoursV2/Canada/CAN_DT_XXXX_20_05.pdf.

40 Royal Commission on National Development in the Arts, Letters and Sciences, *Report of the Royal Commission on National Development in the Arts, Letters and Sciences, 1949–1951* (Ottawa: Edmond Cloutier, 1951), 8, https://www.collectionscanada.gc.ca/massey/h5–406-e.html.

41 "CBC Bans Private Station Outlets for U.S. Television," *Globe and Mail*, 18 May 1948, 1.

42 "Canada Bargains with US Officials on Television Plan," *Globe and Mail*, 27 July 1948, 11.

43 Harvey Hickey, "Ten Dollar Television Set Fee," *Globe and Mail*, 4 November 1948, 1.

44 Blair Fraser, "Why They Won't Let You Have TV," *Maclean's*, 15 January 1949, 12-13, 38-39.

45 "In the Public Interest," *Globe and Mail*, 17 January 1949, 6.

46 "Ample Evidence Available," *Globe and Mail*, 27 January 1949, 6.

47 "Fast Move in Television," *Globe and Mail*, 18 March 1949, 3.

48 P.W. Cook, "A Radio Plebiscite Is Suggested," *Globe and Mail*, 21 March 1949, 6.

49 "Commission Told Radio Will Bow to Television," *Globe and Mail*, 19 November 1949, 5; "Keep Television in Public Hands, Commission Told," *Globe and Mail*, 2 September 1949, 8.

50 "Television in Canada," *Toronto Daily Star*, 18 April 1950, 6.

51 Pierre Berton, "Everybody Boos the CBC," *Maclean's,* 1 December 1950, 7–9, 30, 32–33; "Mailbag," *Maclean's,* 15 January 1951, 47.

52 Allen, "Old Media," supports this conjecture as it covers Canadian print media's reaction to the introduction of radio and emphasizes a level of concern and alarm akin to what was seen in the 1940s among radio executives with the advent of television.

53 Litt, *The Muses,* 140.

54 "Commission Told Radio Will Bow to TV," *Globe and Mail,* 9 November 1949, 5.

55 "Radio Half Year Sees Sharp Swing to Cheaper Sets," *Globe and Mail,* 24 July 1939, 18.

56 "Listening vs Reading," *Maclean's,* 15 May 1938, 4.

57 J.V. McAree, "Radio and Movies Losing Audiences," *Globe and Mail,* 10 December 1948, 6.

58 McAree, "What Television Is Doing to Homes," 6.

59 Peter Whitney, "Television Revolution," *Globe and Mail,* 25 September 1948, 6.

60 Bob Collins, "Remember When Radio Was All the Rage?," *Maclean's,* 15 August 1953.

61 "Television Gives Life to Pages of Newspaper," *Globe and Mail,* 6 November 1943, 20–21, 34–35, 38–39.

62 McAree, "What Television Is Doing to Homes," 6.

63 "TV Not Effective as News Medium, Editor Claims," *Globe and Mail,* 19 May 1952, 11.

64 Alan Harvey, "Candid Camera, Television Intimidates Politicians," *Globe and Mail,* 27 September 1951, 15.

65 "Should the CBC Have the Last Word?," *Maclean's,* 1 September 1951, 2.

66 Royal Commission on National Development in the Arts, Letters and Sciences, *Report of the Royal Commission,* 272.

11

Getting Off the Highway

*Frederick Gardiner and Toronto's Transit Policy
in the Age of the Interstate Highway,
1954–63*

JONATHAN ENGLISH

The 1950s were the age of the automobile. From the prognostications of H.G. Wells, to Frank Lloyd Wright's *Broadacre City* vision of proto-suburbia, to the vision of a future of highways, lower population density, and universal automobility presented to millions of visitors at Norman Bel Geddes's *Futurama* exhibit for General Motors in the New York World's Fair in 1939, the automobile had captured the imaginations of North Americans – their political leaders included.[1] President Dwight Eisenhower, inspired by these visions and his own experiences – both as a young colonel leading an army convoy on a gruelling trip across the country on highways snaking through crowded towns and as an occupation commander marvelling at the modernity and efficiency of Germany's *Autobahnen* – led Congress to pass an Interstate Highway Act in 1956 that provided 90 percent federal funding for a national network of expressways. Although funding was intended ostensibly for long-distance trips, state and local politicians soon clamoured for funding of urban expressway projects too. The Canadian government also funded construction of the Trans-Canada Highway beginning in 1949, though it was not built to freeway standards, and the program did not include funding for urban highway projects.

North Americans, flush with wartime savings and federal government support for the development of suburban housing, abandoned streetcars and buses for cars in droves. Toronto was no exception: from 1952 to 1962, its transit ridership declined by 37.6% – comparable to 38.8% in Chicago, 40.3% in Washington, and 41.0% in Philadelphia.[2] By the time US federal funding began to flow to transit in the late 1960s, there was little left to save, and transit had to be rebuilt from scratch in communities that had been redeveloped entirely around the automobile. Although in the 1950s transit and the "inner city" did not have strong racial connotations, that changed dramatically by the late 1960s, placing a serious further barrier to transit investment.

Toronto, uniquely, was able to reverse this path: it was the only city in Canada or the United States to see overall transit ridership growth between 1946 and 1970.[3] In large part, this was because it had a metropolitan government that subsidized the transit system in bad years, so it did not face the same spiral of fare hikes, service cuts, and ridership decline that affected American transit systems. Many transit systems were still in private hands in the 1950s, but even when they were in municipal ownership they were seen as utilities expected to be self-supporting financially. Toronto had been no exception. However, Frederick Gardiner, the inaugural chairman of the Municipality of Metropolitan Toronto (Metro) beginning in 1953, saw before most that transit could not be self-sustaining in the age of the automobile. If it were to survive and thrive, then it needed at least some government support – as highways were receiving in vast quantities in the 1950s. This decision saved Toronto's transit system, keeping it as a mode used by people with a choice and making the city what it is today.

The task of implementing the autocentric vision was entrusted in cities across the continent to extraordinarily powerful public servants. Ostensibly apolitical, they adopted the mantle of technocracy. Since government planning had triumphed in the Second World War, expectations were strong that comparable attention could resolve the festering problems of the industrial city. Although these individuals were generally disdainful of intellectualized approaches to city building, in practice they generally sought to implement the urban ideals of Clarence Perry, Clarence Stein, Frank Lloyd Wright, Le Corbusier, and Norman Bel Geddes. First and foremost, they focused on the need to reduce population density and increase access to green space.

Many cities in the early postwar years had their own personages in this mould. Technocratic master planners were not a new phenomenon – some North American cities had earlier embraced the "City Beautiful" approach to urban renewal, seeking to emulate the grand boulevards and monumental public buildings of Paris. But in the postwar years, their power was turbocharged by the abundant funds from an increasingly activist federal government in the United States and provincial governments in Canada. Some remained within a single city, whereas others had more itinerant careers, such as Harland Bartholomew, the chief planner in Newark, St. Louis, and Washington, or Ed Logue, who worked in New Haven, Boston, and New York. They worked closely with local business communities and political leaders to advance their plans. Many smaller cities hired them as consultants, like Bartholomew, who produced plans for dozens of American cities, or Jacques Gréber in Ottawa. Unquestionably the most enduring in the public imagination was New York's Robert Moses, immortalized by Robert Caro's excoriating 1974 tome *The Power Broker*.[4] Although that book and others – notably Jane Jacobs's *The Death and Life of Great American Cities* in 1961[5] – later decisively discredited the model of urban technocrat with sweeping powers to implement urban renewal, in the 1950s they were at their peak.

In Toronto, the closest approximation of this role was Frederick Gardiner. Like Moses, he had had an electoral career – as reeve of the small but wealthy Village of Forest Hill, whereas Moses had been an unsuccessful Republican candidate for New York governor – but left it behind in favour of building power in appointed roles. When Leslie Frost appointed him as the first chairman of the newly created Municipality of Metropolitan Toronto, Gardiner was placed in charge of renewing the region's infrastructure – transportation, water and sewer systems, parks, and housing. Moses shared a similarly broad portfolio through the combination of numerous titles – including New York City parks commissioner, New York City planning commissioner, New York State Power Authority chairman, chairman of the Triborough Bridge and Tunnel Authority, and New York City construction coordinator.

The comparison between Moses and Gardiner was drawn at the time. As prominent planner and scholar Hans Blumenfeld remembered, "I came to greatly admire [Gardiner]: I used to say that he had all of the good characteristics of Robert Moses and only a few of the bad ones; in particular, he was able to admit and correct a mistake."[6] Shortly after taking the helm of Metropolitan Toronto, Gardiner visited Moses in New York. At their meeting, the two power brokers discussed their shared distaste for "high-minded advisers." When asked by Moses about his goals, Gardiner responded – startlingly for a Conservative in 1953 – that he planned to be like Stalin, meaning that he would develop a five-year plan and implement it ruthlessly.[7]

However, though their initial views and approaches were similar, Gardiner gradually drifted away from the approach to transportation favoured by Moses and his American counterparts. Instead, he became a skeptic of highways at a time when they were the paragon of modernity, and increasingly he embraced transit when it was widely seen as a relic. The development of interstate highways, and how they shaped American cities, have been significant topics of scholarship. The literature points to the combination of federal funding for highways and federal support for home ownership, along with the unprecedented global growth of cheap energy as new sources of oil in the Middle East were developed,[8] as key factors driving the explosion of both automobile use and geographic expansion of urban areas.[9] They made possible the widespread ownership – at least for white Americans – of a suburban house and car that epitomized the "American Dream" exported by Hollywood around the world. Envy of, and admiration for, this lifestyle were at the foundation of the American Century. In Vice-President Richard Nixon's "Kitchen Debate" with Soviet leader Nikita Khrushchev in 1959, the symbol representing the success of the American political and economic system was a suburban house. It came at a cost, however, in the development of an autocentric transportation system that could not accommodate needed growth without unacceptable social and environmental costs.

Canada followed the American path of suburbanization more closely than most countries. It emerged from the Second World War as one of the world's major industrial powers – having produced more trucks during the war, for example, than all the Axis powers combined.[10] As industries shifted to civilian production, the Toronto area became a major centre for automobile production. Torontonians bought cars with the enthusiasm of their American neighbours: automobile registrations rose from 152,961 in 1940 to 326,009 in 1954, and by 1960 there were more cars than houses registered in Toronto.[11] Of approximately 2.7 million immigrants who arrived in Canada between the end of the war and the mid-1960s, over a quarter settled in Toronto.[12] The growth, however, was concentrated in the newly developing suburbs. From 1946 to 1950, the City of Toronto's population declined by nearly 30,000, or 4.2%, while the suburbs grew by over 100,000, or 48%.[13] This pattern of development nearly proved fatal to transit in most American cities, but thanks in part to Gardiner, Metropolitan Toronto was able to preserve a strong transit system – an asset essential to its functioning in the twenty-first century.

Frederick Gardiner was born as the second son of a dour Methodist family on 21 January 1895. His father, David, had arrived penniless from Ireland but had risen to become a prison guard and small landlord, on whose properties young Frederick worked in most of his spare time. His mother, Victoria, was quite learned and worldly for the time and her station, and she harboured burning ambitions for her sons. Frederick was a somewhat rambunctious young man. His lifelong keenness for gambling and, for many years, alcohol was perhaps a result of chafing under the austerity of his upbringing. He nevertheless excelled as a student after some early hiccoughs, eventually gaining entrance into the University of Toronto. Following service as a flying officer in the First World War, Gardiner entered Osgoode Hall Law School. He graduated first in his class, which he credited to hard work and extraordinary diligence. It was the proudest moment in his life, he often averred, for he had surpassed many young men with far less humble origins.

Working assiduously toward his stated life goal of becoming a millionaire, Gardiner became one of the most prominent trial lawyers in the province, helped by his diligence, outgoing personality, and booming voice. He also entered into an array of businesses. His best financial judgment was selling nearly all of his stocks in early 1929 and, following the stock market crash, investing all of his resources into shares of the Bank of Toronto. Gardiner typified the successful Conservative businessman.

His father had been active in both the Conservative Party and the Orange Lodge and had introduced his son to them at a young age. Frederick worked on a number of campaigns and remained active in the party machinery. These connections proved to be a launching pad for a successful campaign in 1935 for deputy reeve of Forest Hill. This village of about 12,000 was one of the wealthiest residential neighbourhoods in the country. It was home to much of the city's elite as well as its aspiring elite, among whom Gardiner could be counted. Although the campaign was tumultuous, he was able to glean the support of the less affluent North End against an opponent running on a platform of maintaining the exclusivity of the village.

Gardiner long resisted entering electoral politics beyond his small, part-time role as deputy reeve, and later reeve, of Forest Hill. "There is nothing you can do in politics that makes the cash register ring," he said.[14] However, he quickly gained prominence in the Conservative Party's back rooms. A renowned barnstorming orator, Gardiner was in demand from party organizers across the province. In 1948, after refusing entreaties to run for the provincial Conservative leadership, he supported Frost, who won and thus became the premier. Their relationship proved to be important both for Gardiner and for Toronto. Frost shared Gardiner's politics, but his mild, tempered personality and rural origins stood him in marked contrast to Gardiner. Nevertheless, they became allies. Gardiner had been a close friend, and partner in the party machinery, of Frost's brother Cecil, who died at age forty-nine in 1947. Following the loss, Gardiner and Leslie Frost grew much closer.[15]

Gardiner was firmly ensconced in the progressive wing of the party. Despite his pro-business persona, he pressed the Conservatives to adopt a progressive policy on organized labour and even helped to lead the lobbying for changing the party's name to the oxymoronic Progressive Conservative Party.[16] As biographer Timothy Colton describes, Gardiner recognized "that the party could survive as a political force only by fusing its traditional commitment to free enterprise with a new willingness to enlarge the social and economic role of government in favour of the weak and disadvantaged."[17]

Gardiner began with a hostile attitude toward regional government, as one might expect given his parochial political origins in the Village of Forest Hill, a community with the highest assessments of any municipality in Canada and one fiercely determined to maintain its independence.

As late as 1944, he was still referring to the idea of metropolitan government as "poison."[18] Two years later, however, he was appointed by the provincial government to the newly established Toronto and Suburban Planning Board and was soon elected vice-chair and then chair.[19] This role gave him a taste for large-scale planning. It made Gardiner viscerally aware of the desperately inadequate infrastructure in the fast-growing region and the obstacles presented by the patchwork of municipal jurisdictions. He was also becoming disillusioned with the chaotic governance and limited power of York County, on the council of which he served *ex officio* as reeve of Forest Hill.[20] His growing passion for government involvement in social and physical infrastructure placed him well within the mainstream in the wake of the Second World War, and his involvement in regional planning began to change his mind on the importance of regional governance.[21]

As early as 1947, Gardiner was agitating for the Planning Board to include a unified public transit network in its plans. At the same time, he had developed a strong passion for road construction – especially modern expressways – that would do much more to shape the popular historical perception of the man than his work on transit. His impulse to remedy the parlous and fragmented state of the region's infrastructure meant that, within three meetings of his election as chair of the Planning Board in 1949, it voted on a resolution calling for a unified municipality for the metropolitan region. Later that year Gardiner decided against running for re-election as reeve. His new interest in regional planning and big infrastructure had replaced his circumscribed interests in his village, just as he knew that his choice to support amalgamation would put him in danger of defeat in Forest Hill. Gardiner relished the new wider role and quickly threw himself into campaigning for amalgamation, proving to be among its most effective and persuasive advocates.[22]

When the provincial government, in the guise of the quasi-judicial Ontario Municipal Board (OMB), instead recommended the creation of a metropolitan level of government, Premier Frost decided to appoint his friend Gardiner to be the first chairman.[23] Although the role and powers of the chairman were legally amorphous, Gardiner swiftly and assiduously worked to amass power, both through his personality, combining charm with irascibility, and through his absolute mastery of the files before council.[24]

Gardiner's close ties to the provincial government, and in particular his personal relationship with Frost, were key to his power. "There was not a minister in the cabinet who had as much influence as Ted Gardiner," declared Harry Price, one of Frost's closest political advisers.[25] "I always endeavour to meet your point of view," Frost himself wrote to Gardiner.[26] In Canada, all municipalities are commonly dubbed "creatures of the provinces," created and disestablished just as easily with a bill in the legislature. Even if Gardiner did not always prevail in negotiations with the province, his relationships ensured that his position always got a fair hearing – a powerful asset for an Ontario municipal leader.

Soon the Metro Council became little more than a rubber stamp for the plans and policies emerging from Gardiner's small office. These perceptions crystallized when Gardiner went on a vacation to Jamaica and the council seemed to be paralyzed, incapable of making a decision – a situation widely satirized by newspaper cartoonists. They portrayed Gardiner variously as a "Supermayor" flying with cape trailing behind, or, in a style redolent of the era, as an Eastern despot. A contemporaneous magazine writer described Gardiner as "chairman, father image, mentor, sergeant-major and advisor" to the members of the council. "Gardiner, whose features are so craggy that he makes men like Admiral Bull Halsey look effete," he wrote, "is loved, disliked, feared and respected by his flock."[27] Phil Givens, then a Toronto alderman and later the city's mayor, described Gardiner as "a benevolent dictator." The chairman's opinion generally determined that of council: "I feel nothing of any consequence turns without his approval," Givens said.[28] Gardiner's popular nickname "Big Daddy" derived from the patriarch in the Tennessee Williams play *Cat on a Hot Tin Roof,* turned into a film in 1958.[29]

Joseph Cornish, another Toronto alderman and a wartime army officer, was intimidated. "It was with a great deal of reluctance that you would get up in council to disagree with Mr. Gardiner," he explained.

> Here was this big impressive man who had spent all those years in Forest Hill and in the county, who was a friend of the [provincial] government and was well steeped in the ways of Bay Street, who was familiar with every tree and stone and service station in the area we

were talking about. He seemed to know everything about everything. There weren't many who were prepared to dispute a major point with him. It was like putting your nose in a meat grinder.[30]

Facilitated by the amiable but usually ineffectual personality of his only conceivable rival in power on the Metro Council, Toronto mayor Nathan Phillips, Gardiner's primacy on the council was beyond dispute.

His views on transportation were initially orthodox, but growing experience gradually led to an unmistakable shift. Gardiner had championed expressways, including one along the lakeshore that eventually bore his name and, most infamously, the Spadina Expressway, ultimately stopped in 1971 by a citizens' movement that reshaped the city's politics for decades to come.[31] His first role in regional planning was on the Toronto and York Roads Commission, and the difficulty of getting what Gardiner viewed as essential new highways built played an important role in his decision to champion amalgamation and, later, metropolitan government.[32] The "bulldozer" had no qualms about surmounting any obstacle to build highways, and he saw himself as the man "with the courage to say where we should have a street and then plow through the houses and make it long enough."[33] None of these views were out of place for a municipal leader in the 1950s, and Robert Moses easily could have spoken such phrases. But Gardiner's views on transportation became increasingly nuanced as his time in office proceeded. After a few years at the helm of the Metro Council, Gardiner was no longer a single-minded champion of new urban expressways.

Although his early inaugural addresses to the council gave relatively short shrift to transit – in 1955, it was not even mentioned[34] – by 1956 there was a change. He spoke at length about the many arterial road and expressway construction projects that his government had under way. But Gardiner concluded that "a disturbing factor with respect to the provision of these four arterial highways is that we must immediately give consideration to additional rapid transit if our rapidly increasing population is to be moved with anything approaching economy and efficiency." He pointed south with skepticism at the cities that had been models of modernity. "It is the experience of every large city in America," he declared, "that a succession of new expressways is not the answer to efficient and economical movement of traffic. Each successive one is filled the day it is opened. The irresistible fact is that you simply cannot provide sufficient highways and parking space to accommodate every person who desires to drive his motor vehicle downtown and back each day."[35]

Like its American counterparts, the Ontario government was not so progressive in its transportation policies. Gardiner refused to be tempted by the availability of provincial highway funding if it simply meant building highways where transit would do the job better. "It is a snare and a delusion," he said, "to keep on spending tens of millions of dollars on highways because the province will subsidize them 50% when we know that beyond a certain stage that $1 spent on rapid transit is worth $5 spent on more arterial highways and parking facilities."[36]

"The most difficult problem facing Canadian cities is traffic congestion," Gardiner claimed in an address in 1958 to the Canadian Transit Association. This opinion would have found him in the mainstream view of transportation and urban policy in the 1950s. It was only in his prescribed solutions that he differed. Certainly, Gardiner believed in the importance of building a substantial urban expressway network, even at the cost of demolishing homes and businesses in established neighbourhoods. Nevertheless, he said, "it is now painfully obvious that building a succession of expressways each of which will be filled the day it is opened with the traffic it will generate will not solve the traffic and transportation problems of any community. What will solve the problem is a practical and effective combination of expressways and rapid transit."[37]

Gardiner was not merely pandering to his audience. Even when speaking to a body seemingly as transit-unfriendly as the Ontario Good Roads Association in 1956, he stressed the need for investment in public transit. He boasted that "our highways in Ontario have no superior in this country and compare very favourably with the best in America," and he recognized that "there is nothing which gives a man such a feeling of importance as driving down main street in a two-toned automobile plentifully splashed with chrome, even if he had to borrow the down payment from the small loan company and will be married to the finance company for the next thirty months." Nevertheless, he stressed the problems. Although Los Angeles, in the 1950s, was the model city for much of the world, Gardiner claimed that its parking problem was unsolvable. "A man hitched a trailer to his car," he joked, "and when asked what the trailer was for, he said he had to have somewhere to live while he was looking for a place to park." Most importantly, he recognized the importance of transit service quality in attracting automobile drivers. "If you happen to be one of those who makes his living out of public transit," he intoned,

> you can argue until you are blue in the fare box but you will still find that you can't derrick the automobile rider out of his car and into the street car or subway. The only way you can get him there is to coax him with a more convenient and more economical mode of travel with rapid and regular service.

Before the seemingly unsympathetic audience, Gardiner went further: "The day has arrived when our transportation problems can no longer be solved by building a succession of arterial highways. After a basic system of arterial highways has been completed, rapid transit will cost infinitely less and will do the job infinitely better."[38]

Unlike most Conservatives, Gardiner believed firmly in the public provision of transit service – very different from the dominant view in many American cities, where transit was still viewed as a private monopoly with which governments needed to battle. "A transit system operating within a reasonable fare structure is just as important a municipal service as water supply, sewage disposal, arterial highways and education," he declared in his inaugural address in 1956. Gardiner was anxious that rising fares would produce the same vicious spiral that caused transit ridership to evaporate in most American cities. Given the costs of constructing subways, expanding suburban service, and acquiring the former private suburban bus lines, the Toronto Transit Commission (TTC) was no longer profitable. The debt for the Yonge subway line had been borrowed against future revenues from the TTC's fare box, but such a source of funding would be impossible for any future project, not least because the bond market was no longer buying securities issued by the declining transit industry.[39] Gardiner saw subsidies as the only viable alternative. He refused to consider raising fares since, he argued, "in all American cities [fare increases] had resulted in a loss of passenger traffic." Instead, subsidies were needed for a "transition period from a purely city operation in a confined and lucrative area to a metropolitan operation in an immensely expanded area where there were bound to be many deficit areas."[40]

Gardiner mounted a long campaign for transit subsidies from higher levels of government, a theme that would recur in Toronto transit for decades to come. "The cost of rapid transit should be contributed to by both the Dominion and by the Province," he said. "The Province would be wise in its own interest to subsidize rapid transit in lieu of additional highways and expressways which will only confuse the situation and compound the problem." At a time when the Interstate Highway Act was moving through the American Congress, he questioned the domination of the automobile:

> We do not hesitate to spend public money on roads, expressways, and parkways for the convenience of motor vehicles or to subsidize air travel by the building of airports, but for some reason we shy away from the subsidization of public transit ... As millions are spent for the convenience of the motor vehicle, either for its commercial or domestic use, we will likely find that some more millions will have to be spent to subsidize the public transit system. You must move people as well as motor cars.[41]

Gardiner did not abandon the automobile. He still maintained his commitment to completing the network of highways that he had supported since his days on the Planning Board, calling for spending $100 million on four new urban expressways. But he also called for $150 million to be spent on two new subway lines. He favoured a "balanced" system of both highways and transit. This was the approach rhetorically favoured in many North American cities, but in most cases the reality tilted far toward the automobile. In Metropolitan Toronto under Gardiner, the approach genuinely could be termed "balanced."[42]

He couched his radical position in traditional Conservative concern about spending and taxation:

> Granted a six-lane expressway will do a job a two-lane city street can't do, but the $64,000 question is – are we equal to the monumental task and cost of providing the macaroni maze of freeways, cloverleafs and parkways which will be necessary to relieve the present congestion let alone provide for future growth. Traffic engineers say they can do it if they are given the money. As a matter [of] fact that is the engineer's standard answer to everything. Give us the money and we can do anything, even build a stairway to the stars. But the ghost which always haunts us is – can we afford the money? – and the answer is no![43]

Unlike in many American cities, these words were not coming from an idealistic urban planner or a transit activist. They were coming from a Conservative businessman and powerful politician known as Toronto's answer to Robert Moses. A Torontonian Caesar, hand-selected by the provincial government, Gardiner bestrode the new metropolitan government like a colossus. He believed that transit was a better use of government funds than highways, and he had the power – to borrow from Caro's conception of Moses – to change the policy. Despite all his power and connections, it would prove to be neither easy nor quick, but in the end Gardiner almost singlehandedly reshaped provincial transportation policy so that transit would receive equal or greater funding than roads, and, critically, he did so before the prewar transit legacy had disintegrated. This set the stage for the city's multi-decade role as a transit model.

Certainly, there were many critics of a sole reliance on highways, even in those heady days of expressway construction. Some intellectuals and planners noticed the perils of total automobile dependence. Most planners, however, largely embraced the ideology of progress and the inevitability of automobility in the 1950s. Under President Eisenhower, the US Congress passed the Federal Aid Highway Act of 1956, committing to 90 percent federal funding for the construction of a national network of expressways. That funding was increasingly allocated to urban highways intended for daily commuters rather than interstate travel. Soon cities across the United States were bisected by wide highways – often forcing the demolition of entire neighbourhoods, many of them disproportionately home to minorities.

Canada was not much different. Although the federal government was less keen to fund roads beyond a national Trans-Canada Highway, provincial governments – with essentially the same fiscal capacity as the federal government unlike American states – were much more eager to enter the game. In Ontario, for example, urban highway projects were given 50 percent funding from the province, and many local expressway projects were built as provincial highways and therefore funded entirely by Queen's Park.[44]

Harland Bartholomew, the chief planner of Washington, DC and a prominent national figure, presented an American contrast to Gardiner's attitudes toward regional transportation. By the 1950s, he was already in his sixties and had shaped the capital for decades. Although he was sympathetic to transit, he was far less so than Gardiner. In 1950, Bartholomew served as the chief consultant on a regional plan that dismissed the idea of rapid transit: "'Neither the existing nor the probable future population pattern' would provide the densities needed to make rapid transit economically sensible."[45] At the time, however, Washington's population density was 11,738 per square mile, compared with 7,057 in Toronto, where a new subway was then under construction.[46] In 1955, Bartholomew was charged with creating a transportation plan for the region. The plan was to be as technocratic as possible, with minimal community consultation and political involvement, and was led by planners, engineers, and managers under his aegis.[47]

Historian of the Washington Metro Zachary Schrag describes the process as a tug-of-war between different factions – including rail, bus, and highway advocates among the planners and engineers – but he makes clear that the dominance of highways was never in doubt. All of the proposed scenarios in the plan of 1959 included massive highway expansion, not least because much of the study's funding came from federal highway money. Although it included a sop to transit advocates – most prominently eight express bus routes along the new highways without even the benefit of their own lanes and, unusual for the time, two rail routes – it is clear that the planners and engineers saw Greater Washington's transportation future as largely asphalt rather than rails.[48]

The Chicago Area Transportation Study in the late 1950s and early 1960s was a landmark of the "predict and provide" rational approach to transportation planning, and it served as a model for numerous other transportation plans across the United States. Although it recommended a modest expansion of the rail transit system, alongside a massive highway construction program that would produce a "gridiron" of urban expressways, it made no mention of the broader transit network of buses, the only transit available in much of the conurbation. Gardiner, in contrast, spent much time dealing with expansions to suburban bus routes.[49]

His ostensible model, Robert Moses, was even more dismissive of public transportation, refusing, for example, to include rail on his bridges or on the Van Wyck Expressway to Idlewild (now Kennedy) Airport. In remarks at a luncheon of the National Highway Users Conference on 9 May 1962, Moses discussed his commuter rail philosophy at length. Rather than proposing a visionary solution comparable to his approach to road transportation, he merely criticized the private management of the railways and warned governments about the hazards of subsidizing them. His preference for the automobile was evident when he said that "we are becoming hysterical and prodigal about aid to ailing commuter railroads, and tend to exaggerate the advantages of mass transportation."[50]

It was not until the late 1960s when Governor of New York Nelson Rockefeller created the Metropolitan Transportation Authority, which included the suburban commuter railways, that New York made even desultory efforts to improve transit in the new suburbs. Even within the five boroughs, transit funds were devoured by the bottomless pit of deferred maintenance left by the long-insolvent private subway operators.[51]

Some of Gardiner's speeches sound like they could have come from Lewis Mumford, who wrote his article "The Highway and the City" in 1958. That article lamented "the religion of the motorcar" that stood "outside the realm of rational criticism." Mumford, like Gardiner, favoured a "balanced" system of transportation. "The fatal mistake we have been making is to sacrifice every other form of transportation to the private motorcar," he wrote. "We need a better transportation system, not just more highways."[52] He later expanded these themes, but it took several years for such criticism to begin shaping the opinions of most government officials. Gardiner was making the same points as Mumford at the same time.

Opposition from local community activists and intellectuals, however, often was dismissed easily by the powerful advocates of highway construction, including suburban communities, business groups, the automobile industry, and those who simply thought that the car was a much more pleasant way to get around than the streetcar or train that they had been forced to crowd onto in wartime. This is where Gardiner was so unusual. He was neither a radical activist nor a neighbourhood leader acting to preserve his own home – he was a Conservative politician and prominent businessman who had credibility among such groups to get support for highly radical ideas in his day. He had the Conservative credibility to get the kinds of people who would have been powerful opponents of transit in other cities to line up behind its expansion in Toronto.

Gardiner was not so far ahead of his time as one might imagine, however. Already by 1962, President John F. Kennedy had begun to heed intellectuals such as Mumford and to notice that promises of decongested cities made by proponents of expressways had come to naught. Kennedy called for federal assistance to local public transit projects, in line with highway assistance legislated six years earlier. "Our national welfare," he said, "requires the provision of good urban transportation, with the properly balanced use of private vehicles and modern mass transport to help shape as well as serve urban growth."[53] Two years later the Urban Mass Transportation Act was part of a wave of Kennedy-promoted legislation passed amid the outpouring of sympathy following his assassination.[54]

But the difference in timing was decisive. Gardiner saved the TTC from a spiral of fare hikes and reduced service in the early 1950s by securing a modest but timely subsidy. By the later 1950s, he had led the expansion of the subway and taken the capital cost burden off the transit system, giving it considerable fiscal room. By the time American federal money began flowing in the late 1960s, it was too late, because transit had already largely collapsed. While TTC ridership dropped by 30% between 1953 and 1963, a precipitous but survivable decline, American transit systems, on average, hemorrhaged 57% of their ridership in the same period, and in many cities the figure was even worse.[55] Although ample federal capital funding was available, the new rail projects that it typically paid for lacked decent bus networks to extend their coverage and bring in riders. As a result, most were planned as little more than parking shuttles for commuters to an often-dwindling central business district.

As Metro was going through its birth pangs, Gardiner was hesitant to press the issue of transit too hard. Suburban representatives were demanding enhanced service to their constituencies and a flat fare across Metro. He delayed, knowing that both measures would require substantial subsidies and fearing rejection by the provincial government, which was still in thrall to the idea of transit self-sustainability and faced inevitably with similar subsidy demands from all other municipalities.[56] Subsidizing transit was still, in Toronto as everywhere, anathema. Instead, as Harold Kaplan described it, the policy of William McBrien, the widely respected head of the TTC from 1933 to his death in 1954, was to "quiet suburban demands without actually meeting them."[57] The suburban politicians were not fooled; they launched a barrage of motions either to abolish the commission or to force it to improve suburban service. "What saved the TTC in 1954," Kaplan said, "was Gardiner's ability to delay or defeat the suburban motions."[58] Still, Gardiner struck a committee that he chaired to study the question. Although a delaying tactic, it nevertheless engaged him further in the issue.

As his speeches quoted above demonstrate, by 1955 Gardiner had become keenly focused on the transit question. To him, the idea of subsidies was no longer beyond the pale. That year he lobbied Frost to allow Metro to provide an ostensibly one-time $2.5 million subsidy to the TTC to mitigate a fare hike, making the case that the only alternative was to raise fares, which had been proven to drive passengers away and put transit systems into a vicious cycle in the United States.[59] In response to Gardiner's letter, Frost's advisers produced a memorandum opposing the idea. "Officials of the Department of Municipal Affairs believe that if the Metropolitan Council is permitted to make even one grant to cover the deficit of the Toronto Transit Commission ... [then] the municipality will be given the right to underwrite the deficits from then on." They warned that this would destroy the political independence of the commission – maintained even throughout the Depression – and result in the addition of unprofitable service in response to political pressure.[60] They were not wrong in their forecast, but clinging to the old ways of operating had proven to be fatal to transit in many American cities. Despite the opposition, his persuasiveness and relationship with the premier enabled Gardiner to prevail. In so doing, he broke the dam that had long barred governments from subvention of public transit, as Frost's advisers had predicted.

This precedent proved to be the salvation of transit in Metropolitan Toronto. In the United States, a single bad fiscal year meant service cuts and fare increases, which caused riders to abandon the system permanently by buying a car. The City of Cleveland, somewhat larger than Toronto in the 1950s, illustrates the point. Cleveland had municipalized its transit system in 1942, and, flush with a surplus from the busy war years, it embarked on a major program of modernization. It included a brand-new subway, which opened a year after Toronto's in 1955. From that point onward, the two cities' paths diverged. In Cleveland, transit remained dependent entirely on the fare box for revenue through the 1950s and 1960s, and therefore service was repeatedly cut as deficits mounted. By the time the system was regionalized in 1974, it was a husk of its former self: ridership had plummeted from 493 million riders per year in 1946 to 78 million in 1974.

Gardiner was also essential in getting the new subway expanded – an east-west route on Bloor and Danforth to complement the north-south Yonge line, in addition to a branch along University Avenue downtown. The city had long supported the idea, but suburban politicians were far more skeptical of a project that they saw as primarily benefiting city residents. They were still demanding a flat fare for all of Metro in exchange for their assent, viewing the double fare that outer riders paid to get downtown as punitive. Without that fare supplement, however, any hope of supporting the TTC's expenses from the fare box was doomed. Gardiner temporized for several years, hoping for salvation from higher levels of government, until 1957, when he became determined to see the $150 million project through to completion. He declared that he would "pound this thing through with an iron fist."[61]

As usual, he was successful, after rounds of cajoling, bullying, and horse trading with Metro Council. The decision to add a new subway line in 1958 was a decisive moment in the region's transit history. The first subway had been approved with the belief that it would be self-supporting – effectively a continuation of how transit had been run before the war. This time it was different. Transit was no longer a profitable venture. All recognized that direct government support was essential. Transit had shifted from being the principal means of moving people around the city to being seen as an alternative to the automobile. Most North American cities waited until a decade or more later, when their transit system had shrivelled to next to nothing, but Toronto embraced transit's new role while it was still a viable mode of transportation. To a considerable extent, it can thank Gardiner for the shift.

It is impossible to know definitively how Gardiner came to adopt such unorthodox views on transit. The change does not seem to have been sparked by a singular event; he left no memoirs, and his biographer goes into little detail about his motivations. He might have been influenced by William McBrien, the long-time TTC head who was also a respected and influential Orange Conservative. Being a British Canadian, he might also have been more influenced by the mother country than a similar American would have been. London's expansion, Gardiner once said, "followed the extension of the public transportation system. The motor car in England did not have the same revolutionary impact upon the development of their suburban municipalities as has been the case in America."[62]

It might also have been simple pride, for his metropolitan government had been placed in charge of the TTC, and he did not want to be seen as having performed poorly at the task. The comparison with Moses is instructive: transit was one of the few realms of New York infrastructure planning left out of his control. Moreover, transit competed with the toll bridges that were the key financial source of his power. When given the chance to expand his power by having his Triborough Bridge and Tunnel Authority take over the subways in 1952, Moses uncharacteristically opposed the proposal, likely since the money-losing subways would have drained financial resources that he wanted to use for other projects.[63] Gardiner's position might also have been a result simply of his own power of observation triumphing over dogma; even by the 1950s, it had become evident to any dispassionate observer that expressways, as Gardiner often remarked, failed to live up to their promises of reducing congestion.

The precedent established by these policies put in place during the early years of Metro was vital to the survival of transit in its darkest hour. TTC ridership reached its nadir in the late 1950s, stabilized, and then began a steady rise. In contrast, even New York's subway ridership continued to decline until 1977; in other cities, the decline was precipitous.[64] Gardiner effectively had threaded the needle. He secured approval of the new subway through implicit promises of improved service and lower fares for suburban areas. In so doing, he set the stage for the region's transit revival.

Certainly, Gardiner was no perfect friend of transit. Any observer could find numerous quotations with full-throated endorsements of new highways. He delayed the Bloor-Danforth subway construction for the early years of Metro while his first two expressway projects were built. He was always very conservative in the amount that he permitted the Metro Council to borrow for projects, and the demand in the early years for funding for all sorts of construction, ranging from schools to sewage treatment plants, was nearly inexhaustible.[65] Throughout the period, though, he pressured higher levels of government for funding from their more diverse tax bases with limited success. He eventually proceeded with the project anyway, in 1957, and a few years later his lobbying helped to secure the funds from the province needed to accelerate construction.

Gardiner was also not alone in his advocacy for transit. McBrien had done much to establish the credibility of the TTC as a well-run organization and to make the case for subway construction. Many members of the Metro Council from the City of Toronto long favoured subway projects, as did newspapers such as the liberal *Toronto Daily Star,* which hectored Gardiner for delays on subway construction throughout the 1950s.[66] There were also various community organizations that supported transit expansion and lobbied for provincial funding.[67] The Property Owners Association of Toronto, for example, adopted a resolution in 1956 calling for a plan to avoid "the unnecessary extravagance of expressways which past experience has shown simply to end up in a shifting of traffic bottlenecks from one place to another."[68] It was Gardiner, however, with his uniquely forceful personality, his close ties to the provincial government and the Conservative establishment, and his reputation for fiscal probity, who had the power and credibility to prevent transit expansion from being starved for funds or bogged down in endless city-suburban discord.

Despite his contributions to transit, Gardiner is best known for the expressway projects that he championed. Two were built on his watch, and, though they radiated from downtown to the west and northeast, these projects were low-hanging fruit in expressway terms, located in an undeveloped river valley and along the then largely industrial lakeshore. They required minimal land clearance. The next phases of planned expressways were far more destructive, requiring hacking through established residential neighbourhoods with the proverbial meat axe of Moses. By far the most famous was the Spadina Expressway, to cut through a historic neighbourhood and home to much of the city's intelligentsia, notably Jane Jacobs. Gardiner pushed its approval through council as one of his last acts, though construction of its destructive urban section had not begun a decade later. Still, he had delayed, leaving approval of the expressway to the last days before his retirement and the other highway projects deferred to a later date. These were hardly the acts of a self-proclaimed "bulldozer." Gardiner – tribune of small businesses and homeowners – balked at the idea of displacing thousands of members of his base. In the end, none of the expressways was completed after the original two. His plans for transit expansion survived him, but his plans for expressway expansion did not.[69]

Although his views were radically pro-transit for his time, that is not how Gardiner is remembered. Perhaps it is too difficult to imagine a cigar-chomping Conservative Orange businessman with the nickname "Big Daddy" as a pro-transit, anti-car radical. It is perhaps more comfortable to classify him with Robert Moses and other apostles of the automobile. This discordant view likely arises in part because Gardiner remained a character of the 1950s – committed to economic growth and urban development, with his support for transit motivated by efficiency-based concern that highways alone could not meet adequately the ever-increasing demand for mobility. Although Gardiner came to similar conclusions as the activists of the 1970s, his economic focus contrasted sharply with the activists, who became folk heroes for their opposition to highways in the name of neighbourhood preservation and environmental protection.

Respected local transit engineer-turned-writer Ed Levy, in his book examining the history of Toronto transit plans, summarizes the role of Gardiner simply: "During the mid-1950s Gardiner sparred memorably and incessantly with Toronto Mayor Allan Lamport, a tireless proponent of early implementation of the east-west Bloor-Danforth subway. This was in opposition to the former's unerring support for first completing key sections of a US-style urban freeway (expressway) network for the newly constituted metropolitan corporation."[70] Ignoring Gardiner's reversal, and therefore much of his legacy, has gravely distorted the understanding of Toronto's urban history, which tends to embrace an American-style Manichaean struggle between transit-opposing suburbanites and transit-supporting urbanites.

Prominent urbanist and politician John Sewell scarcely mentions Gardiner in his seminal *The Shape of the City: Toronto Struggles with Modern Planning*, which has profoundly shaped how the planning history of Toronto is viewed. Instead, Sewell claims that suburban politicians, with whom Gardiner would certainly be included, were opposed to transit expansion. "City politicians found (almost to their surprise) that their preferred transportation option, public transit, was not readily supported by their counterparts in the suburbs."[71] He wrote in 1978 that public transit was "one of those great discoveries that progressives in local politics have made in the last dozen years," ignoring that Gardiner, no progressive to Sewell, promoted transit a decade earlier.[72] Sewell bluntly declares that "suburban politicians wanted public money put into roads, whereas city politicians preferred transit," even though there are countless examples of suburban politicians, Gardiner foremost among them, who agitated for transit system expansion.[73] From suburbanites, many Toronto transit advocates refused to take yes for an answer. Their understanding of their city, seemingly, was shaped more by the literature on the decline of transit in the United States than by what actually happened a few kilometres away.

Popular memory of Gardiner is much the same. In the *Globe and Mail*'s lengthy obituary after his death in 1983, his catalytic role in the construction of the Bloor-Danforth subway, a project similar in scale to the

St. Lawrence Seaway, was entirely ignored. In contrast, ample space was given to his support for highway projects. The only mention of transit was to state – in the last substantive paragraph of the article – that Gardiner was "an early advocate of the development of the commuter rail system."[74] Likewise, the *Toronto Star*'s obituaries made no mention of his role in transit other than to note a quotation – "you can't derrick the people out of their automobiles and put them on the subway" – without mentioning the following sentence, in which Gardiner argued that drivers had to be coaxed out of their cars with good transit service instead.[75] A retrospective in 1992 in the *Toronto Star* on Gardiner's death described his legacy as encompassing his eponymous expressway "and many others like the Don Valley Parkway, the Metro police force, an amalgamated parks system and public works projects such as pumping plants, roads and sewers." Transit merited not a mention.[76] In 2012, long-time Toronto journalist and transit expert Stephen Wickens wrote a retrospective on the opening of the Bloor-Danforth-University subway and described Gardiner as a figure who "would prefer that expressways get priority" over subways.[77]

Only Gardiner's biographer, Timothy Colton, and Frances Frisken, a York University professor of urban studies, have described Gardiner's role in the region's transit system. Even Colton, who, unlike most, writes favourably of Gardiner's role in transit, notes that Gardiner failed to do enough to make transit strong. But in the North American context, Toronto far outpaced its American counterparts.

As Caro showed, a single individual with a talent for accumulating power and a reputation for expertise could shape profoundly an urban region in the era of rational planning. Whereas Moses used his power to marginalize public transportation in favour of the automobile, Gardiner saw the weaknesses of a car-dominated transportation system and, to an extent as great as possible for an individual, directed Toronto onto a different path.

The 1950s and early 1960s were a period of transit collapse in much of North America amid the entrenchment of car culture. Transit system after transit system faced financial crisis as a result of a vicious cycle of declining revenues, fare hikes, service cuts, and disappearing riders. Gardiner used the power of the new metropolitan system, which he had helped to create, in order to arrest that cycle in Toronto. He won over skeptics, both urban and suburban, to the idea of subsidizing transit to avoid the need for radical fare increases and to permit expansion of transit service into the suburbs. Later he secured the support of Metro council and, through his unique lobbying power, the provincial government for a major new subway expansion. Highways and other emblems of modernity fascinated Gardiner, and the Conservative businessman had long believed in the importance of the TTC's fiscal self-sustainability. At the decisive moment, however, he set aside these beliefs and embraced transit as a long-term solution to the region's transportation problems. The TTC survived its most perilous years, and Frederick Gardiner decisively set the stage for the unprecedented transit revival in the following decades.

NOTES

1 H.G. Wells, "The Probable Diffusion of Great Cities," in *Anticipations of the Reaction of Mechanical and Scientific Progress upon Human Life and Thought* (London: Chapman and Hall, 1902), 33-65; Frank Lloyd Wright, *The Living City* (New York: Horizon Press, 1958); Norman Bel Geddes, *Magic Motorways* (New York: Random House, 1940).

2 Simpson and Curtin Consultants and Joe R. Ong, "Economic Study of Bloor-Danforth Subway and Proposed Extensions," Municipality of Metropolitan Toronto, September 1963, 35.

3 Michael J. Doucet, "Mass Transit and the Failure of Private Ownership: The Case of Toronto in the Early Twentieth Century," *Urban History Review* 6, 3 (1978): 380.

4 Robert Caro, *The Power Broker: Robert Moses and the Fall of New York* (New York: Alfred A. Knopf, 1974).

5 Jane Jacobs, *The Death and Life of Great American Cities* (New York: Random House, 1961).

6 Hans Blumenfeld, *Life Begins at 65: The Not Entirely Candid Autobiography of a Drifter* (Montreal: Harvest House, 1987), 237.

7 Timothy J. Colton, *Big Daddy: Frederick G. Gardiner and the Building of Metropolitan Toronto* (Toronto: University of Toronto Press, 1980), 80.

8 Daniel Yergin, *The Prize: The Epic Quest for Oil, Money and Power* (New York: Simon and Schuster, 1990); J.R. McNeill and Peter Engelke, *The Great Acceleration: An Environmental History of the Anthropocene since 1945,* illustrated ed. (Cambridge, MA: Belknap Press, 2016).

9 There are a number of histories of the development of the American highway system and the accompanying automobile culture, including Mark H. Rose and Raymond A. Mohl, *Interstate: Highway Politics and Policy since 1939* (Knoxville: University of Tennessee Press, 2012); Clay McShane, *Down the Asphalt Path: The Automobile and*

the *American City* (New York: Columbia University Press, 1995); Owen Gutfreund, *Twentieth-Century Sprawl: Highways and the Reshaping of the American Landscape* (Oxford: Oxford University Press, 2005); Kenneth T. Jackson, *Crabgrass Frontier: The Suburbanization of the United States,* rev. ed. (New York: Oxford University Press, 1987), 157–72; Robert A. Beauregard, *When America Became Suburban* (Minneapolis: University of Minnesota Press, 2006); and Tom Lewis, *Divided Highways: Building the Interstate Highways, Transforming American Life* (New York: Viking Penguin, 1997).

10 "Canadian Production of War Materials – Historical Sheet," Veterans Affairs Canada, 20 February 2019, https://www.veterans.gc.ca/pdf/cr/pi-sheets/material.pdf.

11 Murray Jones, "Some Economic and Social Aspects of Modern Metropolitan (Toronto) Man," paper presented at H.R.H. The Duke of Edinburgh's Second Commonwealth Study Conference on the Human Consequences of the Changing Industrial Environment in the Commonwealth and Empire, Toronto, 1962.

12 James Lemon, *Toronto since 1918: An Illustrated History, The History of Canadian Cities* (Toronto: Lorimer, 2002), 113.

13 Committee on Metropolitan Problems, First Report, Section 2, Statistical Appendix (Toronto: Civic Advisory Council of Toronto, 1950), 28.

14 Cited in Colton, *Big Daddy,* 34.

15 Ibid., 29–37.

16 Ibid., 33–34.

17 Ibid., 32.

18 "'City of York' Movement Seen End of York County," *Toronto Daily Star,* 5 February 1944, 8.

19 In 1947, it became the Toronto and York Planning Board.

20 Colton, *Big Daddy,* 46–51.

21 Ibid., 60–65.

22 Ibid., 61–65.

23 Roger Graham, *Old Man Ontario: Leslie M. Frost* (Toronto: University of Toronto Press, 1990), 205; Colton, *Big Daddy,* 72–73.

24 Colton, *Big Daddy,* 104–11; Paul Godfrey, interview with the author, 22 January 2020.

25 Cited in Colton, *Big Daddy,* 128.

26 Leslie Frost to Frederick Gardiner, 15 December 1955, Archives of Ontario (hereafter AO), Leslie Frost Correspondence.

27 John Clare, "The Hectic Story of Canada's Subway," *Maclean's,* 19 July 1958, 18.

28 Cited in Colton, *Big Daddy,* 84.

29 Godfrey, interview.

30 Interview cited in Colton, *Big Daddy,* 109.

31 Danielle Robinson, "Modernism at a Crossroad: The Spadina Expressway Controversy in Toronto, Ontario ca. 1960–1971," *Canadian Historical Review* 92, 2 (2011): 295–322, https://doi.org/10.3138/chr.92.2.295; Ian Milligan, "'This Board Has a Duty to Intervene': Challenging the Spadina Expressway through the Ontario Municipal Board, 1963–1971," *Urban History Review* 39, 2 (2011): 25–39, https://doi.org/10.7202/1003460ar; Steve Penfold, "'People Drive Automobiles': Esther Shiner, the Silent Majority, and the Popular Case for the Spadina Expressway, 1971–1987," *Urban History Review* 49,

GETTING OFF THE HIGHWAY

1 (2021): 30–53, https://doi.org/10.3138/uhr-2020-0009; Richard White, "Jane Jacobs and Toronto, 1968–1978," *Journal of Planning History* 10, 2 (2011): 114–38, https://doi.org/10.1177/1538513210396293; David M. Nowlan and Nadine Nowlan, The Bad Trip: *The Untold Story of the Spadina Expressway* (Toronto: House of Anansi, 1970).

32 Colton, *Big Daddy*, 164.

33 "Bloor Should Get Subway Next – Duncan," *Toronto Daily Star*, 28 April 1953, 1.

34 Frederick G. Gardiner, "An Address to the Inaugural Meeting of the Council of the Municipality of Metropolitan Toronto," 11 January 1955, City of Toronto Archives (hereafter CTA), Metro Chairman's Fonds.

35 Frederick G. Gardiner, "An Address to the Inaugural Meeting of the Council of the Municipality of Metropolitan Toronto," 10 January 1956, CTA, Metro Chairman's Fonds.

36 Ibid.

37 Frederick G. Gardiner, "Sic Transit Gloria Mundi: Rapid Transit – Is It a Thing of the Past or Is It Our Only Hope for the Future," CTA, Metro Chairman's Fonds.

38 Frederick G. Gardiner, "Traffic, Transit and Transportation: An Address by Frederick G. Gardiner Q.C., the Ontario Good Roads Association," 22 February 1956, CTA, Metro Chairman's Fonds.

39 "Raising Fares Won't Protect T.T.C.'s Future Gardiner Told in U.S.," *Toronto Daily Star*, 26 August 1953, 1.

40 Gardiner, "An Address to the Inaugural Meeting," 10 January 1956.

41 Gardiner, "Traffic, Transit and Transportation."

42 Ibid.

43 Gardiner, "Sic Transit Gloria Mundi."

44 Ibid.

45 Cited in Zachary M. Schrag, *The Great Society Subway: A History of the Washington Metro* (Baltimore: Johns Hopkins University Press, 2006), 36.

46 United States Census of Population: 1950, Volume 1: Number of Inhabitants; 1951 Census of Canada, Volume I, Table 2.

47 Schrag, *The Great Society Subway*, 34–35.

48 Ibid., 38.

49 Alan Black, "The Chicago Area Transportation Study: A Case Study of Rational Planning," *Journal of Planning Education and Research* 10, 1 (1990): 27–37.

50 Robert Moses, "The Open Road: Passing Reflections of a Builder," remarks at a luncheon of the National Highway Users Conference, Washington, DC, 9 May 1962, La Guardia and Wagner Archives, City University of New York, Robert F. Wagner Documents Collection.

51 Jonathan English, "Derailed: The Postwar End of New York City Subway Expansion," *Journal of Urban History* 47, 4 (2019), 832–48, https://doi.org/10.1177/0096144219896578.

52 Lewis Mumford, "The Highway and the City," Architectural Record, March 1958, 9.

53 John F. Kennedy, "Special Message to the Congress on Transportation, April 5, 1962," in *Public Papers of the Presidents of the United States: John F. Kennedy, 1962* (Washington, DC: United States Government Printing Office, 1963), 292–306.

54 Michael N. Danielson, *Federal-Metropolitan Politics and the Commuter Crisis* (New York: Columbia University Press, 1965), 177–79.

55 H. Carl Goldenberg, "Report of the Royal Commission on Metropolitan Toronto," June 1965, 44, https://archive.org/details/reportmetrotoroooonta/page/n5.

56 Minister of Municipal Affairs, "Memorandum to Leslie M. Frost Re: Toronto Transit Commission," 27 July 1955, Municipal Administration Correspondence Files – TTC, RG19–43, A; Colton, Big Daddy, 114.

57 Harold Kaplan, *Urban Political Systems: A Functional Analysis of Metro Toronto* (New York: Columbia University Press, 1967), 134.

58 Ibid.

59 "Suburbs Put Up Battle but Grant of $2,500,000 to TTC Is Passed 11 to 6," *Toronto Daily Star,* 9 September 1955, 33; Frederick Gardiner to Leslie M. Frost, 22 August 1955, Archives of Ontario, Leslie M. Frost Correspondence Fonds.

60 Minister of Municipal Affairs, "Memorandum to Leslie M. Frost."

61 Quoted in Colton, *Big Daddy,* 110.

62 Gardiner, "Traffic, Transit and Transportation."

63 Caro, *The Power Broker: Robert Moses and the Fall of New York,* 920.

64 Mitchell L. Moss et al., "Subway Ridership, 1975–2015," NYU Rudin Center for Transportation, March 2017, https://wagner.nyu.edu/files/faculty/publications/State%20of%20Subway%20Ridership%20-%20Mar717.pdf.

65 Colton, *Big Daddy,* 111–17; "Who Is To Blame For Subway Shilly-Shallying?," *Toronto Daily Star,* September 14, 1957, sec. Editorial.

66 "Who Is to Blame for Subway Shilly-Shallying."

67 Kaplan, Urban Political Systems, 131–32; Civic Affairs, Bureau of Municipal Research, "Open Letter: Proposal for Two Diagonal Subway Routes," 18 October 1955, CTA, Fonds 1003, Series 973, Subseries 7, box 145429, file 1.

68 Property Owners Association of Toronto, "Resolution No. 4: Traffic Plan," 9 May 1956, AO, Municipal Administration Correspondence Files – TTC, RG19–43.

69 Colton, *Big Daddy,* 165; "Proposed Don Valley Parkway," October 1955, CTA, Clerk Files.

70 Ed Levy, *Rapid Transit in Toronto: A Century of Plans, Projects, Politics and Paralysis* (Toronto: Neptis Foundation, 2015), 86.

71 John Sewell, *The Shape of the City: Toronto Struggles with Modern Planning* (Toronto: University of Toronto Press, 1993), 216.

72 John Sewell, "Public Transit in Canada: A Primer," *City Magazine,* May–June 1978, 51.

73 Sewell, *The Shape of the City,* 216.

74 Alden Baker, "Frederick Goldwin Gardiner: Metro Steered for 8 Years by First Chairman of Council," *Globe and Mail,* 23 August 1983, 4.

75 "Metro's First Chairman 'a Municipal Churchill,'" *Toronto Star,* 23 August 1983, A10; "Gardiner Left Us Metro Today," *Toronto Star,* 23 August 1983, A8.

76 "Frederick Gardiner 1895–1983: Toronto's Big Daddy," *Toronto Star,* 1 November 1992, 71.

77 Stephen Wickens, "Transit Lessons from the Past: The University-Bloor-Danforth Subway Was Accomplished on Budget, without Provincial Funds. Is Such a Feat Possible Now?," *Toronto Star,* 4 February 2012, IN.3.

12

Talking Jazz at the Stratford Shakespearean Festival, 1956–58

ERIC FILLION

"Well, there we were in our stuffed shirts," the Toronto reporter Gordon Donaldson protested half-jokingly, "sagging slightly at the seams and puffing at the crescendo," while waiting for Princess Margaret to join the 700 people who had gathered in Stratford, Ontario, for a performance by the "aristocrat of North American music – Duke Ellington."[1] The date was 31 July 1958. The concert that night was supposed to be the culmination of a three-year jazz experiment undertaken by the organizers of the city's Shakespearean Festival. In 1956, Ellington had taken part in a multi-concert program on the history of jazz. Fired up, he had returned the following year to premiere *Such Sweet Thunder*, a twelve-part suite based on the work of the "Bard." The news that Princess Margaret planned to stop in Stratford on her month-long tour of Canada in 1958 to attend a performance of *The Winter's Tale* had generated much excitement. Ellington intended to present to her a new composition, titled "Princess Blue," during a concert scheduled to start immediately after the play. The band took the stage at 11:30 p.m., but the distinguished guest, exhausted after a long day of social functions, chose to retire to her room, falling soundly asleep while the music roared on in the nearby arena. The "world king among jazz musicians and composers" and the grand dame did not meet that evening, "like ships passing in the night."[2]

The Stratford Shakespearean Festival officially launched in 1953 with a mandate to activate the art of theatre, thereby putting Canada on the map and elevating its national culture so that it reflected both the aspirations and the self-image of the country's elite. The event soon became a hub of "high art," most of it filtered through the lens of Anglophilic nationalism.[3] Timid efforts to broaden its programming coalesced in 1955 with the inaugural season of the Music Festival, an initiative that failed to generate revenues because of poor promotion and an exclusive focus on "serious music." As a synonym for "erudite music" or "classical music," the term conveyed a bias against so-called vernacular sounds such as jazz, a genre deemed by the elite to be decadent and unsophisticated because of its past association with vaudeville and other forms of Black popular entertainment.[4] The decision to recruit Ellington, Wilbur de Paris and His New New Orleans Jazz Orchestra, the Modern Jazz Quartet, and the pianist Art Tatum, among others, for the 1956 edition of the festival, in the words of the *Stratford Beacon Herald*'s Wendy Michener, was "unusually far-sighted and bold."[5] "Many people who enjoy music," she explained, "are still frightened away from jazz by the illicit surroundings of its beginning and the questionable living habits of some of its exponents and proponents."[6] Yet the experiment was sufficiently successful to warrant two more jazz-infused editions of the Music Festival, with performances by the likes of Count Basie, Billie Holiday, and Dizzy Gillespie, all leading American artists.

On the one hand, the Stratford Shakespearean Festival came on the scene against a backdrop of unprecedented prosperity and collective hope for the future fuelled, in part, by Canada's rising international profile and the rich tapestry of its increasingly diverse citizenry. On the other hand, this apparent coming of age coincided with the beginning of a "critical period" during which the predominantly white members of the country's English-speaking cultural lobby witnessed with apprehension the erosion of the imperial relationship and their nation's waning sense of Britishness in the shadow of the United States.[7] Created in 1949, the Royal Commission on National Development in the Arts, Letters, and Sciences (otherwise known as the Massey Commission) provided this status-anxious elite with a platform for thinking through ways of harnessing postwar changes and rallying the broader Canadian public to its cause. The argument put forward was that "high culture" was fundamental to the pursuit of nationhood and that it was the best safeguard against both the tyranny of totalitarian ideologies and the "illiberal menace of mass culture" pouring over the border.[8] In this context, the presence of jazz – often dubbed a uniquely American art form – at the Stratford Shakespearean Festival, one of the foremost upholders of the Masseyites' vision, was incongruous, to say the least.

The mingling of Shakespeareans and jazzheads formed a formidable paradox in 1950s Canada. The decision to jazz things up in Stratford was arguably informed by the need to increase ticket sales and attract a mass-culture-loving younger crowd that, once on site, could be inculcated with an appreciation of theatre. Yet if Louis Applebaum, the director of music, was able to write jazz into the festival's program, then it was because many of its most ardent ambassadors had already earned their *lettres de noblesse* and made incursions into high culture. Ellington and Canada's Oscar Peterson, for instance, had achieved consecration at New York's prestigious Carnegie Hall in 1943 and 1949, respectively. The Masseyites' linking of high culture and nationalism played out in a number of peculiar ways in Stratford. Not only was the yearly event a venue to feature domestic talent, but also it provided a national stage for projecting leadership and authority to advance the idea of a distinct, if not exceptional, refined Canadian jazz culture. The Stratford elite successfully integrated jazz into their vision by toning down the politics of the music and calling attention to its aesthetic qualities. They underscored the supposed universalism of the idiom while investing it with symbolic value as an expression of Canadianness. Far-sighted, indeed, the jazz-infused editions of the festival constituted a watershed moment that saw the music enter, for the first time, the national discourse on the current state and future of the country's cultural life.

The international music festival format was an ideal medium to exert influence on the production – and to mediate the reception – of "serious jazz" north of the forty-ninth parallel. A relatively novel phenomenon at the time, it helped to foster consensus on canons of taste in addition to energizing participants, musicians and non-musicians alike, in the Canadian cultural public sphere.[9] In other words, it provided a dynamic and clearly defined context within which to think about and experience jazz as one of the nation's modes of expression. In this chapter, I interrogate the paradox of the presence of jazz in Stratford during the mid- to late 1950s, a period during which Canada's elite dealt with the antipodes of optimism and disquietude by thinking creatively about ways to enact their vision of a "vigorous and distinctive cultural life."[10] By the same token, I listen to how the works of Ellington and Peterson, among others, carried added resonance in the wake of the national rethinking spurred by the Massey Commission. At a time when the American cultural presence in Canada was felt keenly, the Stratford Shakespearean Festival demonstrated artfully how to de-Americanize, or rather Canadianize, the music of these eminent ambassadors.[11]

JAZZ IN THE "AMERICAN CENTURY"

"In less than half a century, jazz ... made its way out from the backwoods and the dark corners of the American scene to a position of international recognition as this country's one true native contribution to the arts," wrote the New York–based writer Leonard Feather in his encyclopedia on the music in 1955.[12] Rooted in the blues and ragtime turn-of-the-century experiments of New Orleans African American musicians, jazz was always a "*hybrid* cultural expression."[13] Its development parallelled the expansion of the industrial metropolis, the widening reach of radio, and the advent of mechanical reproduction, notably the phonograph disc record, all of which provided new opportunities for dynamic encounters between and among diasporic communities, above all in 1920s New York (which moved to the synchronous, or rather syncopated, beat of the Harlem Renaissance) and Chicago. A profoundly innovative African American syncretic art form, both in tune with and ahead of the time, jazz soon filled the air in cities throughout the United States. Progressing beyond the blues and ragtime, its practitioners, white and Black, championed innovative approaches to improvisation and composition, in large ensembles or small combos, moving across subgenres, from traditional jazz to swing, bebop, and cool jazz, even venturing toward the realm of classical music. "If the definition of jazz as folk music held true for almost 100% of what was played before [the 1920s] ... it described perhaps 25 to 50% of what was played up to 1940," Feather noted, before adding that it "applies to barely 10% of what is being performed and generally accepted as jazz" in the mid-1950s.[14]

The wide appeal of the music and the recognition that its exponents were both compelling entertainers and legitimate artists inspired promoters to try to organize large-scale events to galvanize excitement. Launched in 1948, France's Nice Jazz Festival was "the touch-paper that lit the fire of enthusiasm for jazz festivals."[15] Held in Newport, Rhode Island, the First Annual American Jazz Festival launched in 1954. Its first edition attracted an audience of 13,000. That number rose to 60,000 by the end of the decade.[16] The importance of the trend was such that Feather commented on it in the 1962 edition of his encyclopedia, noting that festivals were "both cause and effect of a phenomenal upsurge in the general interest in jazz."[17] Only a handful of books and specialized publications with limited circulation had examined the music prior to the 1950s, but the founding of the Newport Jazz Festival changed that. Feather's *The Book of Jazz* and *The Encyclopedia of Jazz* were part of an expanding corpus that included, among others, Barry Ulanov's *A History of Jazz in America,* Marshall Stearns's *The Story of Jazz,* and *The Jazz Makers,* co-authored by Nat Shapiro and Nat Hentoff.[18] Published between 1952 and 1957, these works laid the much-needed groundwork for understanding the history of the art form and detailing how its broad spectrum of sounds and experiences became so integral to cultural life in the United States.

Jazz was the defining sound of the "American Century" not only because of its popularity but also because it was a potent instrument in the cultural Cold War. Gillespie's band was the first to travel overseas in 1956 as part of the State Department's jazz diplomacy, a program of government-funded tours meant to promote, through the medium of improvisation, the ideal of democracy and freedom among the youth in non-aligned and Soviet bloc countries. Occurring as it did in the wake of *Brown v Board of Education,* when the courage of civil rights activist Rosa Parks and the resilience of the Little Rock Nine students seeking to enrol at an all-white school made headlines around the world, President Dwight D. Eisenhower's attempt to instrumentalize the music was also a means of improving the international image of the United States. The irony of promoting racial harmony overseas while Jim Crowism prevailed at home was not lost on jazz ambassadors. At home and abroad, African American musicians spoke directly to the racial politics of the decade by deploying (more or less) subtle ways of celebrating Black identity and conveying messages of social justice in their work, often with the active support of their white colleagues.[19]

Canadians could hardly remain impassive toward these developments, particularly since they possessed a jazz culture of their own, though much of it was informed by cross-border travels and cultural exchanges dating back to the early decades of the century. Touring musicians from the United States – for example The Creole Band, Tennessee Ten, and Morgan Brothers' Syncopated Jaz Band – found receptive audiences in cities such as Winnipeg, Edmonton, and Toronto in the 1910s. The new music might have been a source of anxiety for members of the elite who heard only vacuity and degeneracy in its vaudeville-tinted, free-flowing rhythms, but that did not prevent domestic talent such as Vancouver's George Paris Band and Montreal's Westmount Jazz Band from taking the stage. Canadians such as the Buxton-born pianist Louis Hooper and the Niagara Falls saxophonist Myron Sutton were also making names for themselves in the United States, notably in New York and Buffalo, respectively, during the roaring 1920s. Both moved back to Canada amid the Great Depression. By 1933, Sutton had established the Canadian Ambassadors, possibly the country's first organized Black jazz band, with Hooper behind the piano. There was jazz in Canada, and there was Canadian jazz; the distinction between the two was never clear-cut.[20] However much the State Department trumpeted the idea that it was a uniquely American export, Canadian jazzophiles often thought of the music as a *North* American art form, which only puzzled more those who held nationalist beliefs.

In Canada as in the United States, exceptional talent and world acclaim did not shelter one from the everyday violence of racism. The life of Oscar Peterson is a case in point. Born in 1925 in Montreal's Little Burgundy neighbourhood, he learned to play the piano at a young age with the encouragement of his father, an amateur musician and porter for the Canadian Pacific Railway. Before long, the aspiring artist distinguished himself during performances at church and local community halls, eventually finding his way to the airwaves of the Canadian Broadcasting Corporation (CBC). His nascent recording career received a major boost following an unannounced performance at Carnegie Hall on 18 September 1949. His New York debut, as part of promoter Norman Granz's *Jazz at the*

Philharmonic, made Peterson an immediate star. His experience of Jim Crowism while on tour in the United States deeply marked him, but it did not make him less critical of Canadians' own "bigotry" or their "smugness about race relations."[21] Nor did it keep him from speaking his mind about the "quiet color bar" and the "polite segregation" that made it difficult for members of his family and community to find housing and enjoy equal opportunities.[22] Peterson himself experienced more than his share of incidents of discrimination while playing in Canada, from a Ritz-Carlton manager in Montreal who sought to keep him from manning the piano to a Hamilton barber refusing to give him a haircut.[23] While his co-stars in the United States travelled the world as official envoys of the State Department, Ottawa's Department of External Affairs snubbed Peterson.[24] Racial politics polluted cultural life in postwar Canada too.

Yet things did improve as the 1950s proceeded. Vancouver, Toronto, and Montreal had thriving scenes with their own bands, critics, cohorts of fans, organizations, and combinations of performance spaces – artist-run venues, dance halls, dedicated clubs, and creative workshops – where locals and travelling musicians mingled, thereby furthering the growth of an inclusive and broad-minded, community-oriented jazz culture in Canada.[25] In cities such as Montreal, this bustling activity developed in response to a "symbolic structure" that had essentialized jazz by foregrounding its "foreign and exotic" qualities and amplifying its "rebellious energy."[26] The music's limited but growing presence on the airwaves of the CBC and its repetitive incursions into the Massey Hall performing arts theatre in Toronto – known as "Canada's Carnegie Hall" – were evidence of its wider acceptance.[27] In 1953, the New Jazz Society of Toronto booked the venue for an evening of bebop featuring the now mythical quintet of Charlie Parker, Dizzy Gillespie, Bud Powell, Charles Mingus, and Max Roach. Soon celebrated as "the greatest jazz concert ever," it was an event for the history books that set the stage for the Stratford Shakespearean Festival's programming experiment.[28]

JAZZ FOR CANADIAN HIGHBROWS

The turn of the 1950s was a time of transition epitomized by a conservative Cold War consensus rendered more pervasive because of the ease of cross-border movement, the shared-language reality for much of the population on either side of the forty-ninth parallel, and the massive influx of American cultural products and capital into Canada. It was also the beginning of a new chapter that saw a broader cast of protagonists enter the cultural public sphere to engage in nation building. The Massey Commission was their forum. Established on 8 April 1949, it had as its mandate to report on the significance and state of culture from coast to coast while making recommendations on how best to promote and support those "institutions which express national feeling, promote common understanding, and add to the variety and richness of Canadian life."[29] Through its proceedings, the commission gave voice to artists, administrators, producers, and patrons of the art investing much hope in state support for their high-culture nationalism. For the most part, they were "generally well educated, white, middle-class, and male and their interaction led to friendships which reinforced their shared interests."[30] This was a "moment of cultural consolidation" for them, and they seized the occasion by laying out "measures to further imprint a cultured national design" in accordance with their sense of place in the world.[31] It took several years for some of the Massey Commission's recommendations to be implemented (e.g., the Canada Council for the Arts was not established until 1957), but the "carnival of excitement" that the forum generated was such that it inspired many a cultural entrepreneur to take the lead.[32]

The Stratford Shakespearean Festival was the brainchild of Harry Thomas "Tom" Patterson. A native of the Ontario railway town that carried the name of the English playwright's birthplace, he had served with the Canadian Dental Corps during the Second World War before taking a job as a reporter for Maclean-Hunter's trade magazine *Civic Administration*. He understood that Canada was "ripe for a cultural explosion" in the wake of the Massey Commission.[33] A twofold objective guided his efforts to turn Stratford into a nationally reputed centre for theatre: he wished to enact the vision put forth by the Masseyites while helping to revitalize the town's economy. British-born Tyrone Guthrie, the founding artistic director of the festival, was evidently enthused by the project. He explained to the readers of *Mayfair* that "in its new self awareness" Canada must learn to "talk in tones that are less feeble and tentative and to talk sense."[34] "An occasion like this festival, which provides an opportunity for some tens of thousands of Canadians to participate in a dignified and adult form of artistic expression, is timely," he added.[35] Guthrie's and Patterson's Anglophilic high-culture nationalism was unlikely to hold much appeal for the average Canadian who had learned to live immersed in Americanized mass culture and had no intention of being patronized. Even so, the moment that it debuted on 13 July 1953, the Stratford Shakespearean Festival gained momentum and gathered impressive support among cultural elites.

The idea of pursuing Patterson's twofold objective by using performing arts other than theatre did not take long to germinate. In fact, thanks to the persuasive lobbying of Louis Applebaum, the Stratford leadership had agreed to diversify its offering before it even launched the festival. Born in Toronto in 1918, Applebaum was a graduate of the Faculty of Music at the University of Toronto. He began his career as a film composer at the National Film Board of Canada, where he later served as the music director. Between 1945 and 1949, he followed opportunities to Hollywood and New York. By 1951, he was back in Canada and acting as the vice-president of the newly formed Canadian League of Composers, whose mandate was to place the sonic arts squarely at the heart of the "national tradition of the future."[36] Not long after, Applebaum inherited the job of composer and conductor for the plays to be staged in Stratford. He quickly used "this heaven-sent opportunity to reveal what Canada could do in the field of music" by convincing Patterson and the board of directors to invest in a series of afternoon concerts by the likes of John Weinzweig and Glenn Gould.[37] Unfortunately, the 1953 season was poorly attended and plagued by technical problems and temperamental weather. Not until 1955 was Applebaum permitted to repeat the experience. Wiping the slate clean, he dubbed the revamped Music Festival "The Inaugural Season of Music."[38] Although it was a critical success, it did not do well financially. Still, he and his colleagues were hopeful for the future.

However ludicrous it must have seemed at the time, Applebaum's suggestion that adding jazz artists to the festival's roster would improve prospects was sound. By 1956, the Newport Jazz Festival was already attracting crowds in the range of twenty to thirty thousand. The Stratford leadership was aware of the potential for increased ticket sales, not to mention the possibility of converting younger crowds to its high-culture nationalism.[39] Besides, jazz was already "an acknowledged art form."[40] Its biggest stars were playing concert halls and set to tour the world as impromptu ambassadors on behalf of the Eisenhower administration. Canadian musicians were not quite as fortunate, but this was through no fault of their own; scattered audiences were small, and jobs were scarce north of the forty-ninth parallel. Applebaum could thus confidently make the argument that "the propriety of including good jazz in a festival of fine music is not at all embarrassing."[41] He first proposed to invite prominent pianists such as Art Tatum and Dave Brubeck, or Canada's own Oscar Peterson, to the festival's Summer Music School. Offering classes in improvisation, he argued, "might point towards a special Jazz evening or two."[42] Here was an opportunity to exert power and influence by conferring added legitimacy on an art form that perplexed Canadian arbiters of culture. In February 1956, the Department of Communications announced that the Music Advisory Committee had been given the green light to explore new sounds. "Such highlights as Schubert's 'Die Schöne Müllerin' performed by pianist Rudolf Serkin and baritone Martial Singher, alternating with Duke Ellington concerts, indicates the attitude we are applying to our programming this year," read the press release.[43] "Fine jazz is fine music and its good performers merit attention and respect," Canadians included, Applebaum added.[44]

With these objectives in mind, the director of music and his colleagues opted cautiously for a didactic approach since they believed that it was "perhaps the first time that good jazz" was being "thoroughly integrated into a serious music festival."[45] The jazz concerts of the 1956 season were thus grouped into a survey of the history of the music: first, Wilbur de Paris and his orchestra introduced audiences to the syncopated rhythms of Dixieland; Duke Ellington continued with an illustration of how composition evolved during the interwar years; Calvin Jackson's quartet and Phil Nimmons's ten-piece band then showed how to fine-tune a largely improvised idiom using learned techniques; next Dave Brubeck's quartet and Norm Symonds's octet demonstrated what happens when jazz meets classical music; finally, the Modern Jazz Quartet and Oscar Peterson, a last-minute replacement for the ailing Art Tatum, provided sound bites of the music's recent developments.[46] Augmenting this series were commentaries offered by experts, namely producer John Hammond as well as authors Nat Hentoff and Barry Ulanov. Toronto's Helen McNamara, writing for the *Telegram,* was thrilled to announce that this promised to be "Canada's most important jazz event."[47] Taking her cues from press releases, she borrowed a title from Ellington's repertoire and urged "all good jazz fans to Take the A Train ... to Stratford."[48] Her colleague from Montreal, *La Presse*'s Claude Gingras, provided further enticement when he noted that this "jazz savant," which differed from "[le] jazz commercial qu'on entend à la journée longue à la radio," was unlikely to cause a scandal.[49]

The normative undertones of this initiative were hard to miss, especially if one juxtaposed de Paris's "fine introduction to all that has happened to dance rhythms since they left the jungle" to Nimmons's "educated" jazz.[50] The survey approach made it possible to contain somewhat the enthralling, syncopated sound of Dixieland while easing people into the music. The *Stratford Beacon Herald* did its part with a feature on the musicians, pictured in their best attire feeding swans along the shore of the Avon River, to reassure residents who expressed concerns that jazz was attracting a young "audience that possibly has never walked across Stratford's green."[51] Approximately 700 people attended the group's opening concert. Most were youngsters whose "whistles and shouts of excitement replaced the customary well-mannered applause."[52] The *Toronto Daily Star*'s Stan Rantin captured the scene in colourful fashion: "The ice was officially broken at the Stratford Shakespearean Festival last night – or rather it melted – as 'hot' jazz descended on the staid sanctuary of Mozart and Henry V."[53] Adhering to the discursive framework put forward by the festival, his counterpart from the *Globe and Mail,* John Kraglund, neither a "fanatic" nor an "authority on a complex art," noted that the "excitement was perhaps of a more primitive nature, but it was not unlike that inspired by outstanding performances of so-called classical music."[54] Rantin concurred and commended the group, whose leader prefaced each song with explanatory remarks, for not "stooping to the degrading burlesque performances that mar so many jazz concerts."[55]

The performance that Nimmons's all-Canadian band offered to its 800-strong audience nearly two weeks later was an entirely different proposition.

"Erudition virtually dripped from the stage," wrote the dazzled *London Evening Free Press* correspondent J. Burke Martin.[56] Born in Vancouver, the Toronto-based conservatory-trained clarinetist had put together a stellar group of "serious jazz" musicians capable of holding their own alongside Jackson's quartet, with whom they shared the stage that evening.[57] In addition to playing Nimmons's compositions, they revisited standards, rearranged for the occasion, in a style that exuded both vigour and restraint, wit and sophistication. Their "jazz with a college education" differed from that of earlier concerts because it was "cerebral, cool, and much less emotional."[58] This was the group's first public appearance, and it caught the attention of critics and delighted audiences, including those who listened to the concert on *Wednesday Night,* a CBC Radio series that – exceptionally – substituted "Jazz for Highbrows" for its regular classical music programming.[59] The Philadelphia-born Jackson, a regular fixture of the Toronto scene since moving to the city in 1950, played a solid set on the Baldwin, the official festival piano, but his quartet could not steal the show. The evening's commentator, Ulanov, an expert on Shakespeare and jazz who taught at Barnard College in New York, lauded Nimmons and his musicians, validating with "scholarly" remarks the assertion that the group was the Music Festival's "biggest news."[60] All this attention struck a resounding, nationalistic note bound to please Applebaum and his colleagues.

The Stratford Shakespearean Festival could claim the success of Canadian jazzmen as its own. It had provided, after all, a carefully curated context for the music's production and reception. It was Applebaum's avowed intention to turn the spotlight on "worthy and able Canadians" versed in the more modern and erudite forms of jazz.[61] Applebaum accomplished that by having domestic talent appear on the same bill as world-famous artists. The pairing of the Modern Jazz Quartet with Peterson, an uncontested global star by then, was fortuitous since the slot initially belonged to Tatum, who cancelled because of health complications.[62] The Brubeck-Symonds double bill was intended, however. As for Jackson and Nimmons, their pairing caused some confusion since the former had been busy making his mark on Canadian stages and on CBC airwaves with a group of Toronto-based musicians. Reporters were therefore inclined to recognize him unofficially as an honorary Canadian.

Michener would have none of it. She reminded her *Stratford Beacon Herald* readers that Nimmons, unlike Jackson, "was born in Canada, raised in Canada, and now heads a group of nine Canadian musicians all playing in Canada."[63] She might as well have mentioned that he was also a founding member of the Canadian League of Composers. Be that as it may, Applebaum was satisfied to report that "good jazz played well fits in perfectly with the classics" and that domestic artists can indeed "hold their own with the best from across the border."[64]

Although praiseworthy, the effort to integrate jazz into the high-culture nationalism of the Masseyites was not without shortcomings. Notwithstanding Jackson, whose status as a Canadian was a source of debate, the only Black Canadian to perform in Stratford was Peterson, and he was not even on the schedule when it first came out. The third and fourth annual seasons did not fare better in terms of representing the rich history and diversity of the country's jazzscape: they featured the predominantly white bands of Maynard Ferguson, Moe Koffman, and Ron Collier.[65] It is true that white jazzmen in Canada were more prevalent in the modern field than their Black counterparts. They were also more numerous in cities such as Vancouver and Toronto, where they came to the attention of impresarios or prospective employers in broadcast media. Their formal training, whether it was familiarity with Western canons or notation literacy, best positioned them to secure work and visibility in radio or on television. As John Gilmore explains in his history of jazz in Montreal, many of the pioneering musicians who hailed from Little Burgundy lacked the credentials and experience to thrive in the "impersonal, highly technical environment, [and] split-second timing" of studio work.[66] This was less a reflection of aesthetic choice and cultural predisposition than it was a function of the structural impediments that limited social and economic mobility for Black Canadians in Montreal and elsewhere in Canada.

In engaging foremost with the aesthetics of jazz, those who gravitated toward Stratford neglected to reflect on the racial politics of the music. This resulted in some striking dissonances and missed opportunities. One such instance concerned Billie Holiday's "Strange Fruit," an influential anti-lynching anthem, which the singer performed on 10 August 1957, nearly two years after the racially motivated murder of fourteen-year-old Emmett

Till in Mississippi. Although the audience responded with thunderous applause, reviews of the concert suggest that the "dramatic and emotional realism" with which the singer delivered the piece, rather than the fierce urgency of its lyrical content, was what moved the audience.[67]

The poet Langston Hughes came the closest to initiating a meaningful discussion about race and music, but his visit to Stratford in 1958 turned into a confrontation with the arch-conservative senator Felix P. Quinn, who decried the presence of a left-leaning "blasphemous creature" at a publicly funded event.[68] A leading voice of the Harlem Renaissance, Hughes was scheduled to discuss the history of jazz and read his work to the sound of Henry "Red" Allen's quartet. Quinn, however, wanted the artist banned on the basis of his poem "Goodbye, Christ." His Senate colleagues and the press promptly denounced Quinn for injecting "an unwelcome note of McCarthyism into the Red Chamber."[69] As for Applebaum and Michael Langham, the artistic director that year, they refused to censor one of their guests since they were "purely concerned" with artistic merit, not politics.[70] The performance thus went on as planned, but the controversy dampened the mood and distracted critics from the social issues that Hughes likely had intended to underscore.[71]

Strangely enough, the Stratford Shakespearean Festival's commitment to the principles of art's autonomy and universality was concurrent with its deployment of an Anglophilic nationalism anchored in the twin ideals of high culture and liberal democracy. A towering and familiar figure at the festival, Duke Ellington was an exceptional interlocutor with whom to associate for the purpose of advancing this conflicting agenda. Born in Washington, DC, in 1899, the world-renowned band-leading pianist and composer came from a moderately well-to-do family. His elegant, dignified posture and demeanour earned him the moniker "Duke" when still a boy. It suited him well. Ellington studied piano by attending music school and hopping from one ragtime concert to another. In the 1920s, he moved to Harlem, where he branded himself as a truly brilliant cosmopolitan artist, using a variety of career-building strategies to reach bigger and more diverse publics, gaining recognition as a gifted composer in the process. He knew, of course, how to manage expectations and navigate through different milieus. As Mark Miller explains in a piece published by the *Globe and Mail* on the centenary of the birth of Ellington, "he mixed easily with every level of Canadian society, from the backstage hipsters and hangers-on who turned up at every new city to the Rosedale matrons who invited him to take tea and play bridge in Toronto."[72] His popularity was such that the two concerts that he gave in Stratford in 1956 were filled to 90 percent capacity.[73] Ellington "took an art form and left it enriched," marvelled Martin after one concert.[74] Kraglund concurred by noting that the artist's approach to music making compared with that of composers in other fields. "As for the improvisations of the soloists and the contrapuntal texture that results," he noted approvingly, "one need only remember that Bach was doing similar things in the 17th century."[75]

By maintaining a close relationship with Ellington, the festival was able to further its agenda, especially once it became known that the composer, inspired by his visit to Stratford and experience of the play *Henry VI*, was working on a suite based on Shakespearean characters. The festival organizers were thrilled to report that he would return to perform the new work, titled *Such Sweet Thunder*, during the Third Annual Music Festival. This was a great marketing and branding coup that lent legitimacy to the claim that the former Ontario railway town had grown culturally as a sort of surrogate for England's Stratford-upon-Avon, where Shakespeare was born and lived. The fact that Ellington dedicated his twelve-part suite to the festival reflected well on the Canadian cultural elite in their effort to foster a distinctively unique and resounding jazz culture north of the forth-ninth parallel.[76] Gordon Jocelyn, who temporarily replaced Applebaum as director of music in 1957, pursued his predecessor's campaign to differentiate between "bad" and "fine" jazz by soliciting a text from Ellington for that season's souvenir program. In it, the composer highlighted once again the similarities between some forms of jazz and classical music. More tellingly, he mobilized the "Bard" himself to validate the festival's experiment: "Somehow, I suspect that if Shakespeare were alive today, he might be a jazz fan himself – he'd appreciate the combination of team spirit and informality, of academic knowledge and humor, of all the elements that go into a great jazz performance."[77] Ellington then hypothesized that the playwright likely would "agree with the simple and axiomatic statement that is so important to all of us – when it sounds good, it is good."[78]

Increasingly and in unsuspecting ways, jazz was making it possible for members of the Canadian cultural elite to access their country's depleting reservoir of emotional attachment to Great Britain. The news that Princess Margaret, a fan of the music, planned to visit Stratford in 1958 provided the excuse to invite Ellington once again for a special ball. The invitation came with a request for a composition to commemorate the visit of Queen Elizabeth II's younger sister.[79] The Duke had never met her, but he had jammed informally once with her uncles, the Duke of Windsor on the drums and the Duke of Kent on the piano, while in London back in 1933. Ellington did not like to fly, so opportunities to rub shoulders with members of the royal family were few.[80] Stratford, in contrast, was close to New York, and his recent experiences there were fresh in his mind. Written for Princess Margaret, "Princess Blue," his latest composition, was "suitable for gentle eardrums," he told the *Telegram*.[81] The event enthused Stratford's Shakespeareans, including those who had been reluctant to embrace the festival's jazz turn. Late in the evening of 31 July, they congregated in the arena and listened to the music while waiting for Princess Margaret to grace them with her presence. By the time everyone realized that she was not coming, "the ducal magic" had brought the room to its feet, except for Patterson, who sat at the piano for a lesson from the "very royal Duke."[82] Jazz kept their spirits up and ultimately carried the day.

By the end of the 1958 season, the Shakespeareans could relate to the jazz culture that the Music Festival had put forward. Whether or not jazzophile youngsters had developed an interest in Bachian suites, operatic librettos, and ornate plays, however, was an entirely different question. On the night of the joint Peterson and Modern Jazz Quartet concert in 1956, one reporter noted a "really highbrow remark" coming from behind him: "The theatre audiences here are more *mondaine* in appearance, but I think the musical audiences are more truly *chthonic*, don't you?"[83] Were they more chthonic? To answer that question and others like it, the festival distributed questionnaires at each of the five jazz events held during the 1958 season. One hundred and one festivalgoers handed theirs in – an acceptable response rate of 20.2%. The vast majority were between the ages of eighteen and thirty-five. A little over 40% were under twenty-five. The audience was split roughly evenly between men and women. Most of them came from Toronto (16.8%) and other cities in Ontario (35.7%). A fraction called Stratford home (8.9%). There were also more people visiting from Michigan (14.9%) than the other Canadian provinces combined (10.9%).[84] Ultimately, the data compiled confirmed an observation made in 1956, namely that "the Jazz Concerts attract a different audience than do the other Stratford Festival events."[85] More importantly, they showed un-equivocally that "music and drama are not interdependent."[86] The youth did not flock en masse to theatre stages despite the best efforts of Applebaum and his colleagues.

That said, jazz enthusiasts did embrace aspects of the festival's broader agenda. Not only did they approve of Ellington's take on Shakespeare, but also they readily borrowed from the discursive and symbolic language used in Stratford to distinguish between "bad" and "fine" jazz in addition to adopting the behaviour expected of them as an audience. The expressive and interactive dimension of jazz, Lawrence W. Levine points out, had always eluded arbiters of culture in their attempts to train and discipline audience members to react *"individually* rather than collectively" following proper etiquette.[87] The architects of the Music Festival could thus pride themselves on having instilled discipline and reverence in festivalgoers. Although the youngsters who attended the opening jazz concert of the 1956 season could hardly sit still and hold their applause, for the most part they were compliant and intently focused by 1958. The hallowed setting of the concert hall certainly helped. So did the journalists who reprobated audience members for being too demonstrative or patted them on the back for being exemplarily well behaved.

Rather than making jazz respectable (it already was in the eyes of many), the festival provided a context for Canadians to appreciate the music under a new light, carefully calibrated to match the ambient cultural nationalism of the mid- to late 1950s. The concert hall environment encouraged a certain type of audience engagement, which in turn resulted in favourable conditions for broadcast and recording purposes. Peterson, who had put Canada on the map in the world of jazz, praised Stratford as "the one good festival" for those reasons.[88] At the turn of 1957, Verve Records released *The Oscar Peterson Trio at the Stratford Shakespearean Festival* to great acclaim. In the album liner notes, the pianist explained that festivalgoers "were not only appreciative, but also cooperative, in that they not only were quiet throughout, but withheld their applause until the end of each solo or number."[89] Such a public endorsement vindicated the festival leadership in its decision to expand its musical horizons. McNamara, the doyen of Canadian jazz journalism at the time, agreed that Applebaum and his colleagues were doing important work in elevating the music onto the national stage. Jazzophiles from coast to coast who listened to *Wednesday Night*'s live broadcasts of the concerts were equally thrilled. Bob Steele from Chilliwack, British Columbia, wrote to the CBC after hearing the Nimmons and Jackson groups to express how amazed he was to discover Canadian musicians playing at such a high level. "Never again will you be able to pay feeble lip service to jazz," he commented.[90] At a time when regional scenes had yet to come together under the limelight, the festival's ability to Canadianize jazz in this way was noteworthy.

JAZZ CANADIANA

There were, of course, dissenting voices. Graham George, a British-born organist-choirmaster and Queen's University professor, articulated the misgivings of many regarding Stratford's three-year experiment. According to him, the parallels between this "Negro art" and "serious music" were far-fetched.[91] Conceding that in all probability he would be labelled a "long-haired, ivory-towered bigot" for expressing his views, George argued that jazz – "an art characterised by the unsophisticated emotions of a lovable and childlike people" – hardly qualified as a "full-fledged art-form."[92] Leslie Richard Bell, choir conductor and *Toronto Daily Star* columnist, shared that opinion. If the idiom appealed to people, he insisted, then it was because "serious" composers had failed to devise new ways of engaging concertgoers, too many of whom still wore "long faces and furrowed brows" as if there was "no fun to be found in a symphony or a string quartet."[93] Bell concurred with George that the Stratford leadership was misguided in its desire to make jazz respectable, because the music's aesthetic value was negligible. Unstated but underlying their highbrow criticism was the belief that the promotion of Anglophilic nationalism was incompatible with the dissemination of a music rooted in Black American culture.

Unless jazz concerts helped to balance the budget, the two saw no reason for continuing with the trend beyond 1958.

Jazz, incidentally, did not return to Stratford in 1959. Internal correspondence does not shed much light on the reasons for the decision. Publicly, Applebaum pointed to scheduling issues, noting that the Music Advisory Committee was content with what had been accomplished; the festival had made the music more respectable and provided Canadian artists with a prestigious stage upon which they could stand and perform for the nation. "Stratford has made an important point with its past jazz concerts, but there is no reason to go on with that pattern," he stated.[94] Not to doubt the sincerity of the festival leadership's intentions, but jazz did not quite deliver in terms of ticket sales. Although some of the concerts did bring in profits, they were not enough to balance the budgets. Overall attendance at the jazz component of the 1958 season did not exceed 62%, with losses reaching nearly $2,000.[95] These figures were hardly better than those of 1956, when jazz performances averaged 57.6% capacity.[96] George's and Bell's urging that the music be dropped unless it was critical for budget-balancing purposes apparently fell on receptive ears.

However paradoxical, the presence of jazz in Stratford ultimately helped to communicate the vision of an elite minority to a wider audience. Emphasizing the aesthetics of the music over its politics, the festival leadership resourcefully encoded the works it presented in ways that aligned with the high-culture nationalism of the Masseyites. At the same time, it provided a national stage for Canada's own jazz ambassadors and sympathizers, many of whom readily assimilated much of the discursive and symbolic language deployed in Stratford to promote and mediate the reception of the music. John Norris, the editor of the Toronto jazz monthly *CODA*, echoed McNamara, Peterson, and others when he praised Applebaum and his colleagues for earning "an enviable reputation that no other festival has yet been able to get near."[97] "At Stratford," he wrote, "one could hear good jazz in excellent surroundings, surroundings which inspired the musicians to play really well."[98] Remarking that Canadians have a "far greater appreciation than those south of the border," he spoke for "many others who deprecate the passing of jazz from the Stratford Festival."[99] Emerging as it did in the 1950s, the medium of the international music festival enlivened the cultural public sphere. More significantly, it opened up a space that allowed jazz to reverberate more widely as Canadians stomped headlong into a new decade and toward a much deeper engagement with the music.

NOTES

Acknowledgments: My sincere thanks to Sean Mills for his comments on a previous iteration of this chapter. My gratitude also to Michael Stevenson and Asa McKercher (organizers of the Canada in the Age of Eisenhower Symposium), as well as to Daniel Samson and Elizabeth Neswald (who invited me to share my research as part of the Brock University Department of History Speaker Series) for providing opportunities to discuss – and expand – the ideas that shaped my analysis of the music featured during the Stratford Shakespearean Festival.

1 Gordon Donaldson, "Stiff Shirts, No Jazz: Princess Passes Up Duke," *Telegram,* Toronto, 1 August 1958.

2 E.B.R., "Princess Blue," *Cincinnati Enquirer,* 16 August 1958.

3 For a discussion of the Stratford Shakespearean Festival and the persistence of Anglophilic nationalism during the 1950s and beyond, see Paul Litt, *The Muses, the Masses, and the Massey Commission* (Toronto: University of Toronto Press, 1992); Alan Filewod, *Performing Canada: The Nation Enacted in the Imagined Theatre* (Kamloops: Faculty of Arts, University College of the Cariboo, 2002); Ryan Edwardson, *Canadian Content: Culture and the Quest for Nationhood* (Toronto: University of Toronto Press, 2008); Paul Rutherford, "The Persistence of Britain: The Culture Project in Postwar Canada," in *Canada and the End of Empire,* ed. Phillip Buckner (Vancouver: UBC Press, 2005), 195–205; and Sarah Dougherty, "Touring Shakespeare: The Stratford Festival, Cultural Funding, and Cultural Diplomacy," *Journal of the Canadian Historical Association* 29, 1 (2018): 73–99.

4 Celia Applegate explains that "serious music" emerged as a response to the "status anxiety" felt by intellectual and cultural elites who grappled with the social and structural changes that accompanied modernity and nation building in late-eighteenth-century and early-nineteenth-century Europe. By making "serious music" one of the pillars of their national cultures, those elites claimed that only they had the "technical, intellectual, and emotional resources" to consolidate nationhood. Celia Applegate, "How German Is It? Nationalism and the Idea of Serious Music in the Early Nineteenth Century," *19th-Century Music* 21, 3 (1998): 287, 295. See also Tia DeNora, "Musical Patronage and Social Change in Beethoven's Vienna," *American Journal of Sociology* 97, 2 (1991): 310–46. In his study of Shakespeare and the making of cultural hierarchies in North America, Lawrence W. Levine explains further that the strategies deployed by the elites to impose "cultural order," organize the "cultural sphere," assert "cultural authority," and establish "appropriate means of receiving culture" were concomitant

with similar efforts in the political and economic spheres. Lawrence W. Levine, *Highbrow/Lowbrow: The Emergence of Cultural Hierarchy in America* (Cambridge, MA: Harvard University Press, 1988), 184, 228.

5 Wendy Michener, "New Orleans and Dixieland Style Will Usher in Series of Festival's Jazz Concerts," *Stratford Beacon Herald*, 10 July 1956.

6 Ibid.

7 Phillip Buckner, "Introduction," in *Canada and the End of Empire*, ed. Phillip Buckner (Vancouver: UBC Press, 2005), 9.

8 Litt, *The Muses*, 250.

9 As Jim McGuigan explains, the "concept of a cultural public sphere refers to the articulation of politics, public and personal, as a contested terrain through affective ... modes of communication." Jim McGuigan, "The Cultural Public Sphere," *European Journal of Cultural Studies* 8, 4 (2005): 435. See also Liana Giorgi, Monica Sassatelli, and Gerard Delanty, eds., *Festivals and the Cultural Public Sphere* (New York: Routledge, 2011).

10 Royal Commission on National Development in the Arts, Letters, and Sciences, *Report of the Royal Commission on National Development in the Arts, Letters, and Sciences, 1949–1951* (Ottawa: Edmond Cloutier, Printer to the King, 1951), 18.

11 Canadians were not alone in trying to respond to the idea of jazz as an exclusively American art form, but they faced unique challenges because of their proximity to the United States and the cross-border history of the music. See Mike Heffley, *Northern Sun/Southern Moon: Europe's Reinvention of Jazz* (New Haven, CT: Yale University Press, 2005); Philip V. Bohlman and Goffredo Plastino, eds., *Jazz Worlds/World Jazz* (Chicago: University of Chicago Press, 2016); and Yoshiomi Saito, *The Global Politics of Jazz in the Twentieth Century: Cultural Diplomacy and "American Music"* (London: Routledge, 2020).

12 Leonard Feather, *The Encyclopedia of Jazz*, 1st ed. (New York: Horizon Press, 1955), 32.

13 Nicholas M. Evans, *Writing Jazz: Race, Nationalism, and Modern Culture in the 1920s* (New York: Garland, 2000), 11. See also Fiona I.B. Ngô, *Imperial Blues: Geographies of Race and Sex in Jazz Age New York* (Durham, NC: Duke University Press, 2014); and David Gilbert, *The Product of Our Souls: Ragtime, Race, and the Birth of the Manhattan Musical Marketplace* (Chapel Hill: University of North Carolina Press, 2015).

14 Leonard Feather, *The Book of Jazz* (New York: Horizon Press, 1957), 4.

15 "Nice Jazz Festival," in *The Encyclopedia of Popular Music*, 4th ed., ed. Colin Larkin (New York: Oxford University Press, 2006), 193. For a succinct history of jazz festivals, see George McKay, "Festivals," in *The History of European Jazz: The Music, Musicians, and Audience in Context*, ed. Francesco Martinelli (Sheffield and Bristol: Equinox, 2018), 707–18.

16 Scott Saul, *Freedom Is, Freedom Ain't: Jazz and the Making of the Sixties* (Cambridge, MA: Harvard University Press, 2003), 102. See also George Wein, *Myself among Others: A Life in Music* (Cambridge, MA: Da Capo Press, 2003).

17 Leonard Feather, *The Encyclopedia of Jazz*, 2nd ed. (New York: Bonanza Books, 1962), 50.

18 See Barry Ulanov, *A History of Jazz in America* (New York: Viking Press, 1952); Marshall Stearns, *The Story of Jazz* (New York: Oxford University Press, 1956); as well as Nat Shapiro and Nat Hentoff, *The Jazz Makers* (New York: Rinehart, 1957).

19 On this topic, see Lisa E. Davenport, *Jazz Diplomacy: Promoting America in the Cold War Era* (Jackson: University Press of Mississippi, 2009); Penny M. Von Eschen, *Satchmo Blows Up the World: Jazz Ambassadors Play the Cold War* (Cambridge, MA: Harvard University Press, 2004); Danielle Fosler-Lussier, *Music in America's Cold War Diplomacy* (Berkeley: University of California Press, 2015); and Ingrid Monson, *Freedom Sounds: Civil Rights Call Out to Jazz and Africa* (New York: Oxford University Press, 2007). See also Tad Hershorn, *Norman Granz: The Man Who Used Jazz for Justice* (Berkeley: University of California Press, 2011).

20 For early histories of jazz in Canada, see Mark Miller, *Such a Melodious Racket: The Lost History of Jazz in Canada, 1914–1949* (Toronto: Mercury Press, 1997); and John Gilmore, *Swinging in Paradise: The Story of Jazz in Montreal* (Montreal: Véhicule Press, 1988). See also Robin Elliott, "Ragtime Spasms – Anxieties over the Rise of Popular Music in Toronto," in *Post-Colonial Distances: The Study of Popular Music in Canada and Australia,* ed. Bev Diamond, Denis Crowdy, and Daniel Downes (Newcastle, UK: Cambridge Scholars, 2008), 67–89; Elaine Keillor, *Music in Canada: Capturing Landscape and Diversity* (Montreal and Kingston: McGill-Queen's University Press, 2006), 202–5, 235–38; and Sean Mills, Eric Fillion, and Désirée Rochat, eds., *Statesman of the Piano: Jazz, Race, and History in the Life of Lou Hooper* (Montreal and Kingston: McGill-Queen's University Press, forthcoming 2023).

21 Oscar Peterson, *A Jazz Odyssey: The Life of Oscar Peterson* (New York: Continuum, 2002), 335.

22 Sid Adilman, "Quiet Color Bar Canada's Peril: Oscar Peterson," *Telegram,* Toronto, 12 June 1953; June Callwood, "Famous Families at Home: The Oscar Petersons," *Maclean's,* 25 October 1958, 24–25, 76–78.

23 See Gilmore, *Swinging in Paradise,* 103–5; and Alex Barris, *Oscar Peterson: A Musical Biography* (Toronto: HarperCollins, 2002), 81–82.

24 Barris, *Oscar Peterson,* 183–84. Although Canada's musical diplomacy was still in its early stages, artists did travel overseas on behalf of the Canadian government in the 1950s. Peterson, however, waited until 1974 to perform the role of jazz ambassador in the Soviet Union. See Gene Lees, *Oscar Peterson: The Will to Swing* (Toronto: Prospero Books, 2008); Graham Carr, "'No Political Significance of Any Kind': Glenn Gould's Tour of the Soviet Union and the Culture of the Cold War," *Canadian Historical Review* 95, 1 (2014): 1–29; and Kailey Miller, "'An Ancillary Weapon': Cultural Diplomacy and Nation-Building in Cold War Canada, 1945–1967" (PhD diss., Queen's University, 2015).

25 In her book on the Vancouver scene, Marian Jago decentres the two cities most commonly associated with jazz north of the border with the United States, Toronto and Montreal. Marian Jago, *Live at the Cellar: Vancouver's Iconic Jazz Club and the Canadian Cooperative Jazz Scene in the 1950s and '60s* (Vancouver: UBC Press, 2018). Scholars seeking to learn more about musicians, venues, and record labels in Canada will find the following works useful: John Gilmore, *Who's Who of Jazz in Montreal: Ragtime to*

1970 (Montreal: Véhicule Press, 1989); and Mark Miller, *The Miller Companion to Jazz in Canada and Canadians in Jazz* (Toronto: Mercury Press, 2001).

26 Sean Mills, "Democracy in Music: Louis Metcalf's International Band and Montreal Jazz History," *Canadian Historical Review* 100, 3 (2019): 357. This article examines how an eclectic group of musicians contested this symbolic structure, cultivating an internationalist ethos and enacting the politics of racial justice and democracy through bebop in postwar Montreal. For a discussion of jazz and politics in that city beyond the 1950s: Eric Fillion, *JAZZ LIBRE et la révolution québécoise: Musique-action, 1967–1975* (Saint-Joseph-du-Lac, QC: M Éditeur, 2019).

27 Andrew McIntosh, Timothy Maloney, and Patricia Wardrop, "Massey Hall," in *The Canadian Encyclopedia,* https://www.thecanadianencyclopedia.ca/en/article/massey -hall; William Kilbourn, *Intimate Grandeur: One Hundred Years at Massey Hall* (Toronto: Stoddart, 1993).

28 In reference to the title of a 1973 reissue album of the concert. Charlie Parker with Dizzy Gillespie, Bud Powell, Charles Mingus, and Max Roach, *The Greatest Jazz Concert Ever,* Prestige Records PR 24024, 1973, 33⅓ RPM LP. Miller notes that the recording "has made Massey Hall second only to Oscar Peterson among the most recognizable Canadian names in jazz." Miller, *The Miller Companion to Jazz,* 130. Details about the concert can be found in Mark Miller, *Cool Blues: Charlie Parker in Canada, 1953* (London, ON: Nightwood Editions, 1989); and Kilbourn, *Intimate Grandeur,* 105–9.

29 Royal Commission on National Development in the Arts, Letters, and Sciences, *Report,* xi.

30 Litt, *The Muses,* 21.

31 Edwardson, *Canadian Content,* 57. On this topic, see Maria Tippett, *Making Culture: English-Canadian Institutions and the Arts before the Massey Commission* (Toronto: University of Toronto Press, 1990); Jeffrey D. Brison, *Rockefeller, Carnegie and Canada: American Philanthropy and the Arts and Letters in Canada* (Montreal and Kingston: McGill-Queen's University Press, 2005); and Allan Smith, "From Guthrie to Greenberg: Canadian High Culture and the End of Empire," in *Canada and the End of Empire,* ed. Phillip Buckner (Vancouver: UBC Press, 2005), 206–15.

32 Edwardson, *Canadian Content,* 57.

33 John Pettigrew and Jamie Portman, *Stratford: The First Thirty Years* (Toronto: Macmillan, 1985), 15. See also Tom Patterson and Allan Gould, *First Stage: The Making of the Stratford Festival* (Willowdale, ON: Firefly Books, 1999).

34 Tyrone Guthrie, "Is Canada Ready for Big-Time Theatre?," *Mayfair,* Montreal, October 1953, 27.

35 Ibid.

36 Royal Commission on National Development in the Arts, Letters, and Sciences, *Report,* 4. See also Walter Pitman, *Louis Applebaum: A Passion for Culture* (Toronto: Dundurn Press, 2002), 104–5.

37 Louis Applebaum, "Stratford's Music Festival," in *The Stratford Scene, 1958–1968,* ed. Peter Raby (Toronto: Clarke-Irwin, 1968), 58.

38 Ibid.

39 Louis Applebaum, "Report on the Inaugural Music Festival," 8 August 1955, Clara Thomas Archives and Special Collections (hereafter CTASC), Louis Applebaum Fonds, F0254, 1979–002/026 F-497.

40 Feather, *The Encyclopedia of Jazz*, 1st ed., 25.

41 Applebaum, "Report on the Inaugural Music Festival."

42 Ibid. This particular proposal did not materialize.

43 Cited in "Music Release #2," 29 February 1956, CTASC, Louis Applebaum Fonds, F0254, 1979–002/033 F-622.

44 Louis Applebaum, "Stratford's Second Music Season," in *Souvenir Program*, 1956, Stratford Festival Archives.

45 "Music Release #2."

46 The Second Annual Music Festival (7 July–11 August 1956) featured thirty-four concerts.

47 Helen McNamara, "McNamara's Bandwagon," *Telegram*, Toronto, 7 July 1956.

48 Ibid. In reference to Ellington's signature work, "Take the 'A' Train."

49 Claude Gingras, "Le 'New New Orleans Orchestra' nous a retrempés pendant trois heures dans les origines du jazz," *La Presse*, Montreal, 19 July 1956.

50 See J. Burke Martin, "Cool and Clear: Jazz Comes to Stratford," *London Evening Free Press*, 12 July 1956; and J. Burke Martin, "'Educated' Jazz Holds Stage at Stratford Music Survey," *London Evening Free Press*, 26 July 1956.

51 Wendy Michener, "Jazz Men Feed the Swans and See 'Real Cool' Avon," *Stratford Beacon Herald*, 11 July 1956.

52 Stan Rantin, "Festival Jazz Is 'Gasser,'" *Toronto Daily Star*, 12 July 1956.

53 Ibid.

54 John Kraglund, "Music in Stratford," *Globe and Mail*, Toronto, 12 July 1956.

55 Rantin, "Festival Jazz Is 'Gasser.'"

56 Martin, "'Educated' Jazz Holds Stage."

57 Phil Nimmons "decided to form a group in which the members would have the opportunity to create and produce serious jazz as they felt it," explained the program. Cited in *Calvin Jackson Quartet and Phil Nimmons Group with Paul Draper*, concert program, 25 July 1956, Stratford Festival Archives.

58 W.J. Pitcher, "Jazz Fans Approve Bach by Tap Dancer," *Kitchener Waterloo Record*, 26 July 1956.

59 "Jazz for Highbrows," *Echo-Journal*, Montreal, 5 July 1956.

60 See Pitcher, "Jazz Fans Approve Bach"; and Alex Barris, "Casting About," *Globe and Mail*, Toronto, 30 July 1956.

61 Applebaum, "Report on the Inaugural Music Festival."

62 "Music Release #12," 5 July 1956, CTASC, Louis Applebaum Fonds, F0254, 1979–002/033 F-622.

63 Wendy Michener, "Jackson, Nimmons to Show Contemporary Jazz Ideas," *Stratford Beacon Herald*, 24 July 1956.

64 Cited in Stan Rantin, "Canadian Musicians Feel Festival Jazz Success," *Toronto Daily Star*, in CTASC, Louis Applebaum Fonds, F0254, 1979–002/029 F-559A.

65 Ferguson was working in the United States at the time. His band included African American musicians but no Black Canadians.

66 Gilmore, *Swinging in Paradise*, 214.

67 See Helen McNamara, "The Cats Cool to Billie," *Telegram*, Toronto, 10 August 1957; and Mollie Graham, "Audience Caught by Dramatic Voice of Billie Holiday," Library and Archives Canada (hereafter LAC), Helen McNamara Fonds, R13917, vol. 2, file 11.

68 "Croll Raps Smearing of U.S. Poet; Refers to Canadian 'Hate Sheet,'" *Windsor Daily Star*, 17 July 1958. Quinn represented the division of Bedford-Halifax. His opponents promptly noted that his efforts to have Hughes banned doubled as an ideological attack on the principle of government support for the arts.

69 "Corruption by Poetry an Unlikely Danger," *London Evening Free Press*, 18 July 1958. For a detailed account of the "red scare" in Canada, see Reg Whitaker and Gary Marcuse, *Cold War Canada: The Making of a National Insecurity State, 1945–1957* (Toronto: University of Toronto Press, 1994).

70 "Senator Wants Poet Hughes Banned from Festival Here," *Stratford Beacon Herald*, 16 July 1958.

71 In a text published in the festival's souvenir program, Hughes explained that jazz, because "its deep syncopations" were rooted in "the human soul" of a people who had survived slavery, could never be "a frivolous or meaningless music or merely entertainment, no matter how much it is played for fun." Langston Hughes, "The Roots of Jazz," in *Souvenir Program*, 1958, Stratford Festival Archives. See also Alan Haydock, "U.S. Poet Hughes Defends His Work against Senator," *Stratford Beacon Herald*, 23 July 1958; W.J. Pitcher, "Jazz Poet's Readings Show Religious Tone," *Kitchener Waterloo Record*, 24 July 1958.

72 Mark Miller, "In a Monumental Mood," *Globe and Mail*, Toronto, 13 March 1999. The following biography is enlightening: Terry Teachout, *Duke: A Life of Duke Ellington* (New York: Gotham Books, 2013).

73 Victor Polley, "Report of the Box Office Manager," 20 September 1956, CTASC, Louis Applebaum Fonds, F0254, 1979–002/026 F-497.

74 J. Burke Martin, "Festival Debut Wins Plaudits for Ellington," *London Free Press*, 19 July 1956.

75 John Kraglund, "Music in Stratford," *Globe and Mail*, Toronto, 19 July 1956.

76 The dedication appears on the cover of the album. Duke Ellington and His Orchestra, *Such Sweet Thunder*, Columbia Records CL 1033, 1957, 33⅓ RPM LP.

77 Duke Ellington, "Jazz at Stratford," in *Souvenir Program*, 1957, Stratford Festival Archives.

78 Ibid. For studies dealing with Ellington's interest in Shakespeare, consult David Schiff, "The Moor's Revenge: The Politics of *Such Sweet Thunder*," in *Duke Ellington Studies*, ed. John Howland (Cambridge, UK: Cambridge University Press, 2017), 177–96; Jack Chambers, *Sweet Thunder: Duke Ellington's Music in Nine Themes* (Toronto: Milestones Music and Art, 2020); and Stephen M. Buhler, "Form and Character in Duke Ellington's and Billy Strayhorn's *Such Sweet Thunder*," *Borrowers and Lenders: The Journal of Shakespeare and Appropriation* 1, 1 (2005): 1-10, https://borrowers-ojs-azsu.tdl.org/borrowers/article/view/16/32.

79 See Helen McNamara, "One of His Best," *Telegram*, Toronto, 2 May 1958.
80 Colin Murray, "The Duke's Gift Will Be a Tune," *Telegram*, Toronto, 30 July 1958. The composer reminisced about the encounter in Duke Ellington, *Music Is My Mistress* (New York: Da Capo Press, 1976).
81 Murray, "The Duke's Gift Will Be a Tune."
82 Donaldson, "Stiff Shirts, No Jazz." In a review of the album *Such Sweet Thunder*, Richard J. Doyle referred to the composer as the "very royal Duke." Richard J. Doyle, "It's Recorded: Most Royally the Duke Pays Homage to Bard," *Globe and Mail*, Toronto, 31 August 1957.
83 Robertson Davies, "Stratford Revisited: Amazing Festival," *Saturday Night*, Toronto, 1 September 1956.
84 "Stratford Festival Survey," 1958, CTASC, Louis Applebaum Fonds, F0254, 1979–002/026 F-494.
85 Polley, "Report of the Box Office Manager."
86 Ibid.
87 Levine, *Highbrow/Lowbrow*, 195; Lawrence W. Levine, "Jazz and American Culture," *Journal of American Folklore* 102, 403 (1989): 16.
88 "Stratford Plans Jazz Return," *Toronto Daily Star*, 20 June 1959.
89 See the liner notes for Oscar Peterson, *The Oscar Peterson Trio at the Stratford Shakespearean Festival*, Verve Records MGV-8024, 1957, 33⅓ RPM LP. The following titles also came out of Stratford: Wilbur de Paris, *Live in Canada – 1956*, Jazz Crusade JCCD-3032, n.d., CD; Duke Ellington, *Live from the 1956 Stratford Festival*, Music and Arts Programs of America CD-616, 1989, CD; and Billie Holiday, *Billie Holiday at the Stratford Shakespearean Festival – 1957*, Solar Records 4569920, 2012, CD.
90 "Says Jazz Series Here Opened Canadians' Eyes," *Stratford Beacon Herald*, 14 August 1956. See also Helen McNamara, "McNamara's Bandwagon," *Telegram*, Toronto, 11 August 1956.
91 Graham George, "Music at Stratford: Tail of a Comet," *Canadian Music Journal* 3, 1 (1958): 30.
92 Ibid., 30–31.
93 See Leslie Bell, "Jazz Now Dominates Music at Stratford," *Toronto Daily Star*, 6 July 1957; Leslie Bell, "Why Does Jazz Last?," *Toronto Daily Star*, 31 August 1957; and Leslie Bell, "Frenzy of Jazz Is Incoherent," *Toronto Daily Star*, 9 August 1958.
94 "Report of Music Season – 1958," 21 August 1958, CTASC, Louis Applebaum Fonds, F0254, 2002–009/010 F-010.
95 "Auditors' Report and Financial Statement," 30 September 1958, CTASC, Louis Applebaum Fonds, F0254, 1979–002/026 F-494.
96 Polley, "Report of the Box Office Manager."
97 John Norris, "Editorial," *CODA* 1, 10 (1959): 2.
98 Ibid.
99 Ibid., 1–2.

Afterword

NORMAN HILLMER

In July 2022, as I was reading the manuscript of this book, *Harper's* magazine announced on a red, white, and blue cover that "The American Century Is Over." The article inside, by University of Washington professor Daniel Bessner, described the belief in 100 years of missionary international engagement that originated during the Second World War and grew deep roots in the United States. By the year 2000, "the United States, a nation founded after one of the first modern anticolonial revolutions, had become a world-spanning empire. The 'city on a hill' had evolved into a fortified metropolis." Yet, Bessner argued, the American Century was at its end, the casualty of geopolitics, the rise of China in particular, and inward-facing US nationalist politics. What was to come next no one knew.

North of America discovers the American Century in full bloom in Canada during the fifteen years after 1945. That is the book's subject, with the reader's attention drawn to a country in the shadow of a supremely powerful and confident neighbour. Canadians, in this reading, were vulnerable. They lived so close to and were so invested in the United States that they were at risk.

The focus of *North of America* is on the 1950s, a decade readily glossed over by the temporally minded because it sits between two periods full of texture and obvious significance – the consequential 1940s and the controversial 1960s. The stereotype of the decade-in-between is one of dull stability and consensus presided over by elderly grey men. The authors of this book instead see years of dynamism, change, and complexity. There are the expected chapters on the intricacies of international relations, but the canvas is expanded to take in governance, domesticity, consumerism, race, the movement of ideas, television, transportation and urban planning, and music. The signal contribution of *North of America* is in the variety of its viewpoints.

The meanings of the American Century were not lost on Canadians. They ate up the good life afforded to them by American prosperity, technology, and modernity. They felt safer behind the Cold War shield of US armaments. The United States was unavoidable in politics, economics, international affairs, and culture. Canadians were seldom anti-American, although they could be tempted in that direction from time to time by unscrupulous politicians. Francophone Quebecers moved from early 1900s hostility toward the United States to a realization of the material and psychological benefits of positioning themselves as North Americans. English Canadians, unprotected by language and cultural difference, were more inclined to be skeptical, especially as the 1950s progressed.

Canadian relations with and attitudes toward the United States have always been located somewhere in the tension between admiration and suspicion. The American Century made Canada more like the United States, but it did not make Canadians like America more. Nor did they always want what was on offer from the United States. The report of the Massey Commission in 1951 lamented that Canada was awash in the products of American culture. Frederick Gardiner, the Metropolitan Toronto chief executive, spurned the congestion of automobile-saturated US cities in favour of a balance of highways and publicly funded mass transit. The movement to ease America's hold on the Canadian economy began in the 1950s, not in the 1960s, as is conventionally thought.

Canadians, while following the American lead in world affairs, had their own ideas about how the world should go. Minister of Foreign Affairs Lester Pearson was frustrated by dependence on the United States even as he accepted "the fact that we can't escape this no matter how hard we try." He and his colleagues sought counterweights to the United States in multilateral institutions, and in the ancient connection to the United Kingdom,

AFTERWORD

while building bridges between West and East. Canada was middling in power and influence on the international scene, and its diplomatic temperament favoured dialogue and constraint. The impulse to mediation led to the resolution of the Suez Crisis in 1956, winning the Nobel Peace Prize for Pearson and for Canada.

Exposure to the United States reinforced the desire and need for difference. The drawing of distinctions between the two countries is a staple of Canadian nationalism. This volume's study of anti-Black racism in Dresden, Ontario, demonstrates how the town's violations of the human rights of its Black citizens were depicted in Canada's English-language newspapers as alien to the national experience and traditions. Readers were assured that discrimination and segregation belonged to America, not to the northern paragon. Canadians are expert in moralizing about the shortcomings of the United States, many of which they share.

North of America is dedicated to the memory of Greg Donaghy, the most important Canadian foreign policy scholar of his generation. The book written in his honour addresses international history with the innovation and broad perspective that were his strengths and are his legacy.

Contributors

STEPHEN AZZI is a professor of political management, history, and political science at Carleton University. He is the author of *Walter Gordon and the Rise of Canadian Nationalism* (1999) and *Reconcilable Differences: A History of Canada-US Relations* (2015).

PENNY BRYDEN is a professor of history at the University of Victoria. Her books include *Canada: A Political Biography* (2016) and *"A Justifiable Obsession": Conservative Ontario's Relations with Ottawa, 1943–1985* (2013).

SUSAN COLBOURN is the associate director of the Program in American Grand Strategy at Duke University and a senior fellow of the Bill Graham Centre for Contemporary International History at the University of Toronto. A diplomatic and international historian, she is the author of *Euromissiles: The Nuclear Weapons that Nearly Destroyed NATO* (2022) and the editor, along with Timothy Andrews Sayle, of *The Nuclear North: Histories of Canada in the Atomic Age* (2020).

FRANÇOIS-OLIVIER DORAIS is an associate professor of history at the Université du Québec à Chicoutimi. His books include *L'École historique. Une histoire intellectuelle* (2022) and *Un historien dans la cité: Gaétan Gervais et l'Ontario français* (2016).

CONTRIBUTORS

JONATHAN ENGLISH is a fellow at New York University's Marron Institute of Urban Management. He received his doctorate in urban planning at Columbia University.

ERIC FILLION is an adjunct professor and Buchanan Postdoctoral Fellow in Canadian history at Queen's University. He is the author of *Distant Stage: Quebec, Brazil, and the Making of Canada's Cultural Diplomacy* (2022) and *JAZZ LIBRE et la révolution québécoise: Musique-action, 1967–1975* (2019). He is also the co-editor, with Sean Mills and Désirée Rochat, of *Statesman of the Piano: Jazz, Race, and History in the Life of Lou Hooper* (2023).

NORMAN HILLMER is chancellor's professor of history and international affairs at Carleton University. He is the biographer of O.D. Skelton and the co-author, with J.L. Granatstein, of *For Better or for Worse: Canada and the United States into the Twenty-First Century* (2005).

EMILY LEDUC is a doctoral candidate and teaching fellow at Queen's University. A Canada Graduate Scholarship recipient, her dissertation, "'A Matter of National Necessity': Canadian Television in an American Age, 1950–1990," examines Canadian television broadcasting during its coming of age years and focuses on the unique challenges presented by proximity to American mass culture industries.

BETTINA LIVERANT is an adjunct assistant professor of history at the University of Calgary. Her research projects are situated at the intersection of commerce and culture. She has written extensively on Canadian consumer society, on corporate philanthropy, and on Canadian architecture, and she is the author of *Buying Happiness: The Emergence of Consumer Consciousness in Canada* (2018). She is currently completing a monograph entitled *A Business History of Retail: Going Shopping in the United States and Canada*, under contract with Routledge.

ASA MCKERCHER is an assistant professor of history at the Royal Military College of Canada. His publications include *Canada and the World since*

1867 (2019) and *Canada and Camelot: Canadian-American Relations in the Kennedy Era* (2016).

DANIEL POITRAS is the author of *Expérience du temps et historiographie au XXe siècle: Michel de Certeau, François Furet et Fernand Dumont* (2018) and *L'Université de Montréal : une histoire urbaine et internationale* (2023).

TIMOTHY ANDREWS SAYLE is an associate professor of history and the director of the International Relations Program at the University of Toronto. He is the author of *Enduring Alliance: A History of NATO and the Postwar Global Order* (2019) and creator of the website *Canada Declassified.*

MICHAEL D. STEVENSON is a professor of history at Lakehead University. He has edited or co-edited three volumes in the *Documents on Canadian External Relations* series and has published *Canada's Greatest Wartime Muddle: National Selective Service and the Mobilization of Human Resources during World War II* (2001).

JENNIFER TUNNICLIFFE is an assistant professor of history at Toronto Metropolitan University. She is the co-editor of *Constant Struggle: Histories of Canadian Democratization* (2021) and the author of *Resisting Rights: Canada and the International Bill of Rights, 1947–1976* (2019).

DAVID WEBSTER is an associate professor of human rights studies at King's University College, Western University. He is the author of *Challenge the Strong Wind: Canada and East Timor, 1975–99* (2020) and *Fire and the Full Moon: Canada and Indonesia in a Decolonizing World* (2009), and he is the co-editor of *A Samaritan State Revisited: Historical Perspectives on Canadian Foreign Aid* (2019).

Index

Note: "(f)" following a page number indicates a figure; "(t)" following a page number indicates a table

Acheson, Dean, 17, 22, 23, 102, 128
Act to Limit Slavery, 185
L'action française, 204
L'action nationale, 208–10
Adams, Eric A., 135
Adenauer, Konrad, 52, 55
Adjetey, Wendell, 186–87
advertising: and politics, 246; radio, 211; and radio vs. print industry, 279; and television, 266, 274; US influence in, 246
affluence. *See* prosperity
African Americans. *See* Black Americans
African countries: decolonization in, 32–33; independence, and economic growth, 19. *See also* Bandung (Asian-African) Conference
aid: Canadian, 26, 34; and Colombo Plan, 25–26; and communism, 25–26, 32; US, 26, 27–28
Aird Commission. *See* Royal Commission on Broadcasting in Canada (Aird Commission)
Alaska Highway, 94

Alcoholic Liquor Act, 131
All-African People's Conference (1958), 33
Allen, Gene, 261
Allen, Henry "Red," 328
L'âme américaine (Nevers), 202, 204
American century: about, ix; as Age of Eisenhower, 5; Canadians and, 342; jazz and, 319; Luce on, 3; and new international order, ix; transitions in global power during, 91; US national security state growth and, 17; and US preponderance, 3
"The American Century Is Over" (Bessner, in *Harper's* magazine), 341
American Press Association, 205–6
Americanization: during 1950s, 245; and Canadian identity, 100; and French Canadian nationalism, 205; Maclennan on, 5; and modernity, 225; in Quebec, 207, 209, 226; and Sunday openings, 244; and television, 266, 274. *See also* influence of US
Anderson, Benedict, 188, 200*n*55

347

INDEX

Anglosphere, 90

anti-Americanism: in Canadian identity, 6–7; France-Quebec relationship and, 214; influence of US and, 245–46; and nationalism, 206; in Quebec, 203, 207–8; Second World War and, 207–8

Applebaum, Louis: career, 323; and Hughes, 328; and jazz, 317, 323–24, 326, 327, 331, 332, 333; Jocelyn replacing, 329

Applegate, Celia, 334n4

appliances, household: during 1950s, 239; economic changes and, 168; as end vs. means, 245; industrialization of housework and, 147; integration into home design, 156; in rural vs. urban households, 161–62; Second World War and, 239; and time saving, 165; in urban middle-class homes, 163; in urban working-class homes, 163; women's employment and, 149; and women's leisure, 165

Aquin, Hubert, 221

Armstrong, Bromley, 183–84

Asian countries: aid to, 19; Canada as bridge to, 20; Canadian national security policy and, 72, 77; and China, 23; and Cold War, 21, 33; independence, and economic growth, 19; and Korean War, 22–23; Korean War and association of, 25; non-alignment, 21–25; war and, 72. *See also* Bandung (Asian-African) Conference; Southeast Asia; *and names of individual countries*

Asian Relations Conference, 21

Asian-African conference. *See* Bandung (Asian-African) Conference

Atherton, Ray, 4

Atkinson, Dave, 212

Atlantic Alliance, 44, 45, 48, 51, 56, 57, 58

Atlantic magazine, on Canadian nationalism in 1958 election campaign, 251–52

atomic age. *See* nuclear age/revolution

atomic bomb. *See* nuclear weapons, atomic bomb

Attlee, Clement, 101–2

Australia: and Bandung Conference, 29; and Indonesian civil war, 31–32; in SEATO, 18

automobile(s): during 1950s, 239–40; age of, 288–89; dependence on, 300–1; as end vs. means, 245; in England, 306; Gardiner and, 10, 299, 308; Moses on, 302; ownership, 239, 291–92; production in Toronto, 292; public servants and, 289–90; public transit vs., 288–89, 306; suburban life and, 240; technocracy and, 289–90

Azzi, Stephen, 10, 122, 160

babies. *See* children

baby boom, 8, 141, 143–44, 149

Bach, Johann Sebastian, 329

Baillargeon, Denyse, 163

Baird, John Logie, 263, 264, 267

Bakan, Abigail, 184–85

Balcer, Léon, 250

Bandaranaike, Solomon, 22

Bandung (Asian-African) Conference, 18, 22, 29–30

Bank of Canada, 252

Barbeau, Victor, 206; *La Politique,* 219

Barkway, Michael, 249

Bartholomew, Harland, 290, 301

Barton, W.H., 76; "Canadian National Security," 70–71, 73–74

Beecher Stowe, Harriet, *Uncle Tom's Cabin,* 178, 190, 191, 192

Behiels, Michael, 5

Bel Geddes, Norman, 289; *Futurama,* 288

Bélanger, Damien-Claude, 206

Belgrade Non-Aligned Conference (1961), 33

Bell, Leslie Richard, 332, 333

348

Bender, J.-H., 217
Bergeron, Gérard, 218
Berton, Pierre, 281; on CBC in *Maclean's*, 277–78; "Make Way for the One-Eyed Monster," 269–70
Bessner, Daniel, "The American Century Is Over," 341
Best, Carrie M., 179
Bills of Rights, 130, 131, 133–34, 136
birth rates: during 1950s, 238; during Great Depression, 148
Black Americans: Canadian understandings of, 177; enslavement of, 184; and jazz, 318, 319–20; racial segregation of, 189–90; racism in Dresden vs. as past sanctuary for, 196; shared consciousness with Black Canadians, 186–87. *See also* racial discrimination/segregation; slavery
Black Canadians: absence of history in narratives, 184–85; human rights activism for, 181–84; immigrants, 184; and jazz, 327; in Montreal, 327; newspaper reporting on discrimination against, 189; racial discrimination against, 176, 183, 189; restaurants and, 198*n*35; as second-class citizens, 180; shared consciousness with Black Americans, 186–87; slavery and, 184–85. *See also* racial discrimination/segregation
Black peoples in Canada, 189, 192, 196
Bliss, Richard, 217–18
Bloor-Danforth subway, 309–10
Blumenfeld, Hans, 291
Bohlen, Charles "Chip," 49
The Book of Jazz (Feather), 319
Borduas, Paul-Émile, 215, 216, 221; *Refus global*, 215
Born at the Right Time (Owram), 8
Bouchard, Gérard, 225–26
Bourassa, Henri, *The Spectre of Annexation*, 205
Bourcher v R, 132

Bowley, John D., 193
Bradley, Omar, 54
Brady, Alexander, 4
Brebner, John Bartlet, *North Atlantic Triangle*, 90
Bretton Woods, 238
Britain. *See* United Kingdom
British Commonwealth Air Training Program, 94
British North America (BNA) Act, 122, 123; civil rights and, 131; constitutional culture and, 137; Dawson on, 136; JCPC and, 130, 135; and *Roncarelli v Duplessis*, 131–32; Supreme Court and, 130
Broadacre City (Wright), 288
Brown v Board of Education, 127–29, 132, 133, 319
Brubeck, Dave, 324, 326
Brunet, Michel, 218, 223
Brussels Pact, 98–99
Brussels Treaty, 72
Bryce, Robert, 78, 79, 81, 82
Bryden, Penny, 10
Burma: and Asian neutralism, 21; and Colombo Plan, 19, 26; in Colombo Plan conference, 25; and Korean War, 23
Burnett, Hugh, 177, 181, 182, 183–84
Burns, E.L.M., 112
Burt, A.L., 4

Camisso, Frank and Irene, 166(f)
Campney, Ralph, 73, 74, 77
Canada: Tomorrow's Giant (Hutchison), 243
Canada Council for the Arts, 322
Canada Housing Design Council, 156(f)
Canada's Official Food Rules, 152(f)
Canada-US Agreement (1941), 228*n*17
Canada-US relationship. *See* US-Canada relationship
Canadian Association for Adult Education, 277

INDEX

Canadian Broadcasting Corporation (CBC), 242, 268; Berton in *Maclean's* on, 277–78; bilateral negotiations with US over channel usage rights, 272–73; Board of Governors, 271, 272; federal government and, 274; finances/financing, 265, 273; first two stations, 263; *Globe and Mail* on, 275–76; "Jazz for Highbrows," 326; and licensing fee, 273; as monopoly, 274–75, 283; people's ownership of, 275–76; and Peterson, 320; public vs. private in, 273, 275, 277–78; regulatory control over television, 283; television arm, 259; in *Toronto Daily Star,* 277; *Wednesday Night,* 326

Canadian Forum, on Canada as nation, 9

Canadian League of Composers, 323, 327

Canadian National Exhibition, Marconi television booth, 268

"Canadian National Security" (Barton), 70–71, 73–74

Canadian Negro, on Black peoples in Dresden, 193

Les Canadiens français et leurs voisins du sud (Lanctôt), 209

Cantin, Andréanne, 219

Careless, J.M.S., 245–46

Carnegie Foundation, 222, 223

Caro, Robert, 300, 310; *The Power Broker,* 290

Casey, R.G., 29

Casgrain, Henri-Raymond, 205

Catholic Church. *See* Roman Catholic Church

Cavell, Janice, 34

Central Mortgage and Housing Corporation (CMHC), 155–56

Charbonneau, Robert, 214–15

Charter of Rights and Freedoms, 131, 132

Chartier, Charles, 218

Chatelaine, on "radioitis," 271

Chatham Daily News, 190

Chiang Kai-shek, 23

Chicago Area Transportation Study, 302

Chiefs of Staff Committee, 54, 69, 70, 74

children: babies, 144–45; compulsory schooling, 165; radio and, 271; television and, 212, 269, 282. *See also* families

China: and Bandung Conference, 18, 29–30; Canada and, 76; China Lobby, 20; and communism, 19, 23; Communist vs. Nationalist forces, 76; conflict over coastal islands, 76; declaration of People's Republic of China, 23; India and, 23–24, 30; and Korean War, 23, 24, 25, 101; and Panch Sheel, 23–24; and Philippines, 30; Soviet Union and, 23; Tibet annexation, 24; in UN, 23, 48; US and, 24, 76, 77

Choquette, Robert, 215

Christie, Fred, 179, 181, 189, 198*n*35

Christie, Loring, 135

Churchill, Winston, 92, 95, 98

cities. *See* urban areas

citizenship, Canadian, 8–9

"City Beautiful" urban renewal, 290

Civil Code of Lower Canada, 131

Civil Liberties Association, 131

civil rights: for Black Canadians, 181–84; and *Brown v Board of Education,* 132; in Canada, 180; Constitution and, 134; constitutional culture and, 137; and constitutional role, 129; and courts, 129; Diefenbaker and, 133–34; entrenched, 131–32, 134, 137; federalism and, 131–32; Japanese Canadian deportations and, 189; and legal education, 135; media on, 189; in Quebec, 137; racial discrimination and, 176–77; in *Roncarelli v Duplessis,* 130–33; scholarship, 185–86; Supreme Court of Canada and, 127; trade unions and, 177; in US, 123, 127, 129, 132–33,

350

INDEX

177; US influence on Canadian, 132–33

Clarion: on Black peoples in Dresden, 193

classical music. *See* serious music

Claxton, Brooke, 7, 98, 99

CODA, 333

Colbourn, Susan, 9, 18

Cold War, 8; Asian countries and, 18, 21, 33; Bandung Conference and, 30; Canada and, 34; Colombo Plan and, 19, 27, 28; foreign policy and, 59–60; and Global South, 9; and household spending, 160; and Korean War, 101; as long haul, 43–44, 45, 60; NATO and, 44; and natural resources, 210; neutralism, 17; North Atlantic Triangle and, 91; nuclear revolution and, 70; peaceful coexistence and, 49; Pearson on, 60; Pearson's visit to Soviet Union and, 43–44; policy-making during, 70; Southeast Asia and, 18; Soviet Union and, 44, 45, 54; as stalemate, 54; Stalin's death and, 46; and transformations in international politics, 43–44; US and, 33, 35; and US-Canada relationship, 97–98

Coldwell, M.J., 250

Collier, Ron, 327

Collins, Robert, 281

Colombo Plan, 19, 25–26, 30, 31, 33; conference in Ottawa (1954), 26–28, 52

Colombo Plan conference, 25

Colton, Timothy, 293, 310

Commonwealth: and apartheid South Africa, 112–13; as bridge between Asia and West, 20; and Colombo Plan, 20, 26; Diefenbaker and, 34, 108–9; division in Korean War, 101; Ghana in, 32–33; India and, 20, 25

communism: aid vs., 25–26, 32; Bandung Conference and, 30; China and, 19, 23; Colombo Plan and, 26, 27; Conference on Indonesia and, 22;

domino theory, 31; Indonesia and, 32; McCarthy hearings and, 128; nuclear deterrent and, 83; peaceful coexistence and, 51; SEATO vs., 27; Southeast Asia and, 22; Soviet, 51

Conroe, Irwin, 222–23

Constitution (Canada): Canadian government series on, 136–37; and civil rights, 129, 134; education system and, 135–36; emotions attached to, 121–22, 123; and people's interactions, 132–33; in public consciousness, 137; and *Roncarelli v Duplessis,* 131–32; US judicial activism and, 10

Constitution (US): judicial activism and, 10; public opinion regarding, 127; racial segregation and, 127

constitutional change: constitutional meaning vs., 122; conversations regarding, 122–23; end of JCPC appeals and, 122; Second World War and, 122; US civil rights and, 123

constitutional culture: and BNA Act, 137; British traditions in, 122; *Brown v Board of Education* and, 127–28; changes to, 137; and civil rights, 137; and nationhood, 126; nurturing of, 126; rights rhetoric combined with federalism and, 131; US propinquity and, 122; and US-Canada relationship, 123

Constitutional Law in Canada (Hogg), 136

consumer goods: in homes, 165–66; as household needs, 167; masculinity and, 164–65; in suburban homes, 164; in urban middle-class homes, 163; US provision of, 247. *See also* appliances, household; equipment, household

consumer spending: debt, 157–58; demand, 160–61; and economic growth, 153; by one-person households, 164; postwar, 153–54; recreational, 164;

351

INDEX

regional differences, 164; by seniors, 164; and standards of living, 158; by teenagers, 164. *See also* shopping
continental defence, 72; Canada's position between Soviet Union and US, and, 75; and Canada's stance in Europe, 78; DEA and, 74, 79; defence policy and, 69; DND and, 76, 77–80, 83; joint US-Canadian management of, 75–76; Kennedy and, 112; and NATO, 76, 80; US and, 74
continentalism: economic, 210; Massey Commission and, 272; television and, 262; US and, 215
Convergences (Le Moyne), 220
Cook, Jack Kent, 276
Cook, P.W., 275–76
Cooper, Afua, 184, 192
Cooper, John, *Season of Rage,* 177
Cooperative Commonwealth Federation (CCF), 250
Cormier, Ernest, 222
Cornish, Joseph, 295–96
Corry, J.A., *Democratic Government and Politics,* 136
Coyne, James, 249, 252
Creighton, Donald, 137; *The Forked Road,* 121–22
The Creole Band, 320
Crépault, Ray, 43
Croll, David, 249
cultural elite. *See* elite
cultural imperialism: consumer capitalism and, 142; Massey Commission and, 272; US and, 261, 262, 265–66, 272
cultural industries: as network of mediums, 284; television as, 262; US cultural imperialism and, 261; US cultural influence over, 284
cultural mediums: influence of US on Quebec in, 204; relationship between, 262; television vs. other, 261–62, 278–83; US influence on, 262

Dantin, Louis, 215
Davies, Rupert, 275
Dawson, R. MacGregor, *The Government of Canada,* 136–37
de Paris, Wilbur, 316, 325
Dean, Arthur, 107
The Death and Life of Great American Cities (Jacobs), 290
decolonization, 18, 19, 32–33, 34
defence policy: Canada as buffer in US-Soviet Union war, and, 80; and Canadian air defence, 81; and continental defence, 69; as defence of Canada, 78; deployment in Europe, 67, 69; first objective as defence of Canada and North America, 82–83; Foulkes paper on, 80; Ignatieff paper on, 73–74; joint DEA-DND study, 79; and national security policy, 78–79; in "National Security Policy," 83–84; North American vs. European defence and, 67, 71, 74, 81–82; nuclear revolution and, 67–68, 69–70, 73–74, 83; paper on postwar development of, 82; and reliance on US, 9–10; thermonuclear weapons and, 73; transferral of commitments from Europe to North America, 69, 79–80; and US-China war, 76; and war in Asia, 69; White Paper on, 71; withdrawal of troops from Europe, 67, 71, 74, 81–82. *See also* national security policy
"Democracy in Music" (Mills), 337*n*26
Democratic Government and Politics (Corry), 136
Denison, Merrill, 270
Department of External Affairs (DEA): April 1955 meeting with DND and PCO, 77–79; Barton paper, 69–70, 73–74; and Colombo Plan, 28; and Colombo Plan conference (1954), 27; and Communist vs. Nationalist forces over Chinese coastal islands,

352

76; and continental defence, 69–70, 74, 77–80; on decolonization, 18; and family allowances, 155; and Indonesian civil war, 31–32; and joint study on national security policy, 79; July 1955 joint meeting with DND on national security policy, 81–82; on King's relationship with Roosevelt, 92–93; "National Security Policy," 83–84; and NATO, 79, 82; and North American vs. European defence, 74; and nuclear deterrent, 74–75, 83; paper on atomic age, 53–54; and Peterson, 321; and sale of trucks to Indonesian army, 31–32; and Soviet Union, 45–46, 82; "Study of National Security Policy," 53–54, 69–70; on withdrawal of troops from Europe, 82. *See also* foreign policy; national security policy

Department of National Defence (DND): April 1955 meeting with DEA and PCO, 77–79; on atomic age, 53–54; and Barton paper, 73–74; and continental defence, 76, 77–80, 83; DEA's "nuclear deterrent" paper and, 83; and Ignatieff's questions on national security, 73–74; and joint study on national security policy, 79; July 1955 joint meeting with DEA on national security policy, 81–82; "National Security Policy," 83–84; and national security policy, 54, 76, 82; and nuclear revolution, 69; White Paper, 71; on withdrawal of troops from Europe, 79, 81–82. *See also* defence policy; national security policy

Department of Northern Affairs and Natural Resources, 8

Desmond, Viola, 179, 189

Desrochers, Alfred, 215

Dessaulles, Louis-Antoine, 227n4

détente, 44, 45, 52, 54. *See also* peaceful coexistence

Le Devoir, 204

Dexter, Grant, 7

Diefenbaker, John: and Bill of Rights, 133–34; British speculation regarding government, 104–5; British ties, 105–6; and Commonwealth, 34, 108–9; at Commonwealth prime ministers' meeting, 105; Eisenhower and, 236; and foreign control, 252; Garner on, 105, 109, 113; and Kennedy, 112; Macmillan and, 107–8, 112, 113; and Montreal trade and economic conference, 106, 107–8; and non-alignment, 34; and NORAD, 85; on Northern Vision for prosperity, 8; and nuclear weapons, 85; and Pakistan vs. India, 34; on selling out to US, 250; and South Africa, 112–13; trade diversion proposal, 106, 108, 236; and triangular relationship, 105–7, 109; and UK joining EEC, 112–13; and US, 34, 104–5, 251, 252; world tour, 108–9

Dion-Lévesque, Rosaire, 215

disarmament, 110–11, 112

Dixon, Mort, 213

domestic labour. *See* housework

domesticity: breadwinner-housewife, 146; capital investment in, 167; commoditization of, 159–60; definitions of, 168; demographics of, 143–45; financialization of, 157–58; and fiscal policy, 155; historiography, 141; idealization of, 141, 142, 152; increased comfort of, 168; inequalities in, 168; middle-class families and, 147; new traditions of, 165–68; politicization of, 150–57; rural-urban gap, 161–62; settler colonialism and forms of, 150; television and, 268–70; traditions and practices in, 167, 168. *See also* households

Dominion Bureau of Statistics: on foreign investment, 250; household equipment surveys, 158–60; on new patterns in domesticity, 165; on rurality, 161

Dominion Stores, 160

Donaghy, Greg, ix, xi, 343

Donaldson, Gordon, 315

Dorais, François-Oliver, 10

Dred Scott, 130

Dresden, ON: about, 177–78; as "Alabama of north," 192–93; plebiscite on racial discrimination, 176; population, 178; racial discrimination in, 176, 178–79, 343; as safe haven, 177, 178, 192, 196; as Underground Railway terminus, 176, 178, 190–92. *See also* racial discrimination/segregation in Dresden, ON

The Dresden Story (National Film Board of Canada), 183

Drew, George, 107, 249–50

Drury, C.M. "Bud," 77, 79, 81

Duane Jones survey on impact of television, 279

Dulles, Allen, 31

Dulles, John Foster, 26; on Cold War neutralism, 17; and Colombo Plan, 28; and Diefenbaker's trade diversion proposal, 106; on "Massive Retaliation" strategy, 71–72; and Pearson's visit to Soviet Union, 55; and "secret wars" against communism, 31; and Soviet Union, 47

Duplessis, Maurice, 130, 132, 202, 210, 219

Eaton's department store, 241

economic growth: during 1950s, 238; Asian and African countries, and, 19; Colombo Plan and, 30; as end vs. means, 245; mass consumption and, 153; Second World War and, 96–97; US capital investment and, 247–52

Economist, on Canadian international status, 7

Eden, Anthony, 102–3, 104

education: television and, 282; university enrollment, 238; US-Quebec relationship and, 209

Edwardson, Ryan, 260–61

Egypt: Canada and, 34; and Suez Crisis, 103–4

Eisenhower, Dwight, 26; and Age of Eisenhower, 5, 33; and American Century, 5; and automobile, 288; at Bermuda meeting, 104; and Cold War, 35; and communism, 31; and Diefenbaker's trade diversion proposal, 108, 236; and Dulles' "Massive Retaliation" strategy, 71–72; and highways, 300–1; and intervention in Indochina, 103; and jazz, 319, 324; King and, 95; and Macmillan, 104, 107, 108; on McNaughton's resentment of British colleagues, 94–95; Non-Aligned Movement and, 33; and nuclear revolution, 67–68, 69, 71–72; and race, 129, 319; and Soviet Union, 47, 48; speeches to Parliament, 235–36; and US at crossroads, 128; visit to Canada, 95, 235–36; and Warren Supreme Court, 128–29

elite: and jazz, 317, 320, 329, 330; Massey Commission and, 276, 316–17; and Stratford Shakespearean Festival, 316, 323; and television, 265–66. *See also* high culture

Ellington, Duke, 315, 317, 318, 325, 328–29, 330, 331; "Princess Blue," 330

Emerson, Annie, 183–84

Emerson's Soda Bar Restaurant, 178, 183

employment: earnings levels, 237; hours of work, 164; household members and, 146, 168; postwar, 147–48; resource boom and, 247; sectors, 164; unemployment insurance/benefits, 242; unemployment rate, 238; US ownership of resource industries and, 9. *See also* women's employment

The Encyclopedia of Jazz (Feather), 318, 319

English, Jonathan, 10

Enola Gay, 66

Entezam, Nasrollah, 24

equipment, household. *See* appliances, household; household goods

European Defence Community, 47

European Economic Community, 113

European Recovery Program (Marshall Plan), 96, 97

expressways. *See* highways

Fair Accommodation Practices Act (Ontario), 183, 190, 195

Fair Employment Practices Act (Ontario), 182

fair practices laws, 176, 181–82, 184

Falardeau, Jean-Charles, 223

families: consumer patterns, 10; family allowances, 154–55; income rates, 238; middle-class, 147; nuclear, 10; nuclear as most common household type, 143; single male wage earners and, 149; television and, 279; working mothers, 149; working-class, in Montreal, 146; yearning for traditional family life, 141. *See also* children; domesticity; households

La famille Plouffe, 212–13

Family Allowance program, 154(f)

family allowances, 154–55

Fanon, Frantz, 26

Feather, Leonard: *The Book of Jazz,* 319; *The Encyclopedia of Jazz,* 318, 319

Federal Aid Highway Act (1956) (US), 300–1

Federal Republic of Germany, 57–58; in Atlantic Alliance, 51; and NATO, 51, 72; Soviet Union and, 82

Federation of Musicians of America and Canada, 276–77

Felix the Cat, 263

Female Employees Fair Remuneration Act (Ontario), 182

Ferguson, Maynard, 327, 339*n*65

Fillion, Eric, 10

film/movies: television vs., 280; US influence on Quebec and, 212

First Taiwan Strait Crisis, 72

Fisher, John, 243

Fleming, Donald, 236, 250, 252

Flex We Talent, 197*n*6

Ford, Robert, 46, 49, 54

foreign aid. *See* aid

foreign policy: Canada as middle power and, 7–8; and nuclear deterrent, 74–75; nuclear revolution and, 69–70, 73–74; and Southeast Asia, 18–19; and Soviet Union, 9, 18, 45, 48. *See also* Department of External Affairs (DEA); national security policy

Forest Hill, Toronto, 244, 293, 294–95

The Forked Road (Creighton), 121–22

Foulkes, Charles, 53–54, 74, 77, 78, 79, 80, 81–83, 85

France: and Algeria conflict, 33; and Bandung Conference, 29; and Indochina, 72; and NATO, 82; Quebec relationship with, 203, 209; and UN Declaration on the Granting of Independence to Colonial Peoples and Countries, 33; withdrawal of North American forces and, 79

France-Quebec relationship: and anti-Americanism, 214; artistic, 214; intellectual, 214; metropolitan disengagement in, 225; Second World War and, 214–15; US-Quebec relationship vs., 214, 225–26

Frankfurter, Felix, 129, 134–35

Fraser, Blair, 60; "Why They Won't Let You Have TV," 274–75

Frégault, Guy, 217–18

Friesen, Gerald, 200*n*55

Frisken, Frances, 310

355

INDEX

Frost, Leslie: and fair practices laws, 181–83; and Gardiner, 290, 293, 294–95, 304–5
Fulton, E. Davie, 250
Futurama (Bel Geddes), 288

Gagné, Gilles, 226
Gallup polls: on happiness of Canadians, 243–44; on margarine, 245; on Soviet Union, 59; on US Constitution, 127; on US influence over Canadian way of life, 246
Gardiner, Cecil, 293
Gardiner, David, 292, 293
Gardiner, Frederick, 10, 289, 342; as 1950s character, 308; and automobile, 299–300, 308, 310; and balanced system of transportation, 300, 302, 303; as Conservative, 293, 303, 311; early life and career, 290, 292–93; and economic growth/urban development, 308–9; and Forest Hill, 293, 294–95; Frost and, 293, 294–95, 304–5; and highways/expressways, 294, 296, 297, 298, 299–300, 307, 308, 310, 311; Levy on, 309; and metropolitan government, 290, 294–96, 300; and modernity, 291; Moses compared to, 290–91, 296, 300, 306–7, 308, 310; obituary, 309–10; on Ontario Municipal Board, 294; and provincial government, 295, 297, 311; and public transit, 291, 292, 294, 296–300, 302, 303–11; and road construction, 294; Sewell on, 309; and subway, 305, 306; and Toronto and Suburban Planning Board, 294; on Toronto and York Roads Commission, 296; on traffic congestion in cities, 297; and TTC, 303–4, 306
Gardiner, Victoria, 292
Gardiner Expressway, 296
Garner, Sir Saville, 105, 106, 109, 113

Garson, Stuart, 124, 125
Gauvreau, Claude, 221
Gelber, Lionel, 7
General Agreement on Tariffs and Trade, 108
General Motors, 288
Geneva Conference on Korea and Indochina (1954), 24, 102, 103
Geneva Summit (1955), 53, 56, 57, 60
George, Graham, 332, 333
Gérin-Lajoie, Antoine, 205
Germany, reunification of, 48, 56, 57–58, 79. *See also* Federal Republic of Germany
Ghana, 32–33
Gillespie, Dizzy, 319, 321
Gilmore, John, 327
Gingras, Claude, 325
Givens, Phil, 295
Globe and Mail: on Black peoples in Dresden, 192, 193–94, 195; on CBC, 275–76; on Ellington, 328–29; Gardiner obituary, 309–10; "In the Public Interest," 275; on jazz at Stratford, 325; on Massey Commission, 275; "Now Supreme in Law," 125; on television, 273; television in, 268, 269–70, 272–73; on television vs. audible broadcasting, 281; on television vs. film and radio audiences, 280; on television vs. printed word, 282; on television-newspaper cooperation, 281; on US racial segregation, 127
Gordon, Walter, 249
Gordon Commission. *See* Royal Commission on Canada's Economic Prospects (Gordon Commission)
Gornick, Vivian, 188
Gould, Glenn, 323
Gould, Jack, 269, 282
Gouzenko, Igor, 97, 135
The Government of Canada (Dawson), 136–37

INDEX

Granatstein, Jack, *How Britain's Weakness Forced Canada into the Arms of the United States*, 91
Grant, George, 245
Granz, Norman, 320–21
Great Britain. *See* United Kingdom
Great Depression: birth rates during, 148; domestic consumption during, 150–51; and economy, 96; household loss of appliances during, 163; and social welfare, 8; working-class families during, 146, 163
Gréber, Jacques, 290
Green, Howard, 109–11, 112, 113, 124
Grothe, L.O., 211
Groulx, Lionel, 206–7
Guthrie, Tyrone, 322–23
Gzowski, Jennie, 241
Gzowski, Peter, 241

Haddad, Aaron, 197n6
Halifax, Lord, 95
Hammond, John, 325
Harlem Renaissance, 318, 328
Harper's magazine, "The American Century Is Over," 341
Harvard Law School, 135
Harvey, Alan, 283
Harvey, Jean-Charles, *Marcel Faure*, 212
Hatta, Mohammad, 21
Held, Al, 216
Hémon, Louis, *Maria Chapdelaine*, 205, 212
Henry VI (Shakespeare), 329
Henson, Josiah, 178
Hentoff, Nat, 325; *The Jazz Makers*, 319
Hickey, Harvey, 273
high culture: jazz and, 317; mass culture vs., 317; Massey Commission and, 323, 324, 327, 333; nationalism, 323, 324, 327, 333; and nationhood, 316–17; Stratford Shakespearean Festival and, 316. *See also* elite; serious music

"The Highway and the City" (Mumford), 302–3
highways: balance with public transit, 342; bisecting cities, 301; in Chicago, 302; federal support for, 291; Gardiner and, 294, 296, 297, 298, 299–300, 307, 308, 310, 311; interstate, 291; and Interstate Highway Act, 288; and modernity, 297; provincial governments and, 301; public transit vs., 297; public transit balanced with, 297, 299–300, 302–3; sole reliance on, 300–1; Spadina Expressway, 296; and traffic congestion, 307; and urban areas, 288; in Washington, DC, 301–2
A History of Jazz in America (Ulanov), 319
Hitchcock, William, 5
Hitler, Adolf, 91, 95
Hogg, Peter, *Constitutional Law in Canada*, 136
Holiday, Billie, "Strange Fruit," 327–28
Holmes, John, 32, 43, 56
Holmes, Oliver Wendell, 135
home ownership: and equity, 168; federal support for, 291; masculinity and, 164–65; mortgage financing, 155–56, 166(f); postwar boom and, 8
homes: class, and choices inside, 163; construction, 155, 156–57, 160, 163, 239; integration of appliances in, 156; new, 155, 158; renovations to, 163; shortages, 155; standard of living showcased in, 239; suburban purchasing patterns, 163–64; in suburbs, 239
Honderich, Beland, 248–49
Hooper, Louis, 320
hospital insurance, 242
household goods: as household needs, 167; industrialization of housework and, 147; money spent on, 164; and new traditions in domesticity, 164; in rural areas, 161–62; spending controls, 153–54; statistics of

357

ownership, 158–59. *See also* appliances, household
households: activities transferred to other economic sectors, 165–66; age-segregated, 145; breadwinner-housewife form of, 150; budget management, 167; capitalism and, 167; changing destinations of income, 167; changing economies, 145–47; debt, 157–58; formation rate, 145; Great Depression and, 150–51; ideological constructions of, 145–46; income rates, 149, 150(t); leisure activities, 164–65; as less prosperous in Canada vs. US, 143; masculinity and economically important work outside of, 146; and modernity, 147; national economy, and economies of, 168; non-family, 145; nuclear family and, 143; numbers of earning members, 146, 168; one-person, 164, 168; organizational changes in, 167–68; paid work outside, 167; restrictions on spending, 153; Second World War and, 151–52; senior citizens, 164; size, 143–44; spending, and political identification, 150–51; spending patterns, 160, 167–68; suburban, 163–64; television set ownership, 263; wartime technologies and, 152; women's employment and, 146. *See also* domesticity; families
housework: appliance ownership and, 147; economic value of, 147; industrialization of, 147, 165; as non-market work, 146
How Britain's Weakness Forced Canada into the Arms of the United States (Granatstein), 91
Howe, C.D., 66; and Alberta-Ontario pipeline, 250; on "Anglo-American monopoly," 95–96; and Canadian participation in atomic bomb development, 96

Hubley, Doug, 216
Hudson's Bay Company, 241
Hughes, Everett C., 223
Hughes, Langston, 328, 339*n*71
human rights. *See* civil rights
Hutchison, Bruce, 8; *Canada: Tomorrow's Giant*, 243
Hyde Park Agreement, 92, 97, 228*n*17

identity, Canadian, 10; Americanization and, 100; anti-Americanism in, 6–7; diplomacy of constraint and, 17; Massey Commission and, 100; as mediator, 20–21; racial discrimination and, 186; television and, 261; US influence and, 9, 187; US-Canada relationship and, 216–17
identity, Québécois: Americanness and, 226; Second World War and, 208–9; tourism and, 213
Ignatieff, George, 43, 54, 55, 58, 73–74, 81, 84, 85; "Some Specific Questions on Future National Security Policy," 73–74; "The Strategic Concept of the Nuclear Deterrent," 74–75
immigrants: Black, 184; British, 100; and population growth, 160–61; racist policies, 185; in Toronto, 292
Imperial Oil, 247
imperialism: British, 101, 204; English Canadian, 206; Quebec anti-imperialism, 203; and Quebec nationalism, 204; US, 4–5, 107, 204; US cultural, 261, 262, 265–66, 272
"In the Public Interest" (*Globe and Mail*), 275
income gap, 238
India: and Asian neutralism, 21; Canada and, 19, 20, 21, 24; and China, 23–24, 30; Colombo Plan and, 19; in Colombo Plan conference, 25; Commonwealth and, 20; and Commonwealth vs. neighbours, 25; Diefenbaker and, 34; and Korean War, 21, 23, 102; and law

of sea, 111; and Panch Sheel, 23–24; and Soviet Union, 21; and US, 22, 23, 26; US and, 21, 26

Indigenous peoples: Americans compared to, 220; colonialism and, 179; as slaves, 199*n*40

Indochina: French in, 72; insurgency in, 102–3; partition of, 103

Indonesia: and Asian neutralism, 21; and Bandung Conference, 29; civil war, 31–32; and Colombo Plan, 19, 26; in Colombo Plan conference, 25; and communism, 32; and Korean War, 23, 24; Netherlands rule in, 22; and neutrality, 23; and Soviet Union, 21; and US, 24, 27. *See also* Bandung (Asian-African) Conference

influence of US: in advertising, 246; American Century and, 3–4; and anti-Americanism, 245–46; and Bill of Rights, 134; and Canadian history, 5–6; and Canadian identity, 9, 187; on Canadian life, 236–37; capital investment in economic growth, 247–52; on civil rights in Canada, 132–33; commercialism, 246; constitutional change, 123; in consumer goods, 247; cultural, 10, 122, 186, 261, 262, 265–66, 272, 284; economic, 9, 10, 249–51; European historians on, 6; Gallup Poll on, 246; Luce on, 3; and mass culture, 317; Massey Commission on, 283–84; and materialism, 244; and modernity, 248, 252; and nationalism, 4–5; on Quebec-Canada relationship, 216; and racial attitudes, 177, 189–90, 193; retail stores in Canada, 240–41; in *Roncarelli v Duplessis*, 134–35; as scapegoat, 245–46; shaping developments in Canada, 186; shopping in US, 241; skepticism regarding, 237; Sunday openings, 244; and Supreme Court of Canada, 124, 126; on television, 241–42, 261; values of US and,

237. *See also* Americanization; US-Canada relationship

influence of US on Quebec: in American characters, 212–13; Americanization in, 207, 209, 226; cultural, 204, 210–16, 219–20, 224, 226; economic, 205, 224; European influence in, 219–20; as given of history, 225; intellectual, 219–24; intellectuals on, 206–7; in literature, 214–15; and materialism, 206, 207; "melting pot" in, 217–18; and modernity, 206, 226; in movies, 206, 212; in newspapers, 205–6; openness to, 203; political, 216–19; and prosperity, 204–5, 207; and Quebecers as American beings, 226; in radio, 211–13; and refusal of Americanism, 226; Second World War and, 203–4; structural, 205; in television, 212; in tourism, 213–14. *See also* US-Quebec relationship

Innis, Harold, 4, 246, 260

intercontinental ballistic missiles (ICBMs), 73

International Monetary Fund, 238

International Relations Clubs, 221

Interprovincial Pipe Line, 247

Interstate Highway Act (1956) (US), 288, 299

iron ore, 247, 249, 252

Ismay, Lord, 47–48

Italy: and NATO, 82; withdrawal of North American forces and, 79

Jackson, Milton, 326–27, 332

Jacobs, Jane, 308; *The Death and Life of Great American Cities,* 290

Jaffe, Shirley, 216

Jago, Marian, 336*n*25

Japan: atomic bombs against, 66, 96; and Colombo Plan conference (1954), 26–27

Japanese Canadians, deportations of, 189

jazz: African Americans and, 318, 319–20; as American art form, 335n11; and American Century, 319; as art form, 324; attendance at concerts, 330–31, 333; audience, 330–31; in Canada, vs. Canadian jazz, 320; Canadian culture, 317; Canadian vs. US appreciation for, 333; Canadianization of, 318; commentaries on, 324–25; cross-border history, 335n11; Dixieland, 324, 325; elite and, 317, 320, 330; erudite, 325–26; festivals, 319, 323; and high culture, 317; history of, 318; as hybrid cultural expression, 318; and musical diplomacy, 319, 324, 336n24; musicians in Quebec, 213; as North American art form, 320; politics of, 317; Princess Margaret and, 315, 330; publications on, 319; racism and, 320–21, 327–28; and serious music, 316, 318, 324, 327, 329, 332; Shakespeare and, 329; at Stratford Shakespearean Festival, 10, 315, 317, 318, 323–34; and theatre, 317; ticket sales, 333; white vs. Black Canadians in, 327; youth in audience, 325
"Jazz for Highbrows" (CBC), 326
The Jazz Makers (Shapiro and Hentoff), 319
Jazz at the Philharmonic, 320–21
Jehovah's Witnesses, 130–31, 132
Jocelyn, Gordon, 329
Joint Intelligence Committee, 68, 74
Judicial Committee of the Privy Council (JCPC): and BNA Act, 130, 135; end of appeals to, 122, 124, 125, 126, 133, 137; and precedents, 126, 130

Kabanov, Ivan, 55–56
Kane, Molly, 19
Kaplan, Harold, 304
Kay's Café, 178, 181, 183, 190, 195, 198n35
Keenleyside, Hugh, 7–8
Kennedy, John F., 33, 112, 303

Kennedy, W.P.M., 135–36
Kent, Duke of, 330
Kerouac, Jack, 216
King, William Lyon Mackenzie: on Alaska Highway, 94; American economic/cultural domination under, 122; and Canada in British or US orbits, 91; and Canadian relationship with British, 95; and Churchill's speech at Fulton, MO, 98; and customs union with US, 99; on economic union with US, 97; and Eisenhower, 95; and free trade, 124; and Gouzenko, 97; and Hyde Park Declaration, 92; on keeping English-speaking peoples together, 97; on Korean War, 102; and North Atlantic Triangle, 91, 92; and Ogdensburg Agreement, 92; on PJBD, 97; at Quebec City summits, 95; and Roosevelt, 92–93, 94; and triangular collective security, 99
Klein's department store, 241
Koffman, Moe, 327
Korea: diplomacy of constraint and, 21; East-West division and, 48
Korean War, 68; armistice, 18; Asian states and, 22–23, 24, 25; Canada and, 25, 68; China and, 23, 24, 101; and Cold War, 101; Commonwealth division in, 101; Geneva Conference on, 25; India and, 21, 102; Indonesia and, 23, 24; and Korean War, 25; NATO and, 68; and natural resources, 210; North Atlantic Triangle and, 101–3; nuclear weapons and, 101–2; UN and, 23, 101, 102; US and, 24, 25, 101–3; US-Canada relationship in, 101–3
Kotelawala, John, 25
Kraglund, John, 325, 329
Kresge, 241
Krishna Menon, V.K., 24, 25
Khrushchev, Nikita, 56–58, 291

INDEX

Lambertson, Ross, 176–77, 198*n*24
Lamonde, Yvan, 203, 210, 225–26
Lamport, Allan, 309
Lanctôt, Gustave, *Les Canadiens français et leurs voisins du sud,* 209
Langham, Michael, 328
Laurendeau, André, 209
Laurier, Wilfrid, 124
Laval University, 223; Faculty of Social Sciences, 223
Lavigne, Alain, 219
Le Corbusier, 289
Le Moyne, Jean, *Convergences,* 220
LeBourdais, D.M., 243
LeDuc, Emily, 10
Léger, Jules, 70, 78, 82, 83
Leighton, Alec, 223
leisure, men's vs. women's, 164–65
Lend-Least Program, 96
Leo XIII, pope, 205
Lesage, Jean, 219
Lethbridge Herald, on wide-open Sundays, 244
Lévesque, Georges-Henri, 223
Lévesque, René, 43
Levine, Lawrence W., 331, 334–35*n*4
Levy, Ed, 309
Ligue nationaliste, 204
Little Rock Nine, 319
Liverant, Bettina, 10
Lodge, Oliver, "Will We See around a Corner?," 267
Logue, Ed, 290
London Evening Free Press, on jazz at Stratford, 325–26
Lorenzini, Sara, 29
Lower, Arthur, 7
Luce, Henry, 3–4, 5, 7

MacArthur, Douglas J., 102
Macdonald, D.B., 244
Macdonald, John A., 247
MacDonald, Malcolm, 66
MacKay, R.A., 79, 80

Mackenzie, C.J., 66
Maclean's magazine: on broadcasting vs. print media, 279–80; Gzowskis in New York, 241; "Make Way for the One-Eyed Monster," 269–70; on postwar world, 8; retrospective on broadcast radio, 281; on television, 267–68; on television vs. radio, 283; "What Are They Looking At?," 268; "What TV Will Do to You," 259; "Why They Won't Let You Have TV," 274–75; "Will We See around a Corner?," 267
MacLennan, Hugh, 5
Macmillan, Harold, 104; and Diefenbaker, 107–8, 112, 113; and Eisenhower, 107; and UNCLOS II, 111; visit to Canada, 107–8
Magill, Don, 268–69; "What TV Will Do to You," 259
Make Room for TV (Spigel), 260
"Make Way for the One-Eyed Monster" (Berton/*Maclean's*), 269–70
Malenkov, Georgy, 45
Manhattan Project, 96
Marcel Faure (Harvey), 212
Margaret, Princess, 315, 330
Maria Chapdelaine (Hémon), 205, 212
Marie-Victorin, Brother, 222
marriages, 144–45
Martin, J. Burke, 326
Massey, Vincent, 94, 271–72, 276, 284
Massey Hall, 321
McAree, John Verner, 280, 282
McBrien, William, 304, 306, 307
McGuigan, Jim, 335*n*9
McKay, Morley, 181, 183–84, 190, 195, 198*n*35
McKercher, Asa, 10, 18
McKittrick, Katherine, 185, 192
McLuhan, Marshall, 260
McNamara, Helen, 325, 332, 333
McNaughton, A.G.L., 94–95, 98
media: and agenda-setting/framing, 188–89; and Dresden plebiscite, 182;

and hegemonic ideologies, 188; on racial discrimination, 189; on racial discrimination in Canada vs. US, 196; on racial discrimination in Dresden, 177, 182–83, 185; on rights movement, 189. *See also* cultural mediums; newspapers

Menzies, Arthur, 30

Merchant, Livingston, 104–5

Metropolitan Transportation Authority, 302

Michener, Wendy, 316, 326–27

middle classes: choices inside homes, 163; and consumer credit, 158; and domesticity, 147; families, 147; growth of, 239; income from off-farm employment, 162; and women's employment, 149

middle power, Canada as, 7–8

Miller, L.P., 337*n*28

Miller, Mark, 328–29, 337*n*28

Mills, Sean, "Democracy in Music," 337*n*26

Mingus, Charles, 321

Minneapolis Star and Tribune, on television as news medium, 282

Missed Opportunity: The Story of Canadian Broadcasting Policy (Raboy), 260

Modern Jazz Quartet, 316, 324, 330

modernity/modernization: during 1950s, 244, 245; American century and, 342; Americanism and, 225; in Canada vs. US, 142–43; dissatisfaction with, 8; expressways and, 297; Gardiner and, 291; households and, 147; and Indigenous traditions, 26; influence of US and, 248, 252; influence of US on Quebec and, 206, 226; intellectuals on, 245; Quebec and, 203, 221; and serious music, 334*n*4; television and, 267; US-Quebec relationship and, 224–25

Molotov, Vyacheslav, 52, 54, 56, 57

Montpetit, Édouard, 209, 225; *Reflets d'Amérique,* 209

Montreal: atomic bomb development in, 208; Black Canadians in, 327; as cultural metropolis, 214; jazz in, 321, 327, 337*n*25; Little Burgundy, 320, 327; mafia, 213; trade and economic conference, 106, 107–8; urban working-class homes in, 163; working-class families in, 146

Montreal École Polytechnique, 263

Montreal *Gazette,* on Black peoples in Dresden, 193

Morgan Brothers' Syncopated Jazz Band, 320

Morton, W.L., 91

Moses, Robert, 290–91, 296, 300, 302, 306, 310

mothers' allowances, 150

movies. *See* film/movies

Mowbray, George, 251

Mumford, Lewis, "The Highway and the City," 302–3

music, serious. *See* serious music

Mutual Security Act (1956) (US), 28

"My Place Is Right Here" (play), 177

Nasser, Gamal Abdel, 33

National Broadcasting Company (NBC), 263, 268

National Film Board of Canada, *The Dresden Story,* 183

National Highway Users Conference (1962), 302

National Housing Act (NHA), 155–56

National Policy, 247

national security policy: Barton paper on, 70–71, 73–74; and Canadian air defence, 81; DEA-DND-Privy Council Office meeting on, 77–79; defence of North America vs. European military commitment, 67; defence policy and, 78–79; DND and, 54, 76, 82; Foulkes paper on, 80; Ignatieff paper

362

on, 73–74; joint DEA-DND study, 79; July 1955 joint DEA/DND meeting on, 81–82; military vs. political assumptions regarding, 84; "Study of National Security Policy" (DEA), 53–54, 69–70. *See also* defence policy

"National Security Policy" (DEA/DND), 83–84

National Unity Association (NUA), 177, 181–82, 183, 189

nationalism: Anglophilic, 316, 323, 328, 332; anti-Americanism and, 206; Canada-US relationship and, 93, 99; cultural, 272; economic, 248–49; French Canadian, 204, 205; high-culture, 323, 324, 327, 333; Quebec clerical, 202–3, 226; television and, 262, 265, 277; US influence and, 4–5

nationhood: Canadian questioning of, 9; constitutional culture and, 126; high culture and, 316–17; and serious music, 334n4; Supreme Court of Canada and, 124, 125

NATO (North Atlantic Treaty Organization): advantages for Canada, 99; Canada in, 57, 78, 80, 82–83; Canadian forces in Europe, 69, 71, 72, 79–80, 81–82, 83, 84, 85; Cold War and, 44; continental defence and, 76, 80; DEA and, 79; as deterrent to aggression, 52; disintegration of, 58; and Federal Republic of Germany, 51, 57–58, 72; formation of, 99; German unification and, 57; Khrushchev and, 57; Korean War and, 68; North Atlantic Triangle and, 99; and nuclear deterrent, 69, 77; and nuclear revolution, 71, 72; Pearson's visit to Soviet Union and, 43, 57; Soviet Union and, 46, 47–48, 51, 52, 57, 58–59, 79, 82; strengthening of, 84; and trade, 55; unity of, 83; and US-Canada relationship, 99–100; Washington Treaty and, 68, 71

natural gas industry, 247, 250

natural resources. *See* resources/resource industries

Neatby, Nicole, 213

Needham, Richard, 43

Nehru, Jawaharlal, 23; and "area of peace" (Panch Sheel), 23, 24; on Asian pact resembling North Atlantic Treaty, 22; and Asian Relations Conference, 21; on Canada, 20; and Canada-US relationship, 24; and China in UN, 23; and China-India relationship, 24; and communism, 22; and Conference on Indonesia, 22; invitation to Canada to visit India, 52; Southeast Asian tour, 22

Nepveu, Pierre, 215

Nerone, John, 261

Nevers, Edmond de, *L'âme américaine*, 202, 204

New Jazz Society of Toronto, 321

New York, NY: artistic renewal, 211; diversity in, 218; Quebec General Agency in, 218–19; and US-Quebec relationship, vs. Paris, 215–16; in US-Quebec relationship, 218–19

New York (state), fair practices laws in, 181

New York World's Fair, 288

New Zealand, in SEATO, 18

Newport Jazz Festival, 319, 323

newspapers: on Fair Accommodation Practices Act, 195; framing of racial discrimination, 195–96; importance of, 188; influence of US on Quebec in, 205–6; on Japanese Canadian deportations, 189; and racial discrimination in Dresden, 190–95, 196, 343; on racial segregation in US, 189–90; reporting of racial discrimination, 189; television vs., 242, 281–82. *See also* print media

Nice Jazz Festival, 319

Nimmons, Phil, 325–27, 332, 338n57

INDEX

Nixon, Richard, 291

Non-Aligned Movement, 18, 23, 33

non-alignment, 33–35; in Asia, 19, 21–25; Bandung Conference and, 18; Canada and, 17, 19

Norman, E.H., 104

Norris, John, 333

North American Aerospace Defence Command (NORAD), 84–85

North Atlantic Triangle: about, 90–91; American Century and, 10; and atomic bombs against Japan, 96; British decline and, 100; Canada as mediator in, 91, 92; and Canada's international relationships, 91; Canada's shifting position within, 100; Churchill's Fulton speech and, 98; and Cold War, 91; Diefenbaker and, 104–5; Diefenbaker's Commonwealth tour and, 108–9; Diefenbaker's visits from Macmillan and Eisenhower, 107–8; and disarmament, 112; diversion of Canadian trade from US to Britain, 105–6; economic relationship within, 96–97; fading of, 113; Hyde Park Declaration and, 92, 97; and Indochinese insurgency, 102; intelligence sharing in, 98; Kennedy vs. Eisenhower presidencies and, 112; and Korean War, 101–3; Marshall Plan and, 97; military cooperation, 98–99; and NATO, 99; Ogdensburg Agreement and, 92; PJBD and, 97–98; at Quebec City summits, 95; Ritchie on, 113; and Second World War, 91; and Suez Crisis, 103–4; trade in, 105–6, 108, 109, 112, 236; and UNCLOS, 106–7, 111

North Atlantic Triangle (Brebner), 90

Nova Scotia: Black Americans settling in, 185; racial discrimination/segregation in, 179, 189

"Now Supreme in Law" (Globe and Mail), 125

Nu, U, 22, 23

nuclear age/revolution, 44, 84–85; Canada's dilemma, 67–68; Canadian participation in, 66; and Cold War, 70; and defence policy, 67–68, 69–70, 83; foreign policy and, 69–70; Hiroshima atomic bomb and, 66–67; hydrogen age, 50; and living dangerously, 73; and North American vs. European defence, 71; and reliance on US, 9–10; thermonuclear age, 53

nuclear deterrent: Canadian forces in Europe and, 69; and communism, 83; DEA and, 74–75, 83; defence of, 75; NATO and, 69, 77, 83–84; against nuclear war, 67, 81–82; nuclear weapons as, 77, 83; and Soviet Union, 83

nuclear war: DND on, 84; nuclear deterrent against, 67; and overflights over Canada, 68; Soviet Union and, 68, 75, 84; thermonuclear, 50; and US massive retaliation strategy, 71–72; US-China, 76; US-Soviet Union, 68, 71–72, 80, 81

nuclear weapons: atomic bomb, 66, 68, 96, 101–2, 208; as deterrent to war, 53, 77, 83; development in Canada, 96; development in Montreal, 208; Diefenbaker and, 112; Eisenhower and, 67; equipping Canadian forces with, 85; at Goose Bay, 76; against Japan, 66, 96; and Korean War, 101–2; overflights of Canadian airspace, 53, 68, 76, 78; role of, 68; smaller/"tactical" vs. larger, 77; Soviet Union thermonuclear bomb explosion, 71; thermonuclear, and defence policy, 73; US and, 53, 71

Nye, Archibald, 100

Ogdensburg Agreement, 92, 97–98, 135, 228n17

oil industry, 247, 249, 291

Oliver, Pearleen, 179

364

INDEX

Ontario: Black Americans settling in, 185; fair practices laws, 176, 181–82; Racial Discrimination Act, 180

Ontario Good Roads Association, 297

Ontario Heritage Trust, 177

Ontario Ministry of Labour, 183

Ontario Mothers' Allowances Commission, 150

Ontario Municipal Board (OMB), 294–95

The Oscar Peterson Trio at the Stratford Shakespearean Festival, 331–32

Osgoode Hall, 135

Ottawa Citizen, on Eisenhower's speech to Parliament, 236

Owram, Doug, *Born at the Right Time,* 8

Panch Sheel, 23–24

Pandit, Vijaya Lakshmi, 21

Pannikar, K.N., 23

Papineau, Louis-Joseph, 227*n*4

Paris, George, 320

Paris, New York vs., in US-Quebec relationship, 215

Park Royal shopping centre, 240

Parker, Charlie, 321

Parks, Rosa, 319

Parsons, Talcott, 223

Patterson, Harry Thomas "Tom," 322–23, 330

peaceful coexistence, 33, 44–45, 49–52, 54, 59. *See also* détente

Pearson, Lester B.: Acheson on, 102; on atomic bomb, 66–67; and Barton paper on national security, 70; at Bermuda meeting, 104; and Campney, on continental defence, 77; on Canadian prosperity, 243; on Cold War, 60; and Colombo Plan, 20, 27; on Commonwealth, 20; on dependence on US vs. UK, 342–43; and détente/peaceful coexistence, 45, 52, 54, 59; on dialogue, 60; Eden

meeting with, 102–3; on European vs. US diplomacy, 99; and Federal Republic of Germany, 57–58; and Geneva Summit, 53; as "honest broker," 56; and India, 24; and Indochina, 103; and Korean War, 23, 24; on Korean War, 101–2; on membership in Atlantic group, 34; and national security policy, 53, 54, 82; and NATO, 72; and nuclear deterrent, 74; on Soviet Union, 44, 49–52, 60, 72; Soviet Union visit, 43–44, 45, 52–53, 54–59; and Suez Crisis, 24, 343; and triangular collective security, 99; on US attitude toward Canada, 93; on US-Canada relations, 34; and US-Soviet Union relations, 60, 72

Pearson, Maryon, 43

pension system, 242

People's Republic of China (PRC). *See* China

Permanent Joint Board on Defence (PJBD), 92, 97, 98

Perrault, Pierre, 221

Perry, Clarence, 289

Peterson, Oscar, 318; at Carnegie Hall, 317; as jazz ambassador to Soviet Union, 336*n*24; life and career, 320–21; and Modern Jazz Quartet, 326, 330; and *The Oscar Peterson Trio at the Stratford Shakespearean Festival,* 331–32; and racism, 321; at Stratford, 324, 327, 333

La petite cigarettière, 211

Philippines: China and, 30; and Colombo Plan conference (1954), 26–27

Phillips, Nathan, 296

Pineault-Léviellé, Ernestine, 211–12

Pivcevich, Jean, 220–21

Plessy v Ferguson, 130

Plow, Peter, 245

Poitras, Daniel, 10

La Politique (Barbeau), 219

Pollock, Jackson, 216

INDEX

Polymer Corporation, 240
Pope, Maurice, 66
Popovic, Pierre, 209
population: aging, 145; growth, 238; immigration and, 160–61; postwar growth, 160–61; prosperity, and growth of, 8
poverty, 238
Powell, Bud, 321
The Power Broker (Caro), 290
Prashad, Vijay, 29
Pravda, on Conference on Indonesia, 22
Price, Harry, 295
"Princess Blue" (Ellington), 330
print media: broadcasting vs., 280; on Massey Commission, 276–77; radio and, 279; and television, 261, 262, 267–71, 272, 273–82, 284. *See also* newspapers
Progressive Conservative Party, 293
Property Owners Association of Toronto, 307
prosperity: American century and, 342; as changing way of life, 238; and governments, 242; and happiness, 244; and home ownership, 8; natural resources and, 4, 8; Northern Vision for, 8; and optimism, 242–43; population growth and, 8; postwar, 141–42, 147–48; and Stratford Shakespearean Festival, 316; US-Canada relationship and, 235–36, 237; in US-Quebec relationship, 204–5, 207, 210
provincial governments: Gardiner and, 295; and highways, 301; and public transit, 299, 304, 311
public transit: automobile vs., 288–89, 306; in Chicago, 302; in Cleveland, 305; decline in, 303–4, 310–11; fare levels, 299, 305; Gardiner and, 289, 291, 292, 294, 296–300, 302, 303–11; highways vs., 297; highways balanced with, 297, 299–300, 302–3, 342; inner city and, 289; investment in, 297–98;

Kennedy on, 303; in London, UK, 306; Moses on, 302; in New York, 302, 306–7; population growth and, 297; profitability, 306; provincial government and, 299, 304, 311; public provision/subsidization of, 298, 299, 303, 304, 306, 311; rail services, 310; return to, 289; ridership, 289; as self-supporting utility, 289; subways, 305–6, 307, 309–10; in Toronto, 289, 292; in Washington, DC, 301–2
Purity Flour Mills, 211

Quebec: Anglicization in, 206; anti-Americanism in, 203, 207–8; anti-Semitism in, 218; Black Americans settling in, 185; civil rights in, 137; distinct culture of, 216; in early 1900s, 204–7; "great darkness" period, 202; homogeneity vs. heterogeneity in, 217–18; jazz musicians in, 213; margarine in, 245; and modernity, 203, 221; natural resources, 205, 210; Quiet Revolution in, 202, 218, 221, 223; relationship with France, 203, 209; Roman Catholic Church in, 224, 225; Second World War and, 207–8; working class, 205
Quebec City summits, 95
Quebec General Agency, 218
Quinn, Felix P., 328

Raboy, Mark, *Missed Opportunity: The Story of Canadian Broadcasting Policy,* 260
Racial Discrimination Act (1944) (Ontario), 180
racial discrimination/segregation: of Black Americans, 189–90; against Black Canadians, 176, 183, 189; *Brown v Board of Education,* 127–29, 132, 133, 319; in Canada, 177, 179–80, 186, 194, 320–21, 343; in Canada vs. US, 177, 185, 192–93, 195–96; courts and,

366

179; Eisenhower and, 129; and human rights activism, 176–77; in immigration policies, 185; and jazz, 320–21, 327–28; Jim Crowism, 177, 180, 182, 189, 193–94, 196; media on, 189; newspaper reporting of, 189–90, 195–96; in Nova Scotia, 179, 189; in Ontario, 180; Peterson and, 321; in restaurants, 190; Supreme Court of the United States and, 132; as systemic, 195; in US, 127, 128, 177, 180, 189–90, 191, 343; US influence and, 193; in US vs. Canada, 10, 177, 185, 192–93, 195–96; white settler society and, 179

racial discrimination/segregation in Dresden, ON, 178–79; campaign to end, 181–84; de facto, 184; Dresden as safe haven vs., 192; as exceptional in Canada, 194; media and, 182–83, 185; newspapers and, 190–95, 196; plebiscite on, 176, 182, 190, 193; reference to US in reports on, 191; as representative, 180; in restaurants, 176, 178, 181, 183; as unique, 191; US compared, 193, 194

Radford, Arthur, 54

Radio-Canada, 212

radio(s): advertising, 211; Aird report on, 271; influence of US on Quebec, 211–13; and jazz, 318; Massey Commission on, vs. television, 279; national service, 272; and print industry, 279; private, 276, 277; and "radioitis," 271; and standards of living, 211–12; television vs., 268, 276, 277, 278–82, 283; transistor, 241

Rand, Ivan, 130, 132–33, 134

Rantin, Stan, 325

Rau, Benegal, 24–25

Reflets d'Amérique (Montpetit), 209

Refus global (Borduas), 215

Regina *Leader-Post,* on equal law school facilities in Oklahoma, 189

Reid, Escott, 25; on Asia, 19–20; on Canada-US relationship, 95; on Canadian relationships with UK and US, 93; and non-alignment, 33–34; on Quebec City summits, 95

resources/resource industries, 7, 243; foreign investment in, 247–49; and postwar boom, 8; Quebec and, 205, 210; US and, 4; US demand for, 246–47; US industry ownership, 9

restaurants: Black Canadians and, 198*n*35; Fair Accommodation Practices Act and, 190; racial discrimination in, 176, 178, 181, 183, 190

Revue dominicaine, 207

Riel, Louis, 204

rights. *See* Bills of Rights; civil rights

Rinfret, Thibaudeau, 125

Riopelle, Jean-Paul, 215–16

Rist, Gilbert, 29

Ritchie, Charles, 48, 113

Roach, Max, 321

Robertson, Norman, 93

Robinson, Basil, 105

Rocher, Guy, 223, 224

Rockefeller, Nelson, 302

Rockefeller Foundation, 222

Rockingham, John, 101

Rolph, Gregory, 235, 252

Roman Catholic Church: loyalty toward British Crown and power, 207; in Quebec, 222, 224, 225, 226; US-Quebec relationship and, 207, 225–26

Romulo, Carlos, 22

Roncarelli, Frank, 130–31, 132

Roncarelli v Duplessis, 130–31, 134

Ronning, Chester, 30

Roosevelt, Franklin Delano: bust in Quebec City, 95; and King, 92–93, 94; and New Deal, 127; and Ogdensburg Agreement, 92; and Supreme Court, 127

Rose, Billy, 213

INDEX

Ross, Murray G., 245

Royal Commission on Broadcasting in Canada (Aird Commission), 211, 271

Royal Commission on Canada's Economic Prospects (Gordon Commission), 9, 249, 251, 252

Royal Commission on National Development in the Arts, Letters and Sciences (Massey Commission), 4, 271–72, 322; on American culture, 342; on brain drain, 223; on Canadian cultural content, 283–84; and Canadian identity, 100; on eclipse of Canadian culture, 9; and elite, 316–17; formation of, 271; *Globe and Mail* on, 275; and high culture, 316–17; and high-culture nationalism, 322, 333; and jazz, 333; legacy, 283–84; print media on, 276–77; on radio, 279; reactions to announcement of, 275; report, 283; and television, 265, 266, 271, 275, 278; on US cultural influence, 211, 283–84; and US-Canadian relationship, 100

rural areas: domesticity/households in, 161–62; electrification, 162; land development, 162; off-farm employment, 161–62; rurality as lifestyle, 162; television in, 264

Rutherford, Paul, *When Television Was Young,* 260

Sanborn, John, 123

satisfaction/happiness, 243–44

Saumur v Quebec (City of), 132

Sayle, Timothy Andrews, 9–10, 18, 53

Schrag, Zachary, 301

Scott, Frank R., 131–33, 134, 217–18

sea, law of: conferences on, 111; North Atlantic Triangle and, 106–7

Season of Rage (Cooper), 177

Second World War: and anti-Americanism, 207–8; and Canada as middle power, 7–8; Canada-Britain relations during, 94–95; and constitutional change, 122; and consumer spending, 153; and economic development, 96–97; and France-Quebec relationship, 214–15; and household appliances, 239; households and, 151–52; and North American integration, 4; North Atlantic Triangle and, 91; Ogdensburg Agreement and, 92; and Quebec, 207–9; Quebec City summits, 95; US and, 93–94; and US influence on Quebec, 203–4; and US-Canada relationship, 93–94, 95, 208

Selfridges department store, 263

serious music, 334n4; jazz and, 316, 318, 324, 327, 329, 332; modernity and, 334n4; nationalism and, 334n4

Sewell, John, *The Shape of the City,* 309

Shakespeare, William, 329, 331; *Henry VI,* 329; *The Winter's Tale,* 315

The Shape of the City (Sewell), 309

Shapiro, Lionel, 60

Shapiro, Nat, *The Jazz Makers,* 319

Sharp, Mitchell, 43

shopping: centres/plazas, 157, 240; Dominion Stores, 160; Eaton's department store, 241; Klein's department store, 241; retail stores, 240–41; Selfridges department store, 263; supermarkets, 160, 240. *See also* consumer spending

Shotwell, James, 90

Siegfried, André, 216

Simonds, Guy, 99

Simpson's department store, 239, 240

Simpson-Sears, 240–41

Sklar, Kathryn Kish, 143

slavery: in Canada, 184–85; Dresden as safe haven from, 177, 178, 192, 196; Indigenous peoples and, 199n40; Underground Railway, 177, 178, 184, 185; in US, 177, 178, 184, 192

Smith, Arnold, 33, 34

Smith, Kimber, 216

Smith, Sidney, 20
La soirée au vieux moulin, 211
"Some Specific Questions on Future National Security Policy" (Ignatieff), 73–74
South Africa, Commonwealth, and apartheid in, 112–13
Southeast Asia: Canadian approach to, 18–19; and Cold War, 18; and communism, 22; Nehru's tour of, 22
Southeast Asia Treaty Organization (SEATO): Canada and, 18, 19, 27; Colombo Plan and, 27, 28; communism and, 27; formation of, 18
Soviet Union: and Atlantic Alliance, 57, 58–59; and Bandung Conference, 29; and Canada as buffer in war with US, 80; Canadian communication with, 45; Canadian foreign policy and, 18, 48, 52–53; China and, 23; Cold War and, 44, 45, 54; and Colombo Plan, 27; communism, 51; DEA and, 45–46; and détente, 44, 45, 52, 54; and disarmament, 110; and Federal Republic of Germany, 82; foreign policy and, 9; German unification and, 57–58; Gouzenko affair and, 97; India and, 21; Indonesia and, 21; NATO and, 46, 47–48, 52, 57, 59, 79, 82; nuclear deterrent and, 83; and nuclear war, 68, 75, 84; and peaceful coexistence, 44–45, 49–52, 54, 59; Pearson on, 44, 60; Pearson's visit to, 43–44, 45, 52–53, 54–59; Peterson in, 336n24; public opinion regarding, 59; Stalin's death, and foreign policy, 45–46; thermonuclear bomb explosion, 71; trade agreement with, 43, 55–56; US and, 46, 47, 48, 57, 58–59, 60, 71, 72; war with, 50, 54; Western allies' advantages over, 51; and wheat, 55–56, 58
Spadina Expressway, 296, 308
Special United Nations Fund for Economic Development (SUNFED), 34

The Spectre of Annexation (Bourassa), 205
Spigel, Lynn, 261; *Make Room for TV,* 260
St. Laurent, Louis: on Bandung Conference, 29; at Bermuda meeting, 104; on Canadian participation in Korean War, 101; and Colombo Plan, 26, 27; and Dulles' "Massive Retaliation" strategy, 72; and intervention in Indochina, 102–3; loss to Diefenbaker, 104; and Massey Commission, 271; and national hospital insurance plan, 242; and national security policy paper, 53; and non-alignment, 34; and nuclear revolution, 72; and paper on atomic age, 53; and triangular collective security, 99
St. Lawrence Seaway, 247, 309–10
Stalin, Josef, 19, 44, 45, 46, 48, 49, 291
Standard Oil of New Jersey, 247
standards of living: consumer spending and, 158; costs of living, 150; and happiness, 244; homes showcasing, 239; incomes and, 149; rise in, 167, 237–38, 243; US radio and, 211–12; US-Quebec relationship and, 224–25
Stearns, Marshall, *The Story of Jazz,* 319
Steele, Bob, 332
Stein, Clarence, 289
Stevens, W.P., 282–83
Stevenson, Michael, 10
The Story of Jazz (Stearns), 319
"Strange Fruit" (Holiday), 327–28
Strategic Air Command (SAC), 67, 68, 69, 75, 76, 77, 80, 82
"The Strategic Concept of the Nuclear Deterrent" (Ignatieff), 74–75
Stratford Beacon Herald, 316, 325, 326–27
Stratford Music Festival, 316, 317–18, 323; renaming as "The Inaugural Season of Music," 323
Stratford Shakespearean Festival, 321; cultural elites and, 323; history of,

322–23; jazz at, 10, 315, 317, 318, 323–34; launch of, 315–16; Music Advisory Committee, 324, 333; Summer Music School, 324; and theatre, 315–16

Stratford-on-Avon, UK, 329

Strong, Joanne, 241

Stuart, Reginald, 5

"Study of National Security Policy" (DEA), 53–54, 69–70

suburbs, 291–92; American way of life and, 142; automobile and, 240; households, 163–64; and mass conformity, 141; migration to, 158, 239; proto-suburbia, 288

Such Sweet Thunder, 315, 329

Suez Crisis (1956), 30, 103–4, 343

Sukarno, 26, 29, 31, 32

Supreme Court of Canada: and BNA Act, 130; and British North America Act, 130; changes to, 125–26; and civil rights, 127; and Constitution, 123; costs, 126; image of, 126; and JCPC precedents, 130; as last court of appeal, 124–25; and legal education, 135; and nationhood, 124, 125; and racial discrimination/segregation, 127, 179, 180; and *Roncarelli v Duplessis,* 131–32; and stare decisis, 130; supremacy of, 125; Supreme Court of the United States and, 124, 126; US influence on, 124, 126

Supreme Court of the United States, 127; and *Brown v Board of Education,* 127–28, 132; and civil rights, 123, 127; on equal law school facilities in Oklahoma, 189; and racial segregation, 132; supremacy of, 124; and Supreme Court of Canada, 124, 126; Warren and, 128–29

Sutton, Myron, 320

Symonds, Norm, 324, 326

Taiwan, 23

Taiwan Strait, 18, 72

Tardivel, Jules-Paul, 204–5; *La Vérité,* 204–5

Tatum, Art, 316, 324, 326

television, 188; during 1950s, 241–42; access to US channels, 212; advertising and, 266; Americanization of, 266, 274; bilateral negotiations with US over usage rights, 272–73; CBC operation of, 277; and children, 212, 269, 282; as cultural commodity, 266; as cultural industry, 262; demographics and, 264; and domestic life, 268–70; and education, 269, 282; elites and, 265–66; film vs., 280; financing, 265, 273–75; francophone Canadians and, 264; frequencies, 273, 275; geography and, 264–65; inevitability of impact, 270–71; in influence of US on Quebec, 212; licensing fees, 273; Massey Commission and, 265, 271–72, 275, 279; media on, 10; and modernity, 267; and national identity, 261; national service, 266, 272, 279; and nationalism, 262, 265, 277; as news medium, 282–83; newspapers vs., 242, 281–82; other cultural mediums vs., 261–62, 278–83; physical range of signals, 264–65; politicians and, 283; print media on/and, 261, 262, 267–71, 272, 273–82, 284; print media/industry vs., 278–79, 281–82; private interests in, 266, 272, 273–74, 276–77, 283; private vs. public, 277; public broadcasting of, 266; public-private ownership model, 263–64, 278; radio and, 268, 276, 277, 278–82, 283; regulatory control, 271–73; in rural areas, 264; scholarship on, 259–61; set ownership, 212, 242, 263; and societal beliefs, 259; timing of, 266–67; in urban centres, 264; US content, and Canadian values, 261

370

INDEX

television (British), 263, 267; licensing fees, 273; moderate influence of, 268; public broadcasting model, 266

television (US): as addiction, 269–70; advantages of, 266–67; advertising and, 274; Canadian access to, 212, 241–42, 263, 265; and Canadian values, 261; cultural elites and, 265–66; and family life, 279; influence in Quebec, 212; licensing fees, 273; NBC, 263; private broadcasting model, 266; as social revolution, 268; and timing in Canada, 266–67

Tennessee Ten, 320

theatre: jazz and, 317; Stratford Shakespearean Festival and, 315–16

Théâtre Ford, 211

Thériault, Joseph Yvon, 226

thermonuclear war/weapons. *See entries starting with* nuclear

Thivy, John, 21

Thornhill, Esmeralda, 184

Till, Emmett, 327–28

Time magazine, on US and Canadian sovereignty, 9

Times Colonist, on Black peoples in Dresden, 194

Tocqueville, Alexis de, 221

Toronto: automobile production in, 291; immigrants in, 292; jazz in, 321, 327; metropolitan government, 294–95; Municipality of Metropolitan Toronto (Metro), 289, 290; public transit in, 289, 303; Spadina Expressway, 296; suburbs, 292

Toronto Daily Star: on jazz at Stratford, 325; on television, 277; on transit, 307

Toronto Star, Gardiner obituary, 310

Toronto and Suburban Planning Board, 294

Toronto Transit Commission (TTC), 298–99, 303–5, 306, 307, 311

Toronto and York Roads Commission, 296

trade: Montreal conference on, 106, 107–8; NATO and, 55; in North Atlantic Triangle, 105–6, 108, 109, 112, 236

trade agreements: London-Ottawa-Washington (1938), 228*n*17; with Soviet Union, 43, 55–56

Trans Mountain Oil Pipe Line, 247

Trans-Canada Highway, 288, 301

Treaty of Manila, 18

Tremblay, Marc-Adélard, 223

Triborough Bridge and Tunnel Authority, 290, 306

Trudeau, Pierre, and Canadian troops in Europe, 85

Trudel, Marcel, 223

Truman, Harry, 17; and Churchill's speech at Fulton, MO, 98; firing of MacArthur, 102; and Korean incident, 23; and Republic of China in Taiwan, 23; US-Soviet war possibility, 68

Tumpane, Frank, 194

Tunnicliffe, Jennifer, 10

Tyrell, Ian, 186

Ulanov, Barry, 325, 326; *A History of Jazz in America*, 319

Uncle Tom's Cabin (Beecher Stowe), 178, 190, 191, 192

Underground Railway, 177, 178, 184, 185, 190–92

Underhill, Frank, 92, 246

Unger, Corinna, 19

Union Nationale, 219

United Kingdom: and atomic bomb, 66; and Bandung Conference, 29, 30; Canada's relationship with, 94–95; Canadian exports to, 96; Canadian immigrants from, 100; decline of, 91, 100; diversion of Canadian trade from US to, 105–6, 108, 112, 236; and European Economic Community, 113; Green and, 110; and Indonesian

371

INDEX

civil war, 31; and NATO, 82; in North Atlantic Triangle, 90; postwar economic situation, 96; in SEATO, 18; and smaller vs. larger nuclear weapons, 77; and Suez Crisis, 103–4; and SUNFED, 34; television in, 263; and UN Declaration on the Granting of Independence to Colonial Peoples and Countries, 33

United Nations: Bandung Conference and, 30; China in, 23, 48; Declaration on the Granting of Independence to Colonial Peoples and Countries, 33; and disarmament, 110, 112; Green and, 110, 112; and Korean War, 23, 101; technical assistance scheme, 27; Temporary Commission for Korea, 22

United Nations Association, 21

United Nations conferences on the law of the sea (UNCLOS), 106–7, 111

United States: aid, 26, 27–28; and Asian neutralism, 21; assimilation in, 217–18; and atomic bomb, 66; and Bandung Conference, 29, 30; Bill of Rights, 134; and China, 20–21, 24, 76, 77; civil rights in, 123, 127, 129–30, 132–33, 177; and Colombo Plan, 26, 27–28; and continental defence, 74, 75–76; diversion of Canadian trade to Britain from, 105–6, 108, 112, 236; fair practices laws in, 181; as global power, 91; and India, 21, 22, 23, 26; Indonesia and, 27; and Korean War, 24, 25, 101–3; "manifest destiny" of, 93; "melting pot" in, 217–18; National Security Council document NSC-124, 26; national security state, 17, 33; in North Atlantic Triangle, 90; and nuclear war, 68, 71–72; nuclear weapons, 53; racial discrimination/ segregation in, 127, 128, 177, 180, 189–90, 191; in SEATO, 18; and Second World War, 93–94; "secret wars," 31; slavery in, 177, 178, 184, 192; and

Soviet Union, 46, 47, 48, 57, 58–59, 60, 68, 71, 80, 81; and Suez Crisis, 103–4; and SUNFED, 34; and Taiwan, 23; and UN Declaration on the Granting of Independence to Colonial Peoples and Countries, 33

Université de Montréal, 208, 221, 223; Conroe and, 222–23; students travelling to Europe and US, 221

universities, 221–24

University of Toronto: Departments of History and Political Economy, 135; law school, 135; School of Social Work, 239

urban areas: expressways, 288; highways bisecting, 301; population in, 264; television in, 264; traffic congestion in, 297; working-class homes in, 163

Urban Mass Transportation Act (1964) (US), 303

US-Canada relationship: agreements, 4; American century and influence of US in, 3–4; American economic/ cultural domination in, 122; and brain drain, 223; Canada as buffer in US-Soviet war, 80; Canadian criticisms of US in, 236–37; and Canadian identity, 216–17; Canadian reactivity in, 6; Cold War and, 17, 97–98; and Colombo Plan, 26; consensus within, 5; constitutional culture and, 123; cultural contacts, 4; customs union, 97, 99; and economic control, 249–51; economic relationship within, 96–97; economic union, 4; Eisenhower on, 235–37; English Canadian vs. American in, 216–17; historians on, 5; Hyde Park Declaration and, 92; intellectual contacts, 4; Kennedy and, 112; King-Roosevelt relationship, 92–93; in Korean War, 101–3; Massey Commission and, 100; and "melting pot," 217; military links in, 97–98; nationalism and, 99; NATO

372

and, 99–100; natural resources in, 210; nuclear age and, 9–10; Ogdensburg Agreement and, 92; overflights of Canadian airspace, 53, 68, 76, 78; postwar history, 6–7; and prosperity, 235–36, 237; and SAC, 67, 68, 69, 75, 76, 77, 80, 82; during Second World War, 95; Second World War and, 93–94, 208; Suez Crisis and, 103; and tourism, 4; US industry and, 210; US preponderance in, 3, 6; in US-Soviet Union nuclear war, 81. *See also* influence of US

US-Quebec relationship, 10; American vs. French Canadian literature and, 220–21; Americans coming to Quebec, 213–14; annexation of Quebec, 204, 205, 207, 209–10, 216, 224, 227n4; anti-Americanism in, 203; anti-imperialism in, 203; Catholic Church and, 207, 225–26; changing Quebec vs. sense of self, 220; complexity of, 203; continental roots in, 203; cultural exchanges, 211; economic, 210; and education, 209; French-Québécois relationship vs., 214, 225–26; historiography of, 203; and living standards, 224–25; "melting pot" in, 217–18; and modernity, 224–25; New York in, 218–19; and New York vs. Paris, 215–16; in painting, 215–16; in poetry, 215; in postwar period, 203–4; and prosperity, 210; proximity and, 203; publications on, 209–10; in publishing, 214–15; science in, 222; similarities of rural societies, 225; social sciences in, 223; and Union Nationale election campaign practice, 219; universities/university students in, 221–24. *See also* influence of US on Quebec

Van Wyck Expressway, 302
Vancouver Sun, on Eisenhower's speech to Parliament, 236

La Vérité (Tardivel), 204–5
Verve Records, *The Oscar Peterson Trio at the Stratford Shakespearean Festival,* 331–32
Veterans Charter, 153(f), 155
Victory Bonds, 151(f)
Vietnam, 25, 103
Vinson, Frederick Moore, 127–28

Walker, Barrington, 180, 192–93
Walker, James, 176, 186, 187, 198n24
Warren, Earl, 123, 128–29, 132
Washington Treaty, 68, 71
Waters, Rosanne, 187, 189
Watkins, John, 54–55, 57, 58
Wayling, Thomas, 268
Webster, David, 9, 60
Wednesday Night (CBC), 326
Weil, Simone, 208
Weinzweig, John, 323
Wells, H.G., 288
Westboro United Church, 244
Westmount Jazz Band, 320
"What Are They Looking At?" (*Maclean's*), 268
"What TV Will Do to You" (Magill/*Maclean's*), 259
wheat, 236
When Television Was Young (Rutherford), 260
White Paper (DND), 71
white settler colonial societies: and Black consciousness, 187; and race, 179, 186
Whitman, Walt, 215, 220
Whitney, Peter, 281
"Why They Won't Let You Have TV" (Fraser/*Maclean's*), 274–75
Wickens, Stephen, 310
Wilgress, Dana, 45, 59, 60, 72, 99–100
"Will We See around a Corner?" (Lodge/*Maclean's*), 267
Willoughby, Woodbury, 109
Windsor, Duke, 330

Windsor Star: on Black Canadians in Dresden, 193; on racial discrimination in Dresden, 190

Winks, Robin, 187

The Winter's Tale (Shakespeare), 315

women's employment: in households, 146; labour-saving appliances and, 149; married women and, 148–49; middle-class women and, 149; numbers in paid workforce, 238; paid vs. unpaid, 167; rural women and, 161–62; working-class women and, 149

Woolworth's, 241

working class: choices inside homes, 163; consumer credit, 158; families in Montreal, 146; and household appliances, 163; in Quebec, 205; urban homes, 163; and women's employment, 149

Wright, Frank Lloyd, 289; *Broadacre City,* 288

Wrong, Hume, 67

York Tavern, 179

Zhou Enlai, 24

Zorin, Valerian, 55

Set in Perpetua and Minion by Artegraphica Design Co. Ltd.
Copy editor: Dallas Harrison
Proofreader: Sophie Pouyanne
Indexer: Noeline Bridge